DEVELOPING DEMOCRACY

Comparative research
in honour of J.F.P. Blondel

edited by

Ian Budge and David McKay

SAGE Publications
London • Thousand Oaks • New Delhi

Editorial arrangement © Ian Budge and David McKay 1994
Chapters 1 and 2 © Ian Budge 1994
Chapter 3 © Pamela Johnston Conover and Donald D.
Searing 1994
Chapter 4 © Ivor Crewe 1994
Chapter 5 © David Sanders 1994
Chapter 6 © James E. Alt 1994
Chapter 7 © Gosta Esping-Andersen 1994
Chapter 8 © Michael Laver and Kenneth A. Shepsle 1994
Chapter 9 © Anthony King 1994
Chapter 10 © R.A.W. Rhodes 1994
Chapter 11 © Graham Wilson 1994
Chapter 12 © Arend Lijphart 1994
Chapter 13 © Joe Foweraker 1994
Chapter 14 © Christian Anglade 1994
Chapter 15 © Emil J. Kirchner 1994
Chapter 16 © Ronald J. Hill 1994
Chapter 17 © Peter Frank 1994
Chapter 18 © Kenneth Newton and Nigel Artingstall 1994
Chapter 19 © Anthony Barker 1994

First published 1994

 SAGE Publications Ltd
6 Bonhill Street
London EC2A 4PU

SAGE Publications Inc
2455 Teller Road
Thousand Oaks, California 91320

SAGE Publications India Pvt Ltd
32, M-Block Market
Greater Kailash – I
New Delhi 110 048

British Library Cataloguing in Publication data

Developing Democracy
  I. Budge, Ian   II. McKay, David
  321.8

  ISBN 0–8039–8842–7
  ISBN 0–8039–8883–4 (pbk)

Library of Congress catalog card number 93–085409

Typeset by Photoprint, Torquay, Devon
Printed in Great Britain by Redwood Books,
Trowbridge, Wiltshire

Contents

Contributors

James E. Alt   Department of Government, Harvard University: graduate student, then associate of Blondel at Essex, 1968–79

Christian Anglade   Department of Government, University of Essex: long-standing collaborator with Blondel and founder of Latin American Programme at Essex

Nigel Artingstall   Department of Government, University of Essex

Anthony Barker   Department of Government, University of Essex: long-standing collaborator with Blondel in the Essex Department, 1967–83

Ian Budge   Department of Government, University of Essex: close collaborator with Blondel at Essex and his successor as Director of the ECPR

Pamela Johnston Conover   Department of Political Science, University of North Carolina: long-standing associate of the Department of Government at Essex

Ivor Crewe   Department of Government, University of Essex: close associate of Blondel in the Political Behaviour Programme at Essex

Gosta Esping-Andersen   European University Institute, Florence: associate of Blondel at the EUI, 1986–92

Joe Foweraker   Department of Government, University of Essex: associate of Blondel in the Essex Department from 1972

Peter Frank   Department of Government, University of Essex: collaborated with Blondel in building up the Soviet Programme at Essex, 1968–83

Ronald J. Hill   Department of Political Science, Trinity College, Dublin: research assistant and graduate student at Essex, 1965–69

Anthony King   Department of Government, University of Essex: senior associate of Blondel at Essex from 1965

Emil J. Kirchner   Department of Government, University of Essex: collaborator with Blondel at Essex, 1974–83, and founder of the West European Programme at Essex

Michael Laver   Department of Political Science, Trinity College, Dublin: student at Essex, 1967–72

Arend Lijphart   Department of Political Science, University of California, San Diego: founding editor of the *European Journal of Political Research*

David McKay   Department of Government, University of Essex: associate of Blondel and third Director of the ECPR

Kenneth Newton   Department of Government, University of Essex: associate of Blondel in the ECPR and fourth Director of the ECPR

R.A.W. Rhodes   Department of Politics, University of York: associate of Blondel in the Essex Department, 1979–83

David Sanders   Department of Government, University of Essex: graduate student, then associate of Blondel at Essex

Donald D. Searing   Department of Political Science, University of North Carolina: long-standing associate of the Department of Government at Essex

Kenneth A. Shepsle   Department of Government, Harvard University

Graham Wilson   Department of Political Science, University of Wisconsin: associate of Blondel in the Essex Department, 1973–84

1

Comparative Politics and Reflexive Democracy

Ian Budge

Democracy, perhaps uniquely among all systems of government, is self-referential and reflexive. That is to say, an essential aspect of democratic political life is discussion of, and reflection upon, politics in general and the democratic system in particular. Inevitably this tends towards criticism and suggestions for reform – a tendency encouraged by the inter-party tensions and electoral competition that are a defining aspect of modern mass democracies.

Proponents of the free market-place of ideas see open and frank political discussion as beneficial and self-limiting. It is beneficial because it provokes constructive responses to criticism, which end up by identifying and solving problems and thus strengthening the system. It is self-limiting partly because of the corrective reactions it provokes, but also because a critical discussion takes in not only democracy itself but also its alternatives – a comparison which usually ends by strengthening the case for democracy. Paraphrasing Churchill, we learn to tolerate its imperfections by considering the alternatives.

It is important to realize just how unique democracy is in encouraging this kind of critical reflection on its own presuppositions. Other regimes have used criticism of their agents or of details of procedures as a means of maintaining ultimate control (calls for ideological purity within revolutionary Marxist states are good examples). But such devices have operated strictly within limits and were never intended to reflect on fundamental aspects of the state.

Other systems have tolerated criticism from members of their political class but savagely repressed it from outside. While existing democracies may in practice impose quite sharp limits to open discussion, it is only democracy that, in principle, allows comment to be made at any level without predetermining the truths that must be respected or expressed. Indeed, systems that do not allow for this cannot be recognized as democracies.

While democratic discussion goes on in all sorts of arenas, the media constitute a prime vehicle for its transmission and diffusion. A free press has always been central to democratic demands but in practice it may be restricted and hampered in all sorts of ways (see Chapter 18).

In long-term perspective, an equally important role is that of intellectuals, specialists and academics whose seemingly abstruse deliberations have a knack of identifying crucial problems in the functioning of the system, which in the long run will be taken up by others (see Chapter 19). This has long been true of political philosophy and political theory. In our century the development of a systematic political science has added to speculation about politics a body of empirically grounded description and observation, which enables us to contrast reality with ideal – not only for democracies but for other political regimes as well.

A particularly relevant body of analysis is to be found in comparative politics – particularly but not exclusively in comparisons of democracies among themselves and with alternative systems of government. The point often made about understanding one's own national politics applies also to democracy in general. One cannot really appreciate its peculiarities and norms, its defects and its virtues, without putting it in an explicitly comparative context. Implicit comparative judgements are omnipresent, e.g. in claims that democracy is a particularly libertarian or participatory system. Here one always has general norms of liberty or participation in mind which democracy meets or does not meet. Such norms can be based on comparison with the past but more usually rely on assumptions about the way other types of polity operate in the present.

It is in his clear realization that political judgements always rely on comparison, which to be informed must be made explicit and subjected to systematic analysis, that Jean Blondel most clearly distinguishes himself from his intellectual predecessors and contemporaries. Even his earlier books on British politics draw heavily on theories and findings made in other countries. With the *Introduction to Comparative Government* his use of comparison went much further, to draw in all nation states in the world and to explore variations in their behaviour. A central element in this was the differences between types of regime – democracies and others – which were a key factor in explaining variations in political behaviour at the country level and which themselves also demanded explanation.

It is fitting, therefore, that this book, dedicated to Blondel, makes comparisons between democracies its central focus. In doing so, it puts into comparative perspective the whole process of democratization – both in Europe and in Latin America – which has so dominated this decade.

Blondel's belief has always been that one understands, politically, only by comparing. The rich and exciting material of this book certainly bears him out.

In Part One, 'Research Programmes for Democracy', we trace out Blondel's own professional and research contributions to the development of a comparative political science. We begin analysis proper with Pamela Conover's and Donald Searing's reassessment of the political socialization literature and their argument that it should be reoriented to the study of developing citizenship – a plea that is highly relevant to the needs of the new democratic regimes. In Chapter 4, Ivor Crewe reviews the state of Western election studies thirty years after publication of Blondel's classic account of British voters, and makes explicit generalizations to Eastern Europe.

Part Two, 'Democratic Elections and Capitalist Economics', takes off from Crewe's discussion of short-term economic influences on voting to operationalize these explicitly (Sanders in Chapter 5) and to discuss the interaction between party ideology and actual economic outcomes (Alt in Chapter 6). Esping-Andersen follows this up in Chapter 7 by assessing the effects of democratization on the extension of social welfare provision in Spain and Portugal – particularly relevant, again, in terms of what we may expect to happen in Latin America and Eastern Europe in the future.

The core of Blondel's research of the 1970s and 1980s was directed to the functioning of governments at the cabinet and ministerial level. In this context he has contrasted democratic ministerial careers quite dramatically with communist models (anticipating our later discussions of the transition from communism to democracy in Chapters 16 and 17). It is appropriate, therefore, that the third part of this book focuses on democratic government. In Chapter 8, Michael Laver and Kenneth Shepsle link institutional considerations to formal theories of government coalition (the norm in Western democracies) by showing how their formation and success may be crucially affected by the distribution of ministries between parties and individuals in the cabinet. However, this may vary with the freedom which individual ministers have in relation to prime ministers. This forms an appropriate preliminary to Anthony King's discussion in Chapter 9 of how prime ministerial power itself varies between countries.

Governments themselves function within a framework of supporting institutions which together constitute the state. Part Four of our discussion focuses on state-building (again, with an eye to how Western experience might generalize to the East). Rod Rhodes (Chapter 10) concentrates on the origins of the British democratic experience, which has been an influential role model for the rest of the world. His discussion challenges the generally held assumption that bureaucratization is a necessary precondition for democracy. Use of the British case makes the methodological point that studies of individual countries, within the context of a general theory, can contribute to the general growth of knowledge in comparative politics.

In fact, owing to its world influence as the leading alternative to American 'presidential' models of democracy, studies of the 'Westminster model' can illuminate the workings of politics in many countries. Graham Wilson, in Chapter 11, defines its essential features, abstracted from the specific context of British politics, and analyses its successes and failures in the numerous countries overseas to which it has been transplanted – many of them the 'new democracies' of the earlier post-war period.

The major defect of the Westminster system in many countries is its tendency to exacerbate religious and ethnic divisions by giving all power to the majority. In Chapter 12 Arend Lijphart takes this possibility explicitly into mind in discussing the choice of electoral systems and forms of government in the Eastern European countries. A complementary discussion by Joe Foweraker (Chapter 13) looks at democratization from the bottom up, in Spain and Mexico, where popular utilization of existing institutional forms produced significant concessions from authoritarian systems.

In Part Five, 'New Democracies: Assessments and Prognoses', Christian Anglade follows up Foweraker's emphasis on the popular experience of democratization, by chronicling the woefully inadequate guarantees for the individual produced by institutional reform in Latin America so far. The cautionary note he sounds about the extent of real democratization there, is echoed by Ron Hill in regard to Central and Eastern Europe and Peter Frank in regard to the former Soviet Union (Chapters 16 and 17). Prospects for democracy at least in the old 'outer empire' do however seem better than in Latin America, on Anglade's assessment. In part, this is due to the influence and example of the European Community (discussed by Emil Kirchner in Chapter 15), whose fundamental commitment to democracy is balanced uneasily between national governments and parliaments on the one hand and new transnational institutions on the other.

Although existing democracies form the norm by which we can assess progress in other countries, their own internal processes are not necessarily unblemished or totally open. Our sixth part, 'Diagnosing and Improving Democratic Performance', returns to the reflexive function of political science discussed at the beginning of this chapter, and examines the ways in which Western democracies fall short of their ideal and how they might be brought closer to it. In Chapter 18 Newton and Artingstall examine the extent to which existing governments use censorship to control and manipulate public opinion, showing by reference to the Scandinavian case that this is not an inevitable concomitant of democracy as such, but rather a blemish on the operation of democracy within certain countries. In doing so, they well demonstrate how research can illuminate democratic processes and illustrate some of their problems, fulfilling exactly the kind of self-critical function that democracies need if they are to perform properly. Anthony Barker, in our concluding chapter, follows up this point with suggestions for improving the flow of technical information, in order to facilitate a continuing debate over policy between governments and citizens. As these two chapters make clear, information is in many ways the key both to government accountability and to democracies' ability to tackle the many pressing problems which they face. Unfortunately, this is not recognized (or perhaps even admitted) in most Western democracies.

From this brief review we hope it is clear that the object of this book is to combine the theory with the practice of democracy, in the belief that democratic theory, however prescriptive its conclusions, must always incorporate certain descriptive assumptions about the way democracies actually work. These are as essential to its recommendations as the more normative elements: 'ought' implies 'can'. Like Jean Blondel's research, this book rests on the proposition that only through systematic empirical investigation and comparison can one discover what is practicable for polities in general, and for democracy in particular.

Expanding knowledge of how democracy works is just one sense in which we can understand 'developing democracy'. Another is that of its geographical extension to other parts of the world. In these discussions we hope to show that real consideration of one implies the other. We have to think deeply about how democracy works in order to make recommendations about it, but then we need to consider the success of these recommendations to see if our theoretical ideas were valid in the first place.

All of the 'new democracies' are countries studied under their previous regimes by Jean Blondel (and in some cases by few others) in the 1970s and 1980s. These studies – and above all those of the structures and personnel of governments – are proving increasingly valuable now, when so little is otherwise known of the details of administration and politics in the former Soviet Empire and the Third World, and when so many individuals from the old regimes have carried over into the new.

Blondel, however, has never neglected fundamental research for merely topical results and the balance of our book reflects this. It also covers his eclectic interests and thus forms a suitable tribute to a man whose career has covered both scholarship and administration, the creation both of a major department and of a leading international organization dedicated to political research.

Under all these guises and particularly within the organizations he founded, Jean Blondel has remained a scholar, a populist and a democrat. His own books and the collective research emanating from the Department of Government at the University of Essex, and the European Consortium for Political Research, form part of that ongoing process of reflection on itself which we have identified as characteristic of democracy and indeed necessary to it. We, his colleagues and friends here represented, hope this book too will contribute to democratic self-analysis and in so doing form a fitting tribute to a man who has dedicated his career to the promotion both of political research and of democracy.

2

Blondel and the Development of European Political Science

Ian Budge

In our first chapter, we suggested that political and social science can occupy a position in democracies that complements, and may even be essential to the survival of, elections and representative processes. As political science naturally focuses on the efficiency and validity of political processes it forms a necessary self-corrective to the failings of existing systems of democracy and a necessary spur to self-improvement. The development of political science is thus closely linked with the development of democracy. They are symbiotic in the sense that, in the modern age, one can hardly flourish without the other.

Jean Blondel's career is of both practical and emblematic importance in that it has spanned – and contributed to – a process of development and expansion of European political science which has gone hand in hand with the consolidation of European democracy. When he first took up the study of politics in the 1950s, it was indeed difficult to identify anything that might have been termed political science at all. Apart from a few small departments and centres in Britain and France, the study of politics was carried out by individuals in faculties of law, history or economics. The only branch of the study that had truly consolidated itself was the history of political thought – as the name implies, an essentially descriptive study of past thinkers and how their work related to the contemporary social and cultural context, interesting in itself but explicitly divorced from the development of new insights into political life.

Not only was political science in Europe underdeveloped, it also had little about it that could be characterized as European. There were few meetings or contacts across national boundaries. Each small group of specialists had little contact among themselves, let alone nationally. And to make contacts internationally was practically unheard of. When slight stirrings of activity became apparent from the mid 1950s onward, the British and Germans looked to the United States for inspiration, the French to countries traditionally linked to France – Belgium, Switzerland and Italy. The Scandinavians, though always more open to foreign influences, tended to concentrate on Nordic linkages.

Where the different nationalities at first sporadically and then more frequently began to meet was in American departments and centres, orAmerican dominated organizations such as the American Political Science Association, the International Sociological Association or the International Political Science Association. Meetings organized by Europeans for Europeans were rare even to the end of the 1960s.

The contrast between these disjointed stirrings and the highly integrated state of European political science today, gives some measure of the changes which have occurred in the forty years of Blondel's career – and of his achievement, since he helped forge them. In the early 1990s, the European Consortium for Political Research grouped 150 departments and centres of political science in 16 Western European countries, with the prospect of an influx of new members from Eastern Europe as soon as money could be found. It ran all-European professional meetings and research groups, summer schools and journals. It sponsored two book series which published the results of cross-European research which it had largely initiated and encouraged. It was associated with networks of European data archives and documentation centres. The Consortium was unique in the range and magnitude of its activities, there being no exact parallel to it in other continents or in other social sciences inside Europe.

The corollaries of Consortium activities were:

1   a high output of professional papers and books by European political scientists, with cross-European and comparative research being a major constituent of these;
2   frequent and almost daily links between departments, centres and individual political scientists in different European countries (and even within the same country!);
3   a network of other bodies and institutions fostering cross-European links, with the presence of foreigners as teachers, researchers or students increasingly an everyday phenomenon.

Quantity does not necessarily guarantee quality of course. If we were to nominate classics of European political science these would mostly be books of the earlier rather than the later period – though whether these were read more than the moderns might be a moot point. But if one were to ask almost anyone about the state of European political science today compared with forty years ago, in almost any respect, there would be agreement that it had improved – starting with the fact that there *is* now a European political science.

For this, credit must go to a few major figures of the 1960s – preeminently Stein Rokkan, Rudolph Wildenmann and Jean Blondel. Of these, it was Blondel himself who was most intimately and continuously associated with the organizational development of the discipline – as well as constituting in himself the paradigm of the new European political scientist. To understand how and why this happened we have to go into the details of that career, starting in France in the aftermath of the Second World War.

The Early Years 1950–1964

A Jesuit education early imparted in Blondel a certain very French love of order, logic and formalization which was to come out subsequently in his approach to comparative politics. Later associates were to feel that he had also acquired a mastery of political tactics as well as a formal education from the Jesuits. While this may be, they prepared him well for his exposure to Maurice Duverger and other political specialists at the Institut d'Etudes Politiques in Paris where he studied from 1950 to 1953.

Duverger's *Political Parties*, first published in French in 1950 and only translated into English in the late 1950s, is one of the books – if not the book – which set the basic assumptions of the comparative approach for West Europeans. Indeed, it set the scene for what was to become a characteristic specialization within political science. Its starting point was an institution, the political party, taken as being essentially the same whenever and wherever found (at least in the modern period). Thus, the Belgian Socialists of 1898 were to be discussed in essentially the same terms as contemporary French or Italian Christian Democrats. While such an approach had precedents, notably in Michel's classic of the same name, Duverger's great knowledge of many countries, combined with his quintes-sentially French ability to abstract from comparative description into abstract laws – e.g. 'contagion from the left', or the effects of electoral system upon party system, or the inevitable succession of types of party organizations – was original and new.

His book had an enormous effect on English-speaking political scientists when it was eventually translated, supporting behaviourist tendencies in the United States and shaking many in Britain out of their strictly historical studies of a particular place and time into greater concern for comparison, at least within a European context. For Stein Rokkan it confirmed the existence of general historical tendencies which had shaped European parties and party systems, a conception which was to bear fruit in the 1960s.

Jean Blondel had the benefit of exposure to Duverger's work earlier than the majority of English-speaking political scientists. This bore fruit in his first research work, a thesis on local politics in the state of Paraíba in Brazil, which tried to get behind formal institutions to the real organization of parties and political life. The visit to a still 'exotic' political system in 1954 was itself significant and helped mould an early comparative orien-tation. The thesis was published locally as a book in Portuguese trans-lation, and as an article in the *Revue française de science politique*. (A select bibliography of Blondel's works is given at the end of this book.)

The visit to Brazil was made in the course of studies at St Antony's College, Oxford which resulted in a further degree. Having already differentiated himself from the bulk of his contemporaries in France through these foreign experiences, it was natural to return to Britain after marriage and military service, to take up first a research studentship at

Manchester (1957–8) and then an assistant lectureship and lectureship at the University of Keele. Manchester was, in the 1950s, the uncontested centre of political studies in Britain. Under W.J.M. Mackenzie, it had expanded the frontiers of traditional historical scholarship to studies of British administration, interest groups, and even – very cautiously – political sociology in the shape of community politics. At Keele, a new department in a new university, these interests had in turn been pursued and amplified. It was in these contexts that Blondel initiated studies of public administration in France, with Ridley, and of politics in Reading, with Bealey and McCann.

By the end of the 1950s both the intellectual and the institutional life of British political science was quickening under impulses from the United States. It was Jean Blondel's good luck or good judgement to have started off in Britain on the eve of a great expansion in higher education, which gave political scientists the opportunity to consolidate their discipline in institutional form. In 1962 the Conservative government announced an enormous increase in the resources going to higher education which included the foundation of eight new universities, almost all of which were to have faculties of social science. With the simultaneous creation of departments of political science at many of the older universities, the government initiative more than doubled the number of existing departments in Britain. A chair beckoned for almost every existing member of staff at Manchester and Keele. Blondel responded to the call and in 1962 at the age of 32 was designated founding professor of the Department of Government at the new (and yet to be built) University of Essex at Colchester, 60 miles north-east of London.

Before going to Essex, however, he passed a crucial formative year as a fellow at Yale University. Yale was one of the two leading centres (with Michigan) of the behavioural movement sweeping American political science at the time. Behaviouralists were determined to penetrate behind institutions and organizational forms to the realities of political behaviour. While this aspiration owed something to the earlier muck-raking traditions of American political science, it was favoured by new methodological developments which for the first time allowed direct measurement of individual behaviour in the mass – above all through the social survey.

It was from this heady set of influences that the first of Blondel's two classic textbooks of the 1960s emerged. Although *Voters, Parties and Leaders* was dedicated to the political behaviour of *British* electors, activists and politicians, it drew on the traditions of behaviourism to construct a highly original synthesis of poll data and community studies which was quite new in the British context. One notable feature of the book, however, was that it was not wholly American in inspiration. It also drew on traditions of French electoral geography and of the type of party organizational studies pioneered by Duverger to fill in the gaps which polls did not cover – notably at the higher levels. So the book ends as more of a structural analysis in the older European tradition than it set out to be.

This is probably due more to accident and missing survey information than anything else. It does, however, almost uncannily pre-figure Blondel's later work in comparative politics, which is informed by a similar marriage of American methodological individualism to European styles of structural analysis.

Founding the Department at Essex 1964–1970

Blondel returned to Britain in 1964 charged with the task of creating a new and innovative department at the University of Essex – a hard task at a time when the number of existing departments was being doubled. It was a seller's market, with the limited pool of qualified political scientists in Britain able to pick and choose between posts, with the more talented aiming at chairs. While this created difficulties for any new department, it also created opportunities which would not have occurred in a more stable situation. The solid assets which Essex had were threefold.

The first was a university constructed – alone of the new creations of 1962 – on a wholly novel design. This rested on a limited number (ten) of very large departments, going from literature on the arts side to physics in science, with social science departments linked to each other and to mathematics and computing through common schemes of study. These included area degrees for North America, Latin America and the Soviet Union, thus reinforcing a comparative approach. All departments were to have generously supported research programmes and to make their names as soon as possible through research-based publications. In pursuit of this aim there was an effective tenure hurdle for staff, which facilitated the removal of those who did not perform well. In its first six years, the Department parted with well over half the lecturers it had originally engaged – an action which was unheard of in Britain and which caused the Essex Department to be viewed with suspicion.

The other University contribution to the success of the Department was the personal support of the head of the University (Vice-Chancellor) Albert Sloman – who, once convinced of the need for any initiative, was willing to back it quickly with all the resources at his disposal.

A second advantage enjoyed by the Essex Department was the general availability of government money for research and bursaries. This was channelled through the Social Science Research Council, set up in 1965, which immediately made studentships available for graduate courses in political science. Of course, the money was available for all departments. But only Essex had the necessary flexibility and (it must be said) ruthlessness to recruit twelve MA students in the short time available and enter them for the 1965–6 session. Most failed the year, but the great principle of budgetary inertia meant that departments which had once held studentships continued to get them so long as they had applicants. At one stroke, therefore, Essex acquired the largest graduate school in political science in Britain.

That it did so was due to the tactical dash of its founding professor who, in himself and in the associates he recruited, was the new Department's third great asset. His unusual attributes included a driving energy, which caused him to immerse himself in any project which engaged his attention (usually three or four simultaneously); a strategic conception of what the Department should do and where it ought to go (broadly, to emulate the leading American departments); an ability to provoke and stimulate colleagues to share this objective; and a determination to exploit every opportunity and resource to achieve these ends, regardless of any hesitations which others might have had.

An excellent example of these qualities was the decision to launch the MA programme in 1965. For although the first year's intake was less than impressive, the number and range of courses offered eventually attracted good – and in many cases exceptional – students. By 1969 the MA programme was unambiguously successful.

Blondel's ambition was no less than to make Essex the leading British department and equal to the 'top ten' American ones. He was thus anxious to ward off possible challenges from elsewhere in Britain and pre-empted a possible threat from the behaviourally-oriented department at Strathclyde by recruiting its founder, Allen Potter, in 1965 and its leading behaviouralist, Ian Budge, in 1966.

This provided teaching for Essex's MA in political behaviour. It also provided the necessary logistical basis for the next major landmark in departmental expansion, the foundation of the summer school in Research Methods in 1968. The occasion for holding a Summer School was provided by a UNESCO biennial grant for European departments to host a month-long school in social science. An initial meeting had been held at Paris in 1966. Blondel lobbied intensively to get it for Britain, at Essex; and as few others were interested, he succeeded.

Essex's ambitions, however, went far beyond hosting a one-off meeting on some aspect of political processes or institutions. The money could be utilized to create a summer school modelled on the immensely prestigious and influential research course held each summer at the University of Michigan in the United States, to which increasing numbers of Europeans were being attracted.

Essex had become a member of the Michigan-based Inter-University Consortium for Political Research, the organizers of the Michigan Summer School, in 1966. However, the University's own methodological resources, while enough to make it just feasible to contemplate a smaller summer school on the same lines, were woefully inadequate. A survey analysis package had been written for the University's one mainframe computer in 1967, but did not cover regression. Only one member of the Essex Department had much knowledge of methods; data collections had not been systematized, and teaching materials of all kinds were lacking.

To compensate, Blondel envisaged a joint school with Nuffield College, Oxford, the other major graduate institution in Britain. However, Nuffield wanted a much less advanced course on survey design and analysis, on the grounds that this was all the British were prepared for. Budge, backed by Blondel, argued that the school had to be comparable with Michigan. Blondel then turned to the SSRC Data Archive, just acquired by Essex as the result of another initiative. The Archive felt it had enough to cope with however and pulled out.

In consultation with his colleagues Blondel decided to go it alone and to compensate for Essex's weaknesses by enlisting direct support from Michigan. Anthony King, his most senior associate, secured from Warren Miller, Director of the ICPR, the secondment of an instructor from Michigan to teach the courses. On the strength of this they were advertised throughout Europe.

Lutz Erbring, the instructor in question, brought with him the Michigan suite of computer analysis programs which with the aid of two local assistants he managed to install on the Essex machine. He then taught the courses at the Summer School practically single-handed, with Budge overseeing everything else. With 25 participants from most countries of Europe the courses turned out to be a great success.

In contrast to everyone else, and in the face of indifference from the SSRC, Essex did not see the School as a one-off event, in spite of lacking external finance for 1969. This was grimly squeezed out of internal sources and subsidized by Michigan's altruistic payment of Erbring's salary. There were only 13 participants in 1969, mainly British, but the School kept on and in 1970 attracted a grant from the Nuffield Foundation. The growing number of participants consolidated Essex's reputation in the social sciences and was crucial to the foundation of the European Consortium, as we shall see.

By 1970 the Essex Department had been institutionalized and consolidated. Almost all the first appointees of 1964 had left. A new set of more weighty figures (including many of the Essex contributors to this volume) had arrived. It was they who were to launch most of the departmental initiatives of the next decade, including the foundation of the *British Journal of Political Science* and the acquisition of the National Election Study.

It was in a way the greatest tribute to Blondel that in six years the Department had gone from being a one-man initiative to an institution grouping teachers and researchers who stood in the first rank internationally. The consolidation enabled the Department to survive and indeed flourish in spite of a series of misfortunes which hit the University from the mid 1960s. These included unfavourable reactions to its novel structure on the part of the Universities Grants Council, which resulted in reduced funding at a critical phase; and the wave of student unrest from 1968 to 1974 which made Essex synonymous with radicalism and reduced the undergraduate applications on which funds depended; then the government imposed cuts affecting all British universities during the 1980s. Because of its strong institutional basis and collective morale the Department not only survived but consolidated its teaching and research during these years. That it did so was the achievement of his colleagues, but the credit for attracting them in the first place goes to Blondel.

Blondel galvanized normal British academic life by incessantly stimulating, organizing, and bullying colleagues, administrators, and everyone implicated in any of his initiatives. During the years from 1964 to 1970 he practically lived in the Department. He visited every office daily to enquire what the colleague was doing; he telephoned and visited at the weekends with whatever was uppermost on his mind, capitalizing when it suited him to do so on the fiction that, being a foreigner, he had little knowledge of British academic conventions. Occasionally, these tactics misfired – but they usually worked. In the service of an overall strategic conception of where the Department should go they proved supremely successful.

Comparative Research 1965–1970

Given the way he practically lived in the Department in the late 1960s, it would have been natural for Blondel to have let his own research go, at least for the duration. Many might have done so, but Blondel was very conscious that institution-building, though essential, was not enough. Having immersed himself in collective activities during the week, he retired home to read and write at the weekends – activities interrupted to be sure by telephone calls, visits and exhortations to colleagues. The six-weeks' family holiday in Toulon had also four hours writing a day built into it. Perhaps, indeed, the ferment of ideas in political science, distilled through internal debates at Essex, had to be reflected upon and ordered, so that writing was a necessary complement to his institutional activities.

What emerged from this process of gestation was a work which, parallel to Rokkan's own distinctive contribution, crystallized a new European approach to comparative politics. It should be stressed that it was not Blondel's intention any more than Rokkan's to create a specifically 'European' approach. What he wanted to do was simply to order and systematize the field. Hence, the title of his new book was *Introduction to Comparative Government*. But, in fact, it did more than simply introduce the field of systematic comparative politics: to a considerable extent it defined and formalized it.

The novel feature of the new book was its simple but far reaching assumption that comparative politics covered all countries in the world, each of which counted as one and no more than one. To deal simultaneously with 150-odd national units, Blondel had to have recourse to statistical generalization, and therefore had to collect the same information about all countries (a small data set found in an appendix at the back). The basic information – geographical, economic, social and political – was heavily judgemental in nature and culled from *Keesing's Contemporary Archives* and similar sources.

The statistical methods applied to the information were of the most simple kind: one or two bivariate regressions and a mass of commentary on marginals and cross-tabulations. This was hardly important, however: the shocking or inspiring impact – however one cared to take it – was made by the commitment always to analyse the whole world, by including all countries for which there was information in support of major generalizations.

The approach was original and shocking because comparative government up to then (and for the most part afterwards as well) consisted of detailed treatments of important countries (the Soviet Union, the United States, France, Germany, Britain, Japan) – very often basing any comparison on detailed analysis of each state taken separately and in historical detail. At its most daring it would take an area like Western Europe or Latin America and generalize about social and political trends in the constituent countries.

Contrast this with Blondel's willingness to leap from Togo to China in one breath, while basing comparisons on units as widely separated as Fiji and Poland. While it is true that a limited number of studies had made comparisons at this world level before Blondel, and may have inspired him, these were either very specialized or in the nature of data books, with limited commentary. Blondel's achievement was to go through all political processes, from the initial socialization of populations to the functioning of institutions, without for a moment hesitating in his determination to make world generalizations.

As already noted, two kinds of influence went into the book: one American and behavioural, one European and structuralist. The behavioural influence is easily seen in the use of quantitative data, the 'methodological individualism' implicit in treating countries as single unities, and the broad organization into 'input' and 'output' functions of the polity. The resolute concern for generalization also derives in part from American behaviouralism, but equally from the French tradition of Duverger. Blondel is indeed much less concerned with *a priori* theory and hypothesis than the Americans, and much more with semi-inductive 'laws' based on perceived regularities in his data. The imposition of order and regularity on a seemingly chaotic world is very French and gives the book a distinctive style and approach.

The long-term influence of Duverger may also be seen in the book's attention to institutional regularities – rare in the behavioural literature of the time. Blondel is concerned with electoral systems and party systems like Duverger but extends this concern to contrasts between the presidential and parliamentary systems and the different effects of these institutional arrangements. Moreover he sees in institutional arrangements a powerful force for conscious adaptation and influence among nations – an insight which owes much more to 'constitutional government' traditions of research than to contemporary behaviouralism.

An Introduction to Comparative Government, then, represents a bold and original synthesis of the field which successfully blends American and European, new and old approaches. While much respected and widely read (a new edition was launched in 1992) it did not create a school or stimulate immediate follow-up research as Rokkan's 'developmental' approach to European party systems did. Part of the reason is that Blondel did not seek to create a school. Strangely for one who launched highly successful departmental and international structures, Blondel (for most of his career at least) worked alone on his research. Most comparativists were, in any case, more interested in working on sets of similar countries like Western democracies, or within areas, rather than with all existing states. Blondel's approach has been influential in the sense that within such groupings, each country was treated as a unit amenable to statistically based generalizations.

Perhaps the comparative research for which he is best known came in a concurrent article. 'Party Systems and Patterns of Government in Western Democracies', published in the *Canadian Journal of Political Science* in 1968, proposed a modification to the traditional typology of party systems as having two, three and multiple parties. Blondel brilliantly captured more subtle gradations by proposing a typology of two parties, two and a half parties (the most common form) – with indeed a category of two parties and two half parties, and so on. This has been almost universally adopted by party theorists – to such an extent that they are now hazy about its exact origin, so natural does it seem to classify systems in this way.

Blondel's comparative work in this period represented a landmark in the field, even if it was more admired than emulated (as suggested above, however, it did give a strong impetus to generalizing unselfconsciously across groups of countries without constant reference to national idiosyncrasies). Working on comparative politics perhaps helped to focus his thoughts also on the organizational needs of cross-national research, which were to shape the next major phase of his career.

The European Consortium for Political Research 1969–1979

The Essex Department of Government as it was conceived and developed in the 1960s and 1970s was almost exclusively American in orientation. This was true not only of the type and style of research it did, of its structures like the graduate programme, and of its internal organization and the way it governed itself (rotating Chairman and Department meeting), but also of staff contacts and visits. Two regular exchange programmes (with the University of Wisconsin, Madison and the University of North Carolina, Chapel Hill) functioned over long periods, strengthening the orientation to the United States.

This might seem strange for a department organized in Britain by a Frenchman, and when about a third of the members were of non-British and non-American origin. Differences in background and political experience from the American did work through in some aspects of individual research: the continuity with French approaches in the *Introduction to Comparative Government* is a good example. Collective projects were, however, conceived on American lines and justified as catching up with the United States. This is very understandable given the overwhelming intellectual dominance and professionalization of American political science, especially in relation to the underdeveloped state of the subject in Europe.

Primarily through the assimilation of these influences, political science in the various Western European countries was becoming more vigorous in the late 1960s, focused round new departments organized like Essex itself on American lines. The largest was Mannheim in West Germany, where Rudolph Wildenmann had played an invigorating and organizing role similar to Blondel's own at Essex, with particular attention to creating a whole new generation of scholars destined to take up chairs at the other German universities. Leiden in the Netherlands remained more oriented to the traditional elements in British and American scholarship. Bergen, in Norway, remained somewhere between, but Stein Rokkan's incessant travel, trans-European contacts and intellectual influence made it a place of weight. Other centres – Aarhus in Denmark, Göteborg in Sweden, Strathclyde and Nuffield in Britain – had taken up American-inspired survey research in an enthusiastic way.

At the same time, American conferences and joint research projects were bringing academics of the various European countries into personal contact, an indispensable first step to establishing any collaboration among themselves. The United States, moreover, offered a model of how this might be achieved in the shape of the Inter-University Consortium for Political Research (ICPR).

ICPR was a partnership between the Survey Research Center of the University of Michigan and other universities keen to share its facilities and data. The SRC had been at the centre of the most prestigious research programme of the post-war era in the United States, the first national election studies completed anywhere, which had produced what at the time seemed the definitive work on voting behaviour – *The American Voter* of Angus Campbell, Philip Converse, Warren Miller and Donald Stokes. The immense intellectual prestige won for Michigan by this, and the organizational drive of Warren Miller, led to the idea of the Consortium and the foundation of an annual summer school on research methods, backed by the SRC's suite of computer research programs, rich data resources and skilled personnel. We have already noted the altruistic transfer of some of these resources to the Essex Summer School.

In effect, the ICPR represented an opening of the ongoing activities of the SRC to other universities and institutions, including European ones. It thus focused on meeting the demand for data through a distribution network and the institutionalization of the existing Archive. The Archive was expensive and time-consuming but was the main advantage of membership from the viewpoint of outside members. By the end of the 1960s the ICPR in effect consisted of the Archive and the Summer School.

This was a model which Europeans might very well want for themselves. The occasion to acquire it was a direct result of another expression of American altruism, a decision by the Ford Foundation to aid the development of political science in Western Europe. The crucial point came when the director Peter Janosi toured a number of leading centres in the early summer of 1969 to see what could be done for them. Most, not unnaturally, asked for money or resources for themselves. Blondel suggested that development could be best promoted collectively, by creating a consortium in Europe. Given the increasing number of European members and the great prestige of the ICPR, then at the height of its influence and activity, this seemed a self-evidently good idea.

The crucial test of whether something could be done by Europeans in Europe was the Essex Summer School, then approaching its second summer, with shrunken resources, diminished participants, and no support from funding bodies. Backing a consortium on the basis of the Summer School was constructing a castle in the air on one barely emerging from the sand. But the important point, like the Essex graduate programme before it, was not how it operated but that it was there. Blondel seized on this with his usual flair and dash and obtained the promise of a quarter of a million pounds from Ford for a European consortium, if its feasibility could be demonstrated.

As the model was already there, there was no doubt that the new organization should be based on institutions paying membership fees. Getting these together to agree on its foundation was hard and was delayed by jockeying for position among potential participants. Representatives of eight institutions did, however, come together in 1970 for a foundation meeting: Essex; Nuffield College, Oxford; Strathclyde; Bergen; Göteborg; Leiden; Mannheim; and the Institut de Science Politique, Paris. Blondel's nomination as Executive Director was secured by his Ford Foundation support. Rokkan was elected as Chairman to balance both him and the potential British influence. Representatives of the founding institutions formed the Executive Committee.

The immediate problem was what the new organization could actually do to justify its existence. The Summer School in research methods already existed and it was obvious that, like the ICPR, the ECPR should play a sponsoring role. Continuing along the methodological and data-based analogy with the ICPR, Rokkan wanted a reference publication identifying and detailing European data collections. This was run in the shape of a data information service by the Norwegian Data Archive at Bergen.

Beyond that, however, what was to be done? The other major activity of the ICPR was the Data Archive, but this function had been anticipated in Western Europe by the creation of national archives in many of the countries, which were already making contacts among themselves and with Michigan.

The imperative need to introduce Western Europeans to each other, and even to define the profession, suggested other activities which were taken up with energy by the new Director who, with the Ford grant, had the unusual problem of finding projects to spend money on rather than finding money to finance them. A *Directory of European Political Scientists* was quickly compiled as was a guide to graduate courses in the discipline. A new journal, the *European Journal of Political Research*, was created with the express function of publishing in English research which would normally only be accessible in another language.

Research workshops to bring together academics working on the same topic in different countries could also be used to introduce Europeans to each other, again on American models. A first workshop on coalitions was held in 1971. It was, however, Wildenmann who had the idea which catapulted the Consortium to the centre of professional attention and transformed its prospects: holding several workshops together in a single place for a week, once a year.

The importance of this idea lay in the fact that no body existed to bring European political scientists together as did the big American conventions. Each country had a national association with an annual conference, but these were small, limited in their interests and focused inevitably on national politics. The Joint Sessions of Workshops, held for the first time at Mannheim in 1973, through Wildenmann's pretty well unaided efforts, unleashed an explosion of enthusiasm, European solidarity, and support for the Consortium, unanticipated even by its promoters. Somehow, a critical mass had been established. The Joint Sessions were unusual in a number of respects. *Everybody* attending had to be a member of a workshop and had to give a paper. Workshops, with a specific theme, were spread over five days with morning and afternoon sessions. Hence all participants were expected to contribute on a continuous basis. Special attention was paid to attracting younger members of the profession whose status in the workshops was the same as all other participants bar the chairperson. The chair's role was to select the papers given and to conduct proceedings during the week. This formula worked brilliantly. Membership of the Consortium expanded steadily from the 25 of 1972 to around 100 by 1979 – an achievement which made it self-sustaining financially.

From the first two Joint Sessions (Mannheim followed by Strasbourg in 1974) the Consortium was clearly riding an expanding wave, which made the generation of new projects irresistible, and self-sustaining. Expansion was also built into the organization as a deliberate policy by Blondel, who believed that if it did not grow it would collapse. He therefore invited new ideas from all quarters. Following on the Essex model a premium was put on publishing the results of workshops, and a book series started with Sage to do so. Collaborative programmes of research were funded with a grant from the Volkswagen Stiftung in 1976, owing again to Wildenmann's intervention. However, this was split among a limited number of institutions and the results were less innovative than they might have been. Plans for long-term research groups and joint research sessions, on the lines of the workshops but dedicated to particular projects, were in hand at the end of Blondel's period of office.

This rather institutional account of the Consortium's growth misses out one crucial factor in its success: the evangelistic zeal and frenetic activity of the Executive Director. As he had done with the Essex Department, Blondel lived the Consortium. He travelled incessantly throughout Europe seeking new members and visiting existing ones, soliciting ideas and support and appealing particularly to the younger generation of graduate students and staff. It was this in turn which filled the institutional forms with content and energy. After all, the Consortium would never have succeeded had people not responded to it and it was Blondel who produced and orchestrated the response. As a result, it has become the chief focus of professional life for about 1200–1500 English-using political scientists in Western Europe: the only European professional association which has mobilized its membership to that extent.

The unique features of the Consortium are:

1   The fact that it offers outlets for most aspects of professional life; rather than specializing in conferences or summer schools, it offers these and much more.

2   Its organizing and initiatory role. To an extent unparalleled in professional associations which are mostly rather passive and reactive bodies it offers leads in identifying research projects or new needs or new services. It is more like a *syndicat d'initiative* in French local business than a professional body. This innovatory role owes very much to the stamp Blondel set on the directorship, which he conceived as an energizing rather than an administrative institution.

3   Its federal and autonomous organization. Almost all the activities of the Consortium are carried out through contracts with its members. Thus, even Essex, which hosts the central administration and the Summer School, does so on the basis of a contract. Unlike Michigan, in the ICPR, it is not half the Consortium, but on a par with the other members all of whom share in the editorships of journal or book series and management of the Joint Sessions and research sessions. The internal federalism of the Consortium was, of course, partly forced on it because no one institution was in a position to play a dominant or leading role. But it also reflects the encouraging, hectoring, supportive but never grasping style of Blondel as Director.

The end result of his and his colleagues' efforts of the 1970s was the ECPR as it is today, with over 150 members and an expanding geographical base and range of activities. Much more than through a particular intellectual approach, if European political science can be said to be distinctive it is organizationally, in the strong and comprehensive structure it has created for itself. In the end, the ICPR never developed beyond its initial activities of archive and summer school: the ECPR has covered almost the full range of professional activities in a way which might well be emulated elsewhere. The European Consortium *is* European political science, giving it a firm basis and powerful structure which could not contrast more with its undeveloped state of the 1950s. The achievement is not solely Blondel's but it owes much to him, and it entitles him to be regarded as one of the founding fathers of contemporary political science not only in Europe but in the world.

Research on Government Institutions and Ministers 1979–1993

As remarked above, Blondel's career illustrates the new cross-national mobility of the European profession as well as contributing to it. In 1985 he moved from the University of Essex to the European University Institute in Florence, while remaining Chairman of the Political Science Committee of the British Economic and Social Science Research Council – the major source of funds for research in Britain. The European Institute was founded in 1976 by the European Community as a postgraduate school and research centre for the social sciences. Through its extensive graduate programme and provisions for visitors, it has become an important cross-national meeting point in Europe and – particularly now – a place of contact between East and West. It is an ideal location for Blondel to pursue the research he initiated in 1973 into the governmental structures and processes which had dominated the closing pages of the *Introduction to Comparative Government*. One may see in this growing interest in institutions, norms and practices a long-term working out of older influences in political science. However, it is again combined with an interest in individual ministerial and leadership careers which reflects American behaviourism.

Blondel was convinced that more than theory about governments, what was needed was comparable and detailed data, out of which regularities would emerge. In a whole series of books and monographs, latterly with a group of collaborators, he has tried to fill in the details of government activities, sometimes concentrating on leaders at the top of the system, sometimes on their middle-level colleagues and associates.

Unfashionable when it was initiated in the 1970s, his research into government structures has now moved back into the mainstream. It has enjoyed a symbiotic relationship with formal theories of coalitions and governmental structures, thanks to the development of the 'new institutionalism' emphasizing the stability which legal rules and informal norms impose on potentially chaotic situations. Formal theorists are consequently seeking some understanding of the limits, and potential opportunities, afforded by structures to individual and collective actors. An excellent illustration of how the two lines of research can help each other occurs in Chapter 8, where Laver and Shepsle show how parties dealing in ministries could achieve stable governmental arrangements where parties dealing in policies could not. However, this depends crucially on whether ministries have autonomous fields of action (in which case distributing them to different parties really implies something in terms of policy) or whether they are strictly bound by cabinet decisions (in which case we are back with overall policy packages and predicted instability in coalition arrangements). On these points comparative institutional research, of the kind undertaken by Blondel and his colleagues, has a lot to say, and its findings are being accorded growing significance. His own interests over this period have developed in parallel: from studies of the individual careers of ministers and leaders, still very much in the behavioural tradition of the analysis of elites (though concerned with the dynamics of career development rather than static comparisons of elites and mass), to a growing interest in structure and the rules governing the behaviour of collectivities.

Building Political Science in Europe: an Overview

One could see this development as a return to the grass roots of Duverger and the French tradition, but of course it is much more; what might be termed enriched institutional analysis benefiting from the theoretical developments and empirical findings of the last forty years. In a sense too it has benefited from the organizational developments which Blondel pioneered. It is now possible and indeed increasingly common to build a network of specialists throughout Europe, each of which has a particular expertise in the politics of his or her own country but who can meet regularly to compare similarities or isolate differences in an all-European or indeed world context.

European-level research has characteristically operated under the aegis of the ECPR in precisely this way: country studies, often carried out to a common research design, are grouped together in a volume with introductory and end chapters picking out and commenting on common trends. This is enormously useful. It enables accurate descriptions and analyses of the smaller countries to be made accessible in English. At the same time it does aim at European-level generalizations (and often at generalizing about democracies as such, since until recently most long-lasting democracies were to be found in Western Europe).

However, comparative research cannot stop with country by country studies, however general the framework. It must try to abstract further into relationships between variables (the effects of multi-party systems on government stability for example, rather than the observation that governments are more unstable in Italy and Finland than in other countries). Given his earlier work which aimed precisely at variable-based rather than country-based generalizations, Blondel is well qualified to lead the way here. It would be a fitting culmination to his career if in the 1990s he succeeded in enunciating comparative generalizations of this kind in a way which was widely acceptable. By so doing he would leave even more of a mark on the study of comparative politics than he has already done.

Such a development however still lies in the future. Any assessment of his present achievements must refer itself to the current state of European political science, which Blondel has done so much to shape. A first thing which must be said – and this is well exemplified in his own career – is that there is no distinctive school of political science centred in Europe which has different theories or methods to those prevalent elsewhere. Europeans have different preoccupations from Americans, for example, because they are faced with different historical and contemporary realities – primarily ideologically based parties and social movements, and the importance of self-identities (class, national, religious, regional and ethnic).

All these facts force Europeans into a less individualistic, more collective, and more sociological/psychological approach to politics than Americans. American rational choice theory can afford to base itself on the strategic interactions between individuals with clear-cut and unchanging goals, because these are embedded in a universalistic and individualistic American culture. Those groups and collective values not boiled down in the melting pot can be left to sociologists and cultural anthropologists to explain.

Quite a different set of processes has taken place in Europe which has resulted in collective identities being institutionalized in political parties. To a large extent the political struggle is about which party will render salient which aspect of the multiple identities of most Europeans. Thus, values and identities cannot simply be assumed to be as basic and universal as in the United States. Hence the popularity in Europe of Rokkan's developmental theories of political parties which are as close to a distinctively European theory of politics as can be found.

However, Americans do avail themselves of developmental theories (Lipset after all collaborated with Rokkan in its most influential exegesis) and the application of American-originated theories, models, and approaches by Europeans to their own politics has been manifold. The many lines of cleavage in political science do not divide Europeans from Americans but run through both groups, dividing political theorists from institutionalists and historians, and both from empirical theorists and generalizers.

There is a European political science now, in a sense which did not exist in the 1950s, because there is a sizeable body of institutionally defined political scientists in Western Europe who meet together regularly, collaborate with each other, and read each other's work. These contacts would hardly exist without the European Consortium, which in turn would not exist had not strong departments of political science – Essex, Mannheim, Foundation Nationale de Science Politique, Aarhus and others – not developed in the 1960s and 1970s. Jean Blondel has thus contributed to the creation of European political science at two levels: as founder of a leading national department and as main organizer of the Consortium.

It is wholly characteristic that as late as 1992, Blondel was imploring the ECPR Executive Committee to act fast on the absorption of the universities and centres of Eastern Europe into the organization. At that time Blondel was one of the few to appreciate that the long-term benefits of such an absorption would outweigh the short-term costs.

He himself would wish to be remembered more for the research he has done than for his organizational achievements. But his research, as we have pointed out, has fed into the general discussions of world rather than specifically European political science. His particular European contribution has been organizational, and in this area, pre-eminent. Without him there would not be a European political science. 'Se monumentum requiris, circumspice.'

3

Democracy, Citizenship and the Study of Political Socialization

Pamela Johnston Conover and Donald D. Searing

In the 1960s the main explanation for democratic stability or breakdown, or indeed for the way in which the whole democratic process functioned, was sought in the values and identities acquired by children in their formative years. It was on the supportive attitudes of citizens, learned from parents, friends and schools, that the major institutions – government, parliaments, parties – all rested. This is reflected for example in the organization and initial chapters of Blondel's classic *Introduction to Comparative Government*.

Now things are very different. Political socialization has lost its children, lost its identity, lost its theoretical rationale, and lost its following in the profession.[1] How did this happen? What can be done about it? The alarms have been ringing (Rosenberg, 1985; Cook, 1985; Sears, 1987; Connell, 1987) but there is more agreement about the nature and gravity of the problem than about how to resolve it. Very little research has been done on children in recent years. And most commentators believe that this is undermining the field's identity, for the hallmark of socialization studies has long been their concern with the formation of political ideas during childhood and adolescence (Niemi and Sobieszek, 1977, p.209; Cook, 1985, p.180).

Near the end of the 1970s, socialization researchers reacted to disappointments and dissatisfactions with early theoretical frameworks by turning the field's focus in a new direction: toward attitude change during adolescence and adulthood. The early theoretical frameworks had become highly problematic, but the new directions did not render them less so. Thus, there developed a malaise among researchers in the field, a malaise whose root cause is theoretical. Yet the remedies prescribed thus far have not succeeded and are not likely to succeed. Merelman (1980), for example, has helped by showing how exchange theory can be used to rethink relationships between the family and the polity. Rosenberg (1985) has suggested that we need to take more seriously psychological theories of learning. And Cook (1985) has argued that the theoretical difficulties can best be resolved with the cognitive-developmental models of L.S. Vygotsky.

These three proposals are all desirable but are not by themselves sufficiently powerful to revitalize the field and re-establish it on a convincing foundation. To do that, we need a clear diagnosis of the problem that makes sense to practitioners and a new research agenda that attracts new generations of graduate students into the field. Our diagnosis is that there is not enough socialization in research on political socialization. And the research agenda that we propose takes us back, this time via political philosophy, to the study of citizenship. The first part of this chapter returns to the landmark studies that established the field during the 1960s. It takes a fresh look at the problems that developed with the frameworks found in those studies and tries to see how a new start might be made. The second part of the chapter develops this new start into a research agenda by going back further still: to the study of citizenship as conceived by Merriam and the Chicago school and to debates about citizenship in the history of political philosophy.

The Traditions in the Study of Political Socialization

The founding socialization studies of the 1960s established two distinct research traditions: one associated with David Easton and concerned with the sources of political stability, the other associated with Herbert Hyman and concerned with the sources of political participation (Greenstein, 1965, p. 16; Dennis et al., 1971; Budge, 1971). At the time, Easton and Hess (1962, p. 234) worried that the Hyman tradition, which was indebted to election studies and took many of its variables directly from them (Niemi and Sobieszek, 1977, p. 210), was becoming so dominant that the study of basic dispositions toward the regime and the community might be neglected. That is exactly what happened. And for the emerging field of political socialization, the dominance of the Hyman tradition created both blessings and difficulties. The blessings were that the electoral connection brought instant legitimacy and inspiration through association with an established area and established methodologies. The difficulties were that this led the new field toward political learning and away from political socialization, toward the political system and away from the individual, and toward a narrow conception of citizens and voters.[2]

Political Learning versus Political Socialization

We could save ourselves a good deal of confusion if we renamed the field 'political learning', for this would describe what we currently study more accurately than does the term 'political socialization'. Political learning is a broader concept than political socialization. It refers to the learning of any political beliefs regardless of whether or not such beliefs facilitate adaptation to a collectivity. According to the *Oxford English Dictionary*, the original definition of the verb 'to socialize' is much the same as its contemporary definition in most social sciences: 'to render social, to make fit for living in society'. Thus, all socialization involves learning. But not all learning counts as socialization: to acquire attitudes is not the same thing as to render social. Certainly, Hyman (1959, pp. 9–10) was aware that the process of becoming a member of a collectivity – a group, organization or society – is central to socialization's traditional connotations. But in 1959 there were hardly any political studies of this phenomenon upon which to build. Therefore, he focused his spotlight (and the attention of the field) on the studies that did exist. These were largely studies of dependent variables like political interest, party preference and policy beliefs, variables particularly relevant to electoral contexts and to political learning. Yet, it was difficult in the 1960s to see how this focus on electoral behaviour was moving us away from socialization's distinctive concerns. The truth is that we have not really studied political socialization very much at all. By 1974, Jennings and Niemi, who more than anyone else were carrying forward research in the Hyman tradition, even began to voice scepticism about the utility of the political socialization concept which was not much help with the electoral topics they were investigating. Thus, the title of the first chapter of their first book (1974) replaced the term 'political socialization' with 'political learning'. And, their second book (1981) demonstrated that as the study of political learning moves into the adult years, it requires research designs similar to those found in studies of electoral behaviour.[3] These two books are undoubtedly the field's landmark research efforts after the 1960s. But, we need to investigate socialization too.

System or Individual

The best way to bring back socialization, we shall argue, is to bring back citizenship. From this viewpoint, the debate about political socialization's importance to the political system versus its importance to the individual is at the heart of our current theoretical difficulties. Thus far, the key question has always been: of what relevance is the political socialization of citizens for the political system (Greenstein, 1965, p. 1)? We study political learning among children, in this view, because children will in the future become adult citizens who apply their pre-adult learning to affecting the political system through electoral behaviour and political support.

This is obviously an important topic. But there is another equally important topic that has hardly been studied empirically, a topic that engages socialization *qua* socialization, a topic that is consistent with political education in the history of political philosophy, a topic that has the potential to restore the field's children and its theoretical rationale (see Gutmann, 1987): the making of citizens – not just the making of voters but the making of citizens in a much broader understanding of the term. And this topic draws our attention to the sources of the system's contributions to the individual's experience and character as a citizen in the political community. Here the key question becomes: of what relevance is the political system for the political socialization of citizens? This is not a new idea. Many commentators over the last fifteen years (e.g. Sears, 1975; Cook, 1985; Merelman, 1972; Niemi, 1973; Lindblom, 1982) have said that we should investigate the consequences of political socialization for the individual. But these suggestions have not caught fire because they have lacked a convincing political rationale. We have been unable to discern such a rationale because our gaze has been fixed, by liberal political theory and by election studies, on the citizen as a voter.

Beyond the Electoral Fields

The citizen as voter or political participant is the person Hyman (1959, p. 12) had in mind when he argued that the learning of attitudes related to political participation concerns a central aspect of the role of the citizen (cf. Dowse and Hughes, 1971). Part of the appeal of this approach was its congruence with the liberal theory of democracy which interprets voting as the primary function of the citizen and interprets citizenship in the contractual terms of Hobbes and Locke. The other side of the appeal was that by drawing on concepts and measures already established in the national election studies, socialization research was immediately connected to adult political behaviour and to the systemic touchstones of political relevance. Yet, once the goal became contributing to explanations of adult political participation, it was perhaps inevitable that research on political learning would eventually move from childhood into adolescence and then into adulthood – because we would want to examine the learning of the attitudes that were actually doing the causal work.

By contrast, when we turn to those aspects of citizenship that make people members of the political communities, we encounter attitudes that draw us back to the study of childhood by drawing us back to phenomena that are of direct importance to individuals: matters of identity and experience in the basic bonds between themselves and their collectivities. There is far more to citizenship than the act of voting which has been emphasized so much in the United States. In fact, the act of voting only reflects the second definition of the noun 'citizen' in most dictionaries. The first definition describes citizens as members of political communities to which they owe loyalty. This communal perspective on citizenship, which has been much stressed in Europe, emphasizes not merely political participation, but also the important activities of civility and public service that we shall discuss when we present below this new agenda for socialization research.[4]

The introduction of the subject of citizens as members of their political communities offers us what we need most to revitalize the field: a convincing theoretical and cross-national rationale for studying children. It was Easton and Dennis (1969, pp. 83-4) who argued that the relevance of childhood socialization would vary a great deal by the types of orientations being investigated. Many of the key attitudes that drive political participation, they speculated, might be learned later in life. They thought, however, that feelings of support were more likely to have significant childhood roots. And although support for the political authorities was eventually found to change throughout life more than they had expected, their hypotheses about support for political community and for the regime have never been satisfactorily investigated.[5] These aspects of support are linked via feelings of patriotism and identity to the conception of citizens as members of the political community. The development of such basic psychological bonds, Easton and Dennis (1969, p. 67) argued, takes us back into childhood, for that is where they are learned.

But what are 'significant childhood roots'? Significant for what or for whom? For the system or for the individual? In this case we can answer 'both', since the sorts of citizenship profiles we shall discuss in the second half of this chapter are likely to affect adult political participation. Yet, even if they do not, they will nevertheless recapture childhood for us because although pre-adults may not be voters, they certainly are citizens. And the conceptions of citizenship that they learn as children are significant for their emerging civil identities and for their private identities as well.

The Rapid Rise and Fall of the Study of Political Socialization

Does our diagnosis go to the heart of the matter? The heart of the matter lies in the landmark studies of the 1960s that established the field's framework, and in the disappointments with this framework which began in the late 1960s and have continued on down to the present.

Perhaps the disappointments were so keenly felt because the enterprise had soared so high so quickly. Political socialization was launched in an atmosphere of professional optimism and intellectual ferment. When, thirty years ago, we read Herbert Hyman's (1959, p.vi) observation that 'One seeks far and wide for any extended treatment of political behaviour as *learned* behaviour, despite the fact that this is patently the case', we recognized immediately that he was correct and that a new field had been launched. Enthusiasm rose rapidly on a series of intriguing discoveries about children's images of the political world (Hess and Easton, 1960; Greenstein, 1960). Then, two years later, David Easton and Robert Hess (1962) published an influential essay which seemed to provide a little of everything the fledgeling field needed to get started: a sensible theoretical framework, politically important concepts, and preliminary findings that were startling and provocative.[6]

The findings that most fascinated the profession were those reported by Greenstein and by Easton and Hess about how elementary school children 'idealized' the political authorities. Such findings seemed important because they seemed to be rooted in deep-seated needs concerning authority and because they seemed to be the basis for the diffuse support underlying democratic stability. Yet, very quickly, too quickly, dramatic events and new data shattered confidence in these findings and with it their promise for explaining something basic about the political system (Merelman, 1980).

Events and Data: Childhood Lost

Admiration for the new field began to turn into disillusion when the same generation of children that Greenstein, Easton and Hess had studied in elementary school rebelled against the system when they reached college in the late 1960s and early 1970s (Niemi and Sobieszek, 1977, p. 210). Student protests and anti-war activism by the very children who were supposed to have learned such idealized views and feelings sent shock waves through the field's theoretical foundations (cf. Greenstein, 1975, p. 1373). The early 'deeply rooted' idealization seemed to have evaporated.

New survey data proved equally unsettling. Jaros et al. (1968) found that children in the Appalachian region of eastern Kentucky were remarkably less positive about political authority than were the mainly white, middle-class children studied in previous research. Blacks were rioting in the cities, and it came as no great surprise to see surveys in which, compared with whites, blacks held some views that were less supportive of the system and its leaders (Greenberg, 1970; Sears and McConahay, 1973; Abramson, 1977). In the same vein, Mexican-American children were found to have negative attitudes towards the president (Garcia, 1973). Disturbing data kept coming. In Britain, it was discovered, children likewise held negative attitudes towards party leaders (Stradling and Zurick, 1971). Studies done in other countries found that in some of them no leaders at all were respected by children, while in others children did not even know who their leaders were.

The consequence of this flood of counter-examples was disillusionment with the sanguine launch of socialization research (Niemi and Sobieszek, 1977, pp. 212-14). But the worst result was the beginning of the loss of childhood. Easton and Dennis (1969, p. 6), and nearly everyone else, had assumed that childhood socialization 'had vital consequences for the persistence of political systems'. The discovery that children did not invariably idealize government made us realize that the early research findings had been overgeneralized. It also shattered our hopes that fundamental psychological forces had been discovered during early childhood (Sears, 1975, p. 99).

A decade later, Kinder and Sears (1985, p. 725) would argue that it is extremely difficult to assess the implications of these events and data – because the events were unusual, and because the data turned out to be highly correlated with partisanship. Furthermore, the generation gap between the student rebels and their parents may not have been as great as was supposed at the time (see Jennings and Niemi, 1981, pp. 166–88). Perhaps our reaction to the events and to the associated data had been an over-reaction. Perhaps the idealization thesis had been weakened without its principal claim being invalidated, i.e. that early idealization will affect later supportive feelings when the children become adults. All this was reasonable but ultimately not very persuasive to the profession. It did little to ameliorate the disillusionment of those who began to think that the research operation should be packed up and moved out of childhood (Kavanagh, 1983, p. 39).

Persistence: a Theoretical Rationale Buckles

Growing doubts about the persistence of basic orientations seemed to undermine such counter-arguments, for if the idealized attitudes learned in childhood (whatever their true strength and character) could not persist into adulthood, then it was difficult to see how they could affect the attitudes and behaviour of adults. Socialization seemed trapped in the classic conundrum of historicist methodology. The data and debates on this subject seemed to threaten further the theoretical rationale of studying anyone younger than adult voters – to threaten, in effect, the theoretical rationale of research on political socialization as opposed to political learning. Even scholars within the field began to ask, 'other than studying it for its own sake, is there any justification for studying the political views of pre-adults and especially pre-teenagers?' (Niemi and Sobieszek, 1977, pp. 216–17).

When he started the ball rolling in 1959, Hyman (1959, pp. 21–35), who was a sociologist, apparently did not realize how important it would become to political scientists to be convinced that the political attitudes of children and adolescents were meaningfully linked to the political system via their future impact upon adult political behaviour. Hyman's electoral connection aroused the interest of political scientists. But it also aroused expectations that went beyond his (1959, pp. 18, 74) subtle claims that childhood attitudes should be regarded as 'precursors' (forerunners) of adult attitudes. Although there proved to be some evidence to support the hypothesized persistence (see Sears, 1975, pp. 127–30) the weight of the evidence came down heavily on the other side (Searing et al. 1976). The best data by far were produced by Jennings and Niemi (1974; 1981) who found important changes in most political orientations throughout the life cycle. There were more changes during the first decade of adulthood. And there were substantial changes across the subsequent adult years as well – particularly, Jennings and Niemi (1974, pp. 252–3) argued, for attitudes related to partisan politics.[7]

It was difficult to interpret the evidence about persistence because several quite different models were available for consideration. The most straightforward was the endurance model whereby a political belief learned during childhood endures relatively unchanged into and through-out the adult years. This is the model that most of us have in mind when we evaluate data on persistence. And this is the model under which most observers have concluded that orientations like political efficacy, party identification and political trust fail the test.

More interesting, more confusing, and more difficult to appreciate is the developmental model where beliefs such as political trust are transformed over time, with each new modification being shaped by the previous state of the belief. The difficulty with such developmental models lies in establishing causal connections over very long periods of time. For the short run, the model makes good sense: what we believe today is obviously shaped by what we believed yesterday. But when a belief changes a good deal, is it still reasonable to suppose that what we believe today is 'shaped' by what we believed eight, sixteen, twenty-four or thirty-two years ago? Even if the attitude does not shift direction several times (many do over long periods) and is steady in its rate as well as direction of change, a correlation of 0.30 between any two intervals of eight years might well become 0.09 over three such intervals, and 0.0081 over four.[8]

These doubts about persistence seemed to threaten the theoretical rationale of studying anyone younger than adult voters. The field responded. Some attitudes, it was said, were more likely than others to prove enduring (Miller and Sears, 1985, p. 233). Alternative persistence models, it was said, might not be so seriously affected by the empirical case against the standard models. But the strongest response to the claim that attitudes learned in childhood change a great deal throughout life was the response that set out to study these changes (Jennings and Niemi, 1974; 1981; Sigel and Hoskin, 1981). The results were creative and impressive. But their main contribution proved to be not so much to revitalize childhood socialization research as to shift the focus from political learning during childhood to political learning during adolescence and adulthood (Sears, 1987, p. 8).

Rethinking the Framework

The landmark studies of the 1960s established the basic framework that defined the field of political socialization. The 1970s saw a second generation of studies that criticized some parts of the early work and developed other parts of it, particularly the theories related to electoral behaviour. What is needed now is a third generation of socialization studies that will restore the field's concerns with children and socialization by reworking other parts of the original framework to produce a politically significant and theoretically fruitful research agenda for the next decade. The best way to do this, we believe, is to build on Easton's neglected interest in the political community. Yet, in going back to Easton, it is desirable to extricate political socialization from the systems theory in which he embedded its concepts. Instead, we propose to plant it firmly in the fields of political philosophy by returning to long-standing philosophic debates about the nature of citizenship. In so doing, we will redefine our empirical research topics so that they are relevant to important normative concerns about relationships between children and the political communities of which they are becoming members.

This cannot be done, however, without a new and convincing theoretical rationale for studying the political attitudes of pre-adults. Many think that

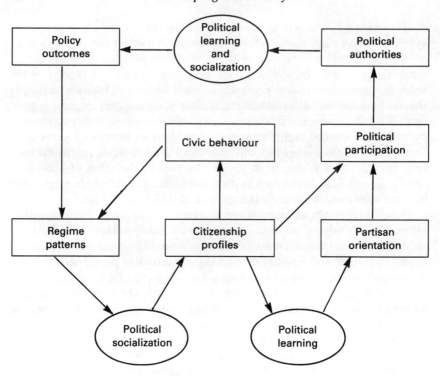

Figure 3.1   *A framework for thinking about the study of political learning*

the way to develop this theoretical rationale is to focus on consequences for the individual rather than on consequences for the system. Yet, as Merelman (1980) argued, to be convincing this new focus on the individual must be linked with a new conceptualization of the relationship between the individual's socialization and the political system. To discover this linkage for citizenship, it is necessary to locate our proposed research agenda in the context of the two other research agendas that are now established in the field.

Figure 3.1 is a map of the field of political learning. Its purpose is to help us see our research agendas in the context of the political system, thus clarifying their theoretical contexts and, above all, their political significance.[9] The top row in Figure 3.1 depicts the research agenda of elite socialization which concerns the ways in which the outlooks of the political authorities are shaped by political learning and socialization. This research agenda was not weakened at all by the problems that beset the study of the public's socialization during the late 1960s and early 1970s. Its only weakness is that it was and still is sadly neglected.[10]

The second established research agenda, political learning during adolescence and adulthood, is depicted on the right-hand side of Figure 3.1 and involves the learning of partisan orientations related to political participation, which, in turn, shapes the selection and behaviour of the political authorities. This is, of course, the Hyman tradition, which has been carried into adulthood so that the political learning involved will have plausible causal connections to electoral behaviour. The partisan orientations in this research include familiar electoral attitudes such as political efficacy, party identification, ideological views of parties and beliefs about policy issues. They also include political trust and support for the political authorities. This agenda is the most advanced theoretically and methodologically and has received by far the greatest commitment from researchers in the field.

The making of citizens, the research agenda that we propose to add to the framework and to develop in the second part of this chapter, is found on the lower left-hand side of Figure 3.1. This agenda departs from previous research in several ways. It draws attention to the fact that citizenship affects not only political participation but also civic behaviour which encompasses both civility and public service. It also involves, as will be seen shortly, a catholic rather than a parochial view of the meaning of citizenship. But, most importantly, it stresses that its key attitudinal variables, citizenship profiles, have important consequences not only for the system through links with civic behaviour and political participation, but also, and of equal if not of greater importance, for the individual – because such attitudes are central components of our identities as public persons.

But where exactly is the new conceptualization of the linkage between the socialization of the child and the political system? One familiar linkage connects citizenship profiles learned as children to political participation as adults. This is precisely the type of hypothesized connection that failed in the first wave of socialization studies. Nevertheless, it is worth investigating again because attitudes involving matters of identity have since been found to be especially enduring (Miller and Sears, 1985). Another much less familiar linkage connects these citizenship profiles learned by children to civic behaviour as children and adolescents as well as to civic behaviour as adults. Most genuine forms of political participation may not be possible until young adulthood, but this is clearly not true of civic behaviour which is a lifelong habit that begins in childhood. Children and adolescents are taught civility first in the home and later in schools. And they engage in civic behaviour through public behaviour in their neighbourhoods and through acts of public service organized by schools, churches and community groups such as scouts, 4-H clubs and YMCAs.

Finally, Figure 3.1 introduces another important new linkage, which has been entirely overlooked in recent socialization research despite the fact that it has long been the principal concern of political philosophers and civic educators: the relationship between regime patterns and citizenship profiles. This is where political philosophers have placed the political relevance in the making of citizens. Different citizenship profiles constitute different sorts of civic identities and ways of public life. And these different citizenship profiles are shaped by different regime patterns. Here, then, is the major new link to the political system for which we have been searching. It needs to be articulated conceptually and investigated empirically. We do not propose to do that here. We propose only to make it plausible. The notion of a 'regime' is a concept whose traditional meaning has been characterized by Easton and Dennis (1969, pp. 59–60) as a 'constitutional order' with three components: rules of the game, institutions and underlying goals.

A regime's *rules of the game*, which consist of the political community's formal constitutional rules and norms, are the rules that define citizenship: they specify the criteria for determining who will be and who will not be considered a citizen. Equally important, they specify the legal rights and duties of citizens as well as their relationships to the political authorities. A regime's *institutions* specify these rights and duties further, but they also do much more. Legislatures, for instance, produce policies that affect racial attitudes, gender attitudes, authority attitudes and scores of other orientations that are central components of citizenship profiles (Niemi, 1973, p. 19). Court decisions do the same: they affect the views that we learn about divorce, relationships among neighbours, even attitudes about the nature of the welfare state and the appropriate degree of competition in the economic system. As for political executives, we need only think of the performances of presidents as tutors to the nation: a Kennedy seeking to lead citizens to appreciate their duties as well as their rights; a Johnson exhorting us to be more compassionate toward our fellow citizens; or a Reagan trying to inject a new spirit of patriotism into the sense of citizenship experienced by Americans. Last are a regime's *underlying goals*: the values, ideals and projects that are widely shared and pursued, sometimes by the political authorities alone, more often by substantial numbers of the public as well. Such goals, different mixtures of freedom and equality for example, characterize a regime and define its ethos. These are the goals of the adult generation which, through political socialization, are passed on to the new generation of citizens.

Having addressed the theoretical problem of the linkage between the political system and the political socialization of children, we can now turn to what everyone concurs is the next step: 'what is needed if pre-adult studies are to be revitalized is a clarification of just what the study of pre-adult socialization needs to concentrate on the most' (Niemi and Sobieszek, 1977, p. 229). What is needed is a new research agenda.

Concepts for the Study of Citizenship

To develop this new research agenda we shall proceed as follows. First, we will examine visions of citizenship in political philosophy. Then, based on this examination, we shall explicate a set of core concepts and a theoretical framework for studying political socialization and citizenship.

Visions of Citizenship

Political philosophers have long been concerned with the making of citizens and have always attributed great importance to the subject. But this strong consensus about the importance of the subject is matched by an equally strong disagreement over the nature of citizenship and over its role in society. In particular, political philosophy has generated two quite different, albeit complementary, visions of citizenship, one 'communal', the other 'contractual'.[11] Each view has developed through centuries of discourse; and each is important to understanding citizenship.

The communal view of citizenship originated in the 'civic republicanism' of Aristotle and other political philosophers of classical antiquity. It was further shaped by medieval and Renaissance thought (Pocock, 1975, Part Two) and found its modern voice in eighteenth century theorists such as Rousseau (Vernon, 1986). At its core, this communal perspective demands an active citizenry and depicts citizenship as being grounded in relationships among friends and neighbours who are bound together by common activities and traditions (Barber, 1984). Politics is, from this viewpoint, a fundamentally public activity that people engage in to pursue the collective good. Moreover, since people usually identify their own personal good with this collective good, civic activity also serves as a source of personal development.[12] Citizens, then, not only have the right to participate in politics but are also expected to do so, both for their own good and for the good of the community. Thus, the quality of communal citizenship depends not just on the act of participation but also on the character of public spiritedness with which this participation is conducted (Daggar, 1981).

By contrast, the contractual vision of citizenship is rooted firmly in liberal political philosophy. John Locke and Thomas Hobbes crafted this viewpoint, and John Rawls (1971) has forged its contemporary interpretation. The contractual vision of citizenship is, at its core, a legalistic account, one which places minimal demands on the public and thus anticipates a passive citizenry (Ackerman, 1980; Daggar, 1981; Murphy, 1983; Portis, 1985; Sullivan, 1986; Walzer, 1970). Citizens are seen as individuals bound together by a 'social contract' rather than as friends and neighbours united by common activity (Barber, 1984; Sullivan, 1986; Wolin, 1986). Within this context, political activity is essentially private in nature, for it is regarded 'principally as a means of protecting and furthering one's private interests' (Daggar, 1981, p. 720). Such activity is purely instrumental; it is neither worthwhile in itself nor a means of achieving some common good.

These, then, are two distinct visions of citizenship which emerge from the dialogues of political philosophy. They are also visions of much contention in vigorous contemporary debates among political philosophers and other political commentators.[13] The ultimate goal of a revitalized sub-field of political socialization will be to provide empirical foundations for such normative assessments by studying the making of citizens. But first we need to identify the concepts that will be central to this enterprise.

Sense of Citizenship

First, of course, is the concept of the citizen. This term has two long-standing interpretations, both in political philosophy and in ordinary language. One is the citizen as a member of a community. The other is the citizen as a bearer of legal rights, a person who has entered into a political contract. These two definitions lead us to think of a people's sense of citizenship, of how they think of themselves as citizens, as having two distinct components: a sense of communal citizenship and a sense of contractual citizenship.

Communal citizenship focuses on the individual's relationship to a community, to a body of individuals that comprises a political entity at either the local, state or national level, individuals who 'seek to solve their problems in common through shared political structures' (Easton and Hess, 1962, p. 233). Because political communities at different levels are embedded within one another, individuals may simultaneously experience several different forms of communal citizenship. Empirically, communal citizenship will be investigated in local communities and in the nation. For now, however, we focus on communal citizenship in general, which has three components that develop in stages beginning in childhood – membership, identification and consciousness.

At a minimum, people are simply members of the community. For most people, this membership gradually becomes imbued with psychological meaning through the development of a communal identity, a sense of attachment and positive affect for the community. Finally, as they mature further, some members develop a sense of communal consciousness, the recognition that others share one's communal identity and that, through this sharing, a 'civic bond' is forged which binds members to one another and to the community as a whole (see Barber, 1984; Gusfield, 1975; and Janowitz, 1983). Communal citizenship has not received much empirical attention from American political scientists. But sociologists, anthropologists and psychologists have investigated related topics such as the nature of communities, community interaction and solidarity, and the development of a sense of community (e.g., Adelson and O'Neil, 1966; Hillery, 1982; Kasarda and Janowitz, 1974; Laumann, 1972; Nisbet, 1969). At the national level, empirical research on the subject includes both national character studies and psychological studies of the development of national identity in children (e.g., Davies, 1968; Jahoda, 1963; Horowitz, 1940; Middleton et al., 1970; Piaget and Weil, 1951; and Tajfel, 1969).

The sense of *contractual citizenship* differs from the sense of communal citizenship in that it involves the individual's relationship to a category or label rather than to a specific community (for a related discussion see

Wolin, 1986). Yet the sense of contractual citizenship nonetheless encompasses similar components which likewise develop in stages. First, people are simply legal citizens of a political entity and become aware of this status. Next, some of them develop a sense of civic identity such that this status acquires psychological meaning: the label 'citizen' becomes part of their personal identity, albeit its importance varies greatly and may only become relevant when one wishes to exercise one's rights or obligations as a citizen. Finally, some people develop a sense of civic consciousness, a recognition that one possesses, as a citizen, certain rights and obligations which are shared by other citizens.[14] There has been relatively little empirical work on contractual citizenship in general or on civic identity in particular. Nevertheless, Jennings and Niemi (1974; 1981) have explored visions of the ideal citizen. And although political scientists have paid little attention to the obligations associated with citizenship (Janowitz, 1983), there is in the United States a well-established research tradition focusing on the rights of citizenship (e.g. McClosky and Brill, 1983; McClosky and Zaller, 1984; Sigel and Hoskin, 1981).

To summarize, we assume that the character of a person's sense of citizenship is defined by the interplay between its communal and contractual components – an interplay that begins in childhood. Moreover, the blending of these two components may assume a variety of forms, the specification of which is best developed through empirical investigations into the nature of citizenship and the course of its emergence during childhood.

Civic Orientations

Recent debates about citizenship in political philosophy suggest the importance of five civic orientations: loyalty, civic virtue, tolerance, political self-development, and civic memory. All of these orientations either influence or are influenced by a sense of citizenship and are likely to have their roots in childhood. Together with the 'sense of citizenship', they define 'citizenship profiles'. Let us consider each one briefly.

As a civic orientation, *loyalty* is often praised (e.g. Janowitz, 1983; Jennings and Niemi, 1981; Marshall, 1977; and Walzer, 1976) and just as often misunderstood (see Sniderman, 1981). At the national level, loyalty becomes synonymous with patriotism, which over the years has been gradually transformed from a love of and devotion to one's country into a sense of national supremacy (see Dietz, 1989; Janowitz, 1983; Karsten, 1978; Pullen, 1971; and Walzer, 1976). The meaning of loyalty therefore requires some reconstruction. This can be done by building on Tocqueville's (1969, pp. 234-5) idea of 'reflective patriotism', a less ardent but more lasting form of devotion to the ideals of the political community – a thoughtful attachment to shared traditions, symbols, geography and political ideals (see Dietz, 1986, p. 266). But regardless of how loyalty is defined, there has been very little empirical research during the last few decades on loyalty in general, or on patriotism in particular (exceptions include Doob, 1964; Lawson, 1963; Pullen, 1971; and Sniderman, 1981).

Civic virtue is less ambiguous than loyalty but certainly no less important. In fact, it has been a key concept in the communal vision of citizenship since Aristotle (see Pocock, 1975). Civic virtue is defined as the willingness to subordinate personal interests to the public good; it is a public-minded spirit that inspires people to place the welfare of their community ahead of their own (see Diggins, 1984, p. 12; Daggar, 1981; Gill, 1987; Landy and McWilliams, 1985; and Murphy, 1983). The concept of civic virtue has played a key role in American political thought (see Diggins, 1984; and Sinopoli, 1987) but not, unfortunately, in empirical political science. Nevertheless, researchers in other disciplines have examined related concepts and have thereby provided material for us to draw upon. For example, both psychologists (e.g. Krebs and Miller, 1985) and sociologists (e.g. Titmuss, 1970) have investigated altruism, which can readily be related to civic virtue in a communal context.

Tolerance is the willingness to endure those whose attitudes, traditions, race, religion, or other attributes differ from one's own. Both communal and contractual visions of citizenship accord tolerance considerable significance. Tolerance may be the closest that contemporary society can get to the ideal of civic friendship suggested by the communal vision of citizenship (Bellah et al., 1985, pp. 203–7; Walzer, 1976). Similarly, when contractual citizenship reaches the point of civic consciousness, it inspires tolerance by encouraging individuals to recognize that others are entitled to the same rights that they themselves enjoy as citizens (Stanley, 1983). Unlike most of our other key concepts, tolerance has been the focus of considerable empirical research in political science. There is, for instance, a rich survey tradition extending from Stouffer's (1955) work in the 1950s forward to research in the 1980s (Gibson and Bingham, 1985; McClosky and Brill, 1983; McClosky and Zaller, 1984; and Sullivan et al., 1982).

Political self-development refers to the acquisition of the skills and information necessary to function as an effective citizen. This is the civic orientation most obviously associated with formal civic education in schools. It has three components: general education, civic literacy and civic wisdom. General education promotes civic literacy and civic wisdom and generally facilitates the exercise of other rights and obligations (Gutmann, 1987; Janowitz, 1983; Marshall, 1977; Merriam, 1966; and Thompson, 1970). The communal vision of citizenship also emphasizes the importance of civic literacy, which is knowledge about and interest in not just the political process but also the political community (Barber, 1984; Janowitz, 1983). The third component of political self-development, civic wisdom, is the most difficult to describe. It presupposes the ability to deliberate, consider alternatives and make decisions (see Gutmann, 1987; Landy and McWilliams, 1985; Hahn, 1984). Civic wisdom involves thinking and talking about politics in terms of the needs of the community (Barber, 1984; Stanley, 1983).

Civic memory refers to the recollection of the 'events, characters, and developments that make up the history' of one's community (Daggar, 1981, p. 729). This is a characteristic of individuals and also of entire communities. Moreover, unlike those civic orientations that are likely to be a consequence of citizenship, civic memory may be a critical factor in shaping citizenship itself (Daggar, 1981; Dietz, 1986; Smith, 1985). Thus, civic memory fosters a sense of citizenship by making the community seem familiar and understandable. And, when widely shared, civic memory 'forges a bond of sympathy, a sense of common life' that encourages a strong sense of community (Daggar, 1981, p. 730). Research dealing with the importance of 'founding' legends and traditions (e.g. Hobsbawn and Ranger, 1983) can serve as the touchstones for our investigations here.

Citizen Behaviour

We now turn to the principal forms of citizen behaviour that appear in the political philosophy of citizenship. These activities can be divided into two broad categories: political participation; and civic behaviour, which encompasses civility and public service. Of the two, *political participation* has been by far the most carefully studied (Almond and Verba, 1965; Barber, 1984; Janowitz, 1980; 1983; Jennings and Niemi, 1981; Marshall, 1977; Murphy, 1983; Verba and Nie, 1972; Walzer, 1983; 1976). It refers to 'acts that aim at influencing the government, either by affecting the choice of government personnel or by affecting the choices made by government personnel' (Verba and Nie, 1972, p.2). Political participation is encouraged by both communal and contractual citizenship, although people are not expected to engage in meaningful political participation before late adolescence and adulthood. Here there is a rich body of research to draw upon (for a review see Kinder and Sears, 1985).

Civic behaviour has received far less attention from political scientists, but it nonetheless has very important implications for the individual and for the regime. Civic behaviour fundamentally shapes the nature of political communities, the quality of life that they inspire and the democratic character of their governments. Consequently, the impact of citizenship upon civic behaviour is a matter of considerable interest that directs attention to the study of children since children begin practising civic behaviour at an early age.

The first of civic behaviour's two components is civility (Janowitz, 1983; Marshall, 1977; Merriam, 1966), which in earlier times had a definite political meaning with reference to the behaviour befitting a good citizen (Walzer, 1976). But, in recent years, civility has come to be defined almost exclusively in terms of the private sphere, in terms of social virtues such as politeness, decency and refinement. As we did with loyalty, we intend to reclaim this concept's political meaning by defining it as 'conformity to the principles of social order, behaviour befitting a citizen' (*Oxford English Dictionary*). Thus, civility will encompass both obedience to the laws and conformity to the social norms governing interactions among people, particularly strangers. This definition makes it clear not only that both communal and contractual approaches to citizenship must nurture civility, but also that this neglected concept is extremely important. As Janowitz (1983, p.13) put it, 'a democratic society rests on civility' – because civility encourages cooperation and, indeed, makes it possible. When civility deteriorates, the government is forced 'to pass more and more laws to regulate citizen behaviour, so that the free society is converted into a system of government coercion' (Howard, 1984, p. 9). In more concrete terms, models of the ideal citizen suggest laws that must be obeyed if people are to fulfil their civic obligations such as paying taxes and performing jury duty (see Janowitz, 1983; Jennings and Niemi, 1981; Marshall, 1977). Likewise, many norms that govern our everyday lives, such as respecting the comfort and privacy of other citizens, are also an important part of civility.

Although civility has not been much studied by political scientists (recent exceptions include Lewis, 1982), other social scientists have conducted relevant research. Of particular interest are the investigations of psychologists, sociologists and economists into what motivates people to obey the law (e.g. Becker, 1968; Kohlberg, 1984; Turiel, 1985). Our challenge is to integrate their work into a theoretical context where obedience and conformity are interpreted as elements of citizenship.

Public service, the other component of civic behaviour that we will consider, has two dimensions, one military, the second civil. Military service is certainly one of the most demanding tests of citizen obligation. It is also one of the most agreed-upon obligations (Walzer, 1976). Yet, in today's world of volunteer forces and unpopular wars, the meaning of military service as an act of citizenship, or as a setting for civic education, has become problematic, something that must be studied empirically rather than taken for granted (Janowitz, 1983; Barber, 1984).

The second dimension of public service, service in the civil arena, refers to voluntary participation in civic organizations or governmental programmes for which the primary purpose is something other than influencing the political authorities. Thus, the realm of public service ranges from local self-help organizations and charities to government-backed programmes of national service such as the Civilian Conservation Corps. Such voluntary public service is at the heart of communal visions of citizenship. From this perspective, volunteerism is one of the major means of exercising civic virtue and thereby enhancing political self-development (Barber, 1984; Sullivan, 1986). Moreover, like civility, public service is meaningfully practised prior to adulthood. Also like civility, it has not received much attention from political scientists. Again, sociological and psychological studies, in this case of volunteerism and helping behaviour, can provide the theoretical and methodological foundation for exploring public service as an element of citizenship (see for example, Eisenberg, 1986; Smithson et al., 1983).

Toward a Theory of Citizenship

To this point, we have defined key concepts from philosophic treatments of citizenship and sketched out a new research agenda for studying the socialization of citizenship. But we are not yet prepared to do this because our present empirical knowledge about citizenship is too thin to support deductive theory construction and far too thin for inductive efforts. Nevertheless, we can take an important step toward the construction of such theories by: (1) specifying the projected patterns of relationships among sense of citizenship, civic orientations, and citizen behaviour; (2) identifying additional key factors that are likely to prove important in shaping the development of the citizenship variables; and (3) suggesting the processes through which these additional factors might be expected to influence citizenship. These tasks are best accomplished by building on Figure 3.1 to develop Figure 3.2 – an analytic framework for theory construction and empirical investigation.[15]

The Politics of Socialization to Citizenship

Most classical theories of citizenship assume that governments have a strong interest in the making of citizens and that the political regime and wider political system have a significant impact upon the nature of citizenship. We are interested in political characteristics at both the national and local level, characteristics which can be divided into several broad categories, as illustrated in Figure 3.2.

First of all, the type of regime is of fundamental importance (Barber, 1984; Mansbridge, 1980). If democratic, is it a direct or representative democracy? Barber (1984) and others argue that direct democracies facilitate the development of communal citizenship. If a representative democracy, is it comparatively 'populistic' or 'elitist' – how much participation does it promote? Communities that are characterized by many opportunities for participation, particularly at the local level, may also encourage communal citizenship (Mansbridge, 1980; Barber, 1984). Furthermore, to what extent does the regime exercise control over civic education (Gutmann, 1987)?

Beyond institutional arrangements, a political system's 'rules of the game' and political leaders are also expected to influence citizenship. Are these rules of the game written or unwritten? Is there a 'bill of rights'? Countries that have formal constitutions and bills of rights provide their citizenry with a tangible basis for contractual citizenship. Do such rules of the game include the initiative and the referendum? Barber (1984), for example, argues that these constitutional devices increase participation and thus enhance citizenship. Political leaders often attempt, through

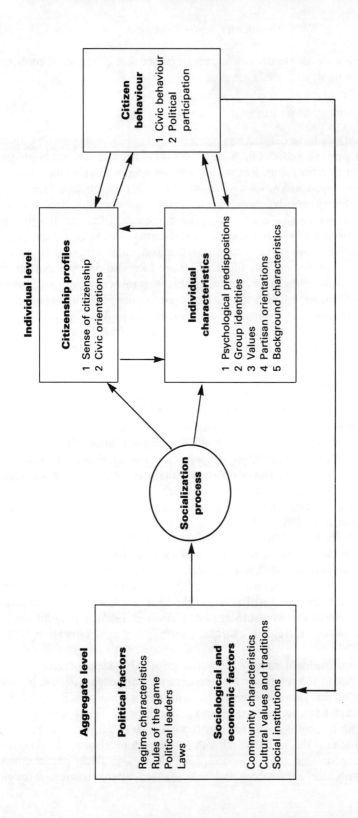

Figure 3.2 A framework for the study of citizenship

speeches and patriotic programmes, to exhort citizens to strengthen their loyalty, civic virtue and civic bonds with their fellow citizens (Barber, 1984). They also use legislation to attempt to shape citizenship profiles and behaviour. Some countries, such as Israel, require public service from their citizens. Efforts to legislate desirable citizen behaviour are also found at the local level when, for example, communities pass legislation governing acts such as smoking in public places.

The Sociology of Socialization to Citizenship

Here we shall focus on three broad categories of social variables: community characteristics, cultural values and traditions, and social institutions.

There are fundamental disagreements among political philosophers about the impact of community characteristics on citizenship profiles and citizen behaviour. Nonetheless, from most viewpoints, the size of a community is a very important community characteristic, because the larger a community is the more difficult it is likely to be to achieve widespread communal citizenship (see for example Barber, 1984; Daggar, 1981; Dahl and Tufte, 1973; Taylor, 1976). Similarly, sociologists have investigated the extent to which urbanization and population density inhibit communal attachments (see Kasarda and Janowitz, 1974; Wilson, 1985; Wirth, 1983).[16] The nature of social organization likewise affects social integration (Kasarda and Janowitz, 1974; Janowitz and Suttles, 1978; and Smith, 1975) and, consequently, is in a strong position to influence the development of citizenship.[17] Is a particular community homogeneous in its social and economic makeup, or does it embody substantial social and economic inequalities (see Gusfield, 1975)? Likewise, a community's ethnic, racial, and religious homogeneity has been said to have substantial effects on the development of citizenship (Gusfield, 1975; Janowitz, 1983; Novak, 1972; Sowell, 1981).

In examining cultural values and traditions, we must be concerned both with the substance of core cultural values and with the consensus they command. Cultural traditions are likewise potentially revealing because they involve symbols that embody the collective 'civic memory' (Merriam, 1966; Smith, 1985). Their existence facilitates the transmission of civic memory from one generation to the next, and from individual to individual (Daggar, 1981). We will therefore want to take into account founding myths, communal celebrations and the representation of political heroes (Barber, 1984; Merriam, 1966; Stanley, 1983). Social institutions, our third broad category of sociological and economic factors, create socialization settings within which people, particularly children, develop a sense of citizenship and civic orientations. These settings are structured by schools, families, churches, youth groups, community organizations and the media. In effect, these social institutions represent the contexts through which other political and social factors exert an influence on the making of citizens (for research on socialization in such contexts, see Jennings and Niemi, 1974; 1981).

The Psychology of Socialization to Citizenship

Essential as it is to investigate the effects of aggregate political and social variables on aggregate patterns of citizenship, it is not possible to understand how citizenship is learned without incorporating the individual level of analysis.

To examine these individual-level, psychological dynamics underlying citizenship socialization, we recommend an information-processing approach that emphasizes the role of cognitive structures and stored affective reactions in shaping thinking and behaviour (see Higgens et al., 1981; Lau and Sears, 1986). From this perspective, the political and social variables reviewed above combine to create socialization settings in which particular types of information are transmitted. Individuals process such cognitive and affective information and store some of it in their memories. Subsequently, this stored information is available to influence their thinking and behaviour. Our information-processing approach to the making of citizens draws on several major bodies of literature: psychological studies of group identities and groups as cognitive categories (see Tajfel, 1981; Turner, 1982; Wilder, 1981); political science applications of these psychological theories in research on group identification and consciousness (e.g. Conover, 1984; 1988; Gurin, 1985; Gurin et al., 1980; Klein, 1984; Miller et al., 1981); and, psychological literature concerning the development of schemata (e.g. Markus, 1977; Markus et al., 1982; Taylor and Crocker, 1981) and moral reasoning (e.g. Kohlberg, 1984).

From this psychological perspective, 'sense of citizenship' is a form of identification, and civic orientations are a form of stored cognitive and affective responses. Citizenship is an identity, a fundamental identity, because it is a way of thinking and feeling about oneself that acts as an anchor in situating oneself in society. Thus, political philosophy's two visions of citizenship constitute different types of identities whose development must be approached somewhat differently. Communal citizenship entails an identification with a community and, in its most developed form, a sense of consciousness about the meaning of that identification. The dynamics underlying the development of communal citizenship parallel those characterizing the emergence of group consciousness.[18] Contractual citizenship is also a type of identity, but its formation is more like self-categorization than like group identification.

The development of any civic identity entails the development of a self-schema – a cognitive structure containing information about oneself (Fiske and Taylor, 1984). By placing oneself in the category of 'citizen' one takes the first step towards developing such a self-schema or civic identity. When this self-schema takes on affective significance, one's civic identity grows in importance. The transition from civic identity to civic consciousness requires individuals to invest their civic identities with meaning. In so doing, many people are likely to make use of their 'citizen prototypes' – their notions about the rights, obligations, and conduct of 'ideal citizens'.[19] In sum, we anticipate that the socialization to both visions of citizenship can be explained in terms of psychological theories concerning identities that are usually shaped in childhood.

Let us turn now to the relationship between a sense of citizenship and civic orientations. Civic orientations can be characterized psychologically as stored cognitive and affective responses which have developed over time in response to repeated experiences in the socialization settings defined by social and political variables. In addition, both communal and contractual citizenship are likely to encourage the development of civic orientations. Thus, when communal citizenship has evolved to the point of consciousness, the individual is expected to develop a sense of commitment to the common good and to the community. This commitment is born out of a recognition of the 'civic bond' among citizens (Sandel, 1984). Moreover, this communal commitment influences how the individual processes information and reacts emotionally.[20] Sympathy and concern for the community and its members thereby become outgrowths of the emergence of communal consciousness (for a related discussion see Conover, 1988). And this sympathy and concern become powerful inspirations for the development of loyalty, civic virtue, tolerance and political self-development.

Contractual citizenship also shapes civic orientations, but it is more likely that duty, rather than a sense of commitment, will prove to be the motivating force underlying its influence. Specifically, civic consciousness involves an awareness of the rights and obligations that we have by virtue of our status as legal citizens. Such obligations act as prescriptions which shape thoughts and behaviour. In psychological terms, the obligations contained in one's citizen self-schema act as expectations which influence thoughts, feelings and, ultimately, behaviour. Hence, when people express loyalty to their country, civic virtue towards their neighbours, tolerance for strangers, or interest in politics, they do so because they feel that this is their obligation as a citizen. As with communal citizenship, there is an aspect of an individual's identity at stake in the relationship between contractual citizenship and civic orientations – but compared with communal identity, this contractual identity is not expected to be as central to the individual's overall self-image.

Finally, we can expect to find reciprocal relationships between citizenship profiles and the individual characteristics in Figure 3.2. Individual characteristics should play a major role in restricting the range of a collectivity's citizenship profiles. Moreover, some of the influence of political and social factors on the development of citizenship will work through their indirect influence on individual characteristics. Reciprocity enters as the developed citizenship profiles turn round to influence individual characteristics. The nature of this influence is most apparent in the communal vision of citizenship where the exercise of citizenship is a process of self-development (Barber, 1984; Daggar, 1981; Sandel, 1982; Sullivan, 1986). When self-development includes developing a sense of citizenship and civic orientations, people may modify elements of their character such as their values and beliefs. For example, cynicism towards strangers might be tempered by the emergence of a sense of communal consciousness; or, racism might be subdued by a tolerance born out of a sense of citizenship. When citizenship and civic orientations shape values and beliefs, civic education becomes not simply a tool for moulding citizens; it becomes, as Merriam (1966) argued, a programme of character development (see Gutmann, 1987).

Conclusions

Political socialization, like political economy, political anthropology and political sociology, has in our discipline perpetual problems of legitimacy. We political scientists import much more from other social sciences than they do from us (Laponce, 1980); but we also demand that the imports continually prove themselves. The test is political relevance. And, by the late 1970s it began to be assumed that political socialization had earned at best a low pass.

The series of disappointments occasioned by counter-factual events and data, and by the collapse of the persistence assumption, turned the field away from childhood and created serious doubts about the entire theoretical rationale that had been developed during the 1960s for studying pre-adults. If our responses to these problems failed to turn the tide, this was not because they were insufficiently reasonable, but rather because they were insufficiently radical. They did not dig deeply enough into the theoretical foundations. In this chapter, we have tried to go to the core of the matter, to the distinctions between socialization and learning, between citizens as members of the political community and citizens as voters, and between consequences for the individual and consequences for the system. We have tried to reanalyse the framework established by the landmark studies of the 1960s and reconstruct it in order to clarify the current position. In so doing, we hope to help the field to regain its children and its theoretical rationale by offering a new and convincing research agenda for studying the making of citizens.

This research agenda is designed to provide new information about the nature of citizenship, and about the differences, similarities and interconnections between citizenship's contractual and communal expressions. Familiar concepts like loyalty, tolerance and political participation can be reconstructed in this atmosphere, while unexplored concepts like civic virtue, civic memory and civility can open up new empirical fields defined by important normative questions. Thus, the purely descriptive side of the research has a significance of its own. What does it mean to be a citizen in a democracy like the United States, France or India? How does one become a citizen in these countries? This process of becoming supplies the focus for the agenda's analytical and theoretical contributions. What is potentially new and significant here is the proposed concentration on the individual and the attempt to set the psychological development of citizenship identities in the framework of aggregate political and sociological variables. Perhaps the ultimate test of the agenda should be whether the results it generates are sufficiently convincing to attract new generations of graduate students to the sub-field of political socialization and thereby bring the enterprise out of its present eclipse.

Finally, the study of the making of citizens also has the potential to help its parent field of political behaviour recover some of its philosophic roots. Too often the concepts in the study of political behaviour seem imprisoned in a mass of empirical findings with little concern for their political meaning. Electoral politics and policy outcomes are very important; but there is much more to political life than what we have incorporated in current studies of these subjects. Thus, by turning our attention to concepts such as civility and civic virtue, we can help reconstruct the field of political socialization and perhaps, in the process, encourage political behaviour to explore new topics that matter politically, topics that are central to philosophic treatments of citizenship.

Notes

This research was supported by a grant from the Spencer Foundation. For comments on earlier versions of the chapter, we would like to thank Ivor Crewe, Peter Lange and the comparative politics discussion group of the University of North Carolina at Chapel Hill.

1   Cook (1985) and Sears (1987) have documented the decline over the past decade in the number of books published on the subject and the number of socialization articles in the *American Political Science Review* and the regional journals.

2   Of course this might have occurred in any event; for although the Easton enterprise seemed designed to study socialization *qua* socialization, and although it took several empirical steps down this path, it actually turned out to study topics that were not so very unlike those in the Hyman tradition. Thus, in retrospect, the Easton and Hyman traditions do not look as different as they did at the time – and, in retrospect, did not prove to be a theoretically critical distinction in the field after all.

3   In their review of socialization research during this period, for instance, Kinder and Sears (1985, pp. 722–3) discuss Markus's (1979) analysis of the impact of Vietnam and racial conflict upon party identification, Jackson's (1975) study of relationships between policy preferences and party identification, and other similar studies which do have a developmental flavour (e.g. comparing effects on two different age groups) would be read by many political scientists as voting behaviour research.

4   At this point, it will suffice to observe that some of the communal dimensions of citizenship have long been in the background of discussions about the political relevance of the political socialization of children (Niemi and Sobieszek, 1977, p. 217). They have been investigated before the emergence of political socialization research under topics such as national identity, nationalism and patriotism (see for example Lasswell, 1925; Horowitz, 1940; Piaget and Weil, 1951; Jahoda, 1963). And, they exist in aspects of the original Easton framework (Easton and Dennis, 1969), the aspects that focus on support for the political

community and regime, which were neglected in favour of research on support for the political authorities (cf. Moore et al., 1985).

5	Hess and Torney (1967, pp. 26–31) did briefly explore citizenship as membership in the political community. They reported on the emergence of a sense of belonging to one's own country, a positive attachment to its principal symbols, and a feeling of being different from people in other countries.

6	Greenstein's book appeared next, in 1965, with more fascinating data about the political beliefs of his New Haven children. Two years later the first major national study seemed to give the field some bottom and produced its share of dramatic as well as detailed and well-documented results. According to the authors, Hess and Torney (1967), political attitudes didn't change much during the high school years. Most children's most important political learning apparently occurred before they arrived there. Two years later again, in 1969, Easton and Dennis's *Children in the Political System* reinforced the findings that young children become attached to the political authorities before they have the information or the ability to evaluate them; and the book cast these early feelings of support as the psychological roots of political legitimacy and stability.

7	Easton and Dennis (1969, p. 186) had speculated that, with the possible exception of party identification, most of the other attitudes that were involved in political participation could probably not 'be traced directly' back to early childhood – even if traces of their first appearances could be found there. But as it turned out, political trust, which was more closely related to their side of the enterprise, didn't prove to be as stable as anticipated either.

8	In fact, Jennings and Niemi (1981) found that for many of the attitudes studied in socialization research, the correlations across eight-year intervals are indeed approximately 0.30. Attributing causality to the seven-year-old's attitude back at the beginning of a long series of changes and turns begins to look like a micro-level example of the logic of macro-level economic or social determinists who argue that the root cause of an event is the cause of that event. Perhaps it is – but it is difficult to accept it as such if the correlations between the steps are 0.30 and there are many other independent and intervening variables along the road.

9	As with all such heuristic exercises, the framework in Figure 3.1 comes with an important caveat: although it is meant to suggest theories by depicting gross relationships among gross sets of variables, it is not itself a theory. Thus, the arrows in the framework do not include all possible relationships among these sets of variables. And, any serious theory about any dependent variable found anywhere in this framework will have to introduce many other variables that are not part of this map.

10	The fact that Hyman's (1959) inventory of socialization research devoted so few pages to elite socialization reflected the scarcity of systematic research on the topic. Genuine socialization research on politicians did appear during the next decades (e.g. Fenno, 1962; Bell and Price, 1975; and Searing, 1986) but such studies have been few and far between.

11	This distinction is quite similar to that presented by Edward Portis (1985) as well as to those noted by Daggar (1981), Kelly (1979), Sullivan (1986), and Walzer (1970). Others (e.g. Mansbridge, 1980; Pateman, 1970) have similarly noted the existence of these two strains of thought, though some (e.g. Barber, 1984) have presented more differentiated accounts than we ourselves find necessary.

12	As Sullivan (1986, p. 157) points out, the notion of self-development embodied in the communal vision of citizenship is the antithesis of contemporary notions of self-development associated with the 'culture of narcissism'. It is a collective experience in which individuals come to develop a 'mutual interdependency' and 'imperative to respond and to care' (Sullivan, 1986, p. 157) as well as a sense of personal autonomy (Daggar, 1987, p. 13).

13	The communitarian critics are a heterogeneous group which includes many who differ sharply among themselves. From our perspective, we would count as communitarians: Barber (1984), MacIntyre (1984), Sandel (1982; 1984), Sullivan (1986), Taylor (1982), and Walzer (1983). As in the case of the communitarians, the defenders of liberalism encompass a variety of distinct interpretations. We would include in this group: Galston (1987), Gutmann (1985), Herzog (1986), and Hirsch (1986).

14	A common criticism of contemporary American culture is that our sense of civic consciousness is too narrow, with too much attention focused on the rights of citizenship and not enough paid to the obligations of citizenship (see Daggar, 1981; Dietz, 1987; Janowitz, 1983). Bruce Ackerman (1980, p. 100), for example, reflects this outlook when he makes no mention of the citizen's obligations in his description of the development of a sense of civic consciousness; instead, he describes civic consciousness as an individual achieving an understanding of himself or herself as 'a person with rights'.

15   In interpreting the analytic framework in Figure 3.2, it should be emphasized that the suggested relationships among variables may involve unusually complex causal patterns. Thus, all the components of our citizenship profiles are not necessarily compatible: the political and social factors that encourage tolerance, for example, may at the same time dampen loyalty and civility (Walzer, 1976). It should also be emphasized that this analytic framework is based on the assumption that socialization processes are the key link between society and the individual. In effect, the political and social systems create 'settings' in which individuals learn what it means to be a citizen. What we need to do, therefore, is to identify these socialization settings, explore the process of learning that occurs within them and examine the individual-level dynamics involved.

16   The other side of this coin concerns the impact of agrarianism (see Daggar, 1981; Tarrow, 1971). And, in the same ecological vein, the clarity of community boundaries has also been found to be important in shaping outlooks related to citizenship (Hillery, 1982; Warren, 1963).

17   In particular, the social organization within a community has been used as an indicator of 'sense of community' (Taylor, 1982). For our purposes, the key question concerns the existence of social networks (e.g. Fischer, 1982; Laumann, 1972; Warren and Warren, 1977) and the extent to which they may facilitate the development of civic orientations (cf. Huckfeldt, 1984).

18   Thus, a communal identity is analogous to a group identity, and the transition from such a communal identity to communal consciousness mirrors the movement from group identity to group consciousness. At the heart of both processes is the development of a collective orientation (see Conover, 1988; Gurin, 1985; Miller et al., 1981).

19   'Prototypes' are schemata in which 'knowledge about a category is composed of a typical or ideal instance ... accompanied by the full range of peripheral or less good examples' (Fiske and Taylor, 1984, p. 146). In effect, people may use their citizen prototypes to help fill in the meaning of their own 'citizen' self-schemata. To understand the making of citizens, we must therefore investigate the nature of citizen prototypes that children are taught through civic education.

20   In psychological terms, the existence of a communal consciousness, in and of itself, has cognitive effects that help stimulate the development of various civic orientations by making community-related matters more salient (see Brewer, 1979; Conover, 1988; and Tajfel, 1978).

References

Abramson, Paul R. 1977. *The Political Socialization of Black Americans: A Critical Evaluation of Research on Efficacy and Trust.* New York: Free Press.

Ackerman, Bruce A. 1980. *Social Justice in the Liberal State.* New Haven: Yale University Press.

Adelson, Joseph and Robert P. O'Neil. 1966. Growth of Political Ideas in Adolescence: The Sense of Community. *Journal of Personality and Social Psychology*, 4:295–306.

Almond, Gabriel A. and Sidney Verba. 1965. *The Civic Culture.* Boston: Little, Brown.

Barber, Benjamin. 1984. *Strong Democracy: Participatory Politics for a New Age.* Berkeley: University of California Press.

Becker, G. 1968. Crime and Punishment: An Economic Approach. *Journal of Political Economy*, 76: 169–217.

Bell, Charles G. and Charles M. Price. 1975. *The First Term: A Study of Legislative Socialization.* Beverly Hills: Sage.

Bellah, Robert N., Richard Madsen, William M. Sullivan, Ann Swidler and Steven M. Tipton. 1985. *Habits of the Heart: Individualism and Commitment in American Life.* Berkeley: University of California Press.

Brewer, Marilyn B. 1979. In-group Bias in the Minimal Intergroup Situation: A Cognitive-Motivational Analysis. *Psychological Bulletin*, 86: 307–24.

Budge, Ian. 1971. Support for Nation and Government among English Children: a Comment. *British Journal of Political Science*, 1: 389–92.

Connell, R.W. 1987. Why the 'Political Socialization' Paradigm Failed – And What Should Replace It. *International Political Science Review*, 8: 215–24.

Conover, Pamela Johnston. 1984. The Influence of Group Identifications on Political Perception and Evaluation. *Journal of Politics*, 46: 760–85.

Conover, Pamela Johnston. 1988. The Role of Social Groups in Political Thinking. *British Journal of Political Science*, 18: 51–76.

Cook, Timothy E. 1985. The Bear Market in Political Socialization and the Costs of Misunderstood Psychological Theories. *American Political Science Review*, 79: 1079–93.

Daggar, Richard. 1981. Metropolis, Memory, and Citizenship. *American Journal of Political Science*, 25: 715–37.

Daggar, Richard. 1987. Autonomy and Community. A Paper Presented at the Annual Meeting of the Midwest Political Science Association. Chicago, IL.

Dahl, Robert and Edward Tufte. 1973. *Size and Democracy*. Stanford, CA: Stanford University Press.

Davies, A.F. 1968. The Child's Discovery of Nationality. *The Australian and New Zealand Journal of Sociology*, 4: 107–25.

Dennis, J., L. Lindberg and D. McCrone. 1971. Support for Nation and Government among English Children. *British Journal of Political Science*, 1: 25–48.

Dietz, Mary G. 1986. Populism, Patriotism, and the Need for Roots. In Harry C. Boyte and Frank Riessman, eds, *The New Populism: The Politics of Empowerment*. Philadelphia: Temple University Press.

Dietz, Mary G. 1987. Context is All: Feminism and Theories of Citizenship. *Daedulus*, 116: 1–25.

Dietz, Mary G. 1989. Patriotism. In T. Ball, J. Farr, and R. Hanson, eds, *Political Innovation and Conceptual Change*. Cambridge: Cambridge University Press.

Diggins, John P. 1984. *The Lost Soul of American Politics: Virtue, Self-Interest, and the Foundations of Liberalism*. Chicago: University of Chicago Press.

Doob, Leonard W. 1964. *Patriotism and Nationalism*. New Haven: Yale University Press.

Dowse, Robert E. and John Hughes. 1971. The Family, the School and the Political Socialization Process. *Sociology*, 5: 21–45.

Easton, David and Jack Dennis. 1969. *Children in the Political System*. New York: McGraw-Hill.

Easton, David and Robert D. Hess. 1962. The Child's Political World. *Midwest Journal of Political Science*, 6: 229–46.

Eisenberg, Nancy. 1986. *Altruistic Emotion, Cognition and Behavior*. Hillsdale, NJ: Lawrence Erlbaum.

Fenno, Richard F. Jr. 1962. The House Appropriations Committee as a Political System: The Problem of Integration. *American Political Science Review*, 56: 310–24.

Fischer, C.S. 1982. *To Dwell among Friends: Personal Networks in Town and City*. Chicago: University of Chicago Press.

Fiske, Susan T. and Shelley E. Taylor. 1984. *Social Cognition*. Reading, MA: Addison-Wesley.

Galston, William A. 1987. Liberalism, Communitarianism, and the Task of Philosophy. A Paper Presented at the Annual Meeting of the Midwest Political Science Association. Chicago, IL.

Garcia, F. Chris. 1973. *Political Socialization of Chicano Children: A Comparative Study with Anglos in California Schools*. New York: Praeger.

Gibson, James L. and Richard D. Bingham. 1985. *Civil Liberties and Nazis: The Skokie Free Speech Controversy*. New York: Praeger.

Gill, Emily R. 1987. Virtue, Commerce, and Liberty: Or, Civic Republicanism, the Moral Sentiments, and Publius. A Paper Presented at the Annual Meeting of the Midwest Political Science Association. Chicago, IL.

Greenberg, Edward S. 1970. Orientations of Black and White Children to Political Authority Figures. *Social Science Quarterly*, 51: 561–71.

Greenstein, Fred I. 1960. The Benevolent Leader: Children's Images of Political Authority. *American Political Science Review*, 54: 934–43.

Greenstein, Fred I. 1965. *Children and Politics*. New Haven: Yale University Press.

Greenstein, Fred I. 1975. The Benevolent Leader Revisited: Children's Images of Political Leaders in Three Democracies. *American Political Science Review*, 69: 1371–98.

Gurin, Patricia. 1985. Women's Gender Consciousness. *Public Opinion Quarterly*, 49: 143–63.

Gurin, Patricia, Arthur Miller and Gerald Gurin. 1980. Stratum Identification and Consciousness. *Social Psychological Quarterly*, 43: 30–47.

Gusfield, Joseph R. 1975. *Community: A Critical Response*. New York: Harper & Row.

Gutmann, Amy. 1985. Communitarian Critics of Liberalism. *Philosophy and Public Affairs*, 14: 308–21.

Gutmann, Amy. 1987. *Democratic Education*. Princeton, NJ: Princeton University Press.

Hahn, Carole L. 1984. Promise and Paradox: Challenges to Global Citizenship. *Social Education*, 48: 240–3.

Herzog, Don. 1986. Some Questions for Republicans. *Political Theory*, 14: 473–93.

Hess, Robert D. and David Easton. 1960. The Child's Image of the President. *Public Opinion Quarterly*, 24: 632–44.

Hess, Robert D. and Judith V. Torney. 1967. *The Development of Political Attitudes in Children*. Chicago: Aldine.

Higgins, E. Tory, C. Peter Herman and Mark P. Zanna. 1981. *Social Cognition: The Ontario Symposium*. Hillsdale, NJ: Lawrence Erlbaum.

Hillery, George A. Jr. 1982. *A Research Odyssey: Developing and Testing a Community Theory*. New Brunswick, NJ: Transaction Books.

Hirsch, H.N. 1986. The Threnody of Liberalism: Constitutional Liberty and the Renewal of Community. *Political Theory*, 14: 423–49.

Hobsbawn, Eric and Terence Ranger. 1983. *The Invention of Tradition*. Cambridge: Cambridge University Press.

Horowitz, Eugene L. 1940. Some Aspects of the Development of Patriotism in Children. *Sociometry*, 3: 329–41.

Howard, John A. 1984. Reopening the Books on Ethics: The Role of Education in a Free Society. *American Education*, 20: 6–11.

Huckfeldt, R. Robert. 1984. Political Loyalties and Social Class Ties. *American Journal of Political Science*, 28: 399–417.

Hyman, Herbert H. 1959. *Political Socialization: A Study in the Psychology of Political Behavior*. New York: Free Press.

Jackson, John E. 1975. Issues, Party Choices and Presidential Votes. *American Journal of Political Science*, 19: 161–85.

Jahoda, Gustav. 1963. The Development of Children's Ideas about Country and Nationality. *British Journal of Educational Psychology*, 33: 47–60, 143–53.

Janowitz, Morris. 1980. Observations on the Sociology of Citizenship: Obligations and Rights. *Social Forces*, 59: 1–24.

Janowitz, Morris. 1983. *The Reconstruction of Patriotism: Education for Civic Consciousness*. Chicago: University of Chicago Press.

Janowitz, Morris and Gerald D. Suttles. 1978. The Social Ecology of Citizenship. In R. Sarri and Y. Hasenfeld, eds, *The Management of Human Services*. New York: Columbia University Press.

Jaros, Dean, H. Hirsch, and F.J. Fleron Jr. 1968. The Malevolent Leader: Political Socialization in an American Subculture. *American Political Science Review*, 62: 564–75.

Jennings, M. Kent and Richard G. Niemi. 1974. *The Political Character of Adolescence: The Influence of Families and Schools*. Princeton, NJ: Princeton University Press.

Jennings, M. Kent and Richard G. Niemi. 1981. *Generations and Politics: A Panel Study of Young Adults and Their Parents*. Princeton, NJ: Princeton University Press.

Karsten, Peter. 1978. *Patriot-Heroes in England and America: Political Symbolism and Changing Values Over Three Centuries*. Madison, Wisconsin: University of Wisconsin Press.

Kasarda, J.D. and Morris Janowitz. 1974. Community Attachments in Mass Society. *American Sociological Review*, 39: 328–39.

Kavanagh, Dennis. 1983. *Political Science and Political Behavior*. London: Allen and Unwin.

Kelly, George Armstrong. 1979. Who Needs a Theory of Citizenship? *Daedalus*, 108: 21–36.

Kinder, Donald R. and David O. Sears. 1985. Public Opinion and Political Action. In Gardner Lindzey and Elliot Aronson, eds, *Handbook of Social Psychology*, vol. 2, 3rd edition. New York: Random House.

Klein, Ethel. 1984. *Gender Politics*. Cambridge: Harvard University Press.

Kohlberg, Lawrence. 1984. *The Psychology of Moral Development*. San Francisco: Harper & Row.

Krebs, Dennis L. and Dale T. Miller. 1985. Altruism and Aggression. In Gardner Lindzey and Elliot Aronson, eds, *Handbook of Social Psychology*, vol. 2, 3rd edition. New York: Random House.

Landy, Marc and Wilson Carey McWilliams. 1985. Civic Education in an Uncivil Culture. *Society*, 22: 52–5.

Laponce, J.A. 1980. Political Science: An Import–Export Analysis of Journals and Footnotes. *Political Studies*, 28: 401–19.

Lasswell, Harold D. 1925. Two Forgotten Studies in Political Psychology. *American Political Science Review*, 19: 707–17.

Lau, Richard R., and David O. Sears. 1986. *Political Cognition: The 19th Annual Carnegie Symposium on Cognition*. Hillsdale, NJ: Lawrence Erlbaum.

Laumann, Edward O. 1972. *Bonds of Pluralism: The Form and Substance of Urban Social Networks*. New York: Wiley-Interscience.

Lawson, E.D. 1963. Development of Patriotism in Children: A Second Look. *Journal of Psychology*, 55: 279–86.

Lewis, A. 1982. *The Psychology of Taxation*. New York: St Martin's Press.

Lindblom, Charles E. 1982. Another State of Mind. *American Political Science Review*, 76: 9–21.

MacIntyre, Alasdair. 1984. *After Virtue*, 2nd edition. Notre Dame, Indiana: University of Notre Dame Press.

Mansbridge, Jane J. 1980. *Beyond Adversary Democracy*. New York: Basic Books.

Markus, Gregory B. 1979. The Political Environment and the Dynamics of Public Attitudes: A Panel Study. *American Political Science Review*, 23: 338–59.

Markus, Hazel. 1977. Self-Schemata and Processing Information about the Self. *Journal of Personality and Social Psychology*, 37: 449–514.

Markus, Hazel, Marie Crane, Stan Bernstein and Michael Saladi. 1982. Self-Schemas and Gender. *Journal of Personality and Social Psychology*, 42: 38–50.

Marshall, T.H. 1977. *Class, Citizenship and Social Development*. Garden City, NJ: Doubleday.

McClosky, Herbert and Alida Brill. 1983. *Dimensions of Tolerance: What Americans Believe About Civil Liberties*. New York: Russell Sage Foundation.

McClosky, Herbert and John Zaller. 1984. *The American Ethos: Public Attitudes toward Capitalism and Democracy*. Cambridge, MA: Harvard University Press.

Merelman, Richard M. 1972. The Adolescence of Political Socialization. *Sociology of Education*, 45: 134–66.

Merelman, Richard M. 1980. The Family and Political Socialization: Toward a Theory of Exchange. *Journal of Politics*, 42: 461–86.

Merriam, Charles E. 1966. *The Making of Citizens*. New York: Teachers College Press, Columbia University.

Middleton, M.R., Henri Tajfel and N.B. Johnson. 1970. Cognitive and Affective Aspects of Children's National Attitudes. *British Journal of Social and Clinical Psychology*, 9: 122–34.

Miller, Arthur, Patricia Gurin, Gerald Gurin and Oksana Malanchuk. 1981. Group Consciousness and Political Participation. *American Journal of Political Science*, 25: 494–511.

Miller, Stephen D. and David O. Sears. 1985. Stability and Change in Social Tolerance: A Test of the Persistence Hypothesis. *American Journal of Political Science*, 30: 214–36.

Moore, Stanley, W., James Lane and Kenneth A. Wagner. 1985. *The Child's Political World: A Longitudinal Perspective*. New York: Praeger.

Murphy, Paul L. 1983. The Obligations of American Citizenship: A Historical Perspective. *Journal of Teacher Education*, 34: 6–10.

Niemi, Richard G. 1973. Political Socialization. In Jeanne N. Knutson, ed., *Handbook of Political Psychology*. San Francisco: Jossey-Bass, 117–38.

Niemi, Richard G. and Barbara I. Sobieszek. 1977. Political Socialization. *Annual Review of Sociology*, 3: 209–33.

Nisbet, Robert. 1969. *Social Change and History*. Oxford: Oxford University Press.

Novak, Michael. 1972. *The Rise of the Unmeltable Ethnics*. New York: Macmillan.

Pateman, Carole. 1970. *Participation and Democratic Theory*. Cambridge: Cambridge University Press.

Piaget, Jean and Anne-Marie Weil. 1951. The Development in Children of the Idea of the Homeland and of Relations with other Countries. *International Social Science Bulletin*, 3: 561–78.

Pocock, J.G.A. 1975. *The Machiavellian Moment: Florentine Political Thought and the Atlantic Republican Tradition*. Princeton, NJ: Princeton University Press.

Portis, Edward B. 1985. Citizenship and Personal Identity. *Polity*, 18: 457–72.

Pullen, John J. 1971. *Patriotism in America: A Study of Changing Devotions 1770–1970*. New York: American Heritage Press.

Rawls, John. 1971. *A Theory of Justice*. Cambridge, MA: Harvard University Press.

Rosenberg, Shawn W. 1985. Sociology, Psychology and the Study of Political Behavior: The Case of the Research on Political Socialization. *Journal of Politics*, 47: 715–31.

Sandel, Michael J. 1982. *Liberalism and the Limits of Justice*. Cambridge: Cambridge University Press.

Sandel, Michael J. 1984. The Procedural Republic and the Unencumbered Self. *Political Theory*, 12: 81–96.

Searing, Donald D. 1986. A Theory of Socialization: Institutional Support and Deradicalization in Britain. *British Journal of Political Science*, 16: 341–76.

Searing, Donald D., Gerald Wright and George Rabinowitz. 1976. The Primacy Principle: Attitude Change and Political Socialization. *British Journal of Political Science*, 6: 83–113.

Sears, David O. 1975. Political Socialization. In Fred I. Greenstein and Nelson Polsby, eds, *Micropolitical Theory*, vol. 2 of *The Handbook of Political Science*. Reading, MA: Addison-Wesley, 93–154.

Sears, David O. 1987. The Current Status of Political Socialization Research. Paper Prepared for the International Workshop on Political Socialization and Citizenship Education in Democracy, Tel Aviv University, 1–7 March.

Sears, David O. and John S. McConahay. 1973. *The Politics of Violence: The New Urban Blacks and the Watts Riot*. Boston: Houghton Mifflin.

Sigel, Roberta S. and Marilyn B. Hoskin. 1981. *The Political Involvement of Adolescents*. New Brunswick: Rutgers University Press.

Sinopoli, Richard C. 1987. Liberalism, Republicanism and the Constitution. *Polity*, 19: 331–52.

Smith, Bruce James. 1985. *Politics and Remembrance: Republican Themes in Machiavelli, Burke and Tocqueville*. Princeton, NJ: Princeton University Press.
Smith, Roland A. 1975. Measuring Neighborhood Cohesion: A Review and Some Suggestions. *Human Ecology*, 3: 143–60.
Smithson, Michael, Paul R. Amato and Philip Pearce. 1983. *Dimensions of Helping Behavior*. Oxford: Pergamon Press.
Sniderman, Paul M. 1981. *A Question of Loyalty*. Berkeley: University of California Press.
Sowell, Thomas. 1981. *Ethnic America*. New York: Basic Books.
Stanley, Manfred. 1983. The Mystery of the Commons: On the Indispensability of Civic Rhetoric. *Social Research*, 50: 851–83.
Stouffer, Samuel A. 1955. *Communism, Conformity, and Civil Liberties: A Cross-Section of the Nation Speaks Its Mind*. New York: Wiley.
Stradling, Robert and Elia Zurick. 1971. Political and Non-Political Ideals of English Primary and Secondary School Children. *The Sociological Review*, 19: 203–28.
Sullivan, John L., James Piereson and George E. Marcus. 1982. *Political Tolerance and American Democracy*. Chicago: University of Chicago Press.
Sullivan, William M. 1986. *Reconstructing Public Philosophy*. Berkeley: University of California Press.
Tajfel, Henri. 1969. Cognitive Aspects of Prejudice. *Journal of Social Issues*, 25: 79–98.
Tajfel, Henri. 1978. *Differentiation between Social Groups: Studies in the Social Psychology of Intergroup Relations*. European Monographs in Social Psychology no. 14. London: Academic Press.
Tajfel, Henri. 1981. *Human Groups and Social Categories*. Cambridge: Cambridge University Press.
Tarrow, Sidney J. 1971. The Urban–Rural Cleavage in Political Involvement: The Case of France. *American Political Science Review*, 65: 341–57.
Taylor, Michael. 1976. *Anarchy and Cooperation*. London: Wiley.
Taylor, Michael. 1982. *Community, Anarchy and Liberty*. Cambridge: Cambridge University Press.
Taylor, Shelley and Jennifer Crocker. 1981. Schematic Bases of Social Information Processing. In E. Tory Higgins, C. Peter Herman, and Mark P. Zanna, eds, *Social Cognition: The Ontario Symposium*. Hillsdale, NJ: Lawrence Erlbaum.
Thompson, Dennis F. 1970. *The Democratic Citizen: Social Science and Democratic Theory in the Twentieth Century*. Cambridge: Cambridge University Press.
Titmuss, Richard M. 1970. *The Gift Relationship: From Human Blood to Social Policy*. London: Penguin.
Tocqueville, Alexis de. 1969. *Democracy in America*, trans. George Lawrence, ed. J.P. Mayer. New York: Doubleday, Anchor.
Turiel, E. 1985. *The Development of Social Knowledge: Morality and Convention*. New York: Cambridge University Press.
Turner, John C. 1982. Towards a Cognitive Redefinition of the Social Group. In H. Tajfel, ed., *Social Identity and Intergroup Relations*. Cambridge: Cambridge University Press.
Verba, Sidney and Norman H. Nie. 1972. *Participation in America: Political Democracy and Social Equality*. New York: Harper & Row.
Vernon, Richard. 1986. *Citizenship and Order: Studies in French Political Thought*. Toronto: University of Toronto Press.
Walzer, Michael. 1970. *Obligations: Essays on Disobedience, War and Citizenship*. Cambridge: Harvard University Press.
Walzer, Michael. 1976. Civility and Civic Virtue in Contemporary America. *Social Research*, 41: 593–611.
Walzer, Michael. 1983. *Spheres of Justice: A Defense of Pluralism and Equality*. New York: Basic Books.
Warren, D. and R.B. Warren. 1977. *The Neighborhood Organizer's Handbook*. Notre Dame, IN: University of Notre Dame Press.
Warren, Roland L. 1963. *The Community in America*. Chicago: Rand McNally.

Wilder, David A. 1981. Perceiving Persons as a Group: Categorization and Intergroup Relations. In David L. Hamilton, ed., *Cognitive Processes in Stereotyping and Intergroup Behavior*. Hillsdale, NJ: Lawrence Erlbaum.

Wilson, Thomas C. 1985. Urbanism and Tolerance: A Test of some Hypotheses Drawn from Wirth and Stouffer. *American Sociological Review*, 50: 117–23.

Wirth, L. 1983. Urbanism as a Way of life. *American Journal of Sociology*, 44: 8–20.

Wolin, Sheldon S. 1986. Contract and Birthright. *Political Theory*, 14: 179–93.

4

Voters, Parties and Leaders Thirty Years on: Western Electoral Studies and the New Democracies of Eastern Europe

Ivor Crewe

The title of this chapter brings together the electoral and comparative interests of Jean Blondel in his two classic textbooks of the 1960s – *Voters, Parties and Leaders* (1963) and *Introduction to Comparative Government* (1969). It does so by taking some of the updated findings and theories of electoral analyses first applied to Britain in *Voters, Parties and Leaders* and considering how far they might now apply to the socially very different democracies of Central and Eastern Europe. In doing this it provides a behavioural basis for some of the suggestions and assessments made in Parts Four and Five of this book: but it also involves reflections on some of the data and theories of participation just discussed in the context of political socialization. For it immediately becomes obvious that any attempt to apply the results of Western voting studies elsewhere also involves reflecting on the Western democratic experience itself and on the foundations of democratic participation in terms of individual and group orientations.

The study of elections in the newly democratized states of Central and Eastern Europe (henceforward CEE) presents students of Western elections with an exhilarating but frustrating challenge. On the one hand, they appear to offer a unique test-bed for the theories of voting, party system development and democratic stability that have evolved with the post-war growth of academic political science. On the other, these theories have been formulated in the West, mainly the United States, where political conditions and research resources are very different from those prevailing now or in the foreseeable future in CEE. They take for granted the existence of a secure democratic order, of long-established parties, of an advanced post-industrial economy and a large private sector. They have been constructed with the aid of a regular series of large national sample surveys, or of long time series of behavioural and attitudinal indicators, which for academic or practical reasons may be inapplicable in other areas of Europe.

There is, it is true, a Western parallel on which the analyst can draw. The democratic revolutions of 1989 resemble in some respects the massive extensions of the franchise that swept through Europe in the aftermath of the First World War. Then, as now, democratic rights were suddenly extended to mass publics in the midst of widespread economic dislocation and, in the case of Central and Eastern Europe, imperial collapse, a discredited old order and rampant nationalism. But the parallels should not be overdrawn. In 1989 democratization came more rapidly and with less preparation. Many of the states that moved to a universal franchise in 1918 had for a generation or more enjoyed some liberalization and experienced competitive elections on a limited suffrage. Most had developed a civil society of independent or at least semi-independent professions, trade unions, churches and social movements which acted as embryonic parties and nurseries for democratic politics. In CEE, with the partial exceptions of Poland and Hungary, there has been no such preparation and thus no time for a liberal, democratic culture to lay down roots.

An account of the major analytical and methodological debates in electoral studies should therefore be selective, not only for sheer reasons of space, but because only some of them are relevant to the situation in CEE. Accordingly, this chapter confines itself to three sub-fields of electoral research:

1   the social basis of party systems;
2   the development of individual partisanship;
3   short-term influences on the vote, especially those of the economy.

These three sub-fields have been selected for a number of reasons. First, each sub-field illustrates a distinct tradition, and stage of development, in electoral studies. Simplifying drastically, these might be described as the 'sociological' tradition of the 1940s and 1950s; the 'socio-psychological' tradition of the 1960s and 1970s; and the 'economic' tradition of the 1980s. Secondly, each sub-field has produced a body of consistently verified propositions, which have a bearing on the long-term prospects of the fledgeling democracies in CEE. The sociological tradition offers insights into the shape of the future party systems of CEE. The socio-psychological tradition provides theories and measures of the electorate's attachment to the parties, and thus the wider political system; and the economic tradition gives a perspective on one of the main short-term threats to the democratic system – economic discontent. Finally, each sub-field has generated methodological and theoretical controversies, which have implications for the way elections should be studied and interpreted.

This chapter will examine the three sub-fields in turn. It describes the underlying assumptions about the nature of voting, lists the core empirical propositions that have withstood the test of time and place, and discusses the methodological and theoretical challenges to the sub-field's assumptions. It then considers what inferences can be drawn for the development of a competitive party system in CEE and whether, in turn, the CEE's experience of 'founding' elections offers lessons for Western electoral studies.

The Social Basis of Party Systems

The Sociological Approach

The founding tradition of electoral studies was sociological and geographical, focusing on the demographic correlates of party choice. It is an *approach* rather than a *theory*. At the micro-level it answers the question 'who votes what?'; at the macro-level the question 'which parties are supported by which groups?' Its emphasis is collectivist rather than individualist: its units of analysis are parties and social categories, not the individual voter, who is regarded merely as a group member. Group voting patterns are interpreted in terms of the group's position in the social order and its relation to political parties; election results are treated as evidence of social divisions rather than the outcome of political processes. These biases probably owe more to the absence of survey-based individual-level data at the time early studies were undertaken than to any Marxist bias on the part of the authors.

This approach has a number of attractions. First, it is the only feasible approach in the absence of a sample survey – a likely situation, for financial and even political reasons, in at least some CEE states for some time. Despite the snares of the 'ecological fallacy' (the illegitimate inference of individual-level behaviour from aggregate-level relationships), multivariate regression techniques can tease out the social correlates of party support at the aggregate level, so long as there are a sufficient number of small units (preferably local election units) for which a variety of uncorrelated social and economic indicators are available (Dogan and Rokkan, 1969).

Secondly, when social attributes correlate with party choice, they are clearly the cause, not the consequence: gender may determine vote, but vote cannot determine gender. In attitudinal models of the vote, the direction of causation is much less clear-cut. Moreover, social structural correlates of the vote always have a substantive significance. Elaborate models often find that political attitudes correlate more strongly than social attributes with the vote; this makes them better predictors of party choice, but not necessarily better explanations.

Thirdly, the sociological approach rests on more reliable data than other theories. The aggregate data are accurate, assuming that returning officers and census officials are honest; and respondents' answers to survey questions about the familiar and enduring demographic facts of their lives are generally more reliable than their instantaneous responses to political questions to which they may have given little prior thought.

Finally, the sociological approach has produced a set of consistently verified empirical propositions about the social basis of the vote and of party systems. There follow a selection of those that have important implications for CEE elections.

Propositions

1 The capacity of social characteristics to predict party choice varies widely and enduringly between countries.

For example, it has always been weak in Ireland and Canada; it has always been strong in Italy, Belgium and the Netherlands. The variation arises from the closeness or absence of 'fit' between the country's party system and its social cleavages; and it endures because both social divisions and party systems are fairly permanent. Why the fit should be tighter in some countries than others has not found a satisfactory theoretical explanation (but see Powell, 1982, for the best attempt). It is likely to be closer where organized communities pre-dated the mass franchise and the formation of the party system and where proportional representation, especially systems with a low threshold, encouraged the separate party representation of distinct religious, national and economic groups. Hence the generally closer fit in the continental European than Anglo-American democracies.

2 The social basis of party systems in uninterrupted democracies is constant over the long term.

This proposition resembles the first but is different. The first said that the capacity of the social structure to determine the vote was enduring. This says that the precise links between social attribute and party choice endure from the foundation of the party system. Summarizing their monumental study of the historical development of party systems since the franchise extensions of the nineteenth century, Lipset and Rokkan (1967, p. 50) concluded with a sentence that has mesmerized political scientists ever since: 'the party systems of the 1960s reflect, with few but significant exceptions, the cleavage structures of the 1920s'. Subsequent studies (Rose and Urwin, 1970; Maguire, 1983; Bartolini and Mair, 1990) have largely confirmed this staggering truth: current party alignments were frozen into shape by the events of over a half a century ago. Thus parties outlive the conflicts which gave them birth (e.g. Ireland's Fianna Fáil and Fine Gael whose origins lie in conflict over the 1920 treaty of secession) and overcome the gradual contraction of their original base. Farmers' parties have outlasted agricultural decline; confessional parties have survived secularization and social democratic parties are adapting to the contraction of the working class.

3 The precise conjunction of social cleavages and party system varies from country to country.

In truth, this is a non-proposition. It concedes that there is no mechanical social determination of party systems. Socially similar countries such as

Norway and Finland or Northern Ireland and Scotland have quite disparate party systems; socially diverse countries such as New Zealand and
Austria or Ireland and Canada have fairly similar party systems. Each
party system is the product of a historically unique combination of factors
at the time the party system emerged, which include the social structure,
the mobilization and organization of social groups, the electoral system,
the pre-democratic party system and, most important of all, decisions
made by individual political leaders to merge or split parties and to seek or
ignore the support of specific groups. Party systems owe far more to
historical accident than to social determinism (Rokkan, 1970).

4 (a) The most *common* social basis of party choice is class.
   (b) The most *important* social bases of party choice are religion and
        language.

These two propositions are juxtaposed to make a point. The pattern of
social cleavages in each country depends on the precise impact of two
waves of conflict that have swept across Western democracies: the
'national revolution' (pitting centre against periphery, state against church
and dominant nation against national minorities); and the 'industrial
revolution' (pitting employers against trade unions and bourgeoisie against
working class) (Lipset and Rokkan, 1967). Some discern two further waves
since the Second World War: the 'growth of the state' (Dunleavy and
Husbands, 1985), generating conflicts of interest between private and
public sector, house owners and tenants, tax payers and state dependents;
and 'post-industrialism' (Inglehart, 1977) which has produced a genera-
tional and educational conflict of values and culture. The first two have had
most impact because they existed when party systems were forming in the
midst of a newly enfranchised and therefore unaligned mass electorate.
Linguistic, national and religious cleavages exist only in those countries
where the national revolution was incomplete when the universal franchise
arrived, i.e. where the state had failed to impose central control, a single
church and a common language. Class cleavages exist in every industrialized country, albeit faintly in some. Where the national revolution was
complete, like Britain and Sweden, class is the only basis of party support;
where it was incomplete, religion and/or language compete with class as
determinants of the vote and are generally more important (Rose and
Urwin, 1970). Lijphart (1979) carried out a 'critical test' on the four
countries where religious, linguistic and class cleavages are all present
(Belgium, Canada, Switzerland and South Africa): religion was the
strongest correlate of the vote in three; language in one (South Africa).

'Religion', it should be noted, encompasses three different cleavages:
clerical versus anti-clerical in homogeneously Catholic countries (Italy,
France, Malta, Austria, Belgium); Protestant versus Catholic in mixed
countries (Weimar Germany, Netherlands, Canada (weakly)); and 'moral
traditionalism' versus 'permissive' in some Protestant countries (United
States, Norway).

5   The probability of voters supporting the 'natural' party of their social
    group is a function of (a) social and geographic mobility; (b) organiza-
    tional ties; (c) the social homogeneity of their environment.

Thus left parties do best amongst those working-class voters born to
working-class parents, belonging to trade unions, working in large plants
and living in largely working-class neighbourhoods. Christian democratic
parties do best among voters born to religious parents, who attend church
regularly, and live in Catholic areas. Where class and religious cleavages
compete, 'group-reinforced' voters (middle-class Catholics, the secular
working class) support their natural party more solidly than the cross-
pressured do.

   Here lies part of the explanation for the greater electoral power of
religion than class. More voters change their class than their religion and
the organizational reach of the church, with a priest in every village,
outmatches that of the labour movement. In addition, emotional ties to
church (and nation) are generally stronger than those to class, for a
complex of reasons including the role of symbol and ritual in early
upbringing.

Empirical, Theoretical and Methodological Challenges

The propositions outlined above have been the subject of empirical,
theoretical and methodological debate. The empirical challenge arises
from evidence of a post-war decline in class (but not religious) voting in
some Western democracies, including Britain, Sweden, the United States
and West Germany; an increase in volatility in some countries; and the
entry into the party system of new, small parties representing the new left,
environmentalism and, across the ideological spectrum, reaction against
Third World immigrants (Crewe and Denver, 1985; Franklin et al., 1992).
All three phenomena can be partly attributed to the emergence in some
economically advanced democracies of the post-industrial cleavage
between the 'post-material values' of the better educated, more affluent
and young and the 'material' values of an older, less privileged generation.
But this is a weak cleavage, based on values not interests, on culture and
not communities, dividing a small minority from the large majority. The
social foundations of party systems in the established democracies have
been shaken by tremors, not destroyed by earthquakes.

   The theoretical debate focuses on the reasons for the social basis of party
choice. The sociological tradition is better at cartography than geography,
at answering the 'who' and 'what' rather than 'why' questions. It tends to
infer that a group votes for a party because it sees the party as representing
its group interest. But social divisions can shape party choice even when
the parties themselves do not exploit or even appeal to those divisions.
Thus Catholics tend to vote Christian Democrat in Germany and Liberal in
Canada even though Catholic–Protestant and state–church conflict barely

exist in either country. To grasp the reasons for social group voting one therefore needs to know the content and origin of the attitudes that link the group to the party.

These attitudinal links form the basis of two types of explanation. One type emphasizes group *identity*: through family upbringing and neighbour-hood tradition the voter learns at an early age that (a) he/she is Catholic (b) Catholics vote Christian Democrat. The voter operates with a simple, often unpoliticized, conception of the group–party tie (Irvine and Gold, 1980). The social alignment is inherited, habitual and almost devoid of group-related content. The second type of explanation emphasizes con-sciousness of group *conflict* and *interests*, inculcated by involvement in group organizations, and attention to party rhetoric and the political media. Such voters possess an elaborate conflict model of the links between their interests, their group and the group's party as well as of the links between the opposing group and opposing party (on two types of class–party ties, see Butler and Stokes, 1969).

The different types of group–party tie have implications for the stability of the democratic and party system in CEE countries. Ties of identity are disproportionately found among the politically less informed and involved, owe their existence to past social conflicts long since depoliticized, and are eroded by social and geographic mobility; they are easily ruptured by charismatic leaders and mass movements. Ties of interest tend to exist among the more 'politerate' voters, are sustained by current party conflict and are thus less easily eroded by new challenges to the party system. Studies of elections in CEE countries need to distinguish between these two types of social alignment.

Methodological debates are largely – and endlessly – devoted to the definition, operationalization and measurement of social class. Unlike any other social attribute social class is an inherently contested concept, overladen with ideological meaning, around which consensus is unlikely to emerge. American election surveys have effectively replaced the concept with that of 'socioeconomic status' which combines income, occupational prestige and education into an interval-level measure. British and conti-nental European election studies attempt to operationalize Marxist or, more usually, Weberian concepts of class (i.e. shared interests or life chances based on position in the labour market) by allocating respondents to one of four or five 'classes' on the basis of their occupation. Each stage of the complex operation is disputed and flawed. First, a large minority of the electorate do not have paid occupations (housewives, the retired, the unemployed, students) and are therefore given surrogate occupations. Secondly, the respondent's description, interviewer's transcription, and researcher's class coding of occupation are all error-prone. Thirdly, the various class schemata – the number and definition of classes – are subject to dispute. Finally, there are doubts about whether occupation alone can capture structured inequalities of life chances. The American practice assumes that inequality exists without classes. The British and continental practice assumes that everybody belongs to a distinctive class. Both assumptions reflect cultural biases.

Some electoral studies attempt to circumvent these problems by relying upon voters' subjective class identity, which usually correlates more strongly than 'objective' class with party choice. But in countries dominated by parties with explicit class ideologies, subjective class may be the effect, not the cause, of party preference: in Britain Labour-voting non-manual workers who call themselves 'working class' are often making a political statement rather than describing their class identity. There is a simple and effective indicator of religiosity – frequency of church attendance. There is no equivalent for class consciousness.

Implications for Central and Eastern Europe

What are the implications of these propositions for the democracies of CEE?

First, the next ten years or so will form, perhaps petrify, their party systems. The fission and fusion of parties and the strategic decisions of party and organizational leaders will be crucial. However, it would be premature to assume that the party systems of CEE already exist in embryo and that the next decade will witness their development along pre-ordained lines. In most of CEE the only national election to have taken place so far was effectively a referendum on the communist regime – a 'founding' election in which parties in the conventional sense did not exist. The transition from authoritarianism to democracy in Spain, Portugal and Greece in the late 1970s and early 1980s suggests that it takes two elections for the party system to take shape. We shall not discern the profile of CEE party systems until the mid 1990s.

But, secondly, judging from West European experience, each country's party system will probably be unique. Much will depend on the contingent decisions of parties to merge or split, cooperate or compete; much on their organizational resources in the early years. There is unlikely to be a CEE 'model' common to all or even several countries in Central and Eastern Europe. We have already seen major differences between countries in the electoral fate of communist parties (compare Czechoslovakia and Hungary with Albania, Bulgaria and Romania).

Thirdly, and following from the above, former communist parties are likely to survive as a significant force where they have retained some legitimacy by having instigated the coup against the party dictator, were not obliterated in the founding election, and have been allowed to retain their assets, patronage networks and access to the media. The National Salvation Front of Romania is the most prominent example, but the former communist parties of Bulgaria and Albania may be in a similar, though less favourable position.

Fourthly, party choice will not necessarily be socially based. It is most likely to be where semi-independent organizations and movements preceded the jump to democracy, as in Poland (the Catholic Church, Solidarity, and farmers' organizations), and least likely where civil society was most thoroughly permeated by the Communist Party, as in Czechoslovakia, Bulgaria and Romania. However, even in Poland, an explicitly Catholic or peasant or trade unionist vote has not, so far, been mobilized. In the first round of the presidential elections in November 1990 the Peasants Party candidate won 7 per cent, and the Catholic Party's candidate 6 per cent, while Solidarity's successful candidate Lech Walesa did not pitch his appeal specifically to organized labour. One cannot be confident that confessional, peasants' and labour parties, comparable in significance to those of many Western European countries, will be established. What is more likely, fifthly, is that parties representing the periphery will be very strong (perhaps explosively so) where the periphery coincides with linguistic and national differences (Transylvania, Macedonia); moderately strong where they coincide with national differences only. The absence of other strong identities makes nationalism especially potent.

Finally, the development of religious and class cleavages is more difficult to infer from the Western experience. Catholic countries in CEE may develop a religious/secular cleavage, which could turn into a clerical/anticlerical cleavage (as in the Third as opposed to the Fifth French Republic). This will partly depend on the role the church seeks to play in society (education, welfare and 'moral' legislation) and on whether or not it establishes a church-based party. One overwhelmingly and devoutly Catholic country, Ireland, where the church symbolized the nation under foreign domination and Catholic teaching is embedded in the constitution, lacks any such a cleavage; Poland may follow the same route.

The future of class cleavages is even more difficult to call. The conventional definitions and measures of class in Western social science, which are anyway so unsatisfactory, are probably inappropriate for societies in transition from a state to market economy. If voters in CEE give themselves a class identity it is likely to be in terms of future expectations, not past experience. In a stimulating essay, Kitschelt (1991) argues that in the CEE democracies a new class division will emerge between potential 'winners' and potential 'losers' in a market economy. 'Winners' will be 'ex-reds' or 'experts' with personal resources to market in the emerging capitalist economy. These resources may depend on incumbency of office (discretionary power; personal networks; access to information; bargaining, coalition building, influence and other political skills) or be independent of office (professional and technical expertise; modest capital accumulation; entrepreneurial ability). 'Losers' will suffer a decline in living standards, economic security, welfare and social status from the privatization of the economy. On one side of the class divide will be former senior party officials, managers, the professions, farmers, small shopkeepers, people in the arts and culture, and skilled service workers (e.g. mechanics, repairmen); on the other, minor state officials, most of the former security and military apparatus, workers in declining industries, unskilled workers, agricultural labourers, and pensioners. Borrowing conventional ideas about occupational status from 'Western' conceptions of social class is unlikely to be fruitful.

The Development of Individual Partisanship

The Socio-Psychological Approach

A socio-psychological perspective on voting succeeded the sociological approach when sample surveys superseded aggregate statistics as the main source of evidence about electoral behaviour. The emphasis shifted from the group to the individual; but the individual voter was treated as the product of a lifetime's socialization, not as an autonomous decision-maker. Voting was expressive not instrumental, an act of affirmation not choice, habitual and hereditary rather than freshly considered at each election. Voters no more 'chose' their party than they chose their religion or nationality. To vote was to demonstrate one's party loyalty, or 'partisanship'. This may appear to make the socio-psychological approach irrelevant to electoral behaviour in CEE, but we shall see that it is not.

Partisanship (or 'partisan self-image' as it is occasionally called) is an enduring psychological identification with a party. When the concept was constructed at the University of Michigan in the 1950s, the American political parties were regarded as a special type of social group to which the voter formed (or inherited) a personal 'identification', a term

> used quite intentionally to express the assumption that the relationship often involves an extension of ego. This is because an important part of the individual's self identity as a political actor is assumed to emanate from the sense of belonging to a political group . . . what happens to the group also happens to the individual; as the group prospers or declines the individual flourishes or suffers, at least in psychological terms. (Miller, 1976)

Thus party identification was regarded as a partial substitute for group solidarity in an individualistic, mobile and plural society where group identities were liable to be weak, fluid and multiple.

In *The American Voter* (Campbell et al., 1960), the classic study of the 1952 and 1956 presidential elections based on the Michigan surveys, partisanship was treated as a long-term influence on voters' party choice and attitudes, enduring across a sequence of elections, as distinct from such short-term, election-specific, influences as the presidential candidates and the issues of the day. It was a stable and pervasively influential attribute of most voters. The authors devised a 'funnel of causality' of the vote running from the most distant influences in time to the most proximate. Closest to the vote were attitudes to the candidates, to domestic and foreign policy, and to group interests. Most distant were the influences of social groups and the family. Partisanship came in between. Yet it proved the linchpin of voters' electoral behaviour and attitudes. On the one hand, it captured the influences of social groups and the family such that their direct impact on party choice, independent of partisanship, was negligible. On the other hand, it channelled its own influence through voters' evaluation of the parties' candidates, policies and benefits to them. The American voter thought the Republican candidates and policies were preferable because he/she was a Republican – not the other way round.

It is significant that partisanship was chosen in preference to other possible long-term, deep-seated influences on electoral behaviour, such as ideology or voters' position on the permanent political issues. The Michigan research showed that the great majority of American voters did not think in ideological or issue-oriented terms. They were unfamiliar with political issues or with parties' and candidates' positions on them, and their own views on issues were highly unstable. Very few organized their political thoughts in terms of a coherent set of general principles which could be described, on a generous definition, as 'ideological' (Converse, 1964). The cornerstone of electoral behaviour from this perspective is not ideology or issues, but partisanship.

Propositions

A set of propositions about the sources, nature and consequences of partisanship has been empirically verified over time and across countries such that one can reasonably speak of the 'Michigan model' of electoral behaviour (Crewe, 1974). It is not a theory of electoral behaviour (i.e. a statement about the empirical relationships predicted to obtain between two or more variables) but a conceptual framework and set of postulates from which a wide range of theories may be derived – including theories about elections in CEE. The most widely applicable propositions are as follows.

Party Identification

1 Most people possess a partisanship, which varies in direction and intensity.
2 Partisanship is the single most *enduring* feature of a voter's political attitudes and behaviour, because:
    (a) it induces a process of partisan selective perception of the voter's political environment and thus becomes self-reinforcing over time; and
    (b) it tends to divide along fairly immutable social cleavages such as religion, nationality and class.
3 Partisan self-image is the strongest predictor of attitudes and behaviour involving the relative evaluation of parties, and particularly
    (a) party choice at a single election
    (b) stability of party choice: strong partisanship is associated with loyalty to party at a single election and consistent support for the

party across a series of elections; weak partisanship is associated with party defection and inconsistent voting;

(c) turnout: the stronger a voter's partisanship the more likely he/she is to vote.

Direction of Party Identification

4 The single variable most associated with the direction of a voter's partisanship is parental partisanship.
   (a) Voters are most likely to inherit their parental partisanship if both parents shared the same, strong, allegiance to the majority party of their social group.
   (b) Voters are least likely to inherit their parental partisanship if (i) their parents had a mixed or weak partisanship; (ii) their parents identified with the minority party of their social group (e.g. if they were black Republicans or working-class Conservatives); (iii) they have experienced intergenerational social mobility, up or down.
5 In the circumstances outlined in 4(b), parental partisanship is still largely bequeathed to children, especially in their early years as electors, but other factors begin to have an important bearing on the direction of partisan image as the voter matures.

Strength of Partisanship

6 Since partisanship is self-reinforcing over time, its strength increases with the length of time it has been held, which is strongly related to but not the same as age. Hence the newly enfranchised, while particularly influenced by their parental partisanship (if any), tend to have relatively weak attachments to a party.

Implications for Electoral and Political Stability

7 Stability of party choice: it follows from propositions 3(b) and 6 that unstable voting is most likely to occur among the newly enfranchised and young voters. Therefore:
   (a) new democracies are more vulnerable than old democracies to electoral volatility, 'flash' parties, the collapse of old parties, and unstable party systems; but
   (b) as new democracies mature the incidence and strength of partisanship in the electorate will grow, *so long as the main features of the party system remain constant.*

Elections in CEE have already furnished support for some of these propositions. For example, while turnout was extremely high in those founding elections that essentially were plebiscites on the dismantling of communism (e.g. 93 per cent in East Germany in March 1990; 96 per cent in Czechoslovakia in June 1990; 90 per cent in Bulgaria in June 1990) it has been low by West European standards in subsequent competitive party elections for the presidency or the national legislature (e.g. 67 per cent in Poland in November 1990 and 65 per cent and 44 per cent in the first and second rounds respectively in Hungary in April-May 1990). The absence of a partisan electorate makes it more difficult, even in the television age, for 'parties' – usually no more than loose political associations anyway – to mobilize followers. Another reflection of the weak or non-existent partisanship in CEE is the success of 'flash' candidates, notably the 23 per cent of the vote obtained (in the space of a four-week campaign) by the politically inexperienced ex-patriot millionaire, Stanislaw Tyminski, in the Polish presidential election. His support came disproportionately from those least likely to have ties with national organizations and thus to have developed any partisanship – the young, the poorly educated, and those living in small provincial towns.

Let us now consider how well the set of propositions has stood the test of time and place, and thus how applicable they are as a whole to the democracies of CEE.

Empirical, Theoretical and Methodological Challenges

The Michigan model of voting, anchored in the concept of partisanship, has been criticized on numerous grounds. These criticisms are encapsulated in four challenging questions that are relevant to the situation in CEE:

1   Is partisanship unidimensional?
2   Is the concept applicable outside the United States?
3   Is the long-term development of mass partisanship linear or cyclical?
4   Is partisanship as deep-seated and long-term an influence as originally envisaged?

Is Partisanship Unidimensional?

At this point one needs to distinguish between the concept of partisanship and 'party identification' which is the measure of partisanship adopted by the Michigan team. The measure was based on answers to a two-part question. The first part asked respondents whether they generally thought of themselves as Republicans, Democrats or independents. The second part asked 'Republicans' and 'Democrats' how strongly they thought of themselves in this way and asked 'independents' whether they 'leant' towards the Republicans or Democrats. Respondents were allocated to one of five categories – Strong Republican, weak Republican, independent, weak Democrat, strong Democrat – which were sometimes expanded to seven categories when independents were subdivided into Democrat-leaning, Republican-leaning and 'pure' independents. Empirical research in the 1970s discovered 'intransitivities' in the expected linear relationship with the vote (Petrocik, 1974) and political involvement (Keith et al., 1986) (although not with split ticket voting or regularity of party choice):

independent 'leaners' were more partisan in their behaviour and attitudes than 'weak' Democrats and Republicans. This is not as petty or technical a problem as it might seem. It illustrated the measure's inability to distinguish between uninterested and uninformed 'non-partisans' who made up the bulk of independents in the 1950s and 1960s, and politically involved and informed 'critical partisans' who joined the swelling band of independents in the 1970s and 1980s. 'Independents' came to encompass both alienated subjects, open to mobilization by anti-system extremist parties and charismatic leaders, and textbook citizens, open to mobilization by pro-system moderate reform movements – a crucial distinction for the new democracies of CEE.

The intransitivities came about for a second reason. The party identification measure regarded partisanship in terms of positive support rather than relative preference. In particular, it did not incorporate a measure of negative partisanship, i.e. strength of antipathy towards one or more enemy parties. Research on Britain and elsewhere suggests that substantial proportions of partisans are more strongly repelled by the enemy party than attracted by their own and that such 'negative partisans' behave electorally in similar ways to the classical 'strong partisans' (Crewe, 1980). In the CEE democracies, where anti-communism (and in places hostility to nationalist parties) is likely to be intense, negative partisanship may be set to play a crucial role in party choice.

Is the Concept Applicable outside the United States?

From the late 1950s members of the Michigan team collaborated with European political scientists in attempts to apply the concept of partisanship to European democracies. The transplant usually took root but often failed to thrive. For one thing, few Europeans thought of themselves as independents; for another, the party identification measure failed to distinguish as clearly between partisanship and vote. Panel surveys revealed that voting and party identification travelled together more in Britain than in the United States and that in the Netherlands party identification was less stable than the vote (Butler and Stokes, 1969; Thomassen, 1976).

Some critics argued that the concept of partisanship worked only in the United States, where the frequency of elections, the existence of multiple-level and multiple-office elections, the practice of 'registering' as a Republican or Democrat in primaries, and the unideological character of the electorate encouraged voters to identify directly with a party. European voters, it was argued, derived their partisan self-image from their social group or an ideology; their vote was a product of the perhaps temporary relation between the parties and their group or ideology.

These are challenges to the standard party identification measure rather than to the concept of partisanship. Nor should the difficulties be exaggerated: the standard party identification measure has been found to be a superior predictor of future voting choice than socioeconomic variables across non-American democracies (Budge and Farlie, 1976). Nonetheless, the defects of the measure suggest that in multi-party systems where a number of parties cluster around the same point of the ideological spectrum (e.g. the Netherlands, Israel) it should encompass multiple-party identification (Van der Eijk and Niemoller, 1983) and where parties constantly merge, split and change their names (e.g. the Fourth Republic) it should consist of identification with an ideological tendency (the left, the centre, the bourgeois parties etc.). Self-placement on an ideological scale and 'feeling thermometers' applied to social groups or parties may prove superior measures of partisanship, although on past evidence they are less stable than party identification among the same respondents. Indeed, an original member of the Michigan team introduced ideological identification ('liberal', 'moderate', 'conservative') into his analysis of American electoral behaviour during the more turbulent and polarized 1964–76 period (Miller and Levitin, 1976). Ideological identification turned out to be almost as stable an attribute as party identification, but only because it was linked by most voters to their identification with, and alienation from, social groups. These criticisms do not, therefore, amount to a refutation of partisanship; they call for a development of multiple and alternative measures to suit local political conditions. In CEE, a rapid turnover of parties in the early 1990s is likely, and two or more parties may occupy the same position on the political spectrum (e.g. the AFD and AFY in Hungary; or the various fragments of the former Communist Party in Poland, Hungary and the Czech and Slovak republics). The development of partisan self-images among voters is therefore likely to involve an identification with a political *tendency* (nationalism, liberal cosmopolitanism, Catholic values etc.) rather than with a particular party.

The Long-Term Development of Mass Partisanship: Linear or Cyclical?

The original Michigan model stressed the role of the family in the transmission of partisanship from one generation to the next. But where did the parents get their partisanship from? Or their parents? Politics had to enter the equation at some stage in the past. The answer was never satisfactorily spelled out: the origins of partisanship appeared to lie partly in traumatic national events such as economic slump, civil war and foreign occupation, partly in the gradual mobilization of the unaligned by party organizations.

Two quite contradictory conclusions were drawn about the implications of family transmission for the long-term development of partisanship in a mass electorate. Converse (1969) constructed an ingenious model which suggested that in a new democratic regime it would take *three generations* before the level of partisanship in the electorate would reach a self-sustaining equilibrium of about 70 per cent. This length of time was needed because in the regime's first generation a substantial majority would remain outside the party system and fail to develop a partisanship to bequeath. If applied to CEE a fully developed stable party system would not be established until about 2050. And if in the early vulnerable years the democratic regime was overthrown the process would have to begin again when democracy was restored, as in West Germany and Italy in 1948.

Converse's model of stabilization was undermined by trends in the mature democracies of the United States and Britain, where the level and strength of partisanship in the 1970s and 1980s declined (Wattenberg, 1984; Crewe, 1984). In the United States the decline arose from the non-existent or weak partisanship of the younger generation; in Britain from a weakening of partisanship across all age groups. These trends prompted Beck (1979) to formulate a cyclical model of partisan development across three generations. Only the generation that directly experiences a new alignment (or realignment) is sufficiently partisan to impart its loyalties to its children. This second generation retains some party loyalties but they are imperfectly bequeathed to the third generation – the grandchildren – whose partisanship is so tenuous that they are available for mobilization by new parties or around new alignments. Applied to CEE this model envisages the development of partisan stability until 2030, after which decline would set in. Thus Converse treats the importance of family socialization as a constant; Beck as related to the stage of a realignment.

Whichever model proves correct, we may assume that the new democracies in CEE consist of first-generation, unaligned electorates awaiting realignment. In the absence of democracy for at least fifty years the generation that identified with the pre-war parties will have largely died out, as is suggested by the low levels of support in Hungary and Romania for the resurrected 'historical' parties that date from the crypto-democratic inter-war and 1945–8 periods. The most aligned electorates are those in Bulgaria and Albania where the communist parties, although defeated in the most recent elections, have retained considerable strength. Ironically, these countries may therefore turn out to have the most stable party systems.

Is Partisanship as Deep-Seated and Long-Term an Influence as Originally Envisaged?

The decline of partisanship in the United States of the 1970s and the apparent upsurge in 'issue voting' led some to question whether party identification was as deep-seated, stable and long-term an influence as originally portrayed. Panel studies revealed considerable instabilities of partisan strength as well as movements between the Democrat/Republican and independent categories (Brody and Rothenberg, 1988). Fiorina (1981) among others (Jackson, 1975; Page and Jones, 1979) showed that party identification was more fluid and more responsive to short-term forces than the Michigan model implied. He reconceptualized party identification as a 'running tally' of retrospective evaluations on the parties combined with the diminishing impact of parental partisanship. With each successive election the impact of inherited partisanship diminishes and the impact of short-term experience increases. Compared with the original Michigan version this reformulation of partisanship gives more weight to 'rational', instrumental ties of calculation and interests, less weight to 'non-rational', expressive ties of emotion and identity.

The work of these revisionists undermined the simple model of partisanship as the cause, not the product, of short-term evaluations of the parties' candidates, policies and performance. The original 'funnel of causality' was unidirectional and sequential. Reality was more complex. When non-recursive modelling techniques were developed it was possible to identify and measure feedback and simultaneity. Findings varied, being sensitive to the structure of the models, and to the validity of the included variables (especially the exogenous ones). They all revealed a two-way flow of cause and effect between party identification on the one hand and each of candidate evaluations, policy evaluations and vote on the other; they all revealed the major independent impact of candidate evaluations on the vote in presidential elections. But party identification remained a crucial, enduring, powerful, independent variable, as the most convincing of these complex models, based on 1972–6 panel data, concluded:

> Partisan predispositions may be outweighed by other model terms at particular stages . . . but these loyalties keep coming back as determinants while the vote decision process unrolls . . . In short, then, while partisan predispositions are unlikely to dominate the process completely at given stages where the candidates are being assessed, these loyalties appear to make repeated inputs of substantial magnitude throughout the process. (Markus and Converse, 1979)

On balance, critics of the original Michigan model have exaggerated the impact of short-term influences on partisanship in the United States. The model needs to be modified, not abandoned. However, complex two-way models have not been constructed for other countries, including those where partisanship is weak. In the democracies of CEE, where partisanship has not had time to develop, parental partisanship is negligible (except to and against the Communist Party) and social group ties are generally weak, we may expect short-term influences, especially evaluations of government performance and presidential candidates, to play a more important role in shaping partisanship. We focus briefly on this element of the electoral process next.

Short-Term Influences on the Vote: Economic Voting

So far this chapter has focused on the sources of long-term party alignments, and thus the shape of party systems. We now turn to an important short-term influence on the vote, and thus on election results: the economy, and voters' perceptions of it.

Economic voting, as we shall call it, is one application of the more general 'economic' or 'rational choice' approach to voting. Like the socio-psychological approach, rational choice models are individualist; but unlike it they treat the voter as a rational decision-maker responding to short-term conditions. They do not invalidate sociological or socio-psychological perspectives on voting: there is no reason why part of the electorate should not act like 'rational' voters while another part conforms to the Michigan model. They assume that voters support the party that is most likely to achieve their political goals but differ on what those goals are ('utility streams', policies, etc.). Economic voting assumes that voters seek economic prosperity for themselves and their country, evaluate the parties' claims to achieve such goals, and vote accordingly.

The burgeoning research literature on economic voting is subject to fierce methodological controversies and has not produced altogether consistent conclusions. More than in other sub-fields of electoral study, findings are highly sensitive to modelling procedures: the methodological tail wags the substantive dog. But from reviews covering research in various countries (Paldam, 1981; and Schneider, 1984) and an important six-nation analysis (Lewis-Beck, 1988) the following propositions appear to apply to the major Western democracies.

Economic Voting: Main Propositions

1 If economic conditions deteriorate (improve), the electorate is more (less) likely to vote against the incumbent party.

Economic voting mainly affects the incumbent party because the government is normally held responsible for the state of the economy. We may expect this to be especially likely in CEE where forty years of socialism has entrenched the idea that the state has responsibility for economic conditions. In the Western economic recession of the mid to late 1970s almost every incumbent government suffered defeat or, in the case of dominant party systems, an abnormal loss of support; the worse the 'misery index' of unemployment plus inflation, the worse in general the government did (Lipset, 1983). In pure two-party systems like the United States, what the incumbent party gains (loses) the 'out' party loses (gains). In other systems, including majoritarian systems with single-party government like Britain, the impact of economic voting on the major as distinct from minor opposition party(ies) has not been satisfactorily modelled. In multi-party systems with coalition government – which are what is likely to emerge in CEE – economic voting tends to be weaker because the accountability of any single party in government for economic conditions is less clear-cut. Moreover, governments can partly escape electoral retribution for economic problems if they can convince voters that responsibility lies elsewhere, such as the previous government (or regime), foreign powers, world economic conditions or subversive domestic forces (e.g. trade unions, bankers, saboteurs).

2   Economic voting is a permanent and major influence on the vote.

'When you think economics, think elections; when you think elections, think economics' (Tufte, 1978, p. 65). Economic variables account for between 20 and 40 per cent of the variation in government popularity, as measured by opinion polls. On the limited time-series data available they were as important in the 1950s and 1960s as in more recent decades. Their impact on the incumbent party's vote, as opposed to its support in the polls, is somewhat less. Nonetheless, economic evaluations are second only to partisanship (and, in a minority of countries, ideology) in their influence on the vote in legislative elections. They are consistently more important than social affiliations or any other current issue. Economic evaluations are therefore both a long-term and short-term force: they operate at every election but favour different parties at different times. In CEE they may prove to be exceptionally important given the weakness of partisanship, ideology and social group ties in these countries.

3   The primary motive behind economic voting is the nation's well-being, not the individual voter's.

Surveys consistently show that 'pocketbook' voting is rare: retrospective personal economic circumstances seldom have a significant effect on the vote. This is because voters either do not hold the government responsible for their personal well-being (as in the United States) or hold the government only indirectly responsible, through the state of the national economy. An exception is the minority of voters who have good reason to blame or praise the government directly for their economic circumstances (e.g. government employees); moreover the economically dissatisfied frequently exert political pressure in non-electoral ways such as strikes and riots. But in elections what moves most voters are evaluations of the government's management of the country's economy as a whole.

4   Economic voting is symmetrical.

Voters are as likely to support the government in good times as to oppose it in bad times.

5   Economic evaluations are prospective as well as retrospective.

Voters judge the government on past economic performance. But they also judge it, independently, on the basis of future expectations, which have an equally strong impact on their vote.

6   The aspects of the economy on which voters evaluate the government vary over time and place, but can be influenced by the government.

There is no one economic indicator that holds the key to government support. Inflation, unemployment, interest rates and per capita real income are usually important but their relative weights depend on economic and political circumstances and, to a small degree, on the sector of the electorate: working-class voters are slightly more sensitive to unemployment, the middle classes to inflation. A government's campaigning resources and influence over the media enable it to influence the voters' criteria for, and expectations of, economic well-being. In the early 1980s, for example, the Conservative government in Britain succeeded in deflecting the public's attention from rising unemployment to declining inflation.

Challenges and Debates

These propositions leave a number of unresolved questions, especially about the mechanisms that link the economy to government popularity. How accurately do voters perceive the state of the economy? Where do they get their information from: personal experience or the media? What standards do voters use when evaluating the government? Do they judge it by absolute levels or by trends? Is an unemployment rate rapidly rising through 10 per cent worse for a government than a stable rate of 15 per cent? Are all economic changes noticed or only big and rapid ones? Do voters distinguish between change, the rate of change, and a change in the rate of change? How short is short term: how far back do voters' memories go – three months, a year, the beginning of the government's term?

Among these questions the one to have provoked most controversy is whether economic variables should consist of objective economic conditions, as measured by official statistics, or voters' perceptions, as measured by survey items. The issue is sharpened by contradictory findings of the two approaches. Models based on official statistics and aggregate election returns (e.g. Kramer, 1971) suggest that the vote for the government fluctuates with changes in real per capita income; whereas models relying on voters' perceptions, as mentioned earlier, fail to find evidence of pocketbook voting (Kinder and Kiewiet, 1981). The former approach benefits from dealing with real votes, not recalled votes or 'voting intention'; it averages out the idiosyncratic factors that affect individual respondents' party choice; and it does not have to cope with the partisan contamination of respondents' economic evaluations (e.g. voters saying the economy has done well/badly out of loyalty to the incumbent/ opposition party). But the survey-based approach benefits from the fact that among voters perception *is* reality.

Implications for the New Democracies

It is uncertain whether propositions derived from studies of the more established Western democracies can be exported to the CEE democracies. If they can, their implications for the stability of party systems and democratic order point in a variety of directions. On the one hand they suggest the possibility of considerable electoral turbulence. In the absence of strong partisanship and a socially aligned electorate we may expect election-specific factors, especially economic evaluations, to have an even stronger impact on the vote than in Western democracies, especially where a single party comprises or dominates the government. The distinct possibility of sudden and serious economic deterioration in the new democracies' early years poses a real threat to the incumbent parties. On the other hand, much depends on the incumbent's capacity to shape expectations. Where the government can convincingly blame the former regime or external constraints beyond its control (e.g. the cutting off of cheap energy from Russia) it may deflect blame for economic problems. Where it can lower expectations it may benefit disproportionately from very modest improvements or indeed from the arresting of further deterioration. The gradual economic improvement from a low base in post-war West Germany was a vital contributor to the popular legitimation of the democratic regime; but the West German government's inflation of East Germans' expectations of the benefits of unification may erode that legitimacy. As always, much depends on the political skills of the party leaderships, on uncontrollable economic forces, and on sheer happenstance. At this point of the story, political scientists must make way for historians.

References

Bartolini, Stefano and Peter Mair 1990. *Identity, Competition and Electoral Availability* (Cambridge: Cambridge University Press).

Beck, Paul Allen 1979. 'The electoral cycle and patterns of American politics', *British Journal of Political Science*, 9, pp. 129–56.

Brody, Richard A. and Lawrence S. Rothenberg 1988. 'The instability of partisanship: an analysis of the 1980 presidential election', *British Journal of Political Science*, 18, pp. 445–66.

Budge, Ian and Dennis Farlie 1976. 'A comparative analysis of factors correlated with turnout and voting choice', in Ian Budge, Ivor Crewe and Dennis Farlie, eds, *Party Identification and Beyond* (London: John Wiley), pp. 103–28.

Butler, David and Donald Stokes 1969. *Political Change in Britain* (London: Macmillan).

Campbell, Angus, Philip E. Converse, Warren E. Miller and Donald Stokes 1960. *The American Voter* (New York: John Wiley).

Converse, Philip E. 1964. 'The nature of belief systems in mass publics', in David Apter, ed., *Ideology and Discontent* (Glencoe, Ill.: Free Press), pp. 206–61.

Converse, Philip E. 1969. 'Of time and partisan stability', *Comparative Political Studies*, 2, pp. 139–71.

Crewe, Ivor 1974. 'Do Butler and Stokes really explain political change in Britain?', *European Journal of Political Research*, 2 (1), pp. 47–92.

Crewe, Ivor 1980. 'Negative partisanship: some preliminary ideas using British data', paper presented to the Joint Sessions of the European Consortium for Political Research, Florence.

Crewe, Ivor 1984. 'The electorate: partisan dealignment ten years on', in Hugh Berrington, ed., *Change in British Politics* (London: Frank Cass).

Crewe, Ivor and David Denver, eds 1985. *Electoral Change in Western Democracies* (London: Croom Helm).

Dogan, M. and Stein Rokkan, eds 1969. *Quantitative Ecological Analysis in the Social Sciences* (Cambridge, Mass.: MIT Press).

Dunleavy, Patrick and Christopher T. Husbands 1985. *British Democracy at the Crossroads* (London: George Allen & Unwin).

Fiorina, Morris P. 1981. *Retrospective Voting in American Elections* (New Haven, Conn: Yale University Press).

Franklin, Mark, Tom Mackie, Henry Valen et al. 1992. *Electoral Change: Responses to Evolving Social and Attitudinal Structures in Western Countries* (Cambridge: Cambridge University Press).

Inglehart, Ronald 1977. *The Silent Revolution* (Princeton, NJ: Princeton University Press).

Irvine, William P. and H. Gold 1980. 'Do frozen cleavages ever go stale? The bases of the Canadian and Australian party systems', *British Journal of Political Science*, 10, pp. 187–218.

Jackson, John E. 1975. 'Issues, party choices and presidential votes', *American Journal of Political Science*, 19, pp. 161–85.

Keith, Bruce E., David B. Magleby, Candice J. Nelson, Elizabeth Orr, Mark C. Westlye and Raymond E. Wolfinger 1986. 'The partisan affinities of Independent "leaners" ', *British Journal of Political Science*, 16, pp. 155–86.

Kinder, Donald R. and Roderick D. Kiewiet 1981. 'Sociotropic politics: the American case', *British Journal of Political Science*, 11, pp. 129–41.

Kitschelt, Herbert 1991. 'The formation of party systems in Eastern Europe', paper presented to the annual meeting of the American Political Science Association, Washington, DC.

Kramer, Gerald H. 1971. 'Short-term fluctuations in U.S. voting behavior: 1896–1964', *American Political Science Review*, 65, pp. 131–43.

Lewis-Beck, Michael S. 1988. *Economics and Elections* (Ann Arbor, Mich.: University of Michigan Press).

Lijphart, Arend 1979. 'Religious vs. linguistic vs. class voting: the "crucial experiment" of comparing Belgium, Canada, South Africa and Switzerland', *American Political Science Review*, 73, pp. 442–58.

Lipset, Seymour M. 1983. 'The economy, elections and public opinion', Working Papers in Political Science no. P-83-1, Hoover Institution, Stanford University.

Lipset, Seymour M. and Stein Rokkan 1967. 'Cleavage structures, party systems and voter alignments', in Seymour M. Lipset and Stein Rokkan, *Party Systems and Voter Alignments* (New York: Free Press).

Maguire, M. 1983. 'Is there still persistence? Electoral change in Western Europe, 1948–78', in Hans Daalder and Peter Mair, eds, *Western European Party Systems: Continuity and Change* (Beverly Hills and London: Sage).

Markus, Gregory B. and Philip E. Converse 1979. 'A dynamic simultaneous equation model of electoral choice', *American Political Science Review*, 73, pp. 1055–70.

Miller, Warren E. 1976. 'The cross-national use of party identification as a stimulus to political inquiry', in Ian Budge, Ivor Crewe and Dennis Farlie, eds, *Party Identification and Beyond* (London: John Wiley).

Miller, Warren and Teresa E. Levitin 1976. *Leadership and Change: The New Politics and the American Electorate* (Cambridge, Mass.: Winthrop).

Page, Benjamin I. and Calvin C. Jones 1979. 'Reciprocal effects of policy preferences, party loyalties and the vote', *American Political Science Review*, 73, pp. 1071–89.

Paldam, M. 1981. 'A preliminary survey of the theories and findings on vote and popularity functions', *European Journal of Political Research*, 9, 181–200.

Petrocik, John R. 1974. 'An analysis of intransitivities in the index of party identification', *Political Methodology*, 1, pp. 31–47.

Powell, G. Bingham Jnr 1982. *Contemporary Democracies: Participation, Stability and Violence* (Cambridge, Mass.: Harvard University Press).

Rokkan, Stein 1970. *Citizens, Elections, Parties* (Oslo: Universitets Forlaget).

Rose, Richard and Derek Urwin 1970. 'Persistence and change in Western party systems since 1945', *Political Studies*, 18, pp. 287–319.

Schneider, F. 1984. 'Public attitudes towards economic conditions and their impact on government behaviour', *Political Behaviour*, 6, pp. 211–27.

Thomassen, Jacques 1976. 'Party identification as a cross-national concept: its meaning in the Netherlands' in Ian Budge, Ivor Crewe and Dennis Farlie, *Party Identification and Beyond* (London: John Wiley), pp. 63–80.

Tufte, E. 1978. *Political Control of the Economy* (Princeton, NJ: Princeton University Press).

Van der Eijk, C. and K. Niemoller 1983. 'Ideology, party identification and rational voting in the Netherlands', paper presented at the 1983 annual meeting of the American Political Science Association, Chicago.

Wattenberg, Martin P. 1984. *The Decline of American Political Parties 1952–1980* (Cambridge, Mass.: Harvard University Press).

PART TWO

DEMOCRATIC ELECTIONS
AND CAPITALIST ECONOMICS

5

Economic Influences on the Vote: Modelling Electoral Decisions

David Sanders

This chapter follows on from the preceding one in taking up the question of short-term economic influences on the vote. It is a commonly held belief among political activists in many democratic countries that, if the governing party 'gets the economy right', it stands a very good chance of being re-elected. This belief, moreover, is generally confirmed by casual observation. It is rare for a government to lose office if it has a strong economic record; and, even when the incumbent party is soundly beaten at the polls, a plausible counter-factual case can frequently be made that 'things would have been very different if the economy had been booming'. Not surprisingly in these circumstances, political scientists throughout the democratic world have attempted to model the possible connections between economic performance and governmental support. This chapter reviews some of the efforts that have been made to develop economic models of voting behaviour. The first section summarizes the simple 'reward/punishment' principle that underlies these models and discusses the main complicating factors that cut across it. The second section describes the different ways in which economic models have been tested against empirical data. The final section presents an illustrative economic model of government popularity in Britain for the 1987–92 period.

The Reward/Punishment Model and its Variants

The primary theoretical assumption that underlies much 'economic voting' analysis is that electors *reward* governments for 'good' economic perform-

ance with higher levels of political support and *punish* them with reduced
support if they perform badly. *Government support* itself is generally
measured in one of two ways: either in terms of votes cast for particular
parties in local and/or national elections or in terms of opinion poll
measures of party or leader popularity. Votes have the obvious advantage
of being unambiguous statements of electors' political preferences; their
disadvantage is that, at the national level, they are usually cast only once
every few years. Opinion polls, on the other hand, are typically conducted
with sufficient frequency to allow monthly or quarterly variations in party
support to be compared with temporal fluctuations in macroeconomic
indicators. The difficulty with opinion polls, of course, is that they are
subject to sampling error and do not necessarily capture 'true' voting
intentions. It is worth noting in the British context, however, that the
average of the major opinion polls conducted in the last few days of the
official campaign has proved a remarkably reliable estimate of government
support in all elections since October 1974 – with the exception of April
1992. *Economic performance* is measured either by asking respondents to
assess the government's economic record directly or else by an examination of movements in the major macroeconomic indicators. In the latter
case, good performance is generally assumed to be associated with lower
levels of unemployment, inflation and interest rates and with higher levels
of GDP and personal disposable income; bad performance with their
opposites.

   On the face of it, given these simple notions of support and performance, it should be a relatively straightforward matter to test the reward/
punishment thesis: government support (measured either as votes or as
opinion poll ratings) should correlate strongly and positively with the
chosen measure(s) of economic performance. In practice, of course, the
connections between performance and support are rather more complicated. At least four sets of confounding factors serve to render the
relationship more ambiguous.

   The first of these is the simple question of *culpability*. How far do
electors hold the incumbent government *responsible* for current economic
conditions? It is entirely possible for voters to realize that the economy is in
poor shape yet for them to attribute the weak performance thus implied to
some agency other than the government of the day. In a Gallup poll
conducted among British voters in January 1992, for example – after six
successive quarters of zero or negative growth – some 50 per cent of
respondents blamed Britain's economic plight on 'the world recession'; 38
per cent blamed 'the Thatcher government' (which had abruptly ended in
November 1990); and only 2 per cent blamed the incumbent government of
John Major.[1] By the same token, of course, it is equally possible that 'good
economic news' may be seen not as the consequence of the government's
policies but as the result of economic processes that are beyond national
government control. In short, whatever the 'objective' economic position,
and whatever its 'objective' causation, the government's economic per-

formance will not *necessarily* elicit a commensurate reward/punishment response if electors do not consider the government to be *responsible* for current economic conditions.

A second confounding factor in the performance–support relationship concerns the question of 'egocentric' versus 'sociotropic' voting. *Egocentric* economic voting is self-centred voting. Individuals who consider that they (and their households) have prospered under the present government, and who are perhaps fearful that they will do less well under an alternative government, will tend to support the incumbent party: they are likely to seek to preserve the very status quo that produced their sense of prosperity in the first place. *Sociotropic* voters, on the other hand, are more society-centred. In making their political calculations, they look not to their own (or their households') economic positions but to the economic condition of the economy as a whole. If the main economic indicators suggest that the economy overall is performing well, they will support the government; if performance is weak, they are likely to oppose it. If all voters were sociotropic, it would in principle be possible to use macroeconomic indicators fairly unequivocally in order to characterize a particular government's economic performance. The likely existence of egocentric voting, however, means that a politically significant number of egocentric voters may wish to reward a government with their support – because they *personally* have benefited from government policy – even though the overall economic performance of the government *for society as a whole* has been lamentable. In such circumstances, an assessment of the links between performance and support necessarily needs to take some account of both egocentric and sociotropic calculations.

The performance–support relationship is complicated further by the *comparisons* that voters may make in order to decide whether a government's current economic performance is satisfactory or not. Several such comparisons are possible. Consider a governing party A, opposed by an opposition party B. Voters may compare A's current performance (its recent 'record') with its own performance sometime in the past. They may compare A's current performance with B's performance when B was last in office. They may compare A's current performance with A's likely future performance. They may compare A's likely future performance with B's likely future performance. They may compare A's performance with the performance of contemporary governments in other countries. Or they may make a number of these (and, perhaps, other) comparisons simultaneously. To complicate matters even more, different groups of voters may make different sorts of comparisons. Clearly, all of these possibilities mean that 'performance' is a difficult phenomenon to specify unambiguously, a conclusion which has obvious implications for attempts to analyse the performance–support relationship systematically.

A final confounding factor is simply that electoral support for political parties is undoubtedly affected by things other than economics. As pointed out in Chapter 4, a number of *social background characteristics* – notably age, gender, social class, region, occupational sector and housing status – have discernible effects on voting behaviour.[2] Similarly, *party identifications* and the ways in which voters perceive *issues*, *leaders* and momentous *political events* are all capable of influencing voting decisions.[3] It follows that, ideally, any attempt to assess the importance of economic voting should attempt to control for the effects of these other correlates of voting behaviour at some stage of the analysis.

What these various confounding factors suggest is that there is no simple way of modelling the relationship between economic performance and political support. Rather, there are a number of alternative ways of modelling the relationship, each of which makes a different set of assumptions about individual electors or groups of electors.

Alternative Approaches to Economic Voting Analysis

The relationship between economics and political support has been investigated at both the individual and the aggregate level. Individual-level analyses, typically based on data derived from 'Michigan-style' election surveys,[4] are obviously able to make precise statistical controls for many respondent characteristics.[5] Using cross-tabulation and, more recently, probit and log-linear techniques, these analyses have sought to establish (a) whether there is any sort of connection between individuals' economic perceptions (about, *inter alia*, inflation, unemployment, the government's economic record, their own financial experiences and prospects, and the prospects for the economy as a whole) and their party preferences; and (b) whether any such connections are still observed when statistical controls for other theoretically relevant variables are applied. It is obviously not possible here even to summarize the huge body of empirical findings about 'economic voting' (and 'non-economic voting') that has been accumulated across the democratic world over the last four decades. Suffice to say that most individual-level studies have found that 'pocketbook' considerations *do* affect the voting decisions of many voters and that very few studies indeed have found economic considerations to be entirely unimportant.[6]

Even the best designed election studies, however, fail to capture one vitally important aspect of 'economic voting'. Such analyses, as noted above, necessarily conduct surveys relatively infrequently. They therefore have no opportunity effectively to track monthly, or even quarterly, movements in government support in the interim periods between elections.[7] This in turn means that election studies are obliged to estimate the effects of economic factors on voting only in the context of the economic conditions that prevail at the time an election is held. The evidence of regularly conducted opinion polls, however, clearly demonstrates that support for political parties can fluctuate very considerably over the electoral cycle.[8] And given that economic conditions *also* fluctuate markedly over the course of the electoral cycle, there is clearly a case for arguing that efforts to investigate the connections between economic factors and political support really need to consider those connections over the entire electoral cycle – not just at election times. One way of circumventing this problem is to employ a 'pooled cross-section' research design which combines individual-level data taken from opinion polls conducted frequently over a given period. Although lack of data availability has meant that few such studies have been undertaken to date, the empirical results that have been reported strongly corroborate the 'economic voting' hypothesis.[9]

The more usual solution to the problem of temporal variations in political support, however, is to use a *time-series* specification which combines aggregate, survey-derived data on political support with aggregate data on the performance of the economy. Monthly or quarterly poll ratings of the governing party (or leader) are compared, over time, with levels of (and/or changes in) various economic indicators. Terms can also be included which measure the effects of extraordinary political events such as wars or leadership changes. The general form of the resultant 'popularity function' is

$$P = f(M, Z) \tag{5.1}$$

where P is a measure of government popularity, M is a measure of economic performance and Z summarizes the effects of extraordinary political events. Following Hibbs,[10] it is generally assumed that the (binary response) choice facing an individual voter j at time t is either to support the government (in which case $P_{jt}=1$) or not (in which case $P_{jt}=0$), and that

$$\begin{aligned} P_{jt}=1 \quad &\text{if } f(M,Z)>c \\ P_{jt}=0 \quad &\text{if } f(M,Z)<c \end{aligned} \tag{5.2}$$

where c is some critical value which may vary for each individual. Aggregating for all individuals, it can be shown that the logit model correctly specifies the relationship between P and $f(M,Z)$. Specifically,

$$\ln(P_t/(1-P_t)) = \beta M_t + \gamma Z_t + \epsilon_t \tag{5.3}$$

where β and γ are vectors of coefficients and ϵ_t is a random error term.[11] If M_t is operationalized as a set of *objective* economic indicators ΣX_{kt}, and Z_t is measured as a set of dummy variables ΣZ_{kt}, it can also be shown that

$$\ln(P_t/(1-P_t)) = \alpha + \rho^i \ln(P_t/(1-P_t))_{t-i} + \Sigma\beta X_{kt-i} + \Sigma\gamma Z_{kt-i} + \epsilon_t \tag{5.4}$$

where α is a constant, i denotes the ith lag and ρ is the 'discount rate' – the rate at which past influences on current popularity are discounted.

It should be emphasized that this represents only one way of specifying the form that the popularity function should take. Some analysts, for example, particularly in the United States, have favoured a Box-Jenkins auto regressive integrated moving average (ARIMA) specification.[12] The crucial features of the general specification, however, are that each individual voter is assumed to be 'an economic voter' and that the 'economic' calculations of each individual can be aggregated up so that hypotheses about the performance–support relationship can be tested at the macro-level. The great advantage of a macro-level specification, of course, is that it can ignore the idiosyncrasies of individuals. As generations of social researchers have found, although it is difficult to predict the behaviour of particular individuals, it is often not so difficult to predict the behaviour of social aggregates, where individual idiosyncrasies frequently cancel each other out. This is not to say, however, that the particular macro specifications favoured by 'popularity function' analysts are unproblematic. One potential difficulty with these specifications lies in their assumption that each elector is indeed an 'economic voter'. This assumption is obviously not entirely consistent with individual-level survey studies. While economic considerations are without doubt important to many people, they are clearly far less important to others, for whom ideologies, issues, leadership images or party identifications may be much more significant. The implicit (and sometimes explicit) response of the popularity function approach is to assert that these alternative motivations are captured in (5.4) by some combination of the constant α, the discount rate ρ, and the error term ϵ_t. It is generally assumed that α contains party identifications and that the magnitude of ϵ_t reflects the extent to which other *non*-economic criteria affect the voting decisions of the electorate.

The other difficulties with popularity functions lie primarily in what they *omit*. Notwithstanding a number of ingenious attempts to overcome the problems thus engendered,[13] popularity functions of the general sort described in (5.4) – which concentrate exclusively on 'objective' economic indicators – have difficulty taking adequate account of the four 'complicating factors' that were identified earlier. These, it will be recalled, were: (a) the culpability problem; (b) the problem as to what comparisons are made in order to assess 'performance'; (c) the question of egocentric *versus* sociotropic voting; and (d) the possibility that the performance–support relationship differs for individuals with different social background characteristics. Lack of suitable time-series data means that there is certainly no *direct* way of evaluating the confounding effects of either (a) or (b). However, while there is also no obvious way of measuring *culpability* indirectly, it *is* possible to identify *indirect* measures of performance which take some account of the *comparisons* that electors might make. If we assume that electors' *perceptions* of the state of the economy reflect the comparisons that are made between current and alternative conditions (whatever those 'alternative conditions' are for any given individual) then (5.4) can be rewritten as

$$\ln(P_t/(1-P_t)) = \alpha + \rho^i \ln(P_t/(1-P_t))_{t-i} +$$
$$\Sigma\beta X_{kt-i} + \Sigma\gamma Z_{kt-i} + \Sigma\delta W_{kt-i} + \epsilon_t \qquad (5.5)$$

where W_{kt-i} is a set of variables which measure electors' perceptions of the economy. It then becomes a simple empirical question as to whether it is the 'objective' X_{kt-i} or the 'subjective' W_{kt-i} which turn out to be the most significant predictors of aggregate popularity; though it may also be important to establish what the connections are between economic perceptions and 'objective' economic performance.

To be able to test the sort of model summarized in (5.5), however, it is clearly necessary to have access to data on aggregate economic perceptions. Fortunately, in the British context at least, good survey-based time-series data on such perceptions do exist. Moreover, the particular measures that are available enable the analyst to distinguish between perceptions of the *general* performance of the economy as a whole and perceptions of electors' own *personal* financial circumstances. This distinction closely matches the sociotropic versus egocentric distinction drawn earlier. In so far as *general* economic perceptions exert a well-determined empirical effect on government popularity, electors would appear to be basing their political preferences on *sociotropic* considerations; a well-determined effect for *personal* economic perceptions, on the other hand, would indicate support for the notion of *egocentric* voting. Although survey data on both backward- and forward-looking economic perceptions are available, previous research has shown that, in Britain at least, prospective perceptions are much more important than retrospective ones.[14] For this reason, the model specification developed here is restricted to prospective perceptions: in other contexts, it might well be appropriate to incorporate retrospective perceptions into the relevant models. In any event, the possibility of distinguishing between general (sociotropic) and personal (egocentric) economic perceptions means that (5.5) can be restated as

$$\ln(P_t/(1-P_t)) = \alpha + \rho^i \ln(P_t/(1-P_t))_{t-i} + \Sigma\beta X_{kt-i} + \Sigma\gamma Z_{kt-i} + \Sigma\eta V_{kt-i} + \Sigma\varphi Y_{kt-i} + \epsilon_t \qquad (5.6)$$

where $\Sigma\eta V_{kt-i}$ and $\Sigma\varphi Y_{kt-i}$ respectively summarize the effects of general and personal prospective economic perceptions.

The final 'complicating factor' noted above is the possibility that different groups of voters may adjust their political allegiances according to different economic calculations. One way of testing this possibility is to estimate the sort of model described in (5.6) for each group of voters separately. A recent study 'disaggregated' British voters according to region, gender, manual/non-manual employment, housing status and trade union membership, and estimated separate popularity functions for each group.[15] The empirical results indicated that the disaggregations were largely unnecessary: although the baseline levels of government support (the constant terms) varied significantly across the different groups, there were very few differences in the way that different groups of voters responded to identical economic stimuli. This in turn suggests that aggregate popularity functions, even if they take no explicit account of the potential differentiations among different groups of voters, are capable of capturing the overall effects of economic performance on popularity just as effectively as more complex, disaggregated models because those effects appear to operate largely independently of the voters' socioeconomic and political milieu.

What all of this implies is that the model described in (5.6) offers a reasonably plausible aggregate specification of the effects of 'economic factors' on governmental support. To be sure, it says nothing of the question of culpability and little of the actual economic comparisons that electors make. However, by including information on the way that the economy is perceived, some assessment of the egocentric/sociotropic question is possible. And, given the lack of empirical differentiation displayed among disaggregated models, the failure explicitly to model the role of 'social background characteristics' need not have a perverse effect on any empirical results that might be obtained.

An Empirical Example: Government Popularity in the UK, 1987–1992

Whenever popularity functions are investigated empirically, the question always arises as to the appropriate length of time over which the function should be estimated. Given that these issues have been addressed elsewhere,[16] I will not debate them here. I merely follow recent practice and confine the estimated function to the lifetime of a single Parliament. This restriction has the considerable advantage of holding constant a large number of personality, issue and other contextual variables, the possible effects of which are otherwise extremely difficult to specify empirically. The period of Conservative government from July 1987 to January 1992, spanning the last Thatcher and (first) Major administrations, was selected as the most recent inter-election period available at the time of writing.

The general form of the model described in (5.6) is clearly based on a logit specification. In fact, the specification reported here is based not on the logit form but on 'raw' popularity scores as follows:

$$P_t = \alpha + \rho^i P_{t-i} + \Sigma\beta X_{kt-i} + \Sigma\gamma Z_{kt-i} + \Sigma\eta V_{kt-i} + \Sigma\varphi Y_{kt-i} + \epsilon_t \tag{5.7}$$

There are three reasons why this particular strategy is adopted. First, as is shown below, in terms of the signs and the significance levels of the predictor variables in the model, the logit and 'raw' score specifications yield identical empirical results. Secondly, the logit specification is normally only considered necessary when there are marked variations in the level of the dependent variable P_t: the logit specification corrects for the probability that, at high levels of P_t, a unit change in any given predictor will not elicit such a large change in P_t as it would do at lower levels of P_t. Given the relatively low standard deviations of the dependent variables examined in the present study,[17] however, this characteristic of the logit specification is not particularly important. Finally, the logit model is eschewed here because it represents, quite simply, an unnecessary mystification for the non-technical reader. Logit coefficients are not particularly easy to interpret at the best of times, and they are certainly not as easy to understand as the coefficients derived from a 'raw score' model. More seriously, the logit specification gives a false impression of the degree of precision that can realistically be expected from popularity function analysis. The raw data in such analyses are, after all, derived partly from opinion polls. And, even if an average of all the major polls is used to measure the popularity of different parties (as it is in the present study), there is bound to be an unspecifiable amount of measurement error in the raw scores. The logit transformation of these scores does not remove this source of measurement error: it merely lends a spurious sense of precision to what is, in reality, an intrinsically approximate estimation procedure.

Model Specification and Estimation

Using the general model described in (5.7), a popularity function for the governing Conservative Party was specified as follows. The 'objective' measures of economic performance contained within the X_{kt-i} term in (5.7) were inflation (*inf*), interest rates (*ir*), unemployment (*un*), gross domestic product (*gdp*) and personal disposable income (*pdy*).[18] Inflation and interest rates were included as nominal values. Because *gdp*, *pdy* and unemployment are all characterized by a unit root,[19] each was differenced in order to render it mean and variance stationary.[20] In the initial specification, each of these X_{kt-i} terms was included at time t, $t-1$, . . ., $t-3$ – on the assumption that any given macroeconomic indicator could take up to three time periods to exert an effect on popularity. The political event terms summarized in Z_{kt-i} in (5.7) included dummies for March 1990 (when the widely resented poll tax was introduced) and for November 1990 (when John Major replaced Margaret Thatcher as prime minister). The aggregate sociotropic measure of prospective perceptions about the economy as a whole ('general expectations') contained in V_{kt-i} was a weighted average[21] of *general expectations* at time t, $t-1$, . . ., $t-4$. The aggregate egocentric measure of prospective perceptions ('personal expectations') contained in Y_{kt-i} was a similarly weighted average of *personal financial expectations* at time t, $t-1$, . . ., $t-4$.[22] Finally, the P_{t-i} term was included as P_{t-1}, with the presumption that, if the error structure of the estimated model demanded it, further P_{t-i} terms could be added at a later stage.

The initial model specification for Conservative Party popularity was:

$$
\begin{aligned}
P_t = \alpha &+ \rho P_{t-1} + \beta_1 inf_t + \beta_2 inf_{t-1} + \beta_3 inf_{t-2} + \beta_4 inf_{t-3} \\
&+ \beta_5 ir_t + \beta_6 ir_{t-1} + \beta_7 ir_{t-2} + \beta_8 ir_{t-3} \\
&+ \beta_{10}\Delta un_t + \beta_{11}\Delta un_{t-1} + \beta_{12}\Delta un_{t-2} + \beta_{13}\Delta un_{t-3} \\
&+ \beta_{14}\Delta gdp_t + \beta_{15}\Delta gdp_{t-1} + \beta_{16}\Delta gdp_{t-2} + \beta_{17}\Delta gdp_{t-3} \\
&+ \beta_{18}\Delta pdy_t + \beta_{19}\Delta pdy_{t-1} + \beta_{20}\Delta pdy_{t-2} + \beta_{21}\Delta pdy_{t-3} \\
&+ g_1 \text{ poll tax dummy} + g_2 \text{ Major accession dummy} \\
&+ \eta \text{ general expectations}_{t, \ldots \, t-4} \\
&+ \varphi \text{ personal expectations}_{t, \ldots \, t-4} + \epsilon_t
\end{aligned} \quad (5.8)
$$

where P_t is the average monthly 'poll of polls' rating for the Conservative Party; Δ represents a first-differenced variable; the coefficient signs on the inflation, interest rate and unemployment terms, since these variables denote relatively poor economic performance, were expected to be negative; the signs on *gdp*, *pdy* and the two expectations terms, since they imply relatively good performance, were expected to be positive; and it was anticipated that the poll tax and Major accession coefficients would be, respectively, negative and positive.

Having specified this model for Conservative popularity, it is a relatively simple matter to specify complementary models for the two main opposition parties, Labour and the Liberal Democrats. Essentially, identical models can be run for these two parties simply by substituting Labour (Liberal Democrat) popularity for P_t in (5.8). The simple expectation in both cases is that, just as the government benefits from good economic performance, so the opposition parties are damaged by it (and vice versa). Accordingly, the *signs* of the various coefficients in the Labour and Liberal Democrat functions should be the *reverse* of those expected in (5.8).

Separate functions as in (5.8) were estimated for the popularity of the Conservative, Labour and Liberal Democrat Parties. Estimation was by ordinary least squares (OLS) using the standard general-to-specific methodology advocated by Hendry and his associates.[23] For each party, the function as in (5.8) was estimated and non-significant predictors were dropped. The model was then re-estimated with only significant predictors retained. At this stage the model was checked for serial correlation and parameter stability. Models are only reported below if (a) all the coefficients are well determined, (b) all the coefficients are stable on the standard CUSUM, CUSUMSQ and recursive coefficient tests and (c) they display no serially correlated error.

Empirical Results

The 'best-fitting' results derived from applying the Hendry methodology to (5.8) for each of the three main UK parties are shown in Table 5.1. (The logit specification for Conservative popularity, as defined in (5.6), is also reported in order to show that the logit and 'raw score' formulations are indistinguishable in terms of parameter signs, significance levels and stability tests.) Several conclusions are suggested by the table. First, it is very clear that the 'objective' measures of the state of the economy hardly figure in the equations at all. No unemployment, inflation, interest rate or *pdy* terms appear in any of the equations. Indeed, the only 'objective' measure that does yield a significant coefficient is (the change in) *gdp*, which has a positive effect ($\beta=1.25$) on government popularity (with a lag of two months) and a negative effect ($\beta=-1.31$) on Liberal Democrat popularity (with a lag of one month). This clearly suggests that, although there may be a minor direct role for 'objective' economic performance in

Table 5.1 *Models[1] of Conservative, Labour and Liberal Democrat popularity[2], July 1987 to January 1992*

Variable	Conservative popularity (raw scores)		Labour popularity (raw scores)		Liberal Democrat popularity (raw scores)		Conservative popularity (logit specification)	
	Coeff.	t-ratio	Coeff.	t-ratio	Coeff.	t-ratio	Coeff.	t-ratio
Constant	17.57	4.89	19.73	4.96	5.45	3.91	−0.13	5.07
Popularity$_{t-1}$	+0.58	6.91	+0.50	4.93	+0.60	5.98	+0.58	6.87
Personal financial expectations$_{t, \ldots, t-4}$	+0.20	3.84	−0.29	4.17	+0.12	3.07	+0.009	3.82
Δgdp_{t-1}					−1.31	2.05		
Δgdp_{t-2}	+1.26	2.04					+0.05	1.96
Poll tax dummy	−4.19	2.62	+3.35	2.13			−0.19	2.88
Major accession dummy	+6.80	4.30					+0.28	4.24
Adjusted R^2	0.90		0.91		0.78		0.90	
DW	2.26		2.17		2.02		2.27	
h	−1.24		−0.94		−0.13		−1.31	
LM(9) χ^2	6.90		6.67		8.04		7.19	

[1] All equations were checked systematically for serially correlated error and pass the standard CUSUM, CUSUMSQ and recursive coefficient stability tests. Each equation represents the empirically determined 'reduced-form' version of (5.8), though the logit specification shown in the fourth column is based on (5.6). All estimation is by OLS using MICROFIT. $N = 55$ throughout.

[2] All popularity measures are monthly averages of opinion poll ratings reported by Gallup, MORI, ICM, NOP, Harris. Personal financial expectations scores are a weighted average as defined in notes 21 and 22. All macroeconomic measures were taken from the CSO's *Monthly Digest of Statistics*.

the determination of party popularity, if economic factors do exert substantial effects on popularity, they must operate in rather more complex ways than is implied by the simple notion that good (bad) macroeconomic performance will automatically produce its own reward (punishment) for the governing party.

A second conclusion suggested by Table 5.1 throws direct light on this very question. A significant predictor of the popularity ratings of all three parties is aggregate *personal* economic expectations. It will be recalled that this measure of subjective economic perceptions is probably the closest that we can get to measuring *egocentric* economic motivations, just as aggregate *general* expectations is the best available measure of *sociotropic* economic motivations. The appearance of the personal expectations term in all three equations in Table 5.1 – even though the Liberal Democrat coefficient has a positive sign[24] – is highly significant. It says much about the way that narrow calculations about economic *self*-interest dominated the political preferences of the British electorate during the late 1980s. Perceptions about *personal* financial prospects were certainly more import- ant than the objective state of the economy as measured by the standard

Table 5.2   *Models[1] of Conservative government popularity, July 1987 to January 1992, comparing the effects of aggregate personal economic expectations and aggregate general economic expectations*

Variable	Conservative popularity (raw scores)		Conservative popularity (raw scores)	
	Coeff.	t-ratio	Coeff.	t-ratio
Constant	10.86	3.60	19.18	4.70
Popularity$_{t-1}$	+0.75	10.67	+0.55	5.68
Personal financial expectations$_{t, \ldots, t-4}$	+0.08	2.99	+0.32	2.82
General Economic expectations$_{t, \ldots, t-4}$			−0.05	0.89
Poll tax dummy	−4.27	2.43	−3.67	2.21
Major accession dummy	+6.59	3.80	+6.07	3.73
Adjusted R^2	0.88		0.89	
DW	2.22		2.10	
h	−0.96		−0.55	
LM(9) χ^2	7.68		10.04	

[1] Both equations were checked systematically for serially correlated error and pass the standard CUSUM, CUSUMSQ and recursive coefficient stability tests. All variable definitions as in Table 5.1. $N = 55$ throughout.

macroeconomic indicators. But they were also more important than perceptions about the prospects for *the economy as a whole*. This is demonstrated by the absence of a 'general expectations' term from all of the equations reported in Table 5.1. It is also shown by the results reported in Table 5.2. This table shows the consequences, first, of substituting general expectations for personal expectations in the equation for Conservative popularity. As the results in the first column indicate, this substitution *appears* to suggest that general expectations *are* important: the general expectations term yields a positive, significant coefficient. The second column of Table 5.2, however, reveals the consequences of including both personal *and* general expectations terms in the same equation. This equation clearly shows that the effects of personal expectations ($\beta=+0.32$) strongly override those of general expectations ($\beta=-0.05$): among the British electorate of the late 1980s and early 1990s, egocentric economic considerations seem to have overpowered sociotropic ones.

A third set of conclusions implied by Table 5.1 concerns the behaviour of the dummy variables. Conservative popularity was clearly damaged by the introduction of the poll tax, with the party suffering a 4 per cent dip ($\beta=-4.19$) in its ratings in March 1990. Labour popularity increased significantly in the same month, though not by quite such a large amount ($\beta=+3.35$). Conservative popularity also benefited by about 7 per cent from the removal of Mrs Thatcher from office in November 1990 ($\beta=+6.80$), though neither of the other parties suffered significantly as a direct result, presumably because the surge in Conservative support derived largely from previously undecided voters.

These results regarding the dummy variable effects, however, need to be seen in the context of the coefficients on the lagged dependent variable in each equation. These coefficients represent, in effect, the discount rate – the rate at which past influences on the dependent variable in question decay. In the Conservative function, the discount rate is 0.58; in the Labour function, it is 0.50; and in the Liberal Democrat function, 0.60. By any standards, given that these are monthly data, these are high discount rates. They suggest that for all three parties, the effect of any exogenous shock to popularity will roughly halve each month as time passes. Thus, for example, the Major accession 'boost' to Conservative popularity was worth 6.80 per cent in December 1990; $6.80 \times 0.58 = 3.94$ points in January 1991; $6.80 \times 0.58^2 = 2.29$ points in February 1991; $6.80 \times 0.58^3 = 1.33$ in March 1991; and so on. Following the same logic, the discount rates reported in Table 5.1 imply that the effects of the introduction of the poll tax on both Conservative and Labour popularity also decayed quite rapidly during the early summer of 1990. The presence of such high discount rates is certainly consistent with accounts of British politics which suggest that the British electorate has become rather more 'volatile' in its political preferences in recent years.[25]

One final point needs to made about the models reported in Table 5.1: how similar they all are. Variations in popularity across all three major parties during the 1987–92 period can be explained quite satisfactorily by a very small set of objective and subjective economic variables (personal expectations and the change in *gdp*), together with two 'political event' variables. To be sure, the adjusted R^2 values indicate that for the Conservative and Labour functions some 10 per cent (and for the Liberal Democrats, just over 20 per cent) of the variation in popularity remains unexplained. However, given the general difficulty of predicting political preferences, these relatively modest levels of explained variance are not unimpressive. Moreover, the models reported all provide well-determined coefficients and pass a battery of stability and other diagnostic tests, suggesting that the results reported are extremely robust. Non-economic considerations certainly played a role in forming British political prefer-ences during the Conservatives' third term; but the relatively small amounts of unexplained variation in the Labour and Conservative models reported in Table 5.1 clearly indicate that economic factors played a very important role indeed.

Modelling Personal Economic Expectations

The foregoing results suggest that, notwithstanding the effects of changes in *gdp*, aggregate personal economic expectations played a crucial role in determining variations in political support across the three major parties. The question that immediately follows, of course, is: what influences aggregate personal expectations? Are expectations conjured from nowhere (which seems unlikely)? Or are *they* perhaps determined by 'objective' macroeconomic movements, even if such movements themselves exert little or no *direct* effect on party popularity? This question can be examined empirically by analysing an 'expectations function' analogous to the popularity function specified in (5.8). In principle, any of the indicators of macroeconomic performance identified in (5.8) could also influence expectations, and with the same potential lag structure. Similarly, it is also possible that expectations could be influenced by unusual political events. The introduction of the poll tax, which itself clearly had important financial implications for many people, and the removal of Thatcher from office (particularly as her removal was so widely seen as an opportunity to abolish the poll tax anyway) were both events, *ceteris paribus*, that could have influenced personal economic expectations. In recognition of both of these sets of possibilities, the initial expectations function specified below includes all of the 'objective' macroeconomic variables specified in (5.8), together with dummy terms for March 1990 (poll tax) and November 1990 (Major accession). The precise specification tested was:

$$
\begin{aligned}
PEX_t = {} & \alpha + \rho PEX_{t-1} + \beta_1 inf_t + \beta_2 inf_{t-1} + \beta_3 inf_{t-2} + \beta_4 inf_{t-3} \\
& + \beta_5 ir_t + \beta_6 ir_{t-1} + \beta_7 ir_{t-2} + \beta_8 ir_{t-3} \\
& + \beta_{10}\Delta un_t + \beta_{11}\Delta un_{t-1} + \beta_{12}\Delta un_{t-2} + \beta_{13}\Delta un_{t-3} \\
& + \beta_{14}\Delta gdp_t + \beta_{15}\Delta gdp_{t-1} + \beta_{16}\Delta gdp_{t-2} + \beta_{17}\Delta gdp_{t-3} \\
& + \beta_{18}\Delta pdy_t + \beta_{19}\Delta pdy_{t-1} + \beta_{20}\Delta pdy_{t-2} + \beta_{21}\Delta pdy_{t-3} \\
& + g_1 \text{ poll tax dummy} + g_2 \text{ Major accession dummy} + \epsilon_t
\end{aligned}
$$

$$(5.9)$$

where PEX_t is aggregate personal economic expectations measured at time *t*. As with the general specification for party popularity, (5.9) was estimated using OLS, the significant predictors were retained and the reduced-form equation was re-estimated. The resultant best-fitting equation (*t*-statistics in parentheses) was:

$$
\begin{array}{llll}
PEX_t & = & 20.56 & + & 0.41 \ PEX_{t-1} & - & 1.93 \ ir_{t-1} \\
& & (4.23) & & (4.33) & & (4.45)
\end{array}
$$

$$
\begin{array}{lll}
& -16.12 \text{ poll tax} & + & 11.50 \text{ Major accession} \\
& \text{dummy} & & \text{dummy} + \epsilon_t \\
& (3.79) & & (2.72)
\end{array}
$$

$$
h = -1.25 \quad LM(9) \ \chi^2 = 7.19 \quad \text{adjusted } R^2 = 0.82 \quad DW = 2.24
$$
Sample: July 1987 to January 1992 $N = 55$ (5.10)

where (5.10) displayed no serially correlated error and satisfied the standard CUSUM, CUSUMSQ and recursive coefficient stability tests.

The results in (5.10), though by no means offering an 'explanation' as to why aggregate personal expectations fluctuate over time, nonetheless suggest that *interest rates* had a very significant (negative) impact on expectations during the Conservative Party's third term in office: expectations rose (fell) by almost 2 per cent for every 1 per cent reduction (increase) in base rates. Expectations were also affected (negatively) by the introduction of the poll tax and (positively) by the removal of Thatcher as prime minister; though the relatively small coefficient on the lagged dependent variable ($\beta=0.41$) suggests that both of these effects were discounted very rapidly in the ensuing months. Equation (5.10) is also important for what it omits. The absence of any terms for unemployment, inflation, *gdp* or *pdy* – which all yielded non-significant coefficients when added, at various lags, to (5.10) – suggests that expectations remained largely unaffected by these factors. In short, with the exception of interest rates, none of the main 'objective' macroeconomic indicators exerted a direct effect on aggregate personal expectations.

Summary and Conclusions

It is widely acknowledged among both scholars and political activists that economic factors exert a powerful effect on democratic voting decisions. Modelling the precise role that these factors play, however, is a highly contentious exercise. Analyses that examine the relationship between economic performance and political support can operate at either the micro (individual) or the macro (aggregate) level. Neither approach, however, is ideal. Micro-analyses are rarely able to specify the effects of changing economic conditions in an effective way. Macro-analyses are obliged to assume that statistical associations uncovered at the aggregate level can somehow reflect the decision calculus of the typical economic voter. Efforts which combine the positive features of both approaches are still, unfortunately, in their infancy because of the difficulty of assembling suitable empirical data.

Because of the importance of relating political preferences to economic *change*, the most successful attempts to evaluate economic models of voting have undoubtedly been at the *aggregate* level, where, for obvious reasons, macroeconomic change can be measured relatively easily. This said, models which simply try to predict movements in (governing) party popularity from a given set of 'objective' macroeconomic indicators necessarily fail to take explicit account of a number of 'complicating factors' that were identified above: whether the government is seen as *culpable* for economic success/failure; what *comparisons* are made in evaluating economic performance; whether electors base their calculations on *egocentric* or *sociotropic* considerations; and whether *social background characteristics* have a confounding effect on the performance–support relationship.

The aggregate specification that has been presented here seeks to take account of some of these 'complicating factors'. To be sure, nothing could be done about the culpability problem. And the potentially confounding effects of social background were dismissed on the simple grounds that previous research has shown that a range of different socioeconomic groups all appear to respond to changing macroeconomic stimuli in broadly similar ways. What differentiates the approach taken here from studies which seek solely to examine the effects of 'objective' macroeconomic changes is its use of survey-based data on aggregate economic *perceptions*. The inclusion of variables which measure the electorate's overall sense of optimism/pessimism, in terms of both personal finances and the prospects for the economy as a whole, enables the analysis to enquire directly into the question of egocentric versus sociotropic calculations. And, because these variables are concerned with electors' *perceptions* about the state of the economy rather than about its 'objective' condition, they are also likely to reflect the impact of the various comparisons – either explicit or implicit – that different voters make when they are deciding how well the economy is performing at present.

The empirical results reported here imply that the British electorate of the late 1980s and early 1990s was, in general, a largely self-serving one. Although major political events did play a limited role, similar *economic* calculations seem to have driven the variations in support for all three main political parties during the 1987–92 period. In particular, the variations in the popularity of the Conservative government can be explained fairly satisfactorily by the operation of two, complementary, economic effects. Support for the government was affected, first, by a very obvious objective indicator of the state of the overall domestic economy: the rate of change in *gdp*. During a period in which the British economy experienced a prolonged recession, it is unsurprising that the government's fortunes should have been adversely affected by the decline in the overall level of economic activity. Unfortunately, it is impossible to say how far this effect resulted from voters making evaluative judgements about the overall performance of the government as an economic manager or how far it reflected a heightened sense of resentment towards the government among individuals who had suffered a reduction in living standards.

The second, and more important, economic effect on government popularity, however, is somewhat easier to interpret. The level of *aggregate personal economic expectations* – what, in British journalistic circles, is sometimes referred to as 'the feel-good factor' – was found to exert a powerful influence on levels of Conservative support.[26] This personal expectations variable effectively measures voters' *egocentric* concerns. When electors' optimism about their own personal financial circumstances was high the government enjoyed high levels of support; when optimism fell, so did the government's popularity. Significantly, the *sociotropic* counterpart to the *personal* expectations variable – expectations about *the economy as a whole* – failed to exert any effect on popularity when controls for personal expectations were applied. What mattered most to British electors, in short, was their perceptions of their own narrow, personal economic interests. In so far as the government was able to satisfy voters by keeping them optimistic about their own financial circumstances, then it was rewarded with a high level of support; in so far as it failed, then support was withdrawn. These perceptions, in turn, were strongly influenced by the prevailing level of interest rates, an economic indicator of peculiar significance in British politics because of the relatively high proportion of the population with variable interest rate mortgages. Applying these factors to a prediction of government support in the April 1992 election,[27] made in December 1990, produced an almost exact correspondence between the predicted percentage (42.5 per cent) and the actual result (42.7 per cent), which increases confidence in the validity of the model.

Notes

1 *Gallup Political Index*, January 1992

2 In the British context, see, for example, Anthony Heath, Roger Jowell and John Curtice, *How Britain Votes* (Oxford: Pergamon Press, 1985); William Miller et al., *How Voters Change* (Oxford: Clarendon Press, 1990). For a crossnational perspective, see Michael Lewis-Beck, *Economics and Elections: The Major Western Democracies* (Ann Arbor, University of Michigan Press, 1988).

3 On the role of party identification, issues and leaders, see Lewis-Beck, *Economics and Elections*; and Bo Sarlvik and Ivor Crewe, *Decade of Dealignment: The Conservative Victory of 1979 and the Electoral Trends of the 1970s* (Cambridge: Cambridge University Press, 1983). On the role of political events, see Helmut Norpoth, 'Guns and Butter and Government Popularity in Britain', *American Political Science Review*, Vol. 81, (1987) pp. 949–59.

4 The seminal study for the United States was Angus Campbell et al., *The American Voter* (New York, Wiley, 1960). The equivalent British study is David Butler and Donald Stokes, *Political Change in Britain*, 2nd edition (London: Macmillan, 1974).

5 In particular, they can make explicit controls for several of the 'confounding factors' identified in the previous section, such as respondents' perceptions of government culpability and the question as to whether respondents are self-centred or society-centred.

6 For a recent review, see Helmut Norpoth, Michael Lewis-Beck and Jean-Dominque Lafay (eds), *Economics and Politics: The Calculus of Support* (Ann Arbor: University of Michigan Press, 1991).

7 Some studies attempt to address this problem by conducting additional survey 'waves' (sometimes panel based) some 18 months or 3 months ahead of an anticipated election. However, such data collection designs still cannot take adequate account of monthly or quarterly fluctuations in macroeconomic indicators.

8 Some analysts have attributed these fluctuations in support to the fact that the questions asked by polling agencies which aim at ascertaining party support change their meaning over the electoral cycle. There is no clear evidence to demonstrate that this inference is either right or wrong: one either *assumes* that the same question has the same meaning over a given period of time, or one does not.

9 See Gregory B. Markus, 'The Impact of Personal and National Economic Conditions on the Presidential Vote: A Pooled Cross-Sectional Analysis', *American Journal of Political Science*, Vol. 32 (1988) pp. 137–54.

10 Douglas Hibbs, *The Political Economy of Industrial Democracies* (Cambridge, Mass: Harvard University Press, 1987).

11 Simon Price and David Sanders, 'Modeling Government Popularity in Postwar Britain: A Methodological Example', *American Journal of Political Science* Vol. 37, No. 1 (Feb. 1993) pp. 317–34.

12 See, for example, Norpoth 'Guns and Butter'; Harold D. Clarke, William Mishler and Paul Whitely, 'Recapturing the Falklands: Models of Conservative Popularity', *British*

Journal of Political Science, Vol. 20 (1990) pp. 63-81. For other specifications, see Nathaniel Beck, 'The Economy and Presidential Popularity: An Information Theoretic Perspective' in Norpoth, Lewis-Beck and Lafay, *Economics and Politics*, pp. 85-102. For a comparison of different specifications, including Box-Jenkins methods, see David Sanders and Hugh Ward, 'Art with Numbers: Timeseries Techniques for Repeated Cross-section Data', in Angela Dale and Richard Davies (eds), *Analysing Social and Political Change: A Casebook of Methods* (London: Sage, 1994).

13   See, for example, Gebhard Kirchgassner, 'Economic Conditions and the Popularity of West German Parties: Before and after the 1982 Government Change' in Norpoth, Lewis-Beck and Lafay, *Economics and Politics*, pp. 103-22; James E. Alt, 'Ambiguous Intervention: The Role of Government Action in Public Evaluation of the Economy' ibid., pp.239–63.

14   David Sanders, David Marsh and Hugh Ward, 'Government Popularity and the Falklands War: A Reassessment', *British Journal of Political Science*, Vol. 17 (1987) pp. 281–313. In the US context, 'retrospective' voting has been found to be much more important. See Morris Fiorina, *Retrospective Voting in American National Elections* (New Haven, Conn.: Yale University Press, 1981).

15   David Marsh, Hugh Ward and David Sanders, 'Modelling Government Popularity in Britain, 1979–87: A Disaggregated Approach' in Ivor Crewe and Pippa Norris (eds) *British Parties and Elections Yearbook* (London: Simon and Schuster, 1991).

16   David Sanders, 'Government Popularity and the Next General Election, *Political Quarterly*, Vol. 62 (1991) pp. 235–61.

17   Conservative popularity varied between 30 per cent and 48.5 per cent during the period analysed, Labour popularity varied between 32 per cent and 53 per cent, and Liberal Democrat popularity between 8 per cent and 20 per cent.

18   These data were all drawn from *Monthly Digest of Statistics* (HMSO, various issues). Unemployment was measured as the UK seasonally adjusted percentage rate; inflation was the annual percentage change in the retail price index; interest rates were measured as the Bank of England base rate; and *gdp* and *pdy* were CSO-supplied index measures (1987=100).

19   See Price and Sanders, 'Modelling Government Popularity', for a discussion of this phenomenon.

20   *pdy*, unemployment and *gdp* were first-differenced in order to achieve stationarity.

21   If general expectations is denoted *GE*, the weighted average, *GEW* was defined as

$$GEW_t = (GE_t + \rho GE_{t-1} + \rho^2 GE_{t-2} + \rho^3 GE_{t-3} + \rho^4 GE_{t-4})/5$$

where ρ is 0.9, the discount rate derived from regressing Conservative popularity at time t on Conservative popularity at $t-1$. Since virtually identical discount rates are obtained for both Labour and Liberal Democrat popularity, the same GEW_t term is employed in both the Labour and Liberal Democrat popularity functions outlined below. The GE_t measure itself is derived from Gallup's regular monthly question: 'How do you think the general economic situation in this country will change over the next 12 months?' The response options are: a lot better, a little better, about the same, a little worse, a lot worse. The percentage of respondents who think the economy will worsen is subtracted from the percentage who think it will improve. The particular weighted average formula employed here was selected because it was a better predictor (results not reported here) of Conservative popularity than similarly constructed weighted averages based on fewer (0–3) lags.

22   The personal expectations index is also taken from Gallup's monthly surveys. Respondents are asked how they think the financial position of their household is likely to change over the next 12 months. The response options are: a lot better, a little better, about the same, a little worse, a lot worse. Again, the percentage of respondents who think that the financial position of their household economy will worsen is subtracted from the percentage who think it will improve.

23   C. Gilbert, 'Professor Hendry's Econometric Methodology', *Oxford Bulletin of Economics and Statistics*, Vol. 48 (1986) pp. 283-307.

24   The personal expectations term in the Liberal Democrat function was predicted to

have a negative sign. In fact, according to Table 5.1, when aggregate personal economic optimism increased (declined) by 1 per cent, support for the Conservatives – as predicted – rose (fell) by around 0.2 per cent. The complement to this tendency was that a 1 per cent rise (fall) in personal optimism was associated – again, as predicted – with a 0.3 per cent fall (rise) in support for Labour. The Liberal Democrats seem to have been *incidental beneficiaries* of this imbalance of benefit/cost between the Conservatives and Labour, which explains the incorrectly predicted sign: a 1 per cent increase (decrease) in optimism was associated with a 0.1 per cent rise (fall) in Liberal Democrat support.

25 Heath, Jowell and Curtice, *How Britain Votes*; Miller et al., *How Voters Change*.

26 These expectations also featured prominently – though with the opposite sign – in the equation for Labour popularity, suggesting a direct tradeoff between Conservative and Labour support as far as changes in expectations are concerned.

27 Sanders, 'Government Popularity and the Next General Election'.

6

Employment versus Inflation: Party Ideology, Information and International Trade

James E. Alt

Following on from the analysis of economic influences on the vote, some consideration of the linkage between this and economic policy is in order. In one of his books of the 1970s, Jean Blondel indicated an appropriate starting point:

> From a consideration, say, of the British Labour Party, one is led to look at socialist parties in other European countries, and to consider all, or at least many socialist parties . . . But we would soon have to recognize that we could not avoid going beyond parties . . . this would inexorably lead us to the question of the broader context of the political system . . . We can imagine that the political system is a large machine designed to turn into policies . . . the various pressures which come from . . . parties. But this is, of course, only an analogy; the danger is that . . . we might get carried away with our analogies. (Blondel, 1976, pp. 136–9)

Well, yes, though in fact the British Labour Party was the second rather than the first example in the expanding literature on political parties and macroeconomic policy. Indeed, nearly two decades have passed since Nixon's 1972 re-election campaign caught everyone's eye and led to theoretical speculation about how general political control of the economy might be. Pioneering work by Nordhaus, Hibbs, and Tufte took this experience and turned it into two sorts of theories of political economy, the political business cycle and the partisan model.

The *political business cycle* is the theory of the pre-election boom, which elevated the cliché of politicians' electorally motivated timing of highly visible and desired projects into a principle of macroeconomic management. If people like good times and reward politicians for bringing them about, then easy money, loose fiscal policy, indeed any window of public spending with deferred taxation requires only a short-sighted electorate (who do not see the coming inflation or taxation) to be good electoral strategy. But can one really expect people to keep falling for this? After all, even if there is a sucker born every minute, in modern America they would comprise less than a fifth of live births! Unsurprisingly, the evidence on political business cycles has always been mixed. There are confirming episodes, in some countries, some of the time, but rarely has rigorous, systematic empirical analysis given consistent support to the theory. Visibility of the intended consequences of policy reduces their electoral effect, which inhibits the temptation to manipulate policy: the 1992 British election-eve budget was classically neutral.

The other branch of the political theory of economic policy, the *partisan model*, originated in the classical 'programmatic parties'' view of democratic government in which elected governments carry out policies voters expect them to enact, to which it added an assumed economic constraint. Hibbs (1977) offered an original, dynamic, cyclical formalization, in which parties of the left and right took different stances *vis-à-vis* a tradeoff between inflation and unemployment, and demonstrated empirical support for the result that left parties, other things equal, reduced unemployment when elected, in data from the United States and Britain. This is a view of demand management as party policy: to set aggregate controllable economic quantities around different partisan goals.

Naturally enough, as Blondel would have had it, the next step was to see if what worked for the British Labour Party also held for other socialist parties. It did, but in ways that pulled the original partisan model in two different directions. One was to view parties as organizations of political entrepreneurs who make strategic calculations even while behaving 'ideologically' by implementing policies that are in the interest of their supporters. This combination of ideology and strategy allows political opportunism back in (like the political business cycle) but adds the possibility of predicting the importance of explicit promises and temporary policy effects. All are synthesized in the newer 'rational' formulations of the partisan model of Alesina and his colleagues, in which the role of information is critical.

The other direction of theoretical development was to see how parties and their supporters might be expected to behave outside the autarkic or essentially non-trade-dependent economies of the original models. Adding concern with the world economy to create an open-economy context has two effects. It greatly increases the information voters need to evaluate the effects of government policy. This happens in part because a new and broader range of economic outcomes are part of the government's economic performance. Also, the transmission of economic shocks among trading partners makes economic outcomes in other countries relevant to evaluating the performance of one's own government, while increasing the constraints under which governments operate. However, the increasing interdependence of countries in a world economy also alters the underlying social basis of the partisan model, replacing class alignments with coalitions reflecting complicated sectoral cleavages formed by competitiveness and exposure to foreign trade. The chapter surveys theoretical innovations and supporting evidence for both these lines of development.

The Partisan Model of Economic Policy

In economic policy, the affirmative answer to the question, 'do parties make a difference?', is so familiar that one can easily forget that from at least three different points of view no significant party differences would be expected. On the one hand, there is Downsian party competition: under some assumptions parties would be expected to converge to common policies. Alternatively, domination of policy-making by permanent bureaucratic advisers could make economic policy unresponsive to the wishes of elected partisan politicians. Finally, policy might be so constrained by the workings of the market economy as to be ineffective. Observing systematic party differences – and in economic policy the partisan model *is* well established – refutes the assumptions of these alternatives.

The foundation of partisan theory is the assumption that each political party has a separate core constituency with its own identifiable interests in economic policy, and that the party acts 'ideologically' to implement policies in the interest of its core constituency. Core constituencies are presumed to be divided along lines corresponding to ownership of the factors of production, capital and labour. Those groups strongest in support of right parties tend to own more financial capital, have higher-status jobs, and in general have jobs that are more secure, more resistant to layoffs in the event of an economic contraction. These groups fear less from economic slack and higher unemployment, but more from high inflation, which particularly devalues returns to those whose ownership of capital takes the form of holding bonds (Hibbs, 1991). Right parties therefore typically promise disinflation, are identified with policies of disinflation, and tend to carry out disinflationary policies when elected, even though these policies create economic slack and increase unemployment.

Just the opposite is true of the core of left parties. Their typically lower-status jobs are on average less secure. They are correspondingly more dependent on earnings from labour, are unlikely to own much financial capital, and are much more exposed economically to the vicissitudes of cyclical downturns, bearing a greater share of the costs of reduced output and increased unemployment. Their condition – relatively and absolutely – improves in times of higher macroeconomic activity. Therefore left parties promise economic stimulation, are identified with such policies, and act to bring them about when elected, even at the risk of raising the inflation rate.

In Hibbs's (1977) original statistical estimates, Democrats (Republicans) in the United States produced a long-run – after eight years – level of unemployment that was about 2.5 per cent lower (higher) as an equilibrium or steady state level than the other party. In Britain the inter-party differences between Labour and Conservatives were smaller (but the overall unemployment rate was considerably lower) though equilibrium differences were achieved faster. In recent work Hibbs has also shown that Democrats produce average rates of growth of real output that are about 1.5 per cent per annum higher than Republicans, at a small inflationary cost. (Of course, since the inflation comes with a lag, with regular four-year alternation between the parties the Republicans inherit most of the inflation from the Democrats.)

Revisions: Mandates, Tradeoffs and Rational Expectations

How general are these results? Predictably, my earliest attempts to replicate the model's political-economic results in other European countries produced both complications and insights (Alt, 1985). First, notably, when a broader range of countries was considered, the expected partisan effects appeared often, but not nearly always. Importantly, they appeared in a way which apparently depended on the existence of *explicit electoral promises*, which necessitated grounding the results for economic policy in mandate theories of party policies, a connection which had not originally been evident. Secondly, it was noticeable that even when the expected partisan effects appeared, they often didn't seem to last very long. This *transitory*, even ephemeral, quality of the outcomes made sense in terms of politicians' strategic behaviour, though that too had not been central in the original form of the argument. Finally, it became clear that, in small countries with trade-dependent economies, the state of the *world economy* imposed on domestic politics to a great extent, both changing politicians' incentives to act and obscuring the consequences of their acts. Hence, indeed, it was necessary to view the broader political and economic context in order to see clearly how the pressures from parties turned into policies, with profound effects for the underlying theory.

Mandates and Honeymoons

There is no doubt, as far as parties' preferences go, the expectations of partisan theory are borne out empirically. Certainly parties of the left are associated more commonly with promises of expansion, other things equal, and parties of the right with disinflation. This fact is confirmed by quantitative studies of party promises (manifestos, platforms) in the United States and many countries in Europe (Budge et al., 1987). But is the translation of a preference – even a standing preference – into an outcome to be taken for granted? That is, do the parties *always* have incentives to act on these standing preferences? Even if such action is costly?

Secondly, even when the promises are there and the policy changes do occur, how long should one expect them to last? That is, should we expect to observe a shift in aggregate unemployment or output growth which is sustained throughout the life of a government (or even longer), or should we expect something shorter-lived? How do we know how long, as well as how big, a change to expect?

Let us think about this in the context of mandate theory. According to this empirical description of contemporary democracies, parties compete for office by offering voters alternative packages of policies or pro-grammes, the winner (in terms of votes) forms the government, and carries out its promised programme, at least partly out of fear of electoral retribution if it does not. Empirical work has established both the importance of economic policies in the predictably distinct packages parties promise and also that, at least most of the time, the promises are carried out.

In theory, if there were economic policy actions that could be taken after an election that would be in the interest of parties' supporters, parties would be expected to promise such actions and carry them out if elected. If such actions to bring about economic change would not be desirable from the point of view of a party's supporters, the party would not promise such actions. If it does not promise them, by the same token, they must not be desirable. Then the partisan effects on economic policy would not be expected automatically, but only when parties had explicitly promised to do these things if elected.

Nevertheless, there are cases in which such partisan action might not be automatic. One is when a party succeeds itself, that is, wins an election as incumbent. Then the question is, why would a party that wished to do something for its core constituency after the election not equally wish to do it before the election? Further, if it was already in office, why wouldn't it just do it? It's different if other parties can oppose, impede, or prevent governing parties from implementing policies as, for example, in the common type of European coalition arrangement (or, more generally, if there are costs to implementing policies, and parties not in the government can increase these costs). Then a party coming to the end of its term might find itself frustrated in its desires to alter the state or direction of the economy. The fact of being re-elected around an explicit policy promise reduces the ability of other parties to oppose or impede government initiatives. It cloaks these initiatives with legitimacy: 'the people have spoken'. It could make possible taking action after re-election that was impossible before, though naturally such 'mandates' must wear off after some 'honeymoon' period.

Formalizing Tradeoffs and Transitory Shocks

Assuming a newly elected party does intervene to change the direction of the economy, how long should such intervention last? This first view, that it should last until the honeymoon is over and it becomes too costly to continue, offers no specific empirical predictions. The evident concern over inflation displayed by left (and right) parties in a number of countries (most notably the United States and Britain between 1975 and 1980) led several authors to propose that the objectives of parties should not be seen only as providing a higher or lower level of employment and/or output, but that inflation should be added to the objectives of both ideological sorts of parties. Instead of being concerned only with unemployment, parties on both sides were now seen as concerned with both unemployment and inflation, which were also still systematically related to each other.

This makes ideologically motivated stimulation and contraction through government policy costly to the government itself. Thus, a left government that stimulates the economy is also assumed to feel the pain of (recognize that its core constituents also dislike) the inflation that results from the stimulation. Symmetrically, a right government that curbs inflation and thereby drives unemployment up or real growth down ultimately stops when its constituents dislike the contraction more than they appreciate the reduced inflation. Thus, partisan changes in the economy come to be self-limiting, and thus transitory as well, though the speed with which they disappear depends on the steepness of the tradeoff between prices and output and on the relative weight each party places on each condition as an objective. In principle, how long the intervention lasts should depend on party preferences and the tradeoff between output and inflation.

Appealing as this modification seems, it is worth noting that its applicability may be limited by at least two empirical regularities observed in the political economy literature. First, as we observed in Chapter 5, 'popularity functions' (quantitative estimates of the effect of economic conditions on popular electoral choices) vary considerably from country to country.

Secondly, as we will see below, including inflation (as well as output) among government targets presumes that governments control these economic variables, at least partially. However, recent work by Grilli et al. (1991) and Alesina and Summers (1992) indicates a close correlation between national inflation rates and the degree of dependence of the central bank's monetary policy on the wishes of elected governments. This does indeed mean that if there is a wholly independent central bank, the government strictly may not control inflation at all. However, if dependence means at least that the government is able to appoint central bankers, Alt (1991) shows circumstances under which the bankers, if they desire reappointment, have incentives to accommodate post-election partisan monetary policy shocks.

Indeed, Hibbs (1992) pushes this interesting possibility further, by assuming that governments also incorporate recent information in their actions: they learn, and particularly they update their beliefs about the economy systematically in every period. Now, partisan governments have their higher and lower output targets, *and* they are concerned about inflation, *and* they revise their beliefs about how inflation and output are related (that is, about the value of the 'multiplier', a measure of how effective their policy interventions are) to take account of the last period's events and outcomes. This makes how long interventions last depend, as above, on the economy and the preferences, but in a way which is dynamic and could vary from administration to administration, depending on adaptation and learning rules.

Rational Partisan Theory

Both the first two revisions focused on the incentives and objectives of the parties and governments. The third revision, rational partisan theory, instead centred on the information and actions of voters and private sector economic agents. The problem posed for the partisan model by rational expectations macroeconomics was to explain why, if the partisan actions of governments were predictable, agents in the private market economy would not forecast these actions as part of forming economic expectations and then make economic choices conditional on these forecasts. This would have the effect of leaving aggregate supply in the economy on a path which either might entirely offset the government's actions, or at any rate be quite different from the path the government sought. In other words, the private sector would get *their* optimal path conditional on the government's actions (which might be offset partly, even entirely). With rational expectations, then, only an intervention (shock) which is unanticipated by private agents could have real effects. But if everyone knew what the parties wanted, and even what they had promised, how could they create an unanticipated intervention?

Alesina (1987; and with various colleagues) proposed the answer that it was the election outcomes that were uncertain. In short, everything about parties and electors would be known to the private sector except what the aggregate outcome would be. Thus, any economic relationship governed by a contract which did not provide for contingencies in the event of different election outcomes would be sticky, and would be adjusted only after the election result was known. These adjustments might be quick once the result was known, so the effects of party interventions on policy will still be transitory, with a length given only by the stickiness of the adjustment process.

Moreover, effects should not appear where the election of one side was certain *ex ante*. Realistically, of course, nothing is ever certain, but it is easy to imagine cases where it seemed particularly likely that a coalition would be returned to office very much as before, and other cases where the results came as a shock to all. Quite reasonably, then, significant contractions followed the elections of Nixon in the US in 1968 (a very close election result, with novel third-party distortions) and Heath in Britain in 1970 (the BBC was so surprised by the result that on election night they had to have studio displays of possible results repainted). Indeed, in the most recent British election, the only certain thing was that nothing was certain. Scrambling in exchange markets during the campaign reflects the difficulty, even in capital markets, of covering positions contingent on the ultimate election outcome.

The Models in Conflict

The original partisan model and its various revisions can be described by a set of half a dozen assumptions, three of which are shared by all versions of the theory, and three of which vary. (This discussion follows closely but non-technically the layout of Alesina and Roubini, 1990.) As they point out, first, all the models assume that inflation is controlled by policy-makers, either directly or indirectly. Secondly, the election dates are fixed or at least exogenously given, or at any rate not determined by (that is, chosen by politicians in view of) the same short-term economic conditions they are needed to explain. Thirdly, the economy can be described by a 'Phillips curve', in which fluctuations of output growth (alternatively, unemployment) around its natural or steady state rate are a function of deviations of price inflation from its expected level. The expectations represent the views of 'typical' economic agents, while the economic measures are averages across the whole economy. This is a highly simplified representation of an economy, but it turns out to be rich enough to provide tests of the main issues at stake.

The models also differ in their characterizations of three things: the process by which expectations are formed, how politicians behave, and how voters decide. For example (outside party politics for a moment) we can see that in the traditional political business cycle model, politicians are *opportunistic* (they care only about holding office and do not have partisan goals), voters are *retrospective* (they may all have the same values, but they vote by judging incumbents according to *past* inflation and output growth, or unemployment), and expectations are *adaptive*, in the sense that they are only partly adjusted for recent expectational errors (all available information is not necessarily incorporated). (The 'rational' political business cycle model of Rogoff, 1990 and others incorporates forward-looking voters and economic agents who form expectations rationally, but still subjects voters to some imperfection or incompleteness of information.)

Traditional partisan theory keeps the three shared assumptions, retains adaptive expectations so that effects of economic policy can persist indefinitely, but bases the behaviour of officials on the substitute assumption that partisan groups of politicians maximize *different objectives*, as described above, and has *forward-looking* voters who differ among themselves in values and choose the party offering the most preferred policy mix, in economic terms also as described above. This produces the implications that sustained changes in the levels of output growth and inflation.

The rational partisan model keeps these voter and politician assumptions of the traditional partisan model, but substitutes the *rational* mechanism for economic agents' formation of inflation expectations. The rational mechanism, again, means that all information available at one time is incorporated in the forecast of prices for the next period. It is this change of assumption which predicts that after a shock, expectations, prices, and wages should adjust immediately, while output and unemployment should remain at their natural levels, or return to them with a delay caused only by their own inherent stickiness, but not by any persisting error on the part of authorities or voters. Shocks are in general expected to be random, with only the exception that the winner of a schedule election is known *ex ante* (and the various possibilities are not covered *ex ante* by contingent labour contracts). Therefore, immediately after an election, partisan governments target output growth or unemployment above or below their natural rates, according to the preference of their constituencies. Since expectations and prices adjust quickly, after some period of adjustment output and employment return to natural levels. However, the price adjustment mechanism makes a left government's initial targeting of output growth above the natural rate produce increased inflation which persists throughout its term. It's a one-time *acceleration* but a sustained change in the level of inflation that attends a transitory change in output.

We can also restate each version as a prediction of what should happen after the election of a (for simplicity) left government. The original partisan model predicted sustained effort by politicians to raise output growth, but did not say anything specific about the inflationary consequences of their doing so. The first modified partisan model predicted that such policy effort would be absent where it would be politically too costly, and that it would be transitory owing to decreasing returns on their activities. These predictions, however, were not explicitly linked to inflationary consequences or to rational models of voter evaluation or expectation formation: both were simply exogenous stipulations. The second modified partisan model acknowledged that since a sustained effort to keep output growth above its natural level would result in accelerating inflation (this is a feature of any natural rate or rational expectations model) the extra inflationary costs would ultimately make politically induced growth rates above the natural rate too costly to sustain. This could ultimately produce testable hypotheses about how long the transitory political interventions should last, given further specification of what information politicians had and how far they used it like sophisticated economic agents.

The rational model predicts shocks to output growth after elections, and allows enough stickiness for a few quarters to pass before the natural rate is restored. Along with the transitory rise and fall of output growth, inflation should reveal a one-time upward acceleration, to a level which would then continue. The prediction of transitory changes in output and sustained changes (but not sustained accelerations) in inflation is unique to this model. Additionally, at least with some further specification of how private sector agents attempt to hedge their uncertainty about post-election behaviour, it might be possible to predict which elections should reveal the largest effects. Since the size of the post-election real effect is related to the size of the last pre-election forecast error, the biggest upsets should produce the biggest effects, and probably in general uncertain outcomes should produce bigger effects. Where governments are re-elected with near certainty (as often happens in multi-party coalition situations), there is less room for real effects. Even in this situation, however, as long as there is some possibility that responsibility for the economy might change (with a different party getting control of the finance portfolio), some element of uncertainty about the economy remains, and with it the possibility of real post-election effects.

The Internationalized Economy

So far, we have presented the partisan model of macroeconomic policy and its revisions in the context of a national economy which was closed, or which did not engage extensively in international trade. This was a good approximation in the early post-war years (and still is, under some circumstances). However, the volume share of traded goods in aggregate world output has been increasing rapidly for the last four decades and world financial markets are increasingly integrated. On the whole it has become harder and harder to talk seriously about macroeconomic policy as though it were only a matter of domestic politics.

The effects of the increasingly internationalized economy on the partisan model are of three sorts. First, there are effects on voters and mandates, in which internationalization increases the information and sophistication required of voters. But it does more than this. Greater trade can also break up the simple class interests stipulated by the partisan model to underlie party systems. The relationship between class alignments and more complex sectoral alignments depends on producer attributes like comparative advantage and asset specificity. Finally, internationalization alters the policy problems facing partisan governments, in ways which depend on these voter and producer characteristics.

Effects on Mandate Theory

Increasing international trade imposes perceptual burdens on voters, which breaks up simpler patterns of accountability. Information is needed to evaluate economic policy which is more abstract, as relatively invisible variables like the balance of payments and exchange rates (even the 'real' exchange rate) come to be relatively more important in policy. Relevant statistics are typically comparative (two flows, two prices, two relative prices) and thus are harder to comprehend and harder to observe.

Moreover, it becomes more important for voters to measure performance on an internationally relative basis. Increasing trade means that there is a lot of shared variation in unemployment and inflation rates across countries. Generally, studies of the business cycle suggest a lot of harmonization. Countries increasingly pool policies behind common tariffs and trade agreements, and import and export to each other their price increases, stimulations, and contractions. This has two consequences. First, what appears to be domestic stimulation of contraction may really be just a reflection of trends in several countries. The current world recession is making headlines not just in the US but in Japan, Britain and elsewhere. But it would be hard to argue that any country made the recession alone, though each might have reshaped the common downturn to some extent.

This appears to be exactly what the half of the British electorate recorded by recent election polls as believing that 'the world' was the cause of their recession had in mind. One hopes they remembered to credit some of the boom of the 1980s which underpinned economic recovery before the previous two elections to the same source. Nevertheless, as the 1992 election took place, the British unemployment rate was within 0.5 per cent of the average of the unemployment rates in France, Germany and Italy, reasonable international comparisons. Whether the British inflation rate was higher or lower depended on whether it was calculated over twelve months or less. However, a quick look at the data would show that the British inflation rate had fluctuated around the OECD industrial country average since the mid 1980s, rarely diverging by more than 1 per cent.

The implication is not that voters should all agree to accept, like, or dislike average performance, though in fact 'comparatively average' unemployment is far better than Britain did from 1980 to 1987, and average inflation since 1985 is far better than the previous decade's performance. But the main point is that if the result of government policy is in fact just part of an internationally shared trend, voters need more information to evaluate this correctly. Moreover, they don't observe this extra information directly unless they travel a lot, and thus they become either more dependent on mediated information or too little informed.

Effects on Classes and Sectors

Recently, a string of writings (Cassing et al., 1986; Alt, 1987; Rogowski, 1989; Frieden, 1991) have described the effects of trade on economic classes and sectors. They unveil complicated questions of asset specificity and comparative advantage, which cause coalitions to change with increasing rapidity, potentially undermining the stability of party alignments to an increasing degree. These efforts reflect a healthy convergence of two previously separate fields: the domestic political consequences of international trade and the international origins of domestic political realignment, always on opposite sides of the same relationships, are together at last.

Arguments in this new literature are not simple, for they make economic interests depend on several variables simultaneously. For example, economic growth (increasing trade, a boom) could harm non-manual or skilled manual workers (or even owners of fixed capital assets) in import-competing industries more than unskilled workers in those same industries, if the skilled represent factors of production less mobile, that is, less transportable to sectors sheltered from foreign trade. Whether it actually does or not can depend on the mobility of factors and assets, which could depend on the nature of the assets or on the nature of the economy (geographical separation, relative transportation or housing costs) or even on institutions (unions can increase the specificity of labour).

It would take a paper rather than a paragraph even to summarize all these possibilities systematically, though one key point is clear. Where time horizons are short (effects are expected quickly), factors are likely to be less mobile, and thus an expansion (boom, increase in trade, stimulation) is likely to have different effects within classes rather than across classes. This would lead to political effects and results in political divisions determined by interests separating industries, say, by exposure to trade (or, even more, among those exposed to trade by whether or not they possess comparative advantage in production and thus can take advantage of increased trade best). This also means that any policy which can stretch time horizons can take advantage of greater possibilities of mobility, or alternatively, must protect against greater possibilities of exit. These relationships have been at the heart of the bargaining described in Scandinavian economic models for many years.

Effects on Government Policy

Both these changes due to increased economic internationalization have consequences for government policy. If voters compare performance internationally, it may be that government targets will also be established relative to other countries. Alesina and Roubini (1990) remark on this possibility but develop it no further. Moreover, clearly, to the extent that trade increases, a government-induced stimulation may have less effect. If imports are a readily available substitute for domestically produced goods, any fiscal or monetary injection of purchasing power may be dissipated abroad.

Garrett (1992) suggests that this substitutability would undermine class-based policy in the short term. It would therefore induce some governments in countries with highly trade-dependent economies to opt for policies of subsidy and investment rather than demand management. This would stretch time horizons, and by doing so, allow for more mobility and thus restore a class-based pattern to the benefits received, stabilizing the class basis of the party system.

Conclusions and Results

So there are some contrasts among models, but they so far require mining some fine margins in the data. Both first modified and rational partisan theory predict that partisan effects should be absent after some elections, but make the predictions on different criteria. The former predicts no change where there is no promise, like mandate theory, and raises the possibility of predicting promises at least in part from economic circumstances; the latter predicts no change where the election outcome was known with certainty *ex ante*, and change as smaller the more clear the outcome was in advance. The rational model can be distinguished from the second modified partisan model according to the contrasting patterns of output growth and inflation they predict: the former predicts a burst of output growth which immediately begins to return to the natural rate and a short acceleration of inflation which levels off quickly; the latter predicts longer duration for the output growth (though not as long as in the original model, which is the case for all the other models) and also for the resulting inflation acceleration. The more foresight politicians are assumed to have in the latter case, however, the more it will converge with the former. Exactly how these predictions need to be amended to take account of internationalization awaits further development.

What empirical results there are don't pick a clear winner from among contending approaches. Alt (1985) showed that economic promises were central to elections about half the time, and significant economic interventions were never found when they had not been promised. They were found less than half the time even when promised, but nearly half the 'missing' cases, cases where the economy was an issue but no actual significant change subsequently took place, were minority governments! Of course, Britain still is a special case where the economy is a central issue every time, but comparative studies of elections provide many examples of cases where economics was a relatively minor theme.

The need to model policy in one country relative to world trends is well established by the data. Even independent of sophisticated controls for the past histories of both unemployment and output series, both Alt (1985) and Alesina and Roubini (1990) show over and over that world trends have a significant impact on domestic economies everywhere. What limited evidence there is also suggests that this impact is roughly proportional to each country's actual dependence on trade. At one extreme is the case of the Canadian economy, where Alesina and Roubini demonstrate that American partisan changes of government have more explanatory power than Canadian partisan changes. At the other, the Scandinavian economies appear to receive shocks from the world with more of a delay (and somewhat less of an effect) than others, but whether this is due to trade patterns, economic structure and political institutions and policies is not known.

Alesina and Roubini provide direct tests of whether politically induced shocks are transitory or permanent, and find that the evidence strongly favours the transitory-shock hypothesis. Most of the clearly 'two-party' countries other than Canada (US, Britain, Australia, New Zealand, France, Germany, but not Sweden) regularly display significant transitory partisan changes in both unemployment and real output. Countries where multi-party coalitions are common (Austria, Belgium, Finland, Ireland, Netherlands, Norway, but not Italy) occasionally show significant transitory effects on unemployment or output. They also demonstrate that the expected pattern of a sustained change in inflation does appear, predominantly in the first group of countries enumerated. To this extent their results also support modified partisan theory.

The best thing is that empirical research and theoretical development have not stood still, but continue to push each other forward. Two main claims about information await testing – the extent to which election surprises produce real shocks and the degree to which policy-makers' actions reflect learning. On the side of internationalization, the task is to specify with greater clarity the interaction of time horizons, specificity, and competitive advantage in determining how economic shocks affect the interests of owners of factors of production in trade-exposed economies.

References

Alesina, A. 1987. 'Macroeconomic Policy in a Two-Party System as a Repeated Game'. *Quarterly Journal of Economics*, 102, pp. 651–78.

Alesina, A. and N. Roubini. 1990. 'Political Cycles in OECD Economies'. Cambridge, MA: National Bureau of Economic Research working paper no. 3478.

Alesina, A. and L. Summers. 1992. 'Central Bank Independence and Macroeconomic Performance: Some Comparative Evidence'. *Journal of Money, Credit and Banking*, 25, pp. 151–62.

Alt, J. 1985. 'Political Parties, World Demand, and Unemployment: Domestic and International Sources of Economic Activity'. *American Political Science Review*, 79, pp. 1016–44.

Alt, J. 1987. 'Crude Politics: Oil and the Political Economy of Unemployment in Britain and Norway, 1970–85'. *British Journal of Political Science*, 17, pp. 149–99.

Alt, J. 1991. 'Leaning into the Wind or Ducking out of the Storm: U.S. Monetary Policy in the 1980s'. In A. Alesina and G. Carliner (eds), *Politics and Economics in the Eighties*. Chicago: University of Chicago Press.

Blondel, J. 1976. *Thinking Politically*. London: Wildwood.

Budge, Ian, D.R. Robertson and D.J. Hearl. 1987. *Ideology, Strategy and Party Movement*. Cambridge: Cambridge University Press.

Cassing, J., T. McKeown and J. Ochs. 1986. 'The Political Economy of the Tariff Cycle'. *American Political Science Review*, 80, pp. 843–62.

Frieden, J. 1991. 'Invested Interests: The Politics of National Economic Policies in a World of Global Finance'. *International Organization*, 45, pp. 425–51.

Garrett, G. 1992. 'Government and the Economy: The Politics of Economic Policy in the Age of Interdependence'. Stanford University, CA, mimeo.

Grilli, V., D. Masciandaro and G. Tabellini. 1991. 'Political and Monetary Institutions and Public Finance Policies in the Industrial Countries'. *Economic Policy*, 13, pp. 341–92.

Hibbs, D. 1977. 'Political Parties and Macroeconomic Policy'. *American Political Science Review*, 71, pp. 1467–87.

Hibbs, D. 1991. 'The Partisan Model of Macroeconomic Cycles: More Theory and Evidence for the United States'. Stockholm: FIEF, mimeo.

Hibbs, D. 1992. 'Partisan Theory after Fifteen Years'. *European Journal of Political Economy*, 8, pp. 361–74.

Rogoff, K. 1990. 'Equilibrium Political Budget Cycles'. *American Economic Review*, 80, pp. 21–36.

Rogowski, R. 1989. *Commerce and Coalitions: How Trade Affects Domestic Political Alignments*. Princeton: Princeton University Press.

7

Budgets and Democracy: towards a Welfare State in Spain and Portugal, 1960–1986

Gosta Esping-Andersen

This chapter takes up a complementary theme to the analysis of inflation and employment in Chapter 6. For although the general well-being may be best served, indirectly, by an optimum balance between these two, a third great issue in industrialized democracies has always been how much the state should spend directly on welfare measures. It is therefore particularly interesting to look at the development of welfare policy, and its effects on democratization in Spain and Portugal during the last thirty years. Such an examination may have some relevance for what we can expect in new democracies elsewhere, though the analogies may be far from exact.

Politics and Social Redistribution

Government budgets are never innocent. In the mid-nineteenth century United Kingdom, 68 per cent of total (non-debt) government expenditure went to defence, administration and the police. By 1975, their share had declined to only 16 per cent while social and related spending accounted for two-thirds. A similar story could be told for most other European countries.[1]

Government budgets are normally divided into a capital and a current expenditure account; in the latter, we distinguish between consumption (tanks, school books, or employee salaries) and transfers (pensions, industry subsidies, and the like). Whom budgets will favour is very specific to nation and period. Some systems are vastly more redistributive than others, but as a rule the massive rise in public spending over the past century has been accompanied by a relative loss for police, military and administration, and a relative gain for social services and redistribution. How did this come about?

A common theme in nineteenth century thinking was that democratization would unleash irrepressible demands for redistribution and, should they succeed, the system of free enterprise would be in jeopardy. Unsurprisingly, the privileged classes – be they conservative or liberal –

advocated curbs to mass democracy so as to prevent the propertyless masses from seizing government for their own redistributive ends. Our political forebears adopted a wide, and quite inventive, range of solutions to this problem: the franchise and parliamentarianism were limited, trade unions and socialist parties were occasionally banned. Alternatively, the potentially disastrous impact of universal suffrage could be contained by the construction of intricate checks and balances that would distance the electoral masses from the centres of power, such as occurred in the American system of federalism. The ultimate and most desperate solution was dictatorship.

Most theories, from de Tocqueville and John Stuart Mill down to modern-day median-voter models, assume that in a democracy, budgets will reflect the weight of electoral preference. Universal suffrage and full parliamentary rule should, accordingly, produce a redistributive profile that mainly benefits the majorities. In this 'simple' version of the democratization thesis, numbers are assumed to translate into power. Hence, the actual party composition of the legislature and cabinet is of minor interest since any party can survive only if it can appeal to majorities. Tocqueville (1969, pp. 208–12) took it for granted that democracy would engender governments that benefited the poorest classes, simply because they would constitute the majority. Indeed, it was precisely this assumption which produced the nineteenth century anti-democratic sentiments. But there were optimists, like Thomas Jefferson and de Tocqueville, who believed that the social order could be made safe from democracy provided that the popular voting masses were secured property ownership. Alas, the spread of mass ownership was in general not part and parcel of early industrialization.

Modern median-voter theories are also optimistic in the sense that they do not typically see full democracy producing a leviathan state. Downs's (1957) model and later applications, such as Jackman (1975; 1986), stress that vote maximization and the need for coalitions will force parties of whatever ideological coloration to embrace policies that do not alienate the median voter. Hence, electoral democracy will safeguard society against extremist policies and may, indeed, produce government 'underspending'.

There are two major alternatives to the 'simple' majoritarian democratic theory. The first holds that budgetary evolution is dictated by largely non-political forces. Adolph Wagner's 'law' emphasizes the role of economic growth, while authors such as Lindblom (1959) and Wildavsky (1964) posit a model of self-reinforcing bureaucratic incrementalism or 'muddling through'. The incrementalist view has considerable merit, at least in the short and medium term, because programmes that spend are anchored in law and entitlements, large shares of expenditure are earmarked, and governments cannot afford to alienate the clienteles that are wedded to any particular budget item. Hence, significant shifts in the budgetary bias are most likely to come via long-run expenditure growth, or following sharp historical breaks, as emphasized by Peacock and Wiseman (1961).

The second alternative argues that democracy is a necessary but insufficient condition for change since the relative size of an electorate may not imply relative power. In this view, numbers will translate into power only under conditions of mobilized and organized party power. Whether one emphasizes the power of working-class parties, as do Korpi (1983) and Stephens (1979), or the weakness of the right, as does Castles (1982), will matter less in this context.

Research on the political determinants of policy has grown over the past decades, but has hardly produced any conclusive answers. The case for a non-political theory of welfare expenditure has been made by Pampel and Williamson (1989) and Wilensky (1975) who, instead, point to the overriding salience of economic growth, bureaucratization and demographic ageing. Yet, their results are only valid when welfare spending is measured as a percentage of GDP. In turn, the case for the causal importance of leftist (or rightist) parties is most convincing when we study the structural characteristics of social policy (Esping-Andersen, 1990). Finally, the 'simple' democracy thesis seems to hold primarily when we study income distribution (Jackman, 1975; 1986).

A common problem with all these empirical studies is that their methodology contradicts their theoretical purpose. Mostly cross-sectional, they rely on post-war data for advanced industrial democracies. This is obviously inappropriate, since the advent of full democracy in most cases emerged many decades earlier. Hence, it becomes impossible to separate the historically specific effects of economic growth, democratization and party cabinet power from one another.

A serious empirical study requires, therefore, very long time series. For some countries such series now exist, but they are rarely complete and, if they are, the data are rarely of the kind required for this kind of analysis.[2] We can, however, benefit from the recent democratization of Spain and Portugal. Their post-war experience presents, in rough form, the basic contours of the dominant European road to modern, democratic and economically developed welfare statism: they have emerged from economic backwardness and dictatorship to the status of relatively economically advanced democracies. This chapter is dedicated to a study of whether, and to what degree, democratization in these two countries influenced the distributional bias of their public budgets.

Government Budgets

It is easy to agree that government expenditures create winners and losers, but it is another matter to pinpoint exactly who gains from what. We can safely assume that agriculture subsidies favour farmers, and that income maintenance favours wage earners. But, how do we decide whom, at any given moment, derives more personal utility than others from military expenditures (aside from the officer corps), the courts, railways, or even education?[3] The intricate problem of how to assign advantages of particular expenditures to specific groups can be sharply reduced if we are willing to agree that the social wage will primarily benefit those groups with least property and economic privilege, that is, those with little or no market power.

Reducing the problem to a question of the social wage shares of total government outlays seems warranted.[4] First, it provides a yardstick of a country's progress towards the welfare state; a minimal definition is that at least a majority of government activity should be devoted to the provision of social welfare and security, as opposed to alternative goals (Esping-Andersen, 1990). It also helps resolve the perennial question of when, precisely, a state is a welfare state. Clearly, imperial Germany of 1910 cannot be considered a welfare state despite the fact that Bismarck's social legislation had, more or less, brought into being the standard array of welfare state programmes.

Secondly, by studying social spending as a share of total government outlays we remain faithful to the issue of democratization and power as it was originally formulated by Tocqueville and his contemporaries; that is, the fear (or hope) that democracy and/or labour party power would allow the masses to colonize the government for their own redistributive ends.

Surprisingly few have, in fact, studied the question in this simple way. The traditional choice of social expenditure as a percentage of GDP was falsely premised on the idea that it mirrored governments' welfare effort. But if the same governments spent an even higher GDP ratio on the military and the police, for example, we would have to conclude that the welfare effort is overshadowed by bellicose concerns.

Those studies which have examined welfare stateness in terms of public budgetary structure fall into two groups. One, following in the footsteps of Lipset's (1960) 'democratic class struggle' and Dawson and Robinson's (1963) party competition model, concludes that parties are decisive for the relative bias in favour of social spending (see, for example, Castles, 1982; Muller and Zimmermann, 1986; Lessmann, 1987; Budge and Keman, 1990). Another, adhering to the bureaucratic-incrementalist thesis, suggests a basic stability in budgetary structure that, in the long haul, will rupture for mainly cataclysmic reasons, be it war or regime change (Peacock and Wiseman, 1961).

An Empirical Model of Social Expenditure Shares

To examine the roots of budgetary change, we develop a fairly simple time-series model for Portugal and Spain from 1960 (the first year in which we can obtain reliable data) to 1986. The model incorporates the major explanations for why the social welfare share of government budgets should grow disproportionately: economic growth, the transition to full democracy, and the nature of party control of cabinets. Budgetary incrementalism is identified via the inclusion of the (one-year) lagged dependent variable (social expenditures as a percentage of total current expenditures). This should tell us to what degree last year's budget is reproduced in the current year.

It will be noted that we propose two alternative measures of democratization: the democracy variable and the transition variable. A shortcoming of the literature is that it has not adequately identified the different implications of the two processes.[5] Leaving aside possible reversals, democratization is to be seen as a permanent change, a consolidated regime change. The transition period forms, of course, part of this change, but is likely to display distinct characteristics. First, by its very nature the transition is a period of political flux in which embryonic political parties seek to profile themselves for the coming electoral competition. It is also very likely a period of unusually intense popular demand to redress previous wrongs and to satisfy long-repressed needs. The hypothesized effect of the two phenomena on spending is different. If it is democratization *per se* which matters, we should anticipate a marked spending shift that becomes permanent. If, in turn, expenditures are mainly a function of the transition period, any observed changes should be temporary.

In brief, the model takes the following form:

$$S/T\,[t] = \alpha + \beta_1(S/T\,[t-1]) + \beta_2(GDPc[t-1]) +$$
$$\beta_3(Dem[t-1]) + \beta_4(Trans[t-1]) + \beta_5(Cab[t-1]) + \epsilon$$

where:

t is from 1960 to 1986.

S/T is social expenditure (including income maintenance, health and social services, but excluding education and housing) as a percentage of total current government outlays, excluding capital accounts.

$GDPc$ is measured as annual percentage change in real GDP, lagged one year to take into account the probability that politicians vote on this year's budget with last year's growth performance in mind.

Dem is a dummy variable for democratization, defined here as date of first democratic constitution. Again, this variable is lagged one year to account for reaction time.

$Trans$ is an alternative democratization dummy variable that takes into account only the years of democratic transition (Portugal 1974–7; Spain 1975–7). Again, this variable should be lagged one year.[6]

Cab is a trichotomous variable for the kind of party in control of the cabinet, and is again lagged one year. A score of 1 was given for cabinets during the dictatorship, a score of 2 for non-socialist cabinets (pre-1982 in Spain, and 1979–83 plus post-1985 in Portugal), and 3 for socialist/left cabinets.[7]

The Budgetary Impact of Democratization

Contrary to the Tocqueville thesis, it has occasionally been held that initial democratization actually diminished the kind of government largesse

Table 7.1 *Budgets in democratic and authoritarian periods: share of total budgets allocated to law and order or social welfare (including education)*

Country and period[1]	Authoritarian regime		Democratic regime	
	Law/Order (%)	Social (%)	Law/Order (%)	Social (%)
Austria 1930			18.5	31.4
1937	27.0	15.3		
Denmark 1901	41.1	21.4		
1929			18.5	37.7
Italy 1900	27.9	3.6		
1921			19.8	10.1
1936	33.2	11.1		
1950			23.8	24.0
Sweden 1913	45.1	14.8		
1922			30.2	30.3

[1] Note: the years lie as close as possible to polity changes, and avoid war.
Source: adapted from Flora et al., 1983

towards the poor that went with paternalistic authoritarian regimes (Dich, 1973; Viby-Mogensen, 1975). One argument has it that early franchise extensions (especially in the mid 1800s) mainly helped empower small property owners and farmers who wished to avoid tax burdens and lower the effective minimum wage. Another argument emphasizes the *noblesse oblige* effect, or the social peace costs, that went with maintaining traditional absolutist and autocratic governments; the 'Bismarck-effect', we might term it.

The two arguments are essentially consistent, but are difficult to validate internationally because we have virtually no reliable data on social spending that span the entire epoch of democratization. We can, however, examine the periods immediately before and after the great wave of democratization in the early twentieth century, and the return to authoritarian regimes in the 1930s. Here it is important to bear in mind that the class structures were radically different in this later context: the small property owners had declined while the working class had grown drastically.

There is considerable, if not especially systematic, evidence that the bias of budgetary expenditure has been sensitive to constitutional regime shifts. Authoritarian and pre-democratic polities are much more likely to favour defence and law and order, while democratization (meaning here universal suffrage and full parliamentarianism) tends to result in a marked shift towards social welfare and educational goals, as shown in Table 7.1. The pre/post-democracy budget shifts presented in the table are not always dramatic, but the trend seems to be quite consistently in favour of a substantial post-democratic redirection from guns to butter. Since we have also tried to limit the time-span between the observations, it is unlikely that our budgetary shifts are explained by economic growth. A major problem, however, is that democratization in most nations coincided with the end of the First or Second World Wars.

Democratization and Budgets in Spain and Portugal

The transition towards a modern welfare state in the advanced European democracies occurred around the late 1950s and early 1960s, at least if by this we mean that the lion's share of government activity was welfare-oriented. This transition, of course, post-dated democratization by anywhere from two to five decades, coincided with a prolonged period of economic growth and near-full employment, and was particularly marked in countries with a strong social or Christian democratic regime.

This entire set of conditions was absent in Spain and Portugal until well into the 1960s (economic growth) or the 1970s (democracy and strong socialist cabinets). Both Spain and Portugal are, furthermore, unique in how these conditions came together historically. Both countries experienced an era of economic stagnation following the emergence of the dictatorships in the 1930s, and the post-war boom of the West passed them by, at least until the 1960s. A relaxation of controls and the opening up of their economies and societies in the 1960s produced, on the other hand, quite spectacular growth rates.

Measured in constant (1970) US dollars, Spain's 1929 per capita GDP equalled Italy's, was two-thirds of Germany's, and half that of the UK. By 1960, this gap had widened considerably, now being two-thirds of Italy's, and less than one-half of Germany's. By the mid 1970s, however, the Opus Dei programme had catapulted Spain to the level of economic development attained by the major European powers a decade earlier.[8] Hence, if the transition to a welfare state presupposes a threshold of economic wealth, this is when we should expect it to unfold.

Compared with the typical trajectory of West European countries, however, the arrival of Spain's economic threshold coincides with democratization (1975–7), and the post-OPEC economic downturn. The latter was particularly severe in Spain where real GDP per capita (in US dollars) remained stagnant (and even declined twice) over six years. Since democratization and 'economic threshold' coincide, it may be difficult to disentangle their relative importance for any eventual welfare shift in the 1970s. The social expenditure data for Spain indicate nonetheless two major waves of social wage growth. The first occurs in the mid 1960s, and is of little interest since it was chiefly a function of administrative budget consolidation.[9] The second occurs in the early 1970s and is of much greater substantive interest. It follows a decade of spectacular economic growth and an internal regime shift in favour of greater liberalization and modernization, and it coincides with the new 1972 Ley de Financiación y Perfeccionamiento (Guillen, 1991).

Comparatively speaking, the democratization process in Spain was gradualist and pragmatic. The party system that emerged with democratization produced, contrary to expectations, neither a strong communist, nor a Christian democratic force. Following the caretaker government of the transition period, a centre–right alliance governed until the advent of the socialist majority government from 1982 onwards. The delay between democratization and socialist cabinets, albeit rather brief, may nonetheless allow us to separate the effects of the two forces in explaining budgetary change.

The Portuguese trajectory appears superficially quite similar. Yet, apart from the timing of democratic transition, most of its components are exactly contrary to those of Spain. First, in terms of economic development, Portugal has always been far behind the rest of Europe, including Spain. Its GDP per head in 1929 was less than half that of Spain, rising to two-thirds by the 1950s and 1960s, but then falling behind again as Spain embarked upon its boom. Indeed, Portugal's GDP per capita in 1973 was more or less equal to Britain's in 1929, Germany's in the mid 1950s, and Italy's in 1960. In other words, Portugal's level of economic development at the period of democratization was far below the magic threshold at which most of Europe experienced its welfare state shift. By 1986, Portugal's GDP equalled Spain's of the mid 1960s, hardly propitious for massive welfare spending if economic development is what counts. As we shall see below, Portugal's 1986 welfare expenditure share is, indeed, quite similar to Spain's in the early 1960s.

Portugal's transition to democracy was far more 'revolutionary', and unique in that it was led by the left. We therefore have a historical coincidence between democratization and a socialist-controlled government. The Portuguese transition cabinets promoted socialism as the official national ideology, and introduced a package of radical social and economic policies, including mass nationalizations. From our point of view, it is also interesting to note that the government budget was implemented without parliamentary approval from 1974 to 1976. Articles 50–72 of the 1976 Constitution (altered in 1982) laid down the parameters for a comprehensive welfare state in terms of citizens' social rights. Hoffman (1983, p. 15) even argues that in no other country's constitution have social policy goals been given such prominence. The left was ousted in 1979, and Portugal was governed by centre–right cabinets throughout the 1980s, except for the centre–left coalition of 1983–4.

Welfare Statism in Portugal and Spain

It is difficult to characterize either the Spain or the Portugal of today as genuine welfare states. Both nations' social policies are rooted in the continental European corporatist-conservative tradition and remained comparatively undeveloped and much less comprehensive throughout the dictatorships. A number of reforms in the direction of a modern social security system were taken towards the end of the dictatorships, especially in Spain, and democratization also gave rise to the introduction of programmes that, during the dictatorships, were non-existent. Thus, unemployment insurance and a national health service were first introduced in Portugal with democratization.[10] Their social safety net is in many places very weak, and coverage and benefit levels are modest. This is perhaps most evident in the case of unemployment where, on the one hand, neither country has been capable of averting high unemployment levels and, on the other hand, the system of unemployment insurance is unable to cover more than about half (or less) of the actually unemployed (Maravall, 1982; Moreno and Sarasa, 1991). But it is also evident in the government budgets. In Portugal, the welfare share (excluding education and housing) of total government outlays remained below 20 per cent until the 1970s, and then experienced a radical jump in the mid 1970s, reaching a maximum of 35.7 per cent in 1978; since then, the share has been stable. Hence, the Portuguese social expenditure climax corresponds to the situation in most European countries in the 1950s.

Reflecting her essentially agrarian and backward economy, Portugese social policy prior to the Salazar dictatorship was limited to a weak system of mutual aid societies. The first step towards an active governmental role occurred with the 1935 social insurance law (Hoffmann, 1983 p. 44). The reform retained the principle of essentially private welfare plans, organized on corporatist principles, but with compulsory membership. Over time, these occupational schemes were gradually extended to more and more groups. But they remained precarious, relying basically on member contributions. A first step towards consolidating the myriad corporatist plans was taken in 1962 but, until the 1974 'revolution', social protection was residual at best. If we combine means-tested assistance and civil service benefits, we arrive at 50 per cent of total public welfare outlays in 1960 (ILO, 1974; 1983)! Thus, only 20 per cent of the population was actually insured, and even if they were, the system hardly guaranteed much protection. The insured, for example, paid roughly 30 per cent of hospital costs themselves (Hoffmann, 1983, p. 47).

The huge social welfare void inherited from the dictatorship may help explain why the 1976 Constitution and subsequent reforms promoted such a strong social policy profile. Besides the introduction of unemployment insurance (1975, 1977), and national health care (1979), a guaranteed social minimum income was passed in 1980. In other words, Portugal experienced its single biggest leap towards the modern welfare state concept in the period of democratization and leftist cabinets.

In comparison with that of Portugal, Spanish social policy has evolved more gradually. Social security under Franco was more advanced although, internationally speaking, definitely a laggard. As with the Salazar dictatorship, the first decades of the Franco regime could hardly be accused of excessive welfare promotion; they were surely not of the welfare-paternalist kind. As late as 1950, defence-related expenditures accounted for one-third of total (central) state outlays, and transfers to the church equalled spending on health (calculated from Carreras, 1989, Tables 10.18 and 10.29). In the early phase of the dictatorship, social protection policies were presented in the Catholic organicist tradition of *obras sociales*, relying (as in Portugal) on corporatist welfare funds, the subsidiarity principle and charity. The Falangista wing of the dictatorship favoured a more centralized and statist approach, and it is in this light that we should understand the introduction of the 1939 pension scheme, and the 1942 sickness insurance plan. The net result was a patchwork of voluntary and compulsory protection, of corporatist and state insurance. Its capacity to ensure broad social protection was weak (Moreno and Sarasa, 1991; Guillen, 1991). Government's direct responsibility for social protection was mainly biased in favour of its own civil service.

The period of rapid economic development that followed with the 1959 stabilization plan included also a significant shift towards modern principles of welfare statism. The most important step was the 1963 Basic Law of Social Security that mainly provided for a consolidation of the previously fragmented corporatist mutual societies and the state schemes (Comin, 1988a, pp. 886ff.; and Guillen, 1991).[11] The 1972 Social Security Law led to a substantial increase in expenditures, mainly because coverage and benefits in the pension system were raised (Moreno and Sarasa, 1991). But, the social security system remained inadequate in many important respects until democratization (Maravall, 1982; Tamames, 1982; 1986; Moreno and Sarasa, 1991; Guillen, 1991). As these authors indicate, the existing system covered only two-thirds of the population, and it hardly functioned as a guarantee of adequate income maintenance.[12] Post-democratization governments (both non-socialist and socialist) took many initiatives to fill some of the principal gaps in the system, especially with regard to health care, social services, pensions and unemployment protection. Articles 41–9 of the 1978 Constitution stipulate the principle of universal popular social rights. As a share of total outlays, the welfare share climaxed around 1976–7, but has declined significantly since. Surprisingly, the welfare share (excluding unemployment benefits) has not increased over the post-1982 socialist cabinets. This, of course, implies not so much a militant anti-welfarist campaign on the part of the socialist governments as a redirection of budgetary growth in favour of alternative purposes, the economy in particular. Total public spending has grown markedly, but in terms of our chosen measure of welfare statism, the Spanish budget has, during the 1980s, slipped back to its Francoist structure. Accordingly, it is difficult to believe that the transition to socialist majority cabinets will have a significantly positive effect on welfare state development in Spain. Instead, the trend lends support to the many voices which claim that the Spanish socialists, favouring anti-inflationary policies over social citizenship, are not comparable to Northern European social democrats (Estevill and Hoz, 1990; Merkel, 1989; Paterson and

Thomas, 1986). It is also against this backdrop of relatively falling social spending that we should understand the 1988 trade union revolt against the government.

In our Portuguese–Spanish comparison, there are several factors which suggest that we should expect a rather different causal trajectory. In Spain, the process of democratization was fairly gradual; the inherited social safety-net was, compared with Portugal's, relatively well established; and post-democratic social policy has continued more or less along the traditional lines of the Franco era. In contrast, democratization in Portugal was more radical and produced a qualitative jump in terms of social legislation. In other words, we would expect the incrementalist effect to be far stronger, and the democratization effect to be weaker, in Spain than in Portugal. And, we would expect democratization and transition to be of far greater importance for budgetary change in Portugal. Since left cabinets and democratization coincide in Portugal, they will be statistically inseparable in our analysis.

A Statistical Test of Democratization and Budgetary Change

Table 7.2 presents the results of our time-series analyses. A first problem lies in the degree to which multi-collinearity prohibits a test of the full model (see the high zero-order correlations between the cabinet variable and democratization in the Appendix). To resolve this problem, our approach was to compare partial models in order to establish which of the two collinear variables remained the most robust. In the case of Portugal, the cabinet variable is systematically inferior to democratization, not only in terms of significance levels but also in terms of model performance. Hence, our final Portuguese model omits the cabinet variable. In Spain, the situation is contrary: the democracy variable performs systematically poorly, and is therefore omitted from the final model.[13] The two models shown in Table 7.2 are not econometrically perfect owing to some worrisome deviance from the normality assumption. Nonetheless, considering the limited years and the 'noise' that inevitably characterizes political reality, one can consider them quite acceptable.

The results for Portugal are very clear. As we know, the party composition of cabinets has had very little influence on budgetary behaviour. Instead, the shift towards welfare spending is the product of economic growth, incrementalism, the transition period and democracy. But it is the latter which is, by far, the most salient force. In other words, democratization in Portugal brought about a permanent welfare shift.

The Spanish model indicates an entirely different set of forces at work. Here spending development is mainly driven by bureaucratic incrementalism. The modest but significant effect of the transition variable (noting the systematic insignificance of the democracy variable) tells us that the years of transition produced a temporary welfare shift that, however, was

Table 7.2 *Portugal and Spain: the determinants of social expenditure change, 1960–1986 (OLS estimates, T-statistics in parentheses)[1]*

	Portugal	% variance explained	Spain	% variance explained
Intercept	8.684		13.312	
	(3.33)		(2.95)	
S/T[−1]	0.345	22.9	0.732	44.8
	(2.35)		(0.732)	
GDPc[−1]	0.516	15.9	−0.116	8.6
	(2.64)		(1.15)	
Dem[−1]	9.427	47.3		
	(4.02)			
Trans[−1]	5.166	13.9	4.392	19.0
	(3.03)		(3.65)	
Cab[−1]			−1.554	27.6
			(3.32)	
R^2 (adj.)	0.912		0.873	
Lagrange autocorrelation	0.138		0.873	
Rho	−0.02		−0.07	
Heteroscedasticity	0.001		0.078	
(prob. value)	(97.09)		(77.97)	
Jarque-Bera normality test	1.210		0.130	
(prob. value)	(54.60)		(93.71)	

[1] Dependent variable: social expenditure as a percentage of total general government spending, excluding unemployment transfers.

subsequently cancelled. Cabinets play an important role in Spain, but one that runs counter to traditional theory: socialist cabinets depress the welfare share. Comin (1988a) argues that social expenditure growth until democratization was mainly fuelled by economic growth. He may be right, but this is not confirmed when we study budget shares. Economic growth has had absolutely no significant effect in Spain.

It is evident that both countries' budgetary structures have been substantially affected by democratization, yet in opposite ways. In Portugal, democracy as such introduced a sharp break in favour of a sustained higher level of social welfare spending. In Spain, the forces of incrementalism have been very strong; the years of transition produced a modest jump in the budget's welfare bias, but democracy engendered no permanent budgetary shift.

Conclusions

The long era of Spanish and Portuguese dictatorship was obviously motivated by fears beyond mass demands for welfare and redistribution. Still, this almost certainly played an important part in the regimes' policies. As numerous authors have documented, both the Salazar and the Franco

Table 7.3   *Correlation matrix: Portugal*

	S/T	S/T[−1]	GDPc[−1]	Dem[−1]	Trans[−1]	Cab[−1]
S/T	1.000	0.889	−0.491	0.923	0.360	0.901
S/T[−1]	0.889	1.000	−0.444	0.880	0.889	0.810
GDPc[−1]	−0.491	−0.444	1.000	−0.680	−0.433	−0.574
Dem[−1]	0.023	0.880	−0.680	1.000	0.312	0.904
Trans[−1]	0.360	0.889	−0.433	0.312	1.000	0.497
Cab[−1]	0.901	0.810	−0.574	0.904	0.497	1.000

Table 7.4   *Correlation matrix: Spain*

	S/T	S/T[−1]	GDPc[−1]	Trans[−1]	Cab[−1]
S/T	1.000	0.876	0.223	0.390	−0.602
S/T[−1]	0.876	1.000	−0.444	0.889	0.810
GDPc[−1]	−0.491	−0.444	1.000	−0.433	−0.574
Trans[−1]	0.390	0.187	−0.240	1.000	0.976
Cab[−1]	−0.602	−0.488	−0.723	0.976	1.000

regimes were thoroughly adverse to major social reforms (Maravall, 1982; 1991; Guillen, 1991; Hoffmann, 1983). Until the 1970s, at least, neither regime was of the Bismarckian kind that willingly paid the social policy price for social peace. At best, they were indifferent to the 'social question'. This attitude did change towards the 1970s, but it is very difficult to ascertain whether the enhanced concern for social policy was due to economic buoyancy, the process of tentative political liberalization, the desire to join Europe, or simmering social unrest. Most likely, the truth lies in a combination of all these forces.

In both countries, democratization – be it by the left or not – heralded a noticeable shift towards social security; powerful and permanent in Portugal, modest and temporary in Spain. On balance we would have to conclude that those who remain faithful to the doctrines of nineteenth century anti-democratic thought would have little to fear from democratization in terms of radical redistribution. Even the revolutionary zeal of the leftist transition government in Portugal fell, in the end, victim to the median-voter constraint.

Appendix: Data Sources and Tables

The social expenditure data for both Spain and Portugal (Table 7.3 and 7.4) derive mainly from the United Nations *National Accounts* series, but with some adjustments in the case of Spain. First, the United Nations series for Spain is incomplete. To complete the series for the 1980s (1983–6), I have extrapolated using the SEEPROS (EEC-based definition of social expenditure) series for the 1980s as the baseline. For the years 1967–

9, the same procedure was followed using the ILO social expenditure data. Since the difference between the ILO and UN data on the one hand, and the ILO and the SEEPROS data on the other hand, is minuscule, this system of extrapolation approach seems justified. Total government (non-capital) expenditures are, for Portugal, taken from the United Nations *National Accounts*; for Spain, from Comin (1988b, p. 455). The Spanish social expenditure data were adjusted for unemployment benefit outlays and the 1967 budget consolidation with data from Banco de España, *Boletín Estadístico* (current issues).

Notes

I am grateful to Antonio Tena, Andres Pose and the participants of my European University Institute seminar for help and comments on this chapter.

1 Estimates based on Flora et al. (1983).

2 For the more advanced European countries, the main source is Flora et al. (1983). In addition, many nations have now compiled more or less complete compendiums of historical statistics, including the United States, Canada, Spain, Italy and the United Kingdom.

3 For a detailed discussion of how to classify budgetary outlays by their client-specific target, see Saunders and Klau (1985) or Lessmann (1987).

4 In this study we define the social wage as comprising social security transfers, social services and health services. We have chosen to exclude education since (a) it is not redistributive, and (b) its strongly human capital aspect implies that it may be more of a common collective good than in the interest of a particular social group or class.

5 The distinction proposed here is inspired by the analysis of Perez-Diaz (1990).

6 Both statistically and substantively the two alternative democratization variables have their own distinct logic. The democracy dummy separates the era of dictatorship from the era of democracy, suggesting that once democracy is installed the budget will be given a permanently new structure. Statistically, the democracy variable will identify the existence of a 'structural break' or parameter shift.

In contrast, the transition variable is motivated by the assumption that governments during the transition period will be particularly prone to change the budget structure, even in ways that are not sustainable in the long run. First, the period of transition is likely to unleash a chorus of previously repressed redistributive demands that, given the need for legitimacy, will be difficult to ignore. Secondly, the transition period is also a period in which the embryonic political parties will find it necessary to invest in their future electability, and we can safely assume that they will seek to profile themselves favourably with the low-income electorate. Transition cabinets are therefore likely to engage in a burst of social spending that, *à la* Mitterand, later might necessitate claw-backs. The transition variable, in other words, taps the possibility of temporary budgetary effect. It is certainly possible that both variables may operate additively.

7 As an alternative measure of the party power variable, I ran parallel models with a left-party share of seats in the legislature. The cabinet variable is preferred since it also captures the period prior to democratization.

8 The comparative GDP data for both Spain and Portugal derive from Carreras (1989).

9 During the 1950s, the Franco regime nourished the evolution of a double social policy: one part integrated in the public social security administration, the other semi-autonomous in mutual benefit societies. The two systems were merely combined in 1967, and we can therefore not speak of a real social expenditure jump (for a discussion see Tamames, 1982; Comin, 1988b; and Guillen, 1991). To remove this false spending jump from the United Nations expenditure series used in this study, the 1960–7 data have been adjusted with data from the Banco de España, *Boletín Estadístico*, current volumes.

10   This was in fact an implementation of the 1976 Constitution (Kohler, 1982, p. 242, note 160). For a detailed discussion of Portuguese social policy, see Hoffmann, (1983). This is also more or less the only available international study of the Portuguese case. See also, however, the briefer overview in Weber and Leienbach, (1989).

11   As noted earlier, this consolidation led to a dramatic jump in the expenditure series in 1967, thus requiring adjustments.

12   Moreno and Sarasa (1991) point out that in 1973 only 20 per cent of the registered unemployed actually collected benefits; as late as the early 1980s, the average pension was only 71 per cent of the official minimum wage.

13   The results of these many partial analyses are not shown for reasons of space.

References

Budge, I. and Keman, H. 1990. *Parties and Democracy*. Oxford: Oxford University Press.
Carreras, A. (ed.) 1989. *Estadísticas Históricas de España, Siglos XIX–XX*. Madrid: Fundación Banco Exterior.
Castles, F. 1982. *The Impact of Parties*. London: Sage.
Comin, F. 1988a. Reforma Tributaría y Política Fiscal. In J. Delgado (ed.), *España Economía*. Tomo II, Madrid: Espasa-Calpe.
Comin, F. 1988b. Las Administraciones Públicas. In J. Delgado (ed.), *España Economía*. Tomo II. Madrid: Espasa-Calpe.
Dawson, R. and Robinson, J. 1963. Inter-party Competition, Economic Variables and Welfare Policies in the American States. *Journal of Politics*, 25: 265–89.
Dich, J. 1973. *Den Herskende Klasse*. Copenhagen: Borgen.
Downs, A. 1957. *An Economic Theory of Democracy*. New York: Harper & Row.
Esping-Andersen, G. 1990. *The Three Worlds of Welfare Capitalism*. Cambridge: Polity Press.
Estevill, J. and Hoz, de la J. 1990. Transition and Crisis: The Complexity of Spanish Industrial Relations. In G. Baglioni and C. Crouch (eds), *European Industrial Relations*. London: Sage.
Flora, P. et al. 1983. *State, Economy and Society in Western Europe, 1815–1975*. Frankfurt: Campus.
Guillen, A.M. 1991. Social Policy in Spain from Dictatorship to Democracy, 1939–1982. Unpublished Paper, Instituto Juan Marsh.
Hoffmann, G. 1983. *Sozialpolitik in Portugal*. Frankfurt: Haag and Herchen Verlag.
ILO. 1974. *The Cost of Social Security*. Geneva: ILO.
ILO. 1983. *The Cost of Social Security*. Geneva: ILO.
Jackman, R. 1975. *Politics and Social Equality: A Comparative Analysis*. New York: Wiley.
Jackman, R. 1986. Elections and the Democratic Class Struggle. *World Politics*, 39: 123–46.
Kohler, B. 1982. *Political Forces in Spain, Greece and Portugal*. London: Butterworth.
Korpi, W. 1983. *The Democratic Class Struggle*. London: Routledge and Kegan Paul.
Lessmann, S. 1987. *Budgetary Politics and Elections: An Investigation of Public Expenditures in West Germany*. Berlin: de Gruyter.
Lindblom, C. 1959. The Science of Muddling Through. *Public Administration Review*, 19.
Lipset, S.M. 1960. *Political Man*. New York: Doubleday Anchor.
Maravall, J. 1982. *The Transition to Democracy in Spain*. London: Croom Helm.
Maravall, J. 1991. Economic Reforms in New Democracies: The Southern European Experience. Instituto Juan March Working Paper, June.
Merkel, W. 1989. Sozialdemokratische Politik in einer Post-Keynesianischen Ära? Das Beispiel der Sozialistischen Regierung Spaniens. *Politische Vierteljahresschrift*, 30: 629–54.
Moreno, L. and Sarasa, S. 1991. Catholicism and Socialism in the Development of the Spanish Welfare State. Paper Presented at the Workshop on Comparative Studies on Welfare State Development. Helsinki, 29 August.

Muller, F.G. and Zimmermann, K. 1986. The Determinants of Structural Changes in Public Budgets. *European Journal of Political Research*, 14: 481–98.

Pampel, F. and Williamson, J. 1989. *Age, Class, Politics and the Welfare State*. Cambridge: Cambridge University Press.

Paterson, W. and Thomas, A. (eds) 1986. *The Future of Social Democracy*. Oxford: Clarendon Press.

Peacock, A. and Wiseman, J. 1961. *The Growth of Public Expenditure in the United Kingdom*. London: Allen & Unwin.

Perez-Diaz, V. 1990. The Emergence of Democratic Spain and the 'Invention' of a Democratic Tradition. Instituto Juan March Working Paper, June.

Saunders, P. and Klau, F. 1985. *The Role of the Public Sector*. Paris: OECD Economic Studies, 4.

Stephens, J. 1979. *The Transition From Capitalism to Socialism*. London: Macmillan.

Tamames, R. 1982. *Introdución a la Economía Española*. Madrid: Alianza Editorial.

Tamames, R. 1986. *The Spanish Economy*. London: C. Hurst.

Tocqueville, A. de 1969. *Democracy in America* (1848). New York: Doubleday Anchor.

Viby-Mogensen, G. 1975. *Socialhistorie*. Copenhagen: Akademisk Forlag.

Weber, A. and Leienbach, V. 1989. *Soziale Sicherung in Europa*. Baden-Baden: Nomos Verlag.

Wildavsky, A. 1964. *The Politics of the Budgetary Process*. Boston: Little, Brown.

Wilensky, H. 1975. *The Welfare State and Equality*. Berkeley: University of California Press.

PART THREE

8

Cabinet Ministers and Parliamentary Government: a Research Agenda

Michael Laver and Kenneth A. Shepsle

Political parties link governments to elections. In fact, in parliamentary democracies, the political identity of the executive is typically defined by the partisan composition of the cabinet. This definition is used informally by lay commentators who talk of a 'Conservative government' in Britain, for example, when the Conservative party controls all cabinet portfolios, or of a *pentapartito* administration in Italy when portfolios are shared by a particular coalition of five parties. The high priests of political science have adopted the same usage. There is some debate within the profession over which particular events signal a change of governments. All authors agree however that a change in a party composition of the cabinet means that a new government has taken power. Beyond this the cabinet plays surprisingly little role in the main theoretical accounts of party competition and government formation in parliamentarian democracies. This is because very few of these theories have any real concern for what governments actually do after they have taken over the reins of power (as opposed to what they promise they will do).

Theoretical neglect of the cabinet is not confined to the literature on elections and party competition, however. While the cabinet as a political institution has been the subject of intensive study in its own right, relatively little theoretical attention has been paid by people working within this case-based 'cabinet studies' tradition to the role of the cabinet in the process of party competition. This is despite the fact that the political complexion of the cabinet is obviously the key output of any given cycle of the process of party competition, as well as being the key input to the next electoral cycle.

Thus relatively little attempt has been made to analyse the political role of the cabinet in a more comprehensive theoretical framework. This neglect is in many ways quite remarkable. The legislative investiture of a cabinet is the formal climax of the process of parliamentary democracy in many countries. The legislative defeat of the cabinet on a motion of no confidence is, similarly, a fundamental defining characteristic of parliamentary democracy. Any theoretical account of this must therefore incorporate some systematic method of forecasting what any proposed cabinet will do if invested, and what the incumbent cabinet will do if not defeated.

This chapter sets out to lay some of the groundwork for a theoretical account of the role of the cabinet in parliamentarian democracies. The first section briefly reviews the current theoretical state of play. The following section briefly summarizes a new theoretical approach to the politics of government formation, based on the notion that the policy outputs of any given government can be forecast once we know the identity of the cabinet ministers with jurisdiction over key policy portfolios. Three further sections elaborate a range of theoretical and empirical issues that must be resolved before such an approach can be developed comprehensively. These matters have to do with legislative–executive relations, with the autonomy of individual cabinet ministers and with collective cabinet decision-making. The final section presents our conclusions.

The Role of the Cabinet in Theories of Party Competition and Government Formation

Rational choice theories of elections and party competition developed in the Downsian tradition assume that politicians maximize votes and/or pluralities, while voters try to improve the vote and/or seat shares of parties whose professed policies are closest to their own. Those working within the more social-psychological approach of the Michigan school assume that people vote as an expressive act, with no real concern for the effective political consequences. Either way, there is very little to be found on the business of government formation in the literature on voting and party competition, with a couple of recent and honourable exceptions (Austen-Smith and Banks, 1988; Schofield, 1993). Thus there is almost no concern among party competition theorists for what a government might actually be and what it might actually do. Consequently there is almost no concern for the political role of the cabinet.

Theories of government formation, on the other hand, treat the cabinet in surprisingly different ways. Early approaches, working on the basis of some form of minimum size principle, suggested that the cabinet would be as 'small' as possible while still controlling a legislative majority (Gamson, 1961; Leiserson, 1966; Riker, 1962). These approaches were based upon the assumption that control over government was some sort of fixed prize to be shared between those in power. The larger the number of actors who were involved in the government, the smaller the share of the prize available to each actor. The nature of this prize was often left rather vague but, when it was made explicit, it tended to be described in terms of a particular sack of political trophies, prominent among which were cabinet portfolios. Thus authors who analyse the 'payoffs' of coalition bargaining have often denominated these payoffs in terms of control over a fixed set of cabinet portfolios (Browne and Feste, 1975; Browne and Franklin, 1973; Browne and Frendreis, 1980; Budge and Keman, 1990). It has been shown that, because of their policy interests, different parties value the same portfolios in different ways, so that portfolio allocation becomes a variable-sum game (Browne and Feste, 1975; Budge and Keman, 1990). But 'payoff theorists' mostly treat cabinet membership as something to be consumed in and for itself. In effect, they treat the political game as ending, and the 'payoffs' as being distributed, at the moment when parties take control of cabinet portfolios. They do not consider at all what happens after this moment (an exception is Budge and Keman, 1990, Chapter 5).

Another group of theorists writing about the formation of coalition governments effectively ignore the cabinet altogether, concentrating instead upon the policy position of the government that takes office, however this government might be construed (de Swaan, 1973; McKelvey and Schofield, 1986; 1987; McKelvey, 1979; Schofield, 1983; 1993; Baron and Ferejohn, 1989; Baron, 1991). They too treat the political game as ending when the government is invested, assuming in effect that the incoming government takes office and immediately implements everything that it promised during the formation negotiations. In such models, indeed, the political identity of the cabinet is quite irrelevant. The equilibrium processes that are described are assumed to generate the same government policy output, whoever is in the cabinet.

Notwithstanding this long-term theoretical neglect, some recent developments in the theory of government formation have placed a heavy emphasis on the political role of cabinet ministers, and in particular on the level of autonomy enjoyed by ministers over policy outputs within their jurisdiction (Austen-Smith and Banks, 1990; Laver and Shepsle, 1990a; 1990b; 1991). This new approach puts the cabinet at centre stage, and is grounded on the assumption that control over government policy is to a large extent exercised by cabinet ministers in their role as the heads of major government departments. These cabinet ministers have both the ability and the incentive to affect policy output in areas under their jurisdiction. Thus, the effective policy of any government depends upon the allocation of cabinet portfolios between politicians. Knowing the policy preferences of cabinet ministers, and the process of interaction among them, it is possible to forecast the policy outputs that will emerge from a particular cabinet once it has taken office. Knowing these, in turn, it is possible to assess the political implications of having one government take office rather than another, and thereby to make strategic calculations about party competition and government formation.

For these reasons, we regard what we call the 'portfolio allocation' approach to government formation as a more realistic theoretical account of the role of cabinet ministers in parliamentary democracy. However, this approach forces us to consider a range of issues that have hitherto been ignored by those concerned with government formation. Before we can develop the portfolio allocation approach into a comprehensive model of cabinet politics, therefore, we need to make realistic assumptions about a number of matters. The main body of this chapter reviews, and discusses the theoretical implications of, these alternative assumptions.

The Political Role of Cabinet Ministers: an Overview

From our perspective, the most important aspects of the role of cabinet ministers have to do with the extent to which individual ministers can affect government policy outputs in areas under their political and administrative jurisdiction. If a cabinet minister has at least some autonomy to determine policy outputs within the jurisdiction of his or her portfolio, then ministers who differ in their policy preferences may make different decisions when occupying the same portfolio. If ministers behave in predictable ways, that is, bring commonly known reputational baggage to their jobs, then we can forecast the consequences of allocating a given portfolio to a given minister. This in turn means that those involved in government formation negotiations do not need to rely upon 'mere' promises about future government policy. Policy proposals can be underwritten by making an appropriate ministerial nomination. Thus a hard-line defence policy can credibly be underwritten by nominating a well-known hawk as defence minister. Professing a hard-line defence policy while nominating a dove as defence minister is far less credible. The appropriate ministerial nomination makes a policy promise more credible, precisely because the minister has some autonomy within his or her jurisdiction. If the minister had no autonomy, it would make no difference at all who was nominated to any given portfolio.

A second effect of the assumption of ministerial autonomy is that, since there is a finite number of possible portfolio allocations between senior party politicians, there is a finite number of possible cabinets, each associated with a particular policy forecast. This means that negotiations over government formation and maintenance deal only with a finite set of alternatives. A consequence of this is that we can forecast equilibrium governments in many circumstances in which alternative approaches, implausibly in our view, forecast chaos (Laver and Shepsle, 1990a; 1990b; 1991). Overall, then, the assumption that cabinet ministers can act autonomously within their respective jurisdictions gives us considerable theoretical leverage over the process of government formation and maintenance.

The notion of individual ministerial autonomy must obviously be set in the context of ministerial relations with the legislature, with the cabinet as a collectivity and with the civil service. Obviously, if the cabinet has no freedom of action against policy decisions taken by the legislature, then the notion of individual ministerial autonomy means little. Even if the cabinet totally dominates the legislature, however, individual ministers may have little autonomy if the scope of collective cabinet decision-making is very wide and if collective cabinet decisions can be enforced at the departmental level. Thus the balance between individual ministerial autonomy and collective cabinet decision-making in any given country is crucial to our ability to forecast government outputs in a particular policy area from the preferences of the cabinet minister with jurisdiction over it. Even if the executive is strong while the collective authority of the cabinet is weak, individual ministers may have little autonomy if the real seat of power lies in the professional civil service. If the civil service dominates government decision-making, then once more it will make little difference which senior politician is nominated to which particular portfolio. In what follows, we explore some of the implications of relations between cabinet and legislature and between individual minister and the cabinet as a collectivity, leaving for later work the relationship between ministers and the permanent civil service.

The Role of the Cabinet in Legislative–Executive Relations

Bagehot's seminal statement of the doctrine of cabinet government, originally published in 1867, is worth stating at some length:

> The efficient secret of the English Constitution may be described as the close union, the nearly complete fusion, of the executive and legislative powers. No doubt by the traditional theory, as it exists in all the books, the goodness of our constitution consists in the entire separation of the legislative and executive authorities, but in truth its merit consists in their singular approximation. The connecting link is *the Cabinet*. By that new word we mean a committee of the legislative body selected to be the executive body . . . The legislature chosen, in name, to make laws, in fact finds its principal business in making and in keeping an executive . . . The Cabinet, in a word, is a board of control chosen by the legislature, out of persons whom it trusts and knows, to rule the nation. (Bagehot, 1963, pp. 66–7: emphasis in original)

Bagehot was writing about nineteenth century Britain, and important details obviously change with shifts in place and time. Nonetheless, we take his general definition of cabinet government to remain in force today for most if not all of the Western European parliamentary democracies with which we are concerned.

The essential feature of Western European parliamentary democracy is that the executive both is responsible to, and can be dismissed by, the legislature. At the same time, the executive can typically dissolve the legislature should it want to do so. The result of all this is that changes in the balance of forces in the legislature, such as those brought about by elections whether these are actual or anticipated, change the balance of forces that sustain the executive in office. In this way voters, through their chosen representatives, have an impact on government.

This intimate interaction between legislature and executive highlights a number of important matters upon which we require more information if we are to build a workable model of the process of cabinet government. Here we elaborate upon three questions to which we need systematic answers:

1 What are the procedures for proposing and voting upon motions of confidence and no confidence in the government? Can the government control these procedures? Can any legislative actor propose such a motion at will?
2 Can the legislature unilaterally impose policy decisions upon an unwilling cabinet? Can it unilaterally impose decisions upon an individual unwilling cabinet minister?
3 To what extent does the cabinet control the substantive legislative agenda?

Procedure on Confidence Motions

The fundamental basis of Western European parliamentary democracy is that the executive must retain the support of the legislature. 'The executive' is almost invariably operationalized in particular constitutions as the set of cabinet ministers chaired by a prime minister. 'The support of the legislature' is almost invariably operationalized in terms of votes of confidence and no confidence and also, in some countries, in terms of votes of investiture. Governments may choose to resign for all sorts of reasons, of course, including losing votes on particular pieces of legislation. But they are constitutionally obliged to resign if they lose a legislative motion of confidence or no confidence.

An analysis of the procedures for getting a vote of no confidence on to the legislative agenda is therefore a neglected but vital part of the mechanics of parliamentary democracy. Obviously, such a motion cannot be debated while the parliament is not in session. (Thus, in most Western European countries, parliamentary democracy is effectively suspended when the legislature is not in session, notably during the long summer recess.) Even while parliament is in session, however, it may be more, or less, difficult for different actors to get a motion of no confidence on to the legislative agenda. If the incumbent government can use its agenda power to block or delay such a motion, then it can effectively prolong its own life. On the other hand, if every legislative actor can costlessly propose such a motion at every possible opportunity, then parliament will effectively sit in a permanent debate on the future of the government.

The situation in most countries doubtless lies somewhere between these extremes, with most governments having some worthwhile power over the legislative agenda which they can use to protect their position, yet most being susceptible sooner or later to the wrath of the legislature. In the same way, most opponents presumably face some costs if they choose to devote their legislative energies to the continuous proposing of votes of no confidence. In most countries, furthermore, there are procedural constraints on the frequency with which such votes can be proposed. All of this means that, in any one legislative session, only a limited number of attempts can be made to unseat the government with a vote of no confidence. Thus, before we can model the processes of cabinet government in any particular parliamentary democracy, we need to set out carefully the rules of procedure that govern the treatment of motions of confidence and no confidence in the incumbent administration. The Laver-Shepsle model assumes that opposition parties do not find it difficult or costly to propose motions of no confidence. The more difficult and/or costly it is to propose such motions, the more likely it is that a particular government can remain in office after some change in the strategic environment that would otherwise cause it to fall. And the more likely it is that others can anticipate, in advance of investiture, the difficulty of ridding themselves of an unwanted incumbent government.

Legislative Control of the Cabinet

Notwithstanding Bagehot's comment, cited above, that the legislature's 'principal business' is 'in making and in keeping an executive', most legislatures do also legislate. Obviously, if every detail of public policy were to be settled by parliamentary legislation, then the role of the cabinet would be limited to the mechanical oversight of policy implementation. In the extreme, the partisan composition of the cabinet would be irrelevant, since substantive policy outputs would be determined by the balance of partisan forces in the legislature. (As we indicated earlier, certain models of government formation do implicitly make this assumption.) At the opposite extreme, a legislature might have almost no power to set *de facto* policy. This might result from permissive conventions about the scope for ministerial interpretation in the implementation of legislation, conventions that presumably would need to be supported by the system of administrative law if the minister were not continually to be brought to book. It might also result from tight government control over the legislative agenda, a matter to which we return below.

What is clear is that, before we can model the political role of the cabinet in any given country, we need to know the extent to which cabinet ministers are constrained by the legislature in their ability to set policy. The key question here concerns whether it is possible to enact legislation in a particular policy area that binds either the cabinet as a whole or the relevant minister, in the face of active opposition from either the cabinet or the minister concerned. If it is possible for the legislature to do this, then the legislature can allow a particular minister to occupy a particular portfolio in the knowledge that this person can be directly constrained should the need arise. In this event, the minister is not autonomous. If, on the other hand, the legislature cannot realistically expect to bind a minister in this way, then the minister can be taken as autonomous within his or her jurisdiction, at least as far as relations with the legislature are concerned.

The Laver-Shepsle model assumes that cabinet ministers can indeed act autonomously within their policy jurisdiction as far as the legislature is concerned and that, following Bagehot, the main political job of the legislature is making and keeping an executive. In contrast, the greater the ability of the legislature to constrain cabinet ministers, either individually or collectively, the less salient politically is the actual partisan composition of any given cabinet.

Cabinet Control of the Legislature

Intimately related to the matter of legislative control of the cabinet is the matter of cabinet control of the legislature. One of the most striking manifestations of such control is the constitutional power, wielded by most governments, either to dissolve the legislature directly or to recommend a dissolution to a head of state who is almost certain to comply. This power effectively enables governments to get rid of legislatures and call elections at will. (Norway is the only serious exception to this rule among Western European parliamentary democracies; Norwegian elections take place according to an immutable four-year cycle.)

The power of the incumbent government to call an election at will allows it to threaten to impose the costs of an election on its opponents. It also gives a vital role to opinion polls, both published and private, since the government is continually provided by such polls with an estimate of the distribution of weights in the legislature that will result from an immediate election. This means that the government can calculate its strategies either on the basis of actual legislative weights as they currently exist, or on the basis of the weights that are forecast to result from an election, whichever weights are the more favourable. Each of these factors means that the executive's power to dissolve the legislature loads the relationship between legislature and executive in favour of the executive. A popular government can always call an election and improve its legislative position. An unpopular government can remain in office, no matter what the opinion polls say, provided it does not lose its current legislative majority.

The second important element of cabinet control over the legislature has to do with the process of legislation itself. If the government has a tight grip on the parliamentary timetable and a near-monopoly of both the information and the drafting skills needed to prepare legislation, then it may be very difficult for opposition parties to get significant draft statutes on to the legislative agenda. In such situations, incumbent governments may effectively legislate at will, constrained only by their need to retain the confidence of a majority of the legislature. In this event, cabinet ministers are autonomous, subject only to the sanction that they cannot implement policies that provide the legislature with the incentive to defeat the government as a whole.

The Laver-Shepsle model assumes that cabinet control over the legislature is sufficient to ensure that the only really effective way in which the legislature can affect government policy outputs is related to the threat to defeat the government in a vote of confidence. The more that the legislature can set policy directly, the less salient is the partisan composition of the cabinet.

The Autonomy of Individual Cabinet Ministers

Even if cabinet ministers are not much constrained by the legislature, they may still be constrained by collective cabinet decisions. An individual cabinet minister is not only a member of the cabinet, however; he or she is also typically the head of a major government department, charged with both formulating and implementing policy within a particular jurisdiction.

There is intense pressure of work on an individual cabinet minister, who is after all the person with overall responsibility for government policy in a particular area. Within each government department, the minister is able to draw upon a considerable pool of specialist expertise, oriented towards the policy area in question. Given the pressure of work and the lack of access to specialist expertise in other departments, it seems unlikely that many cabinet ministers will be able successfully to poke their noses very deeply into the jurisdictions of their cabinet colleagues. This gives each minister the ability to act in his or her own department independently of other members of the cabinet. Since individual ministers will each have a private agenda, each also has the incentive to act autonomously. There is thus a potential tension between the collective decisions of the cabinet and the individual decisions of its members. Our model of cabinet decision-making must take account of this. Once more, important questions require systematic answers:

4   In what circumstances, both in theory and in practice, can cabinet ministers make decisions within their jurisdiction independently of the collective views of the cabinet? In what circumstances must they seek cabinet approval for such decisions?
5   Can ministers ignore collective cabinet decisions without other cabinet members realizing this? What happens when ministers publicly defy such decisions?

Each of these questions relates to the ability of an individual cabinet minister to go against the collective wishes of his or her cabinet colleagues. Our model of cabinet decision-making will be very different, depending upon whether we assume that cabinet ministers have scope in their own departments to act autonomously of the cabinet as a whole, or whether we assume that ministers must obey collective cabinet decisions relating to their own departments, even when they disagree with these.

If we assume that ministers are always bound by the collective decisions of the cabinet, then we must model this collective decision-making process before we can forecast government policy outputs. If we further assume that there is a diversity of preferences both within and between government parties, we could locate cabinet members within a continuous policy space. Some decision rule would select an outcome from that space. The cabinet, in effect, can be treated as a microcosm of the legislature as a whole, though we are not aware of any author who has developed a fully elaborated model of cabinet decision-making in these terms. The problems facing such a model would be the same as the problems facing models of government formation in continuous legislative policy spaces. If cabinet decisions are taken by majority vote and there are two or more salient policy dimensions, for example, then such a model would predict that there is no equilibrium government policy, since any policy that might be selected would be such that there is some alternative policy that is preferred by a decisive coalition of cabinet members. The model would predict decision-making chaos within the cabinet as a direct analogue of decision-making chaos within the legislature.

An alternative assumption about cabinet decision-making is that, regardless of what is formally decided at cabinet meetings, it is possible to forecast government policy in a given area from the identity of the cabinet minister with jurisdiction over this area. The most extreme version of this assumption is that ministers are policy dictators in their own jurisdictions, but it is not necessary to go this far. It is simply necessary to assume, taking account of constraints such as the power of the civil service and existing contractual obligations, that having a particular politician in charge of a particular ministry has particular consequences that can be forecast, and that having a minister with different preferences in charge of the same ministry is forecast to have different consequences.[1]

The assumption that we can forecast the effect of putting a particular senior politician in charge of a particular cabinet portfolio has powerful theoretical consequences. Perhaps most important of these is that government policy programmes are underwritten by nominating appropriate politicians to the portfolios concerned and are in this way largely self-policing. As we indicated above, policy packages underwritten in this way do not need to rely for their credibility upon assertion and bluster, upon mere words. Rather, they rely upon giving *de facto* power over a particular salient policy dimension to a politician whose preference is to carry out the programme in question on this dimension.

Another striking consequence of the assumption of ministerial autonomy, as Laver and Shepsle (1990a; 1990b; 1991) have shown, is that a model can be developed that predicts equilibrium governments in a wide range of circumstances and when any number of policy dimensions are salient. (Traditional spatial models predict chaos whenever two or more dimensions are salient.) One of the reasons for this is that the autonomy of cabinet ministers within policy jurisdictions gives a structure to bargaining over government formation that is equivalent to the structure provided by US congressional committees to bargaining over legislation (Shepsle, 1979). Another reason is that there is a finite number of possible governments, because there is only a finite number of ways to allocate a fixed set of portfolios to a fixed set of politicians. This number may be dramatically reduced, furthermore, by considering only the most import-ant cabinet portfolios as being critical, and by considering their allocation only to a cadre of senior politicians.

A further consequence of the assumption of ministerial autonomy is that, for cabinets with the same party composition, different allocations of portfolios between the same set of politicians have different consequences for government policy. Indeed, the allocation of a set of portfolios between a particular group of senior politicians becomes one of the most critical features of the entire government formation process, since each different allocation underwrites a different forecast of government policy. To return to Bagehot:

> The leading Minister . . . has to choose his associates, but he only chooses among a charmed circle. The position of most men in Parliament forbids their being invited to the Cabinet; the position of a few men ensures their being invited. Between the compulsory list whom he must take, and the impossible list whom he cannot take, a Prime Minister's independent choice in the formation of a cabinet is not very large; it extends rather to the division of the Cabinet offices than to the choice of Cabinet Ministers. (Bagehot, 1963, p. 67)

Thus we might see the real business of cabinet formation as being the allocation of a limited number of key portfolios among a small set of 'cabinet-rank' politicians. The ability of each cabinet minister to take independent action within his or her own bailiwick means that each different allocation of cabinet portfolios generates a discrete and credible statement of government policy.

Figure 8.1, for example, describes the forecast policy outputs that result from nominating any one of a charmed circle of six senior politicians to one of two key cabinet portfolios, finance and foreign affairs. There are three parties, A, B and C, and two senior politicians in each party, A_1, A_2, B_1, B_2, and C_1, C_2. There are 36 possible allocations of two portfolios between six politicians, each described as a point on the 'lattice' in Figure 8.1. Thus, if A_1 takes the finance portfolio and B_1 takes foreign affairs, then the forecast government policy output is A_1B_1. If B_1 takes finance and A_1 takes foreign affairs, then the forecast output is quite different, at B_1A_1. This means that parties A and B can find eight different ways to allocate the two portfolios between them (A_1B_1, A_1B_2, A_2B_1, A_2B_2, B_1A_1, B_1A_2,

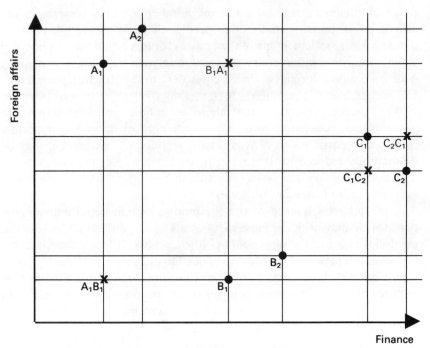

Figure 8.1   *Credible cabinet policies in a three-party system*

B_2A_1, B_2A_2). Only these eight points are credible policy outcomes of a coalition between A and B; other policy packages can of course be promised, but they are not credible.

Another important implication of the assumption of ministerial autonomy relates to party policy. If a party spokesperson is taken as being the person held out by the party as its proposed cabinet minister in the jurisdiction concerned (and note that any other assumption implies that some other person is held out as its proposed minister) then party policy in a given area is, in effect, the policy associated with its spokesperson in that area. This means that, if a party wishes to change its policy, it must change its spokesperson – something that highlights the interaction between intraparty politics and the process of forming and maintaining a cabinet (Laver and Shepsle, 1990b). Thus, in Figure 8.1, if C_1 is the party C spokesperson on finance and C_2 the party spokesperson on foreign affairs, then party policy is effectively at C_1C_2. The party's position can be moved to C_2C_1 by switching the responsibilities of the two spokespersons.

Overall, then, we can make considerable progress in developing a model of cabinet government by making an assumption that each senior politician is associated with a forecast of what government policy would be on a particular dimension if he or she were to become the relevant minister. It is important to stress once more that this does not amount to an assumption that ministers are dictators within their own jurisdictions. Rather it is an assumption that the policy effects of appointing a particular politician to a particular ministry are predictable.

Collective Cabinet Decision-Making

The notion of individual ministerial autonomy stands in contrast to the notion of collective cabinet decision-making, though not necessarily to the notion of collective cabinet responsibility. Ministers may bear collective responsibility for a set of decisions, each of which is taken by an individual minister within his or her own jurisdiction. Indeed this will inevitably be the case for many decisions relating to policy implementation. Nonetheless, the notion of collective cabinet responsibility is often taken to imply *de facto* collective decision-making by the cabinet on at least some issues. This, if it is to mean anything, carries the further implication that cabinet ministers who lose their case in cabinet can thereafter be forced in their own departments to implement policies that they personally oppose.

In certain circumstances, collective cabinet decision-making is inevitable. Most obviously, if different government departments come into direct conflict with one another, then it will not be possible for each of the ministers concerned to act autonomously, and such conflicts must be resolved if deadlock is not to result. In addition, certain policy problems, for example urban regeneration, will be intrinsically 'inter-departmental' in character and will require coordinated policy-making and implementation. Last but not least, new issues will emerge that do not automatically fall within the jurisdiction of an existing portfolio. These must be disposed of somehow, either directly by the cabinet or indirectly by assigning the problem to the jurisdiction of some particular portfolio. Overall, therefore, if the cabinet as a collective entity did not exist, then someone would have to invent it.

All of this is easy to say, of course, but the hard question that remains to be answered concerns how cabinet decisions can be made to stick, if we take seriously the autonomy of individual ministers. While, as we have seen, government policy positions based upon the assumption of ministerial autonomy are credible because they are self-policing, collective cabinet decisions must depend upon some other enforcement mechanism. The nature of this mechanism is an important empirical matter. Before we can make any progress towards understanding it, however, a series of questions need to be addressed:

6 How is it determined which matters are decided by cabinet and which by individual ministers?
7 What is the decision rule for collective cabinet decision-making?
8 What mechanisms are available to reallocate policy areas between departmental jurisdictions?
9 In the event of a ministerial resignation, how is the relevant portfolio

reallocated? How, in general, are ministers replaced and portfolios 'reshuffled'?

These questions address three basic issues concerning the decision-making regime of the cabinet. The first is the locus of the power to set the cabinet agenda; the second is the decision rule itself; the third is the locus of control over the structural and partisan composition of the cabinet.

Power to Set the Cabinet Agenda

Obviously, a crucial feature of decision-making within any cabinet concerns who sets the political agenda. In particular, this centres upon who determines what, on the one hand, is to be discussed and decided in full cabinet, as opposed to what, on the other hand, is to be decided within individual ministries. On the face of it, this power over the cabinet agenda appears to be a very important role for the prime minister (PM), but we obviously need much more systematic evidence on this. If it is possible to forecast the outcome of a particular decision when this is taken by the full cabinet, and to compare this with the forecast outcome when it is taken within the department controlled by a particular minister, then obviously the power to determine who takes any given decision is a power well worth having.

At the same time as the PM is setting the cabinet agenda, however, we must not forget that members of the cabinet may well have some considerable say in the political future of the PM. Prime ministers are not dictators, notwithstanding a formal constitutional position in most countries that gives them a reasonably free rein to sack cabinet ministers at will. As Margaret Thatcher found to her cost, the internal structures of most political parties are such that even strong prime ministers can be forced unceremoniously out of office as a result of losing the support of senior party figures. The extent to which any PM can successfully manipulate the political agenda to generate outcomes that are opposed by cabinet colleagues is therefore an interesting empirical matter. In the extreme, any PM can be defeated by a disciplined cabinet revolt that forces a legislative vote of no confidence in the PM and immediately offers an agreed alternative administration. This bottom line possibility will of course be anticipated by seasoned politicians who will not press matters to their bitter end. The full-dress constitutional procedure will rarely, therefore, be needed. The very fact that it is available, of course, means that there is a major constraint upon the agenda power of the PM.

In its most dramatic form, power over the cabinet agenda includes the power to organize the allocation of responsibilities between government departments, and to enforce comprehensive administrative reorganizations from time to time. If we wish to generate a completely general model of cabinet decision-making, therefore, we should not take any particular administrative structure, together with its associated allocation of policy dimensions to particular portfolios, as being 'given'. We should rather see the allocation of policy dimensions to portfolios as the output of a complex political process. Indeed it is possible to apply the portfolio allocation model to this process. Forecasts can be made of policy outcomes under every possible allocation of policy dimensions to portfolio jurisdictions. The choice facing the legislature when deciding upon a government can be seen, not just as the allocation of portfolios, but as the choice of a particular jurisdictional structure, combined with an allocation of portfolios to senior politicians. Those forming a new cabinet can in principle decide to reorganize the entire structure of government departments as a part of the deals that they make between themselves. However, it probably makes sense to defer systematic consideration of this more complex possibility until a more fully developed model of cabinet decision-making is available.

The Cabinet Decision Rule

The ability to forecast the outcome of collective cabinet decisions obviously depends upon knowing the decision rule that the cabinet uses. If cabinet decisions are taken by simple majority vote, for example, then the cabinet is in effect a second-order legislature. This would have a number of consequences, including making the smaller partner in a two-party coalition very weak, leaving it with no more than the ultimate threat to resign and bring down the entire government. For coalitions of three or more parties, a simple majority decision rule would set up a second-order coalition game within the cabinet.

Insider accounts of cabinet decision-making rarely discuss in these terms, however, tending to portray such decisions as a more complex interaction between a number of criteria, including weighted majorities (some ministers being more powerful than others), partial vetoes and many more things besides. Obviously, modelling such a decision rule in its full glory presents an almost impossible task. The empirical question that remains, therefore, is whether there are two or three features of the *de facto* cabinet decision rule that are sufficiently important and general that we can use them as sensible approximations of what is going on.

Control over the Structural and Partisan Composition of the Cabinet

A key element of control over the composition of the cabinet is in the hands of each individual cabinet minister and derives from the ability of cabinet ministers to resign, either individually or *en masse*. Just as no politician can be forced into the cabinet against his or her will, none who is determined to leave can be forced to stay in it. An individual resignation may impose two types of cost on the cabinet. First, the individual concerned may have a reputation that is needed by the cabinet in order to underwrite a particular policy position. The departure of a hard-line monetarist finance minister, for example, may generate an unwanted signal about the government's monetary policy if markets assume that the resignation implies that this is being relaxed. The knowledge of this gives the finance minister some bargaining leverage, since other ministers may make concessions rather than see him or her resign. Each senior politician has a policy reputation that is a valuable part of his or her stock in trade. Each minister has been brought into the cabinet, in terms of this reputation, as an optimum choice to underwrite some policy position. His or her voluntary departure is therefore bound to result in a suboptimum choice of minister for the same portfolio, and thereby generate costs. These costs may be particularly evident if the resignation of an individual minister destabilizes an equilibrium policy position.

A second set of costs is less tangible. If a ministerial resignation is seen by the outside world as a sign of cabinet disunity, then people may revise their assumptions about the stability of the government. This increased uncertainty may be damaging to the incumbent administration. Individuals, therefore, can impose costs upon the cabinet by resigning, and this gives them some bargaining power at the cabinet table. Different individuals may be able to impose different levels of cost, and thereby have different levels of bargaining power.

One of the key questions that arises from any ministerial resignation, of course, concerns the reallocation of the portfolio concerned. (Note that it is the need to reallocate the portfolio concerned that makes such a resignation potentially disruptive.) As we have seen, the portfolio allocation that characterizes any government is perhaps the single most important element of the government formation process. In a real even if not in a *de jure* sense, therefore, a government must be formed again after every ministerial resignation. In particular, if the minister who resigned had been holding one of the top portfolios, it may not be possible to find someone from outside the cabinet with a reputation sufficient to fill the vacant position. Rather it may be necessary to promote an existing cabinet member, which might set off a chain reaction of appointments and promotions that could amount to a full cabinet reshuffle (see below). Particularly within coalition cabinets, therefore, the procedure by which cabinet vacancies are filled is a vital empirical matter.

Resignation *en masse* from the cabinet by all members of a particular party is a different kettle of fish entirely in the minds of most observers, since it effectively signals the end of the incumbent administration. It is difficult to see how ministers could expect to have more, rather than less, influence on government decisions after having resigned from the cabinet. Thus the reasons for such resignations must have to do with more than the short-term content of government policy outputs. One plausible reason has to do with the next election. Parties may resign from government because they feel that this is to their subsequent electoral advantage. Before we can take this much further, however, we need to be able to specify what happens to the government when a party resigns from a cabinet.

There are two basic possibilities. If the party concerned holds the prime ministership then, on almost any *de jure* or *de facto* definition, the government is at an end. Since the country cannot be left without a government for any period of time, even if only to sign the cheques, a caretaker administration will take over. This may even be led by the outgoing prime minister, and will typically operate under strict constitutional conventions that constrain its freedom of action. Unfortunately, since almost nothing has been written about caretaker governments, there is little comparative information about how these constraints operate in practice. On the face of things we can assume that such constraints preclude a caretaker government from initiating new policy or taking any controversial policy decision, but this is obviously an important matter for systematic comparative research.

If the party that is resigning from the cabinet does not hold the prime ministership then, at least in a *de jure* sense, it may be possible for the party to pull out without bringing the government down about its ears. Such a resignation is nonetheless always an extremely destabilizing political event. We argued above that the reallocation of a single portfolio after even an isolated resignation amounts to a *de facto* reconstitution of the government. Obviously, after the resignation of a group of ministers belonging to a single party, such a reallocation will be a far more serious matter. The key empirical question concerns how their portfolios are redistributed.

Despite the fact that an actual resignation from the cabinet imposes costs on the government, it seems unlikely that this is enough in itself to explain the logic of resignation from the point of view of the actor resigning. A party might resign from the cabinet, having threatened to do so if certain demands were not met, so that threats to resign from future cabinets of which it was a part would be taken more seriously, but somehow this seems rather unrealistic. It seems more plausible to argue that parties see something more substantial to be gained from resigning in certain circumstances, and the most likely reason for this has to do with the expectation of subsequent electoral benefits.

If parties fight elections on the basis of policy promises to voters, and if they then go into governments that enact policies which differ from those promised, they may fear a loss of credibility among voters at subsequent elections. Another interesting empirical question to which we have no systematic answers thus has to do with whether voters discount the credibility of coalition members in relation to the whole of government policy, or whether they discount the credibility of parties in relation only to promises broken in the areas over which they had ministerial control. On the former assumption, a point may well come at which the short-term benefits of staying in a particular government are outweighed by the longer-term electoral costs. (Though once more this process has not, to our knowledge, been systematically modelled.) At this point, it may become rational for the party to resign with an eye to the next election.

A further feature of the decision-making regime within cabinets has to do with the power of the PM to sack ministers and reshuffle portfolio

Table 8.1 *Frequency of cabinet reshuffles*[1]

Netherlands	2.33
Iceland	2.40
Spain	2.40
Israel	2.63
Malta	3.86
Finland	3.93
Austria	4.00
Italy	4.00
Germany	4.11
Ireland	4.41
France	4.50
Norway	4.50
Belgium	4.60
Denmark	5.00
Sweden	5.11
New Zealand	5.46
Canada	5.63
Australia	5.76
Portugal	5.86
USA	5.90
Japan	6.00
Britain	6.33
Greece	8.40

[1] 1 = low, 9 = high.
Source: Unpublished data from expert survey reported in Laver and Hunt (1992)

allocations during the life of an administration. As we have already indicated on a number of occasions, any reallocation of portfolios – whether as a result of a resignation, a sacking or a reshuffle – amounts *de facto* to a new government formation. The formal position under most constitutions gives the PM quite swingeing powers in this regard, but in practice reshuffles are likely to be destabilizing events in coalition systems, changing the equilibrium portfolio allocations that had underpinned the incumbent administration at the time of its formation. This is much less significant for one-party majority cabinets (Budge, 1985). Provided that firm party discipline prevents the government from behaving as a coalition of factions, the portfolio allocation approach suggests that precise allocation of cabinet portfolios in a one-party majority cabinet is not critical.

Table 8.1 shows expert judgements on the frequency of cabinet reshuffles in a range of different democratic systems. It is quite striking that the countries with the highest estimated frequency of reshuffles tend to be those in which one-party majority government is the norm and the precise allocation of cabinet portfolios is less critical to the stability of the government. In countries in which coalition governments are the norm and the allocation of portfolios is much more critical to government stability, cabinet reshuffles seem to be far less common. In short, both the portfolio allocation approach and the available evidence seem to suggest that the *de jure* power of the PM over the fate of individual cabinet ministers, in relation to both sackings and reshuffles, will be severely constrained by *de facto* politics in coalition cabinets.

Conclusions

The research agenda in this chapter, and any attempt to address it, must balance two forces that pull our attempt to understand the cabinet in opposite directions. One force impels us in the direction of simple, elegant and parsimonious theory. Despite the obvious advantages of this route, we run the risk if we take it of ignoring too much substantive detail generating an account that is simplistic, trivial and lacking in substance. The other force impels us in the direction of complex, subtle and detailed case studies. Despite an understandable reluctance to suppress any of the magnificent subtleties of the real political world, the price we risk paying if we go the route of 'thick description' is that we will not be able to see the wood for the trees. Swamped in detail, our general appreciation of the essential processes at work will be diminished.

In our view, most existing theoretical accounts of government formation have suppressed too much important institutional detail. At the same time, most work in the case-based 'cabinet studies' tradition has suffered from a lack of theoretical sophistication.

We are acutely aware that it is far easier to criticize what others have done than it is to do things well ourselves. And we do not wish to produce yet another long list of tasks that functions as a substitute for actually doing anything at all. Rather, what we hope we have set out in this chapter is a realistic agenda for cooperation between those whose prime interest in the cabinet is theoretical and those whose prime concern is with elaborating particular cases.

The theoretical approach that has informed this chapter is based on the idea that institutional detail is important, that no simple theory of government formation and maintenance can be sensibly used by those with absolutely no knowledge of political institutions in the country being studied. What we are really arguing for, therefore, is a much closer cooperation between theorists and country specialists in the field of cabinet politics. The portfolio allocation approach is based on a serious attempt to address the well-founded concerns of country specialists that the earlier generation of coalition theory was in many ways sterile and, when the chips are down, no help in developing an understanding of cabinet politics in any particular country. The essential message in this chapter is that we believe there is now a generation of theories of government formation and maintenance that country specialists might want to pay attention to, if only to provide constructive criticism and productive suggestions for revision.

Our theoretical investigations have highlighted a range of important substantive matters, listed in the previous three sections, which we feel it would be useful to discuss from a comparative empirical perspective. At the same time, we are sufficiently enthused by what on the face of things seems to be the power and elegance of the portfolio allocation approach that we commend it to country specialists as an aid to the more systematic elaboration of the cases about which they have so much detailed knowledge. Just as theorists have opened themselves to the concerns of country specialists, we hope that country specialists will open themselves to the concerns of theorists.

Note

1   The most elaborate version of this type of assumption would be that government policy in a particular jurisdiction can be forecast only from the identity of the entire set of cabinet ministers – since interaction effects mean that a change in the minister for education may conceivably affect foreign policy, for example. We do not pursue this possibility, however, since the modelling exercise involved would be extremely complex.

References

Austen-Smith, David and Jeffrey Banks. 1988. Elections, Coalitions and Legislative Outcomes. *American Political Science Review*. 82, 405–22.
Austen-Smith, David and Jeffrey Banks. 1990. Stable Portfolio Allocations. *American Political Science Review*. 84(3), 891–906.
Bagehot, Walter. 1963. *The English Constitution*. London: Fontana.
Baron, David. 1991. A Spatial Bargaining Theory of Government Formation in Parliamentary Systems. *American Political Science Review*. 85, 137–65.
Baron, David and John Ferejohn. 1989. Bargaining in Legislatures. *American Political Science Review*. 83, 1181–206.
Browne, Eric and Karen Feste. 1975. Qualitative Dimensions of Coalition Payoffs: Evidence for European Party Governments 1945–70. *American Behavioural Scientist*. 18, 530–56.
Browne, Eric and Mark Franklin. 1973. Aspects of Coalition Payoffs in European Parliamentary Democracies. *American Political Science Review*. 67, 453–69.
Browne, Eric and John Frendreis. 1980. Allocating Coalition Payoffs by Conventional Norm: An Assessment of the Evidence for Cabinet Coalition Situations. *American Journal of Political Science*. 24, 753–68.
Budge, Ian. 1985. Party Factions and Government Reshuffles. *European Journal of Political Research*. 13, 327–34.
Budge, Ian and Hans Keman. 1990. *Parties and Democracy: Coalition Formation and Functioning in Twenty States*. Oxford: Oxford University Press.
de Swaan, Abram. 1973. *Coalition Theories and Cabinet Formation*. Amsterdam: Elsevier.
Gamson, William. 1961. A Theory of Coalition Formation. *American Sociological Review*. 26, 373–82.
Laver, Michael and W. Ben Hunt. 1992. *Policy and Party Competition*. New York: Routledge.
Laver, Michael and Kenneth Shepsle. 1990a. Coalitions and Cabinet Government. *American Political Science Review*. 84(3), 873–90.
Laver, Michael and Kenneth Shepsle. 1990b. Government Coalitions and Intraparty Politics. *British Journal of Political Science*. 20, 489–507.
Laver, Michael and Kenneth A. Shepsle. 1991. Divided Government: America is not 'Exceptional'. *Governance*. 4(3), 250–69.
Leiserson, Michael. 1966. *Coalitions in Politics*. PhD, Yale University.

McKelvey, Richard. 1979. General Conditions for Global Intransitivities in Formal Voting Models. *Econometrica*. 47, 1085–111.

McKelvey, Richard and Norman Schofield. 1986. Structural Instability of the Core. *Journal of Mathematical Economics*. 15, 179–98.

McKelvey, Richard and Norman Schofield. 1987. Generalised Symmetry Conditions at a Core Point. *Econometrica*. 55, 923–33.

Riker, William. 1962. *The Theory of Political Coalitions*. New Haven: Yale University Press.

Schofield, Norman. 1983. Generic Instability of Majority Rule. *Review of Economic Studies*. 50, 696–705.

Schofield, Norman. 1993. An Empirical Analysis of the Conditions for Stable Coalition Government. *European Journal for Political Research*.

Shepsle, Kenneth. 1979. Institutional Arrangements and Equilibrium in Multidimensional Voting Models. *American Journal of Political Science*. 23, 27–60.

9

'Chief Executives' in Western Europe

Anthony King

At some early stage in the history of the United States the American people got into the habit of referring to the president of the US as the nation's 'chief executive' or 'chief magistrate'. The syllogism was simple. The American government has three separate branches. One of them is the executive branch. Within the executive branch one person is in charge. The 'executive power' of the United States is vested by the constitution in that one person. Ergo, the president of the US is the 'chief executive' of the United States.

Europeans have a different conception. Europeans are less bound by the doctrine that governments should consist of three separate branches. The judiciary in all European countries stands at a distance from the other organs of government; but, unlike in America, the executive – or at least the executive's purely political component – is normally dependent on the legislature and its members are frequently drawn from the legislature. In addition, the executive in almost every European country consists not of one person but of several. European governments are managed by collectivities, usually called cabinets. As Jean Blondel has pointed out, the existence of these collective executives is one of the defining characteristics of European systems: 'a large number of rules and of modes of behaviour – of political understandings – are common to Western European countries while these rules, modes of behaviour and understandings do not apply to most other countries of the world' (Blondel and Müller-Rommel, 1988).

Nevertheless, despite their collective character, all systems of government in Europe recognize the special status of one individual who is, in some sense, 'the head of the government' and who normally, though not invariably, presides over cabinet meetings. In Austria and Germany this person is known as the chancellor, in Ireland as the *taoiseach*, in Spain as the *presidente del gobierno* and in Italy as the *presidente del consiglio*, but prime minister is the term used in most countries and is the generic term that will be used in this chapter. It is the prime minister who usually represents his or her country at summit meetings, and in many countries the prime minister gives his or her name to the government of the day – as in 'the Andreotti government' or 'the Thatcher government'.

Prime ministers might be expected to be rather important people. They are often in the public eye. They are usually mentioned and accorded a special status in their country's constitution. Yet oddly little is known about them. In most European countries there is no book – or often even a substantial learned-journal article – that describes their role; and genuinely comparative writings on prime ministers were, until quite recently, almost non-existent. The only volumes that describe the prime ministerial role in different countries in some detail, and also attempt a degree of comparative analysis, are *Presidents and Prime Ministers* (Rose and Suleiman, 1980), *Cabinets in Western Europe* (Blondel and Müller-Rommel, 1988) and *West European Prime Ministers* (Jones, 1991). These three volumes will be drawn on heavily (and at some points exclusively) in what follows.

Because the same or a similar term, prime minister, is used in so many different countries, there is a temptation to suppose that the persons known as prime ministers in different countries must have similar powers and play similar roles. Nothing, it turns out, could be further from the truth. If the prime ministers of different European countries were to devote one of their summit sessions to comparing notes on their different offices, they would probably get a considerable shock. A power that one prime minister takes for granted is beyond another's wildest dreams.

This chapter begins by offering a tentative rating of European prime ministers in terms of their ability to exert influence. It then goes on to focus on three possible determinants of prime ministerial influence that have tended to be neglected in the academic literature. The aim is not to be dogmatic. On the contrary, it is, as the English say, 'to push the boat out' – to see whether there are new lines of enquiry that might be worth pursuing. There is so much still to learn.

Prime Ministerial Influence

It goes without saying that some prime ministers are more influential than others within their own systems of government. In some European countries, the prime minister is the boss; ministers and civil servants defer to him, and he is expected to initiate policy and to reconcile disputes between ministers and departments on his own terms. In other countries, the prime minister is little more than a non-executive chairman or coordinator, someone who is seldom, if ever, looked to for leadership or policy initiatives. The key phrase is 'within their own systems of government'. Someone may be the prime minister of an important and influential country yet have relatively little clout within his own cabinet, bureaucracy and parliament. Equally, someone else may be the prime minister of a tiny and unimportant country yet be the dominant political figure within that country. In assessing prime ministerial influence, one needs to 'control for country' – to discount the fact that countries differ considerably in their international prestige, economic wealth and military power.

The point also needs to be made here that we are comparing prime ministerships, that is offices, rather than prime ministers, that is individual holders of those offices. It again hardly needs to be said that, within one country and one prime ministerial office, some men and women are going to be more influential than others. Personalities vary; so do circumstances. Large people can walk on small stages. But the history of Western Europe since the war suggests that Rose (1991) is right to emphasize the fact that, in terms of influence, the office usually matters far more than the holder: 'differences between national political institutions create more variation in the office of prime minister than do differences of personality and circumstances within a country.' In other words, it makes sense to compare Spain and Germany and not just González and Kohl.

On the basis of the existing literature (and a certain amount of personal observation and enquiry) it seems possible to divide European prime ministerships into three very rough categories – high (I), medium (II) and low (III) – based on assessments of the capacity of the prime minister within each country to influence events and developments within his or her potential sphere of influence. The categorization is admittedly unidimensional, but the single dimension is reasonably easy to interpret and speaks to something that politicians as well as political scientists can readily understand. The British prime minister would not want to change places with the Norwegian. There is an informal hierarchy of headships of government just as there is an informal hierarchy of ministries within governments. (The French and Finnish prime ministers have been omitted since they share power in somewhat idiosyncratic ways with the French and Finnish presidents.)

An obvious choice to represent the category I prime ministers is the Irish *taoiseach*. The *taoiseach* is the cock of the walk in Irish politics and within the Irish system of government. He coordinates the work of the government. He has extensive patronage powers. He is looked to for leadership. He is 'the figure to whom ministers naturally turn for advice and guidance' (Moynihan, 1960). Farrell (1988) is emphatic: 'It is the *taoiseach* who exercises ultimate authority. It is a function not merely of the office but of the multiplicity of roles thrust upon him – simultaneously chief executive, government chairman, party leader, national spokesman, principal legislator, electoral champion and media focus.' O'Leary (1991) goes even further: 'Within his own political system the Irish prime minister is potentially more powerful than any other European prime minister, with the [single] exception of his British counterpart.'

At the other end of the range, the Norwegian prime minister provides a vivid illustration of the category III head of government. He or she is less cock of the walk, more one of the farmyard chickens. The Norwegian cabinet is a highly collegial body which meets frequently and at length. Individual ministers have their own contacts and bases of support among interest groups and in the political party to which they belong, both in the country and in the Storting. The prime minister's influence in the cabinet scarcely exceeds that of his colleagues. As Eriksen (1988) points out:

> The [Norwegian] Prime Minister has few formal powers *vis-à-vis* his other colleagues. He or she can require any piece of information from colleagues, but

Table 9.1   *Prime ministers ranked according to their degree of influence within government*

High (I)	Medium (II)	Low (III)
Germany	Austria	Italy
UK	Belgium	Netherlands
Greece	Denmark	Norway
Ireland	Sweden	
Portugal		
Spain		

is not empowered to issue instructions. He or she cannot dissolve the Storting, call elections, establish or abolish ministries or reshuffle their jurisdictions. Like other ministers he or she is subject to the final, collective authority of the cabinet.

Olsen (1980) remarks somewhat ruefully that Norway's prime minister is a 'political organizer but no superstar'.

Between these two extremes come the category II premierships, which allow the prime minister of the day more influence than in Norway but significantly less than in Ireland. A good example of a category II prime ministership is that of Denmark. On the one hand, the Danish cabinet is highly collegial, and the parties that make up a typical Danish coalition have considerable say over the allocation of ministerial portfolios as well as over the government's programme; but, on the other, the Danish prime minister has the power to hire and fire individual ministers and acts as ultimate arbiter of inter-departmental disputes in cases where the cabinet as a whole cannot reach a decision. According to Schou (1988), 'the overall equilibrium [in Denmark] is markedly dependent on the leadership of the Prime Minister, who carries considerable weight.' Against that, the Danish system accepts only 'a moderate level of leadership by the Prime Minister' (Schou, 1988). Denmark thus falls easily into the medium category.

Table 9.1 allocates all the Western European prime ministerships (except those of France, Finland and the minuscule Luxembourg) to one or other of our three categories. Some readers may feel that there have been some misallocations; for example, some might want to assign the Austrian chancellorship to category I instead of category II. But most of the assignments are probably fairly uncontentious, and it seems doubtful whether anyone would want to shift any of the prime ministerships by more than one category.

So much for taxonomy. The interesting question that immediately arises is: what accounts for the fact that some countries' prime ministers are more influential within their own systems of government than others? What is there about the UK's institutions or culture that makes its prime minister-ship more influential than that of Belgium? What is there about Belgium's institutions and culture that makes its prime ministership more influential than that of its neighbour, the Netherlands? We need some kind of theory;

or, if a fully fledged theory is not available, then we need some guidance about how we might begin to construct one.

And one undoubted element of such a theory at once presents itself. It is evidently the case, and is not denied here, that, other things being equal, the prime minister of a single-party government is likely to be more influential than the leader of a multi-party government, especially if, as is usually the case, the prime minister of the single-party government is also the acknowledged leader of that single party. The prime minister of a single-party government rules alone. By contrast, the prime minister of a multi-party government has to share his authority with the leaders of the other parties that make up the coalition. They are dependent on him, but he is dependent on them; and the more parties that make up the coalition, the more likely it is, other things being equal, that the prime minister will find himself, not a significant influence wielder but rather a mere influence broker, a passive referee or, in Rose's (1991) term, a 'juggler'.

Coalitions are inimical to strong prime ministerial government. That proposition is not denied. Yet if one looks again at Table 9.1 one sees that the presence or absence of governmental coalitions cannot entirely account for the presence or absence in individual countries of prime-minister-centred government. To be sure, most of the countries in category I are countries that usually have single-party governments or else coalition governments in which one party is, by a considerable distance, the strongest partner. But Germany's government is, nevertheless, usually a coalition government, and Irish governments have been coalitions on occasion. Similarly, the Austrian and Swedish prime ministerships would appear to belong in category II, but both Austria and Sweden have had periods of single-party government, in the case of Sweden prolonged periods. Norway, too, frequently has single-party government, but its prime ministership, as we have seen, falls firmly into category III.

In other words, the presence or absence of multi-party coalitions gives one a good deal of purchase on the problem, but there is considerable slippage nevertheless between what a theory that relied solely on multi-partyism would predict and what one actually finds. Hence the frequent use of the phrase 'other things being equal' in the previous paragraphs.

Let us consider three other possible elements of explanation. They are neither exhaustive nor mutually exclusive, but they would appear to have some degree of explanatory power, and comparative research into them would certainly be worthwhile.

Control of Careers

A bald statement of the first possibility would go something like this: that prime minister will have the most influence within his or her system of government who has the most control over the careers of the other politicians within that political system. Imagine a country in which large numbers of politicians – and possibly non-politicians – desperately want ministerial office. Imagine, further, a country in which the prime minister has sole control over the distribution of such offices. He or she decides who will be appointed to office; he or she decides who will be dismissed; he or she decides who will, and will not, be advanced in the ministerial hierarchy. Such a prime minister is not likely to find it too difficult to bend other ministers – and would-be ministers – to his or her will. The hungry sheep look up and are, or are not, fed; and the prime minister is in sole charge of the feeding. That is power indeed.

The relationship just described clearly has two aspects. One concerns the number of people in the country who want ministerial office and how desperately they want it: is ministerial office a particularly desirable commodity among the politicians in the country in question? The other concerns the prime minister's powers in this regard: does he or she in fact have sole control over the distribution of ministerial offices, or is his or her control in some way shared or seriously constrained? In other words, the relationship has both a demand side and a supply side, and both sides need to be looked at.

There is an additional aspect: that of what might be called the prime minister's 'reach'. How many ministerial offices are there for him or her to control? The larger the number of offices to which the prime minister makes appointments, the greater the prime minister's patronage power and the greater also the prime minister's control over the activities of the government as a whole. A prime minister who appoints only a country's foreign minister is likely to exercise less day-to-day influence than one who appoints not only the foreign minister but, in addition, a number of under-ministers or 'junior' ministers in the foreign affairs ministry. In such a system, the person whom these junior ministers – and all would-be junior ministers – will want to impress is not the foreign minister but the prime minister.

It is relatively easy to identify the countries in Western Europe that fall at the two ends of the range of prime ministerial 'career control'. In no country is the prime minister's control over ministerial appointments more complete or more extensive – or more useful to the prime minister – than in the UK. The British prime minister has a large number of ministerial appointments to make, some 90–100 altogether, including cabinet ministers, so-called 'ministers of state', who occupy the second ministerial tier in each department, and parliamentary under-secretaries, who occupy the third tier. In making all these appointments, the British prime minister is constrained only by the normal exigencies of politics; he or she does not even have to consult the ministerial heads of the departments in which these various junior ministers will serve.

Moreover, to pursue the metaphor from economics, the British prime minister is not merely a monopolist with regard to ministerial appointments; he or she is the central figure in what has become a strong buyers' market. In the age of the career politician (King, 1981; 1991), the number of those who want to become ministers greatly exceeds the number of governmental posts available to be filled. It follows that the British premier can use his or her almost unfettered power of appointment not merely to exert influence within the ranks of the government itself but also, to a considerable extent, to discipline non-ministerial members of the governing party in the House of Commons. Their hopes of office are his or her instruments of control. The situation in Ireland is similar to that in the UK, and the Spanish prime minister's powers of appointment and dismissal are also quite formidable.

The position in a number of other European countries, however, is completely different. An extreme case at the other end of the range from the UK is that of the Netherlands. Whatever the demand for ministerial office in the Netherlands, the Dutch prime minister certainly does not control the supply. The parties that make up coalition governments in the Netherlands first decide, collectively, which portfolios will be allocated to which parties and then decide, individually, which members of each party should take on the portfolios that have been assigned to that party. The parties thus make the key decisions at both stages; the prime minister is largely a bystander. As Andeweg (1991) puts it:

> In the Netherlands the prime minister has little or no influence on the composition of his own cabinet. He may belong to the core group that determines the ministerial team from his own party, but the ministers from other governing parties owe their nomination to their own party's leadership and pay only a ritual visit to the prime minister-designate before being sworn in by the Queen.

Moreover, the Dutch prime minister can neither reshuffle his cabinet nor dismiss individual ministers. During the Second World War, the prime minister of the Dutch government in exile in London dismissed two members of his government. He was criticized severely at the time for this display of 'Persian constitutional morals', and after the war a parliamentary commission of enquiry confirmed the view that the head of a government in the Netherlands has no right to sack his ministerial colleagues (Andeweg, 1988; 1991). The Dutch prime minister is thus, as a matter of routine, denied a political weapon that British prime ministers take for granted and regard as crucial to their role. The Italian prime minister, in practice, is just as hamstrung as the Dutch.

It is obvious that to some extent prime ministers' control of careers is a function of whether or not their governments are coalitions. The head of a single-party government is much more likely than the head of a multi-party government to have a monopoly of the control of ministerial appointments; the head of a multi-party coalition is much more likely to be tied down. The British and Dutch cases are straightforward illustrations of the point.

But there is more to it than that. In the first place, prime ministers in some countries where coalition governments predominate appear to have greater control over ministerial appointments than in others. The German chancellor and the Irish *taoiseach*, for example, are expected to play a leading role in the making of cabinet appointments even when (as is usually the case in Germany) their own party is in coalition with others. The decisions are not made by the coalition parties entirely on their own. In the second place, there are some countries where, even when the government is controlled by only one party, the prime minister's room for manoeuvre is, nevertheless, severely constrained. In Norway, to take the extreme case, the prime ministers even in single-party governments (normally Labour governments) are expected to consult widely among party and interest-group leaders before making 'their' cabinet appointments. In 1973, when Trygvie Bratteli formed his second government, he was compelled to renounce some of his own choices and to accept into his cabinet persons he was reluctant to have there (Eriksen, 1988).

Finally, it is worth noting that, within a single political system, the prime minister's 'reach' – the number of ministerial posts that he or she personally controls – may vary significantly through time. In the UK the prime minister's reach has been greatly extended in the course of the past century. The British prime minister from the late eighteenth century onwards has had the right to make core cabinet appointments. Since then the number of ministerial posts has greatly increased and, in addition, the prime minister's reach has been extended to include all of them. Cabinet ministers once chose their own junior ministers. They do so no longer. The prime minister has been the beneficiary. For all these reasons, prime ministers' control over ministerial appointments, their control of careers, should be regarded as having an independent effect on their ability to exercise prime ministerial influence. It is not enough to look at whether a country's governments are mainly coalitions or not.

Unfortunately, although it is possible to give examples of countries like the UK at one end of the career-control range and the Netherlands and Norway at the other, it is not possible at the moment to paint a complete career-control picture for most European countries. Political scientists writing about a specific country almost invariably refer to the prime minister's degree of control over cabinet appointments, but they usually say little either about the demand for such appointments (how many sheep are looking up to be fed and how hungry they are) or about the extent of the prime minister's reach (how much ministerial or other sustenance the prime minister has available). A really rigorous comparative study would require more data about both.

Public Visibility and Prime Ministerial Power

Most students of prime ministers and cabinets are aware of the importance of prime ministers' control or lack of it over ministerial appointments, even if they do not pursue the matter very far. But there is another possible explanation for variations in the degree of prime ministerial influence; and that has to do with the prime minister's public visibility or lack of it. In a rather subtle way, public visibility in and of itself may be a source of influence.

It is widely believed, and is probably true, that in countries where the prime minister is a highly visible public figure his or her influence within the government is likely to be partially dependent on his or her standing with the general public. A popular prime minister who is expected to lead his or her party to victory at the next election is likely to be more influential than an unpopular prime minister who is expected to lead his or her party to defeat. Even if an election is not in the offing (or for some reason the head of government cannot stand for re-election), a favourable public rating is likely to rebound in the prime minister's favour. If the public feels good about the prime minister, his colleagues are likely to feel good about him too. Long ago Neustadt (1960) drew attention to the importance of this factor of 'public prestige'. He suggested that Washingtonians' responses to an American president were powerfully conditioned by their beliefs about his current public standing. Standing and influence thus 'track together'.

This line of argument takes for granted, however, that the prime minister or other head of government is indeed 'a highly visible public figure' in his country. Highly visible public figures who are, in addition, popular are implicitly being compared with highly visible public figures who are not popular. But what happens if we compare, not these two situations, but rather a number of different countries in which the prime minister of the day is, and is not, highly visible? Not all heads of government, after all, are as conspicuous as American presidents.

Suppose the prime minister of a given country is highly visible to the general public. He appears often on television and radio. He speaks frequently and answers questions in the national parliament. His photograph is published several times a week in the newspapers. Most voters know the prime minister's name and would recognize him if they saw him in the street; and, more than that, they have opinions about him, whether favourable or otherwise. In such a country, the prime minister is likely to come to personify his government, to be praised for everything that goes right, whether or not he is actually responsible for it, and to be blamed for everything that goes wrong.

The mere fact that the prime minister under these circumstances is uniquely the object of both praise and (more particularly) blame is likely, in itself, to have consequences for the internal workings of government. If the prime minister is going to be *held* responsible for whatever happens, he is likely to want to *be* responsible – that is, to be able at will to intervene in other ministers' affairs when he judges that *their* actions may influence *his* reputation. Moreover, other ministers under these circumstances are likely to accord him at least some such right of intervention. They can see that he, more than they, will suffer if things go wrong; to that extent, he becomes in an almost feudal way their protector and shield. Equally important, they can also see that the reputation of the government as a whole – and therefore to some degree (probably) their own future success – is intimately bound up with the prime minister's. Therefore, it is in their interests to cooperate with the prime minister and, within limits, to accede to his wishes. Visibility alone may in this way be conducive to influence.

Alas, hard data on the visibility of prime ministers in many Western European countries, and on the connections between their visibility and their influence, are lacking; but it is probably no accident that all of our category I prime ministers are celebrities, household names, media stars, within their own countries. There can scarcely be a German who does not know the name of Kohl, an Irishman who does not know the names of Haughey and Reynolds, or a Greek unfamiliar with the names of Karamanlis, Papandreou and Mitsotakis. To be sure, these prime ministers are probably famous partly because they are men of weight within their own governments, but it seems at least as plausible, perhaps more so, to argue that their weight is partly a function of their fame. One of Margaret Thatcher's cabinet ministers drew attention to the central point: 'The [British] Prime Minister . . . carries the full responsibility: an error by a minister is the Prime Minister's responsibility, just as much as the minister's' (Ridley, 1991).

Some European prime ministers, however, are not nearly so visible and, not being so visible, cannot translate their public standing into a political resource for themselves. A paradigm case is that of the Italian premier. Hine and Finocchi (1991) write of him:

> The expected brevity of a prime minister's tenure, combined with the dual leadership that results from the prime minister/party secretary tandem, ensures that Christian Democrat prime ministers can rarely create an identity in voters' minds between their own political status and that of the party. There is thus no significant coat-tails' effect. Prime ministers cannot easily take *personal* credit for government performance, translate it into personal popularity and use it as a resource with which to build up a position of dominance in the party.

Sensing this to be true, at least one post-war Italian prime minister, the Socialist Bettino Craxi, set out to identify himself in the voters' minds with the achievements of his 1983–7 administration. Whether he succeeded or not is beside the point here. What matters from our point of view is his recognition of the visibility–influence link. It is a link that European political scientists might care to explore further.

The Legacy of History

There is a third possible element of explanation for variations in prime ministerial influence among different Western European countries. It is one that must have struck anyone who has read even cursorily in the comparative literature. Today's political cultures of executive leadership seem to be derived directly from different countries' historical experiences – not necessarily their history in general (e.g. their experience of the Second World War), but their specific experiences with their prime ministership or other headship of government. It would be a fair first approximation to the truth to say that European prime ministers are most influential today where their predecessors were most influential a century or more ago.

Some of our category I premiers do not conform to this general rule, of course; the post-Franco Spanish prime ministership, for instance, was deliberately designed so that the new *presidente del gobierno* would have greater autonomy and be more influential than prime ministers under the pre-Franco regime. But most strong prime ministerships today are the lineal descendants of strong prime ministerial offices in the nineteenth century. The British prime ministership is still recognizably the same office that it was a hundred years ago, and Irish expectations that their *taoiseach* would dominate the Irish government were fuelled by their experience of the old, pre-1918 United Kingdom.

Germany is a particularly striking case of a country with a long tradition of strong executive leadership, a tradition that has survived both the Hitler period and the post-war era of coalition governments. The German constitution of 1867 created the imperial chancellery and decreed that the chancellor alone was to be responsible for the policy of the empire. The Weimar constitution perpetuated this *Kanzlerprinzip*, as it quickly became known, though in the context of a revived cabinet form of organization. And the Bonn constitution has perpetuated it still further. Not only has the title of chancellor been retained, but he and he alone is elected by the Bundestag, and the constitution declares that it is the chancellor who 'determines and bears responsibility for the general policy of the government'. At least as important is the fact that, quite apart from formal constitutional requirements, German politicians (and the German public) expect the chancellor to be an assertive and effective national leader. Those chancellors who conform to expectations, like Konrad Adenauer and Helmut Schmidt, are held in high esteem. Those who do not, like Ludwig Erhard, Kurt Georg Kiesinger and (frequently) Helmut Kohl, are held in some contempt. Just as John Major in the UK is the lineal descendant of Disraeli and Gladstone, so Kohl in Germany is the lineal descendant (whether or not he would relish the comparison) of Bismarck.

By contrast, most of the countries that stretch in a belt from Belgium in the south-west to Sweden in the north-east have undergone a different constitutional evolution. In most of those countries, the king gradually delegated his powers to a number of different ministers or to a collective of ministers. The office of prime minister was frequently slow to emerge; and, when it did emerge, the prime minister was often little more than the chairman or coordinator of the collective. In the Netherlands, the office of prime minister (or minister president) was not created until shortly after the First World War. Before 1922 the chairmanship of the council of ministers was not a permanent office but rotated, either by means of election by the whole cabinet or on the basis of seniority. Andeweg (1988) explains:

> Any attempt to introduce a Prime Minister worthy of that title met with strong opposition. Ministers saw it as a violation of the principle of ministerial equality. Members of Parliament feared it would destroy the individual responsibility of Ministers and would thereby weaken Parliament's influence. Moreover, there was some anxiety that it would restore influence to the King, as he would appoint the Prime Minister.

Even after 1922, and until after the Second World War, the Dutch prime minister was not usually only prime minister but held some other ministerial portfolio. Similarly in Belgium the term prime minister was not used until the 1890s and was not used officially until 1918.

In view of the apparent importance of the history of the prime ministership in different Western European countries, it is a pity that, with very few exceptions, so little is known about that history. Even in the case of the UK for example, little is known about the process by which prime ministers extended the reach of their appointments power to include all ministerial offices, and there remains a considerable mystery about how the prime minister, and the prime minister alone, came to be responsible for determining when parliament should be dissolved and national elections held. Political scientists in Europe might wish to consider turning historians, as Milkis and Nelson (1990) have done to advantage in the United States.

Convergence?

Are there any signs that in the 1980s and 1990s the prime ministerships of the countries of Western Europe are beginning to converge, that the influence of the category II and, especially, the category III premierships within their own systems of government is tending to increase?

There are two reasons for supposing that it might be. One has to do with television. Before television became the predominant channel of political communication in the late 1950s and 1960s, it was somewhat more difficult for politics to be personalized in the way it has subsequently become, and it was certainly possible for a prime minister – especially a prime minister in a country without a pervasive national press – not to be 'a highly visible public figure'. The prime ministers of some European countries could, and did, ride on a tram or train without being noticed. That is no longer possible, and increased public visibility might be expected to be leading to the consequent increases in influence that were referred to earlier.

The other factor that might be tending towards convergence is 'summitry', the increasing tendency for prime ministers from different countries to meet and do business with one another, especially under the aegis of the

European Community. Prime ministers seldom met before the Second World War; the prime minister of a large country like the UK or France would not have known the names, let alone the faces, of the premiers of neighbouring but smaller countries. Now Europe's prime ministers are colleagues. Summitry increases public visibility, as voters see their national leaders entering conference chambers in Rome, Madrid, Brussels or wherever. It may also increase prime ministers' influence in a more direct way if the circumstances of international negotiation require cabinets in individual countries to give their prime ministers at least limited powers of agency in dealing with their prime ministerial opposite numbers. The bargaining power of a nation may be weakened if its principal bargainer cannot engage in actual bargaining.

Certainly many of those who write about Western European prime ministerships claim to detect signs of convergence. None suggests that the influence of the prime minister in any country is actually decreasing, and some believe the prime minister's influence is increasing. Pridham (1983) believes that there is some secular tendency for the office of the Italian prime minister to become more important. Frognier (1988) believes that the same has been true of Belgium since the mid 1970s as a result of the forceful premierships of Leo Tindemans and Wilfrid Martens. Even the Dutch prime minister may be fractionally less insignificant than he was.

That said, the bulk of the evidence does not point to any very great changes since 1945 (even in the Netherlands). On the face of it, the combined forces of party politics, constitutional provisions and national traditions appear to be considerably greater than those of summitry and even television. Apart from those countries that were not yet democracies, Table 9.1 would have looked very similar in the 1950s or the 1960s to the way it looks today; and the gap between category I and category III countries would have been very nearly as great then as it is now. American state governors tend to occupy similar offices because American state governorships are all derived from the same constitutional tradition. There are few signs in Europe of the spread of any similar uniformity. The few signs there are probably owe more to the temporary rise to prominence of outstanding individual prime ministers – Craxi in Italy, Tindemans and Martens in Belgium, Ruud Lubbers in the Netherlands – than to any genuinely long-term trends. Europe seems likely to remain as various as ever in its political institutions and therefore to continue to offer political scientists the intellectual equivalent of an adventure playground.

One additional advantage of studying European prime ministerships comparatively is that it further reduces any temptation one may have had to refer to them collectively as chief executives. The term can reasonably be applied to, at most, our category I prime ministers. As a description of the prime ministerships in categories II and III, it is obviously a complete misnomer. As Blondel (1982) pointed out a decade ago, 'team governments' and 'consociational governments', not 'leader-based governments', remain the European norm.

References

Andeweg, Rudy B. 1988. 'Coalition Cabinets in Changing Circumstances', pp. 47–67 in Jean Blondel and Ferdinand Müller-Rommel (eds), *Cabinets in Western Europe*. London: Macmillan.

Andeweg, Rudy B. 1991. 'The Dutch Prime Minister: Not Just Chairman, Not Yet Chief', pp. 116–32 in G.W. Jones (ed.), *West European Prime Ministers*. London: Frank Cass.

Blondel, Jean 1982. *The Organization of Governments: A Comparative Analysis of Governmental Structures*. London: Sage.

Blondel, Jean and Müller-Rommel, Ferdinand (eds) 1988. *Cabinets in Western Europe*. London: Macmillan.

Eriksen, Svein 1988. 'Norway: Ministerial Autonomy and Collective Responsibility', pp. 183–96 in Jean Blondel and Ferdinand Müller-Rommel (eds), *Cabinets in Western Europe*. London: Macmillan.

Farrell, Brian 1988. 'The Irish Cabinet System: More British than the British Themselves', pp. 33–46 in Jean Blondel and Ferdinand Müller-Rommel (eds), *Cabinets in Western Europe*. London: Macmillan.

Frognier, André-Paul 1988. 'Belgium: A Complex Cabinet in a Fragmented Polity', pp. 68–85 in Jean Blondel and Ferdinand Müller-Rommel (eds), *Cabinets in Western Europe*. London: Macmillan.

Hine, David and Finocchi, Renato 1991. 'The Italian Prime Minister', pp. 79–96 in G.W. Jones (ed.), *West European Prime Ministers*. London: Frank Cass.

Jones, G.W. (ed.) 1991. *West European Prime Ministers*. London: Frank Cass.

King, Anthony 1981. 'The Rise of the Career Politician in Britain – and its Consequences', *British Journal of Political Science*, 11: 249–85.

King, Anthony 1991. 'The British Prime Ministership in the Age of the Career Politician', pp. 24–57 in G.W. Jones (ed.), *West European Prime Ministers*. London: Frank Cass.

Milkis, Sidney M. and Nelson, Michael 1990. *The American Presidency: Origins and Development, 1776–1990*. Washington, DC: CQ Press.

Moynihan, Maurice 1960. *The Functions of the Department of the Taoiseach*. Dublin: Institute of Public Administration.

Neustadt, Richard E. 1960. *Presidential Power: The Politics of Leadership*. New York: John Wiley.

O'Leary, Brendan 1991. '*An Taoiseach*: The Irish Prime Minister', pp. 133–62 in G.W. Jones (ed.), *West European Prime Ministers*. London: Frank Cass.

Olsen, Johan P. 1980. 'Governing Norway: Segmentation, Anticipation, and Consensus Formation', pp. 203–55 in Richard Rose and Ezra N. Suleiman (eds), *Presidents and Prime Ministers*. Washington, DC: American Enterprise Institute.

Pridham, Geoffrey 1983. 'Party Politics and Coalition Government in Italy', pp. 200–30 in Vernon Bogdanor (ed.), *Coalition Government in Western Europe*. London: Heinemann.

Ridley, Nicholas 1991. '*My Style of Government*': The Thatcher Years*. London: Hutchinson.

Rose, Richard 1991. 'Prime Ministers in Parliamentary Democracies', pp. 9–24 in G.W. Jones (ed.), *West European Prime Ministers*. London: Frank Cass.

Rose, Richard and Suleiman, Ezra N. (eds) 1980. *Presidents and Prime Ministers*. Washington, DC: American Enterprise Institute.

Schou, Tove Lisa 1988. 'Denmark', pp. 167–82 in Jean Blondel and Ferdinand Müller-Rommel (eds), *Cabinets in Western Europe*. London: Macmillan.

10

State-Building without a Bureaucracy: the Case of the United Kingdom

R.A.W. Rhodes

The administrative temper was in being before there was an administration to give it effect. (Young, 1960 [1936], p. 41)

The gentry has saved England from the bureaucratization which has been the fate of all continental states. (Weber, 1948, p. 93)

This chapter challenges Jean Blondel's methodological assumptions about *comparative* government by arguing that case studies are a comparative method which produce valid *generalizations*. The contrast with his preference for quantitative methods is deliberate. I do not argue that his approach is invalid. My aim is constructive: to increase the number of research strategies used in 'middle-range analysis'.

The argument focuses on three questions. What role did bureaucracy play in state-building in Western Europe? Why, in sharp contrast to the rest of Western Europe, did Britain fail to develop a bureaucracy until the late nineteenth century? What contribution can the case method make to the study of bureaucracy and state-building?

The first section of the chapter outlines briefly Blondel's approach to comparative government. It pays particular attention to his criticisms of the case method. The second section identifies the theoretical propositions in the existing comparative literature about bureaucracy and state-building in Western Europe. Using a case study of the 'administrative revolution' in Britain in the nineteenth century, it criticizes these propositions. The final section describes and defends the comparative case method.

The case study draws on the massive literature about the distinctive 'administrative revolution' in British government in the nineteenth century. This chapter does not explore 'the mists of time': medieval bureaucracy is a mystery to me and will remain so. Nor does it provide a chronology of events, laws and personalities – for which readers are referred to the relevant texts (see the extensive references). Finally, it does not explore nation-building, as distinct from state-building, in the United Kingdom. To employ S.E. Finer's (1975, pp. 85-8) terminology, England began to acquire the characteristics of a nation in the later Middle Ages. There was a community 'based on self-consciousness of a common *nationality*' and in which members 'mutually distribute and share duties and benefits'. State-building, as distinct from nation-building, involves developing a defined territory, functional specialization of government organs, and national sovereignty. Although state- and nation-building are interconnected processes they are not identical: common consciousness can promote political organization, or the other way round (see also LaPalombara, 1963; Marx, 1963, pp. 62-95). For example, it is a mistake to assume that developing a modern civil service is a necessary condition for developing a nation state.

Although a discussion of the development of bureaucracy in nineteenth century Britain may seem arcane and of little relevance to the present day, state-building is of contemporary importance. The break-up of the Soviet Union and Eastern Europe has brought a growing concern with the contribution of constitutional and institutional reform to democratic stability. The neutral, expert bureaucracy is often seen as one of the keys to successful state-building. Indeed, it played this role in many West European states. This chapter cautions against the too easy association of bureaucracy with state-building and democratic stability. As ever, mono-causal, unidirectional explanations are inadequate. There is no single, let alone best, way of state-building. The great virtue of the British case is that it is deviant and helps to identify the range of conditions under which state-building does and does not occur.

Jean Blondel and Comparative Government

Blondel's (1969a, pp. ix–x) approach to comparative government was 'general and analytical':

> We shall not consider particular countries; we shall not examine the 'historical accidents' which lead to particular regimes. We shall consider . . . , the general conditions which lead to the development of types of political systems and the more detailed factors which account for the characteristics of political structures, whether groups, parties, governments, assemblies or bureaucracies.

Blondel (1990, p. xvi) quotes this passage and reasserts that the objective of comparative government remains the 'genuinely cross-national study of the institutions of government and of the interconnections between these institutions'. So, 'one is inclined to look for "causes" and, more generally, for regularities' (p. 4).

In an ideal world, the comparative method would try:

to measure the relative weight of all the variables and to describe as precisely as possible the extent to which a particular variable accounts for the characteristics of a political system. (Blondel, 1969b, p. xvii)

However, the subject is ' "messy" and somewhat unscientific' and 'the development of quantification in political science does depend in part on an "act of faith" ' (Blondel, 1981, pp. 107–8 and 168; see also Blondel, 1969a, p. 13). Nonetheless, the use of quantification to identify regularities is an important ambition. Otherwise, the subject will remain 'descriptive', 'superficial' and 'indistinguishable from journalism' (Blondel, 1981, p. 109).

The development of comparative government is hampered by limited knowledge and too few facts (see for example Blondel, 1969a, p. 14; and 1981, pp. 175, 185 and 195). Consequently, ' "middle range" or "partial systems" comparisons' are the best way of tackling 'the persistent problem of political institutions'. General models of the political system are too ambitious. Comparative government requires a general analysis of structures; of such institutions as political parties, legislatures, bureaucracies, the military and the judiciary (Blondel, 1981, p. 163, and pp. 178–85, 190 and 197; 1990, pp. 357–9; see also LaPalombara, 1970). In sum, Blondel focuses on middle-range comparisons, employing quantification whenever possible to identify genuine cross-national regularities. (For examples of middle-range quantification see Blondel, 1980; 1982.)

There are certain 'key' words in this brief summary of Blondel's approach to comparative government: for example, 'quantification', 'systematic' and 'regularities'. They have a dual significance. They are not only the objectives of the comparative method but also criticisms of other methods, most notably case studies. Blondel has consistently argued that both historical and case study methods are limited not only by lack of data but also by their inability to compare and explain systematically the structure and behaviour of governments (Blondel, 1969a, p. 5; 1976 pp. 68–72). The case method is suitable for the description of unique events and great men but it does not allow generalizations. It does not:

provide guide-lines by which to abstract from reality the 'critical' elements which would provide the material for comparisons on a large scale. (Blondel, 1981, p. 67; Blondel, 1981, p.101 concedes that the combined efforts of historians and political scientists can produce systematic analyses)

Thus, following Riggs (1962, p. 11), quantitative, middle-range analysis is a *nomothetic* approach (that is, it is systematic and fosters generalizations) whereas the case study method is an *idiographic* approach (that is, it is descriptive and focuses on the unique). The final section of this chapter discusses the case method in more detail. It is sufficient to note here that Blondel's characterization of the strengths and limits of the case method is inadequate.

I do not want to argue that quantitative middle-range analysis is an inappropriate research strategy. Rather, I argue that it is only one of a range of possible research strategies. Blondel's approach to comparative government is widely employed (see for example Lane and Ersson, 1990, p. 75). However, the approach has limitations. For example, Dogan and Pelassy (1990, p. 116) comment:

> Many books could be mentioned, the results of which have proven disappointing because the segments were extracted from such different political systems that their comparability is very low. The book by Jean Blondel on *World Leaders*, which considers all 'heads of government in the postwar period', has such weaknesses; the chapter devoted to 'routes to leadership', for example, raises problems due to its lack of consistency. What sense is there in comparing the 'regular ministerial career' in the Middle East and in the Atlantic and communist worlds? Aren't we here misled simply by verbal similarities? What is the meaning of comparatively studying the 'duration of leadership' when the nature of leadership is so different?

Blondel recognizes the validity of this criticism and it does not justify the conclusion that quantitative, middle-level analysis should be abandoned. However, it does suggest that we need complementary research strategies. In the next two sections, I seek to show that the 'heuristic case study' is one such.

The Development of Bureaucracy in Britain

Patterns of Development

The relationship between bureaucracy and state-building is a source of problems for any analysis of the British state because 'Britain in her state-building period neither possessed nor developed a civil service as it is defined in the text books.' In fact, 'a modern civil service was established only in the nineteenth century, when "state-building" . . . had already come to a final stage' (Fischer and Lundgreen, 1975, p. 459; see also Jacoby, 1973, pp. 165–6). State-building without a bureaucracy runs counter to the experience of the rest of Western Europe. Thus, Eisenstadt (1963, p. 105) sees bureaucracy as central to political unification and modernization in Western Europe and, in a similar vein, Krygier (1979, p. 3) concludes that:

> The growth of powerful, hierarchical and centralized administrative institutions in Europe was a crucially important element in the development of the modern European nation-state and in the consolidation of several hundred more or less independent political units in 1500 into twenty-odd states in 1900.

In Tilly's (1990, pp. 5–16) view, statist accounts of state-building are the most common, although explanations of the variations in the kinds of state in Europe range from 'straightforward economic determinism to assertions of the complete autonomy of politics'. These variations are also seen as the outcome of events internal to the state and as determined by external events. Tilly himself (1990, p. 14) places 'the organization of coercion and preparation for war squarely in the middle of the analysis' while he sees civil bureaucracies as 'more or less inadvertent by-products' (p. 26) of creating and supporting standing armies. On the other hand, Badie and Birnbaum (1983, p. 135) argue that 'the state was the political response that some European societies were forced to make to an increasing division of labour coupled with strong resistance to social change on the part of certain elements of feudal society.' Marx (1963, p. 74) stresses 'the obvious though usually neglected point that the history of modern government and the evolution of the merit bureaucracy are inextricably intertwined' because they helped 'to provide [managerial] capacity', thereby 'making the contemporary state'. Finally, Blondel (1969b, p. xlvii) notes that 'bureaucracies . . . play an early and large part in developing as well as developed nations'. (On the proposition that bureaucracy was a key factor in state-building see, among others, Alford and Friedland, 1985, pp. 185–98; Barker, 1944, Chapter 1; Finer, H., 1946, p. 1290; Finer, S.E., 1980; Heady, 1979, pp. 128–33; Kamenka, 1989, p. 89; Nash, 1969; Page, 1990; Rueschemeyer and Evans, 1985; Skocpol, 1979; 1985; Tilly, 1975b; and Weber, 1948.)

There is, therefore, a broad consensus that, for continental Western Europe, bureaucracy played a key role in state-building. Why then, did bureaucracy not emerge in Britain until the late nineteenth century? To focus on bureaucratic development in Britain is to examine a 'deviant' case. As Dogan and Pelassy (1990, p. 123) argue, such cases are of interest because they can 'disclose new causes and oblige the observer to develop or reformulate his theory'. Following Eckstein (1975, pp. 104–8), I also treat it as a heuristic case study because it challenges existing theories (see pp. 182–4 below for a more extended discussion).

As a first step, it is helpful to identify the stages in the development of the British civil service. Fischer and Lundgreen (1975, p. 466) identify the following three 'crucial' periods of innovation:

1 1080–1230, the Anglo-Norman period: the centralized feudal state governed by the King and his household;
2 1470–1560, the Yorkist to mid-Tudor period: the establishment of government departments as separate institutions run by great officers of the King who recruited personnel by patronage;
3 1780–1870, the Victorian period: the creation of the modern government machine with departments responsible to Parliament, staffed by non-political servants, recruited by open competition.

Following Dicey (1914, pp. 62–9) this latter period is itself conventionally divided into three:

(a) 1800–1830 was an era of legislative quiescence or an era of old Toryism. Even so, it saw the reports of various commissions into public accounts which sought to abolish sinecures, increase efficiency and introduce public servants paid for out of funds voted by Parliament. Perhaps more important, the foundations for nineteenth century reform were laid with the emergence of the cabinet, Treasury control and the growing separation of politics and administration.

(b)   1825–1870 was typified by the Benthamite spirit of inquiry and the Northcote-Trevelyan Report which sought to improve the quality of civil service personnel by abolishing patronage and introducing entry by open competition, and promotion by merit.

(c)   1865–1900 was termed the era of collectivism by Dicey. It may perhaps more accurately be seen as 'a period of consolidation and coordination' (Cohen, 1965, p. 21; and MacLeod, 1988, p. 9; see also Drewry and Butcher, 1988, pp. 34–7; and Hennesy et al., 1988, pp. 50–5). Nonetheless, it witnessed the extension of open competition (starting with the 1870 Order in Council) and the unification of the service.

The twentieth century saw the continuing evolution of the civil service. During the inter-war years there was created that 'blend of intimacy and informality which has characterised the higher echelons of Whitehall' (Chapman and Greenaway, 1980, p. 113; see also Beloff, 1975). Between 1939 and 1975 there came a massive extension in both the numbers of civil servants and public spending with the introduction and consolidation of welfare state services – a growth which combined vertical functional (or service) centralization with horizontal functional fragmentation.

Finally, since 1975, the civil service has been reduced in size and has experienced a degree of politicization. The civil service unions were 'deprivileged'. There was a sustained attempt to improve management in the civil service in the guise of the 'three Es' of economy, efficiency and effectiveness. There was a shift in the balance of power between ministers and their advisers. In short, there was an attempt to break with the immediate past and reintroduce the 'minimalist state' (Drewry and Butcher, 1988, Chapters 10 and 11; Hennessy, 1989, Part IV). Table 10.1 shows the slow growth of government in the nineteenth century, the massive acceleration to 1959, and the steady decline of the 1980s.

Having considered the background, we can now focus on the central issue of when, how and why Britain developed a 'constitutional bureaucracy'. This term 'constitutional bureaucracy' refers to:

> an unpolitical civil service whose primary connection is with the Crown, and which, while subordinated to party governments, is unaffected by their changes: the two permanent elements, the Crown and the civil service, which not by chance together left the political arena, supply the framework for the free play of parliamentary politics and governments. (Namier, 1974, p. 14; cited in Parris, 1969, p. 49)

By the end of the nineteenth century, Britain had developed a permanent, neutral, anonymous, generalist body of officials. It is necessary to answer three questions to explain this pattern of development. Why did Britain not develop a strong central bureaucracy before the nineteenth century? Why did it develop in the late nineteenth century? Why did it take the form of a 'constitutional bureaucracy'?

Table 10.1   *Size of the civil service*

Year	No. of civil servants	Year	No. of civil servants
1797	16,267	1901	116,413
1815	24,598	1911	172,352
1821	27,000	1914	280,900
1832	21,305	1922	317,721
1841	16,750	1939	387,400
1851	39,147	1943	710,600
1861	31,943	1951	1,075,000
1871	53,874	1961	1,008,000
1881	50,859	1971	700,100
1891	79,241	1981	689,600
		1986	594,400

Sources: Cohen, 1965, pp. 19, 23 and n. 1, 164, 166; Drewry and Butcher, 1988, pp. 48 and 59; Mackenzie and Grove, 1957, p. 7.

Explaining Developments before 1800

There are six interrelated explanations for the late development of a central bureaucracy in Britain: geography; the lack of a large standing army; a uniform institutional structure; social mobility; local self-government; and the separation of state and civil society. I will briefly explain each one.

First, Britain is an island and this simple geographical fact gave secure borders. Thus, Namier (1961, pp. 6–7) suggests that:

> The historical development of England is based upon the fact that her frontiers against Europe are drawn by Nature, and cannot be the subject of dispute; that she is a unit sufficiently small for coherent government to have been established and maintained even under very primitive conditions; that since 1066 she has never suffered serious invasions . . . In short, a great deal of what is peculiar in English history is due to the obvious fact that Great Britain is an island. (See also Barker, 1944, p. 30; and Finer, H., 1946, pp. 1290–1)

Secondly, England did not have a standing army with the related needs of the monarch for high taxation, direct coercive ability and bureaucratic control. Thus, it

> has not known, as France and Prussia have known, the effects of military exigency in producing an organized administration to cope with the task of providing not only recruits and taxes, but also the general system of internal control which a great army needs as its basis. (Barker, 1944, pp. 29–30; see also Braun, 1975; Namier, 1961, pp. 6–7; Finer, H., 1946, p. 1290; Finer, S.E., 1975, pp. 109–24)

Instead, England looked outwards to the colonies and developed a powerful navy.

Thirdly, England had a uniform institutional structure. Thomas (1978, pp. 47–9) argues that England 'achieved national identity at a very early stage'. Its unity was a product of: the development of common law; the 'triumph' of vernacular English; a nationwide customs system; a unified coinage; national weights and measures; 'national representative institutions, organized, not as a meeting of "estates", but on a territorial basis'; absence of provincial assemblies; and the growth of London as the capital of the economy and the home of Parliament.

Fourthly, English society was characterized by social mobility and the balance of social forces in Parliament. Moore (1969, Chapter 1) stresses 'the role of the enclosure movement and the rise of industry in the violent destruction of the peasantry' in England. He also recognizes the importance of political structures such as Parliament:

> Perhaps the most important legacy of a violent past was the strengthening of Parliament at the expense of the king. The fact that Parliament existed meant that there was a flexible institution which constituted an arena into which the new social elements could be drawn as their demands arose and an institutional mechanism for settling peacefully conflicts of interest among these groups. (p. 29)

Landed society absorbed the new social groups into its ranks. In short, the gentry kept the balance of social forces in Parliament and by its presence in the country (Finer, H., 1946, p. 1290; see also Barker, 1944, p. 30; Dowse and Hughes, 1986, Chapter 5; Fischer and Lundgreen, 1975, pp. 464–5; Moore, 1969, Chapter 1).

Fifthly, England had developed a strong habit of local self-government by the gentry. There was no invasion of England after 1066, but that was no guarantee of political stability. As Thomas (1978, p. 45 and citations) points out, 'Until the eighteenth century England was notorious for her political instability.' Stability was not enforced but bought, by allowing the gentry a substantial measure of local self-government. By the late eighteenth century England had developed a

> system of remarkably weak central control, remarkably autonomous local bodies, and remarkably small units of local government. Thus power in local matters (the power which affected men most immediately in the nineteenth century) rested to an extraordinary degree upon the unreformed corporations, parish vestries and justices of the peace – upon small town merchants, farmers and the gentry and parochial clergy. There were some 25,000 petty instruments of government largely independent of each other and of the central authority in England and Wales . . . This system of local government . . . had come to seem . . . part of the natural and eternal order of things. It was deeply embedded in the old system of politics through patronage. (MacDonagh, 1977, pp. 12–13; see also Barker, 1944, p. 33; Chester, 1981, Part I; Finer, 1946, pp. 1290 and 1292; Fischer and Lundgreen, 1975, p. 558; Greenleaf, 1987, Chapter 2; Thomas, 1978, pp. 67–8 and 77; and Sidney and Beatrice Webb, 1963, p. 309)

Finally, the state and civil society were separated in England. Dyson (1980, p. 43) argues that Britain paid 'little or no attention . . . to the state as a political concept' and it is scarcely surprising, therefore, that Adam Smith's separation of state, economy and civil society – each governed by its own laws – took root in Britain (Braun, 1975, p. 296). Similarly, British politics has a distinctive 'operating code', rather than formalized, elaborated procedures. Under this code, bargaining between court and country in Parliament rested on a distinction between 'high' and 'low' politics with the former reserved to the court (Bulpitt, 1983, Chapter 3; see also Dyson, 1980, pp. 38 and 49). These political ideas, or central operating code, were the counterpart of political structures in a polity characterized, at the end of the eighteenth century, by the diffusion of authority and limited power of the state:

> The power of the state . . . was effectively limited by the universally accepted principle that all administration was essentially the mere fulfilment of duties imposed by common or statute law. Such a principle left little or no room for the imposition of direct administrative control by the central government over local authorities . . . The eighteenth century was an era of almost complete autonomy for the local institutions of the country. Their duty was to carry out the law and not to obey the commands of the central executive. (Keir, 1961, p. 312; see also Chester, 1981, p. 66)

It is important to stress that Britain is an aberrant case. It is incorrect to treat it otherwise. For example, Fischer and Lundgreen (1975, p. 459) argue that the term 'civil service' has to be redefined to cover 'experienced servants of the king'. In this way Britain 'acquires' a civil service for the relevant periods. However, equating a part-time, amateur, decentralized administrative system with a permanent, anonymous, neutral and generalist service serves no useful purpose. As Parris argues:

> The 'permanent civil service' prior to that time (1780–1850) differed from its modern counterpart in three significant ways. It was not permanent, it was not civil, and it was not a service. (Parris, 1969, p. 22; but for an important qualification see Chester, 1981, p. 299)

Above all, many interesting intellectual puzzles arise from Britain's late development of a modern civil service. They must be confronted, not avoided in an attempt to reinstate civil service expertise as an essential condition of state-building. As I have shown, there are many, clear reasons for the late development of a modern civil service. There is no standard pattern of state-building. So, the next step in the argument is to explore how and why Britain developed a 'constitutional bureaucracy' in the nineteenth century.

Explaining Developments in the Nineteenth Century

Ancient Toryism and its 'Gothic administration' (Finer, S.E., 1952a, p. 333) may have died hard, but it buckled and eventually crumpled under the continuous onslaught of pragmatic collectivism. (For general histories of the period see Kitson Clark, 1950; Thompson, 1950; Young, 1960 [1936].) By the end of the nineteenth century, Britain had a central bureaucracy comparable, in many respects, to its continental counterparts and recognizable in its outline, terminology and informal customs to twentieth century counterparts and commentators alike. This section of the chapter discusses the several explanations for this 'administrative revolution'. (Relevant surveys of this revolution include Chapman and Gree-naway, 1980; Chester, 1981; Cohen, 1965; MacDonagh, 1977; Parris, 1969; Smellie, 1950. Useful collections of articles include Cromwell, 1977; Stansky, 1973; and Sutherland, 1972.)

Dicey's division of the nineteenth century into the three areas of old Toryism, Benthamite individualism and collectivism (see pp. 169–70) was the conventional point of departure. More recently, MacDonagh's 'model' of administrative growth has been the controversial, historiographic focal point. Dicey stressed the relationship between legislation and public opinion. MacDonagh draws attention to various socioeconomic factors. Most important, and of particular relevance to the themes of this chapter, he also emphasizes the impact of the internal dynamics of government, especially the bureaucracy, in fostering administrative growth. A critical appraisal of MacDonagh's work will serve to highlight the competing interpretations of the administrative revolution (MacDonagh, 1973 ([1958]; 1961; 1977).

MacDonagh's first proposition is that the 'peculiar concatenation of circumstances' of the nineteenth century provided 'very powerful impulses' for change. These circumstances included: the social problems created by industrialization and mass migration to the cities; developments in techni-cal and scientific knowledge which provided solutions to these problems; the widespread influence of humanitarian sentiments and intense public pressure to deal with the problems; and the recognition that it was the responsibility of government to introduce legislation to deal with them (MacDonagh, 1973, pp. 12-13). These circumstances triggered the follow-ing legislative-administrative process, termed a 'model' by MacDonagh:

1 This process begins with the exposure of an intolerable social evil which generates public pressure for legislation. The affected interests dilute the legislation as it is enacted and enforced. Nonetheless, a precedent for intervention has been created.
2 The legislation is ineffective. Executive officers are appointed to remedy the defects.
3 The executive officers demand both fresh legislation and a superintend-ing central body.
4 The solution lies no longer in legislation, or increasing numbers of staff, but in growing expertise and closing legislative loopholes by continuous review and experiment.
5 The officers demand and obtain broad administrative discretion which, allied to systematic inquiry, leads to a dynamic approach to adminis-tration and increased intervention. (paraphrased from MacDonagh, 1973, pp. 13–17).

I consider the criticisms of this model under four headings: the influence of Benthamism; the status (and accuracy) of the 'model'; the functional imperatives of bureaucratization; and social class interests in administra-tive reform.

The Influence of Benthamism

MacDonagh challenges Dicey's interpretation of nineteenth century administrative history. He rejects both the influence of Benthamite ideas on legislation in the period 1830–70 and Dicey's conclusion of increased central control between 1865 and 1900. Parris has convincingly argued, however, that:

> It would be absurd to argue that Bentham revolutionized the British system of government by power of abstract thought alone. His ideas were influential because they derived from the processes of change going on around him. He was working with the grain. But it does not follow that the same solutions would have been reached had he never lived. (Parris, 1973, p. 55; see also Rosen, 1983; and Hume, 1981)

In particular, Parris criticizes the identification of Benthamism with *laissez-faire*, arguing that the principle of utility was its central doctrine. This latter principle did not preclude an extension of state intervention but required that the merits of any government action be judged by its results. So, there is no necessary contradiction between Benthamite ideas and intervention.

The debate is wide-ranging. Hart (1965, pp. 39–61) objects to 'the denigration of the Benthamites'. She criticizes MacDonagh for generalizing from a single case study (of emigration control); and for identifying Benthamism with *laissez-faire*. Alan Ryan (1972, p. 61) argues that:

> There is no such thing as *the* utilitarian view of bureaucracy, either in the advocacy of more rather than less government or in pressing the claims of expertise against those of public opinion – and vice versa.

Finer has identified the possible transmission mechanisms for Benthamite ideas (Finer, S.E., 1972, pp. 11–32). Given the range of opinions expressed in the literature, the temptation is to agree with Perkin (1969, p. 267) that this is a 'scholastic dispute about an unverifiable question' and 'the influence of Benthamism or Evangelicalism upon the middle classes remains uncertain' (Thomas, 1978, p. 77). Nonetheless, it is impossible to ignore the role of ideas in the growth of nineteenth century government.

The Status of the Model

Several authors have challenged the accuracy of MacDonagh's model. Thus, Parris (1973, pp. 43–52) concludes from a study of ten branches of administration (other than the emigration service) that 'not one has been found where there is even a reasonable degree of fit between model and reality'. Dunkley challenges MacDonagh's view that the emigration service developed through its own internal momentum, claiming that 'development was more fortuitous than logical, self-generating, or inevitable' (Dunkley, 1980, p. 379). Hart (1965, pp. 49–50) argues that MacDonagh's claim that ' "intolerability" was the master card' in stimulating action against social evils is tautologous. There was 'no agreement' as to what was 'intolerable' and the thesis 'is so elastic that it can never be proved false'.

The Functional Imperatives of Bureaucratization

MacDonagh sees nineteenth century administration as 'creative and self-generating'; as an 'independent historical process in operation' (Mac-Donagh, 1973, pp. 7, 20 and 355; see also MacDonagh, 1961, pp. 16, 346–7 and 348). He is seeking to add the internal dynamics of government to such explanatory factors as, on the one hand, individuals, ideas and events and, on the other hand, social, economic and political forces. Hart (1965, pp. 59–61) criticizes this argument because it denies the efficacy of collective action; 'there were men behind the abstractions'; it is one of 'the great alibis' removing men's culpability for their actions; and it reflects a Tory interpretation of history in which social progress takes place without human effort.

Social Class Interests in Administrative Reform

MacDonagh (1977, p. 202) argues that civil service reform 'was promoted by the middle class'. The objective was 'the further loosening of the aristocratic hold on government' (see also MacDonagh, 1973, p. 21). The Fabian school shares this view of nineteenth century administrative history (for example, Hart, 1965; 1972). In short, reform was the product of the rise of the middle class, the spread of democracy, technological change, and the complexity of public administration (Gowan, 1987, p. 6).

There is, however, great disagreement about the class interests served by reform. For example, Kingsley (1944, pp. 60ff.) sees the Northcote-Trevelyan Report as a product of pressure from the rising, educated middle classes seeking jobs. (For a summary of the Northcote-Trevelyan Report see Chapman and Greenaway, 1980, pp. 36–53; and Committee on the Civil Service, 1968, Appendix 3, pp. 108–31. For summaries of nineteenth century views on the report see Rhodes, 1973; and Hughes, 1949.) Hart (1972, pp. 63–81) dismisses this claim, showing there was no shortage of jobs. Mueller (1984, Chapters 3 and 5) argues that the report sought to protect not only the aristocracy but also the gentry and, as Gowan (1987, pp. 19–20) argues, the gentry was that part of the middle class which 'had long mingled with the aristocracy, . . . had places . . . as poor scholars at the top public schools and Oxbridge, . . . entered the church, the bar and the army along with the aristocracy'. He dismisses MacDonagh's claim that Northcote sought to overthrow the ancient regime as 'preposterous', and asserts that social class and class conflict are crucial in any satisfactory explanation of administrative change. As Gladstone argued at the time:

I do not hesitate to say that one of the great recommendations of the changes in my eyes would be its tendency to strengthen and multiply the ties between the higher classes and the possession of administrative power. (cited in Mueller, 1984, p. 215)

It is possible to dismiss the MacDonagh 'model', therefore, on various grounds. It would be a mistake to do so, especially given its later revision. Parris (1973, pp. 54–5) suggests the following stages to the nineteenth century administrative revolution. First, it was a response to socio-economic change. Secondly, the nineteenth century divided into two periods with the dividing line about 1830. Thirdly, contemporary ideas influenced the response to socioeconomic change and utilitarianism was dominant after 1830. Fourthly, contemporary ideas influenced the utilitarianism and its application increased both state intervention and the spread of *laissez-faire*. Finally, the officials appointed to administer the law generated further legislation which increased their own powers.

MacDonagh (1977, pp. 1–8) has also revised his position, distinguishing between 'the main forces tending to promote and the main forces tending to retard centralization and the extension of state power'. The prime cause of the administrative reforms was the 'changes in the size, distribution and economic functions of the population' which created 'the modern problems of an industrial proletariat and of urban aggregation'. He classifies the promoting forces into the technical, the political and the theoretical. Technical forces refer to improvements in technical knowledge, the empirical investigation of social questions and the creation of a corps of 'trained, examined and tried men' allied to a system of communication which promoted centralized expertise.

Political forces refer to the emergence of the middle classes and their attendant wish for efficient, comprehensible government; the growing legislative role of the executive with the accompanying need for administrative instruments to implement policy; and the investigative role of select committees and royal commissions, exposing social evils. The theoretical forces cover humanitarianism and Benthamism. McDonagh focuses on three themes of Benthamism: applying 'the devastating test of utility to every branch of government'; devising universal administrative schemes; and developing incentive schemes to 'induce men to behave in especial fashions for the general good' (the quotations are from McDonagh, 1977, pp. 1, 2, 4 and 8 respectively).

The key retarding forces were: social and economic assumptions (a phrase which covers both possessive and aggressive individualism and the piecemeal, pragmatic nature of collectivism); political conventions (covering, for example, 'the survival of the local tradition of government'); and vested and class interests (most notably the new manufacturing and commercial class which opposed collectivism and centralization) (Mac-Donagh, 1977, pp. 8–19).

The emergence of constitutional bureaucracy was the product of various forces and its consolidation was not guaranteed. Two points are relevant in the present context. First, the administrative revolution was 'as much a

consequence of industrialism and urbanization as the rise of class itself'
(Perkin, 1969, p. 320. see also Barker, 1944, p. 35; Finer, H., 1946,
p. 1294; and Thomas, 1978, p. 77). Secondly, the new bureaucracy carried
within it the seed of the modern concept of public service. But still further,
'such a government instrument . . . implied a government or state policy,
something continuous and constant and apart from and above the alternat-
ing ministries' (MacDonagh, 1977, p. 6). In other words, to return to
earlier themes, Britain got a strong central bureaucracy, not as an
instrument of state-building, but in response to the pressures of industrialization and urbanization – and, once it was obtained, the interests of this
bureaucracy further fuelled the trend towards centralization and collectivism; bureaucracy became its own cause.

The Distinctive Features of 'Constitutional Bureaucracy'

I have tried to explain why Britain did not develop a modern central
bureaucracy until the nineteenth century and have summarized the various
explanations of the administrative revolution in that century. But why did
this revolution take the form of a 'constitutional bureaucracy'? There are
four explanations for this pattern of development: the doctrine of ministerial responsibility; the pragmatic, evolutionary pattern of administrative
growth; the 'dual polity', and the pattern of elite competition.

It is a commonplace of British administrative history that the Northcote-
Trevelyan reforms created the neutral, anonymous civil servant. They did
not. Subordinating permanent officials to a minister responsible to Parliament can be traced to the early years of the nineteenth century (Kitson
Clark, 1973, p. 69; see also Taylor, 1927, Chapter II; and Finer, S.E.,
1956, pp. 377–96). The convention has its roots in Parliament's ascendancy
over the Crown (see Chester, 1981, pp. 93–4 and 120–2). Rejecting the
concept of the state for the notion that sovereignty was vested in the
Crown-in-Parliament not only reveals remarkable continuity with the
medieval roots of court versus country but also personalizes government by
conferring powers on the ' "over-life-size" role of ministers' (Dyson, 1980,
pp. 40–1). As a result, public servants are no longer 'closct statesmen'
(Kitson Clark, 1973, p. 87; see also Finer, S.E., 1952b).

Administrative growth followed no grand plan but trod a wary path
between the contending ideals of *laissez-faire* and collectivism. The
administrative response to 'intolerable social evils' was pragmatic. Boards
of all shades of independence flourished between 1832 and 1855 but,
eventually, Parliament became convinced

> that the device which offered the best means of ensuring that administration was
> carried out in accordance with its wishes was that which had already grown up
> during the previous half century or more – the individual responsibility of
> Ministers. Once this idea had been accepted in practice – Bentham had been
> advocating the virtues of 'single seatedness' for some time before 1832 – it soon
> became one of the features by which the British system of government is most
> widely characterised. (Willson, 1955, pp. 48–9)

The combination of constitutional convention, Benthamite single-mindedness and practical experience proved irresistible.

Bulpitt (1983) describes the territorial settlement within the UK as a 'dual polity'. It was created between 1870 and 1926. Its defining characteristic is centre autonomy in high politics, with operational control of low politics conceded to local and regional authorities (see also Dyson, 1980, pp. 41–2). However, Bulpitt (1983) concludes that the price of this autonomy was loss of contact with the periphery. Most important, the dual polity continued to accord a role to the Gothic administration of the localities. As MacDonagh (1977, p. 19) makes clear, municipal reform handed the towns over to the middle class without reforming the patchwork quilt of authorities. And these parvenus defended their domains against central authority as vigorously as their predecessors defended the ancient regime, often with disastrous results in the large cities.

This dual polity had several implications for the central bureaucracy. First, it called for a non-executant civil service. The consequent lack of 'hands-on' expertise of services increased dependence on sub-central authorities. The reliance on 'hands-off' controls, in contrast to the Napoleonic systems of the continent, limited the civil service's ability to control sub-central authorities. This functional insulation of centre and periphery was only one of several political strategies for managing the periphery. Thus, Birch's (1989, pp. 79–80) list of strategies includes: full representation of the periphery in Parliament; recruiting peripheral elites to the centre; allocating public expenditure to the periphery; discouraging minority languages but keeping other symbols; and hiving-off administration to the periphery. In sum, combining elite incorporation with administrative decentralization produced a depoliticized relationship which further heightened the centre's insulation from the periphery. The combination of these functional and political factors was to have dramatic results for managing centre–periphery relations in the twentieth century (Rhodes, 1988, pp. 93–4, 253–4, 396–7 and 408–10).

The characteristics of the elite coalition provide the final distinctive twist to constitutional bureaucracy. It is commonplace to describe the administrative reforms of the nineteenth century as technocratic, concerned with efficiency and favouring the middle class at the expense of the aristocracy. Thus, abolishing patronage and reforming the civil service are interpreted as attacks on the ancient regime. However, as Parris (1969, p. 50) points out:

> The establishment of permanence might seem to imply the end of patronage . . . Yet patronage did survive . . . the decline of the old system was long and slow.

> They thought it dying when it slept
> And sleeping when it died [*sic*]

> The exact moment of its death is not important . . . What is important is that neither the Northcote-Trevelyan report, nor the setting-up of the Civil Service Commission (1855), nor the introduction of Open Competition (1870) killed it.

Also, the reforms protected the aristocracy and gentry. As MacDonagh (1977, p. 206) concedes in his reassessment of the Northcote-Trevelyan Report:

> there is a good reason to suspect that nothing less was aimed at than the exclusive preservation of the vital sphere of civil administration for the educated upper and upper-middle classes, while there was still time to beat the oncoming democracy to the gun. (see also Gowan, 1987, p. 33; Mueller, 1984, Chapter 5)

The reforms sought not only to preserve the privileges of the gentry, but also to forge a link between the higher civil service and the humanities provided at Oxbridge (MacDonagh, 1977, pp. 206 and 213). They protected an exclusive elite in the (initially incipient) guise of the generalist civil servant – a development consistent with the long-standing preference for amateur administrators. Simultaneously, the specialist official was drawn into the departments and subordinated to the generalist (MacLeod, 1988). This trend was to exercise a profound effect on the government of the twentieth century (see Balogh, 1962; Ridley, 1988; and Committee on the Civil Service, 1968). In its outlines, this bureaucracy was to remain unchanged, if not unchallenged, until the late 1980s.

In Defence of the Comparative Case Method

The rest of this chapter discusses the theoretical lessons learnt from the case study and argues for developing the case study from a heuristic to a comparative tool.

Conditions for State-Building

It is informative to contrast the British experience with that of the rest of Western Europe. In the most important single collection on this subject, Tilly (1975a, pp. 632–3) summarizes the conditions favouring European *nation*-building as follows:

> (1) the availability of extractable resources; (2) a relatively protected position in time and space; (3) a continuous supply of entrepreneurs; (4) success in war; (5) homogeneity (initial or created) of the subject population; (6) strong coalitions of the central power with the major segments of landed elite.

He then adds four conditions specifically concerned with state-building:

> (7) the high cost of state-building; (8) the intimate connection between the conduct of war, the building of armies, the extension and regularization of taxes and the growth of state apparatus; (9) the large role of alternating coalitions between the central power and the major social classes within the subject population in determining the broad forms of government; and (10) the further effect of homogenization – or its absence – on the structure and effectiveness of government.

The most significant feature of this summary is that it omits a great many factors relevant to the British case, as outlined earlier. Thus, Britain failed to develop a bureaucracy because it: (1) was an island with secure boundaries; (2) lacked a large standing army; and (3) had a uniform institutional structure. Allied to these factors were (4) social mobility leading to a merger of the landed aristocracy, the gentry, professions and merchants; (5) a decentralized system of local self-government; and (6) a separation of state and civil society. As a result, British bureaucracy was underdeveloped. When it did develop a bureaucracy in the nineteenth century, it did so because of: (7) the impact of industrialization and urbanization; (8) the growth and centralization of technical knowledge; (9) the professionalization of government and the impact of this administrative leadership on policy; (10) the political influence of the middle class; and (11) the impact of Benthamite and humanitarian ideas. It took the form of a 'constitutional bureaucracy' because of (12) parliamentary ascendancy over the Crown and the attendant rise of the doctrine of ministerial responsibility; (13) the pattern of pragmatic administrative growth; (14) the dual polity with a non-executant centre; and (15) the need to preserve the interests of the gentry. On a generous estimate, Tilly's summary covers only points (1) to (4), (9) and (10), and then not always in the same form.

The lessons of the case study are as obvious as they are important. First, the interrelationship between bureaucracy and state-building is not one of direct cause and effect. Bureaucracy was not a necessary condition of either state- or nation-building in Britain. However, bureaucratic interests help to explain the scale and speed of administrative growth in the nineteenth century, as described earlier (for a general discussion see Alford and Friedland, 1985, Part II).

Secondly, the case study identifies many conditions which influenced state-building in Britain, prompting the conclusion that any monocausal account, whether it stresses the impact of the international system or of war, will be inadequate. It also highlights a major dilemma. What does it mean to study 'the conditions of state-building' when 'state-building', indeed the nature of 'the state', varies so much even within such a relatively homogeneous area as Western Europe?

Thirdly, the case study discloses two causes of state-building absent from many statist accounts. Industrialization and urbanization were probably the most important causes of bureaucratization in Britain, and their significance is not restricted to that country, but they are missing from many statist accounts of state- (and nation-) building (the notable exceptions are Mumford, 1966; and Tilly, 1990). The British case also draws attention to the influence of the centre's operating code (and of central elite strategies) on the form of bureaucratic development (on the latter see also Alford and Friedland, 1985, p. 189).

Finally, looking to contemporary application of these lessons there are no easy generalizations about the relationship between bureaucratic development and political stability in Eastern Europe. Indeed, a pessimistic reading of the literature suggests that a large standing army, disputed boundaries and internal social diversity would foster bureaucratic growth which would provoke, in turn, territorial opposition. On this view, state-building is a cause of instability, and such a conclusion is consistent with current trends.

These arguments illustrate the long-standing conflict between proponents of comparative analysis and its critics. The former search for regularities. The latter denounce the exercise for its superficiality and disregard of cultural specificity and historical tradition (see for example Dogan and Pelassy, 1990; Holt and Turner, 1970; Ragin, 1987). Thus, the cultural traditions and concrete historical experiences of Britain simply confound existing generalizations about bureaucracy and state-building. Such a critique is both too severe and underestimates the potential of the case study as a nomothetic method.

Developing the Comparative Case Method

Eckstein provided the earliest and best discussion of the case study method in political science (the following paraphrases Eckstein, 1975, pp. 92–123). He distinguishes five 'species' of case study. *Configurative-idiographic studies* are the conventional case studies of political science which provide comprehensive descriptions of specific subjects: for example, political parties, bureaucracies. *Disciplined-configurative studies* base their interpretations of cases on explicit theories; that is, general laws or statements of probability are applied to particular cases. *Heuristic case studies* do not take the existence of general laws for granted but use case studies for 'discerning important general problems and possible theoretical solutions'. Such case studies are directly concerned with theory-building and 'can be conducted seriatim, by the so-called building-block technique, in order to construct increasingly plausible and less fortuitous regularity statements' (p. 104). *Plausibility probes* are case studies conducted as preliminary tests, or trials, of the validity of hypotheses. *Crucial case studies* test theories and are virtually equivalent to 'decisive experiments'. Eckstein (1975, p. 116) argues that:

> in principle, comparative and case studies are alternative means to the end of testing theories, choices between which must be largely governed by arbitrary or practical, rather than logical, considerations. (italics in original)

Had Eckstein's chapter been read more widely, and with the care and attention it deserves, the political science community might have been spared much criticism of case studies and their alleged inferiority to quantitative methods (or 'comparative studies' in Eckstein's terminology). By definition, case studies are neither descriptive nor divorced from theory. They can and do test theories. They can and do permit generalizations. They constitute an alternative to quantitative methods, not a poor relation.

Eckstein shows the relevance of the case method to the construction and testing of theory. Yin (1984) shows how to use it for comparative study.

Following Eckstein's analysis of crucial case studies, Yin (1984, p. 39) argues that the

> *analogy to samples and universes is incorrect when dealing with case studies*. This is because survey research relies on *statistical* generalization, whereas case studies (as with experiments) rely on *analytical* generalizations. (italics in original)

He proposes (pp. 108–9) the following 'iterative' research design for explanatory case studies:

- making an initial theoretical statement or an initial proposition about policy or social behaviour;
- comparing the findings of an initial case against such a statement;
- revising the statement or proposition;
- comparing other details of the case against the revision;
- again revising the statement or proposition;
- comparing the revision to the facts of a second, third or more cases; and
- repeating this process as many times as is needed.

Explanatory case studies involve a multiple-case design (pp. 47–52 and 107–9) using a standard protocol (pp. 64–72). It is crucial to emphasize the underlying *replication logic* of these procedures, as distinct from the sampling logic underlying statistical generalization:

> Each case must be carefully selected so that it either (a) predicts similar results (a *literal replication*) or (b) produces contrary results but for predictable theoretical reasons (a *theoretical replication*). (Yin, 1984, pp. 48–9)

Within a multiple-case design, compiling a number of case studies is directly analogous to conducting a series of experiments and, in a like manner, it is possible to produce valid generalizations.

This chapter has employed the heuristic case method and shown that it can play a productive role in testing theory. However, this view does inadequate justice to the case study method. To discuss Eckstein and Yin is not to digress but to show that the comparative case method is a genuine alternative to quantitative methods in the study of comparative government. Eckstein makes the general case. Yin describes the research design and procedures. The weakness of the case method stems not from its intrinsic nature but in misunderstandings of both its scope and its application (see for example Evans et al., 1985, pp. 348–50 on 'analytical induction'). There are examples of its skilful use in political science (my own favourites include Allison, 1971; Bauer et al., 1972; Lowi, 1964; Pressman and Wildavsky, 1984; Sundquist, 1968; but see the bibliography in Yin, 1984 for a more comprehensive listing).

The case study method is also capable of fostering the link between the historian and the political scientist; it can relate the historian's 'what-questions' to the political scientist's 'why-questions'. As Kavanagh (1991, p. 490) points out, political scientists rely on the accounts provided by historians. The problem is to combine description and analysis. The comparative case method is one way of bringing the two together productively (and the work of Grew, 1978; Moore, 1969; Skocpol, 1979; and Tilly, 1975b all show the value of the marriage). In sum, the comparative case method is a complementary research strategy to quantitative methods in the study of comparative government. Most important, it is of particular use 'when it is important to investigate complex phenomena and to develop and build hypotheses out of a rich contextual framework' (Agranoff and Radin, 1991, pp. 229–30). In other words, it combines cultural specificity and historical tradition with the capacity to generalize.

'Whether comparative government has reached the "positive" age is a matter of judgement.' However, for Jean Blondel, 'the discipline has now taken off' and 'knowledge is being acquired and systematic analyses gradually replace historical accidents as the basis for most explanations' (Blondel, 1990, p. 360). The aeroplane of comparative government may have 'taken off' but it will never reach its destination as long as the false antitheses between quantitative and case studies, systematic and historical analyses, bedevil its methodology. Eckstein (1975, p. 96) makes it clear that case studies are 'very demanding, implying great rigour of thought and exactitude of observation'. They require:

> More thought, more imagination, more logic, less busy-work, less reliance on mechanical printouts, no questions about sampling, possibly firmer conclusions (including that rarity in political study, the conclusively falsified hypothesis). (p. 123)

The comparative case method, in alliance with the historian, has a key role to play in the future of comparative government.

Note

I would like to thank: Keith Alderman (University of York); Ian Budge (University of Essex); Hans Daalder (University of Leiden); John Peterson (University of York); and Vincent Wright (Nuffield College). They all commented on an earlier version of the chapter.

References

Agranoff, R. and Radin, B.A. 1991. 'The Comparative Case Study Approach in Public Administration' in J.L. Perry (ed.), *Research in Public Administration: A Research Annual*. Greenwich, Connecticut: JAI Press, pp. 203–31.
Alford, R. and Friedland, R. 1985. *Powers of Theory: Capitalism, the State and Democracy*. Cambridge: Cambridge University Press.
Allison, G. 1971. *Essence of Decision*. Boston: Little, Brown.
Badie, B. and Birnbaum, P. 1983. *The Sociology of the State*. Chicago: Chicago University Press.
Balogh, T. 1962. 'Apotheosis of the Dilettante' in H. Thomas (ed.), *The Establishment*. London: Ace Books, pp. 72–115.
Barker, Sir Ernest. 1944. *The Development of Public Services in Western Europe, 1660–1930*. London: Oxford University Press.
Bauer, R.A., Pool, Ithiel de Sola and Dexter, L.A. 1972 [1963]. *American Business and Public Policy*. Chicago: Aldine, Atherton (second edition).

Beloff, M. 1975. 'The Whitehall Factor: The Role of the Higher Civil Service 1919–39' in G. Peele and C. Cook (eds), *The Politics of Reappraisal 1918–1939*. London: Macmillan, pp. 209–31.

Birch, A.H. 1989. *Nationalism and National Integration*. London: Unwin-Hyman.

Blondel, J. 1969a. *An Introduction to Comparative Government*. London: Weidenfeld & Nicolson.

Blondel, J. (ed.) 1969b. *Comparative Government: A Reader*. London: Macmillan.

Blondel, J. 1976. *Thinking Politically*. London: Wildwood.

Blondel, J. 1980. *World Leaders*. London: Sage.

Blondel, J. 1981. *The Discipline of Politics*. London: Butterworth.

Blondel, J. 1982. *The Organization of Governments*. London: Sage.

Blondel, J. 1990. *Comparative Government: An Introduction*. London: Philip Allan.

Braun, R. 1975. 'Taxation, Sociopolitical Structure and State Building: Great Britain and Brandenburg-Prussia' in C. Tilly (ed.), *The Formation of National States in Western Europe*. Princeton, NJ: Princeton University Press, pp. 243–327.

Bulpitt, J.G. 1983. *Territory and Power in the United Kingdom*. Manchester: Manchester University Press.

Chapman, R.A. and Greenaway, J.R. 1980. *The Dynamics of Administrative Reform*. London: Croom Helm.

Chester, Sir Norman. 1981. *The English Administrative System 1780–1870*. Oxford: Clarendon Press.

Cohen, E.W. 1965. *The Growth of the British Civil Service*. London: Cass.

Committee on the Civil Service. 1968. *Report* (Fulton). Cmnd 3638, London: HMSO, Appendix 3.

Cromwell, V. (ed.) 1977. *Revolution or Evolution*. London: Longman.

Dicey, A.V. 1914. *Lectures on the Relations Between Law and Public Opinion During the Nineteenth Century*. London: Macmillan (second edition).

Dogan, M. and Pelassy, D. 1990. *How to Compare Nations: Strategies in Comparative Politics*. Chatham, New Jersey: Chatham House (second edition).

Dowse, R.E. and Hughes, J.A. 1986. *Political Sociology*. London: Wiley (second edition).

Drewry, G. and Butcher, T. 1988. *The Civil Service Today*. Oxford: Blackwell.

Dunkley, P. 1980. 'The Emigration and the State, 1803–1842: The Nineteenth Century Revolution in Government Reconsidered'. *The Historical Journal*. Vol. 23, pp. 353–80.

Dyson, K.H.F. 1980. *The State Tradition in Western Europe*. Oxford: Martin Robertson.

Eckstein, H. 1975. 'Case Study and Theory in Political Science' in F.I. Greenstein and N. Polsby (eds), *Handbook of Political Science. Volume 7: Strategies of Inquiry*. Reading, Mass.: Addison-Wesley, pp. 79–137.

Eisenstadt, S.N. 1963. 'Bureaucracy and Political Development' in J. LaPalombara (ed.), *Bureaucracy and Political Development*. Princeton, NJ: Princeton University Press, pp. 96–119.

Evans, P.B., Rueschemeyer, D. and Skocpol, T. 1985. 'On the Road Towards a More Adequate Understanding of the State' in P.B. Evans, D. Rueschemeyer and T. Skocpol, (eds), *Bringing the State Back In*. Cambridge: Cambridge University Press, pp. 347–66.

Finer. H. 1946. *The Theory and Practice of Modern Government* (two volumes). London: Methuen (second edition).

Finer, S.E. 1952a. 'Patronage and the Public Service'. *Public Administration*, Vol. 30, pp. 329–60.

Finer, S.E. 1952b. *The Life and Times of Sir Edwin Chadwick*. London: Methuen.

Finer, S.E. 1956. 'The Individual Responsibility of Ministers'. *Public Administration*. Vol. 34, pp. 377–96.

Finer, S.E. 1972. 'The Transmission of Benthamite Ideas 1820–50' in G. Sutherland (ed.), *Studies in the Growth of Nineteenth Century Government*. London: Routledge & Kegan Paul, pp. 11–32.

Finer, S.E. 1975. 'State and Nation Building in Europe: The Role of the Military' in C. Tilly (ed.), *The Formation of National States in Western Europe*. Princeton, NJ: Princeton University Press, pp. 84–163.

Finer, S.E. 1980. 'Princes, Parliaments and the Public Service'. *Parliamentary Affairs*. Vol. 33, pp. 353–72.

Fischer, W. and Lundgreen, P. 1975. 'The Recruitment and Training of Administrative and Technical Personnel' in C. Tilly (ed.), *The Formation of National States in Western Europe*. Princeton, NJ: Princeton University Press, pp. 456–561.

Gowan, P. 1987. *The Other Face of Reform*. London: unpublished MA thesis, London School of Economics and Political Science. All page references are to the thesis. A shortened version was published as: 'The Origins of the Administrative Elite'. *New Left Review*. No. 162, pp. 4–34.

Greenleaf, W.H. 1987. *The British Political Tradition, Volume 3: A Much Governed Nation (Part 1)*. London: Methuen.

Grew, R. (ed.) 1978. *Crises of Political Development in Europe and the United States*. Princeton: Princeton University Press.

Hart, J. 1965. 'Nineteenth Century Social Reform: A Tory Interpretation of History'. *Past and Present*. No. 31, pp. 39–61.

Hart, J. 1972. 'The Genesis of the Northcote-Trevelyan Report' in G. Sutherland (ed.), *Studies in the Growth of Nineteenth Century Government*. London: Routledge & Kegan Paul, pp. 63–81.

Heady, F. 1979. *Public Administration: A Comparative Perspective*. New York and Basel: Marcel Dekker (second edition).

Hennessy, P. 1989. *Whitehall*. London: Secker & Warburg.

Hennesy, P., Jay, A., Michael, J., Wolstencroft, A., McPherson, A., Raab, C.D., Theakston, K. and Walker, D. 1988. 'Symposium: the Civil Service'. *Contemporary Record*. Vol. 2, pp. 44–55.

Holt, R.T. and Turner, J.E. (eds) 1970. *The Logic of Comparative Research*. New York: Free Press.

Hughes, E. 1949. 'Sir Charles Trevelyan and Civil Service Reform 1853–55'. *English Historical Review*. Vol. 64, pp. 52–8 and 206–34.

Hume, L.J. 1981. *Bentham and Bureaucracy*. Cambridge: Cambridge University Press.

Jacoby, H. 1973. *The Bureaucratization of the World*. London: University of California Press.

Kamenka, E. 1989. *Bureaucracy*. Oxford: Blackwell.

Kavanagh, D. 1991. 'Why Political Science Needs History'. *Political Studies*. Vol. 39, pp. 479–95.

Keir, Sir David Lindsay. 1961. *The Constitutional History of Modern Britain Since 1485*. London: Black (sixth edition).

Kingsley, J.D. 1944. *Representative Bureaucracy*. Yellow Springs, Ohio: Antioch Press.

Kitson Clark, G. 1950. *The Making of Victorian England*. London: Methuen.

Kitson Clark, G. 1973. ' "Statesmen in Disguise" : Reflections on the History of the Neutrality of the Civil Service' in P. Stansky (ed.), *The Victorian Revolution*. New York: Watts, pp. 61–88.

Krygier, M. 1979. 'State and Bureaucracy in Europe: the Growth of a Concept' in R. Brown et al., (eds), *Bureaucracy: the Career of a Concept*. London: Edward Arnold, pp. 1–33.

Lane, J.E. and Ersson, S. 1990. 'Comparative Politics: From Political Sociology to Comparative Public Policy' in A. Leftwich (ed.), *New Developments in Political Science*. Aldershot: Gower, pp. 61–81.

LaPalombara, J. (ed.) 1963. *Bureaucracy and Political Development*. Princeton, New Jersey: Princeton University Press.

LaPalombara, J. 1970. 'Parsimony and Empiricism in Comparative Politics' in R.T. Holt and J.E. Turner (eds), *The Logic of Comparative Research*. New York: Free Press, pp. 125–49.

Lowi, T. 1964. 'American Business, Public Policy, Case Studies and Political Theory'. *World Politics*. Vol. 16, pp. 676–715.

MacDonagh, O. 1961. *A Pattern of Government Growth: the Passenger Acts and the Enforcement, 1800–1860*. London: MacGibbon and Kee.

MacDonagh, O. 1973 [1958]. 'The Nineteenth Century Revolution in Government: A Reappraisal' in P. Stansky (ed.), *The Victorian Revolution*. New York: Watts, pp. 5–25 and 355–8. The paper appeared originally in the *Historical Journal*, 1958. Vol. 1, pp. 52–67.

MacDonagh, O. 1977. *Early Victorian Government*. London: Weidenfeld and Nicolson.

Mackenzie, W.J.M. and Grove, J.W. 1957. *Central Administration in Britain*. London: Longmans, Green.

MacLeod, R. 1988. 'Introduction' in R. MacLeod (ed.), *Government and Expertise*. Cambridge: Cambridge University Press, pp. 1–24 and 255–66.

Marx, F.M. 1963. 'The Higher Civil Service as an Action Group in Western Political Development' in J. LaPalombara (ed.), *Bureaucracy and Political Development*. Princeton, NJ: Princeton University Press, pp. 62–95.

Moore, B. 1969. *Social Origins of Democracy and Dictatorship*. Harmondsworth: Penguin Books.

Mueller, H.E. 1984. *Bureaucracy, Education and Monopoly: Civil Service Reforms in Prussia and England*. London: University of California Press.

Mumford, L. 1966. *The City in History*. Harmondsworth: Penguin Books.

Namier, Sir Lewis. 1961. *England in the Age of the American Revolution*. London: Macmillan (second edition).

Namier, Sir Lewis. 1974. *Personalities and Power*. Westport, Connecticut: Greenwood Press.

Nash, G.D. 1969. *Perspectives on Administration: The Vistas of History*. Berkeley, Ca.: Institute of Governmental Studies, University of California.

Page, E. 1990. 'The Political Origins of Self Government and Bureaucracy: Otto Hintze's Conceptual Map of Europe'. *Political Studies*. Vol. 38, pp. 39–55.

Parris, H. 1969. *Constitutional Bureaucracy*. London: Allen & Unwin.

Parris, H. 1973 [1969]. 'The Nineteenth Century Revolution in Government: A Reappraisal Reappraised' in P. Stansky (ed.), *The Victorian Revolution*. New York: Watts, pp. 29–57.

Perkin, H. 1969. *Origins of Modern English Society, 1780–1880*. London: Routledge & Kegan Paul.

Pressman, J. and Wildavsky, A. 1984 [1974]. *Implementation*. Berkeley: University of California Press (third expanded edition).

Ragin, C. 1987. *The Comparative Method*. Berkeley, Ca. and London: University of California Press.

Rhodes, R.A.W. 1973. ' "Wilting in Limbo": Anthony Trollope and the Nineteenth Century Civil Service'. *Public Administration*. Vol. 5, pp. 207–19.

Rhodes, R.A.W. 1988. *Beyond Westminster and Whitehall*. London: Unwin-Hyman.

Ridley, F.F. 1988. *Specialists and Generalists*. London: Allen & Unwin.

Riggs, F.W. 1962. 'Trends in the Comparative Study of Public Administration'. *International Review of Administrative Science*. Vol. 28, pp. 9–15.

Rosen, F. 1983. *Jeremy Bentham and Representative Government*. Oxford: Clarendon Press.

Rueschemeyer, D. and Evans P.B. 1985. 'The State and Economic Transformation: Toward an Analysis of the Conditions Underlying Effective Intervention' in P.B. Evans, D. Rueschemeyer and T. Skocpol (eds), *Bringing the State Back In*. Cambridge: Cambridge University Press, pp. 44–77.

Ryan, A. 1972. 'Utilitarianism and Bureaucracy: The views of J.S. Mill' in G. Sutherland (ed.), *Studies in the Growth of Nineteenth Century Government*. London: Routledge & Kegan Paul, pp. 33–62.

Skocpol, T. 1979. *State and Social Revolutions*. London: Cambridge University Press.

Skocpol, T. 1985. 'Bringing the State Back In: Strategies of Analysis in Current Research' in P.B. Evans, D. Rueschemeyer and T. Skocpol (eds), *Bringing the State Back In*, Cambridge: Cambridge University Press, pp. 3–37.

Smellie, K.B. 1950. *A Hundred Years of English Government 1832–1939*. London: Duckworth (second edition).

Stansky, P. (ed.)·1973. *The Victorian Revolution*. New York: Watts.

Sundquist, J.L. 1968. *Politics and Policy: The Eisenhower, Kennedy and Johnson Years*. Washington, DC: The Brookings Institution.

Sutherland, G. (ed.) 1972. *Studies in the Growth of Nineteenth Century Government*. London: Routledge & Kegan Paul.

Taylor, Sir Henry. 1927 [1836]. *The Statesman*. Cambridge: Heffer.

Thomas, K. 1978. 'The United Kingdom' in R. Grew (ed.), *Crises of Political Development in Europe and the United States*. Princeton: Princeton University Press, pp. 41–97.

Thompson, D. 1950. *England in the Nineteenth Century*. Harmondsworth: Penguin Books.

Tilly, C. 1975a. 'Western State-Making and Theories of Political Transformation' in C. Tilly (ed.), *The Formation of National States in Western Europe*. Princeton, NJ: Princeton University Press, pp. 601–38.

Tilly, C. (ed.) 1975b. *The Formation of National States in Western Europe*. Princeton, New Jersey: Princeton University Press.

Tilly, C. 1990. *Coercion, Capital and European States, AD 990–1990*. Oxford: Blackwell.

Webb, S. and Webb, B. 1963 [1906]. *The Parish and the County*. London: Frank Cass.

Weber, M. 1948. *From Max Weber*. London: Routledge & Kegan Paul.

Willson, F.M.G. 1955. 'Ministries and Boards: Some Aspects of Administration Development since 1832'. *Public Administration*. Vol. 33, pp. 43–58.

Yin, R.K. 1984. *Case Study Research: Design and Methods*. London: Sage.

Young, G.M. 1960 [1936]. *Victorian England, Portrait of an Age*. London: Oxford University Press.

11

The Westminster Model
in Comparative Perspective

Graham Wilson

The British political system whose evolution we have just described, and which became the subject of Jean Blondel's scholarship in the 1950s, was a system whose citizens either celebrated or took for granted its advantages compared with the others. As we shall see, some of the features of the British political system are unique; the hereditary element in the House of Lords has (fortunately) no equivalent elsewhere. However, the essential features of the British political system can be abstracted to form a particular version of democracy, the *Westminster model*. The Westminster model was passing through one of its periods of highest prestige during Blondel's early academic career in Britain. Not only was it celebrated at home; it was also praised overseas. The report of a committee of the American Political Science Association early in the 1950s, *Toward a More Responsible Party System*,[1] so admired the Westminster model that it proposed to modify the US system in its general direction. Although the report prompted a generation of patriotic American political scientists to spring to the defence of their country's party system,[2] the report reflected an American esteem for the model that can be traced back to Woodrow Wilson's writings and has yet to disappear completely.

During Blondel's early career, the Westminster model not only was admired by academics but was being spread throughout the world. As the Europeans scrambled to wind up their empires in the 1950s and 1960s, the British exported it complete with bewigged speakers and judges to their former colonies. The federation of the West Indies, Ghana, Nigeria and the other former African colonies joined the 'white Commonwealth' (Canada, Australia, New Zealand) in being governed under Westminster arrangements. No other nation's system of government – certainly not the United States's – has been copied so extensively in such a wide variety of societies and continents. The sun had set on the British Empire but not on Westminster-style government.

Essential Components

Had Jean Blondel continued to direct his considerable talents to the study of British government, his strong comparative instincts would undoubtedly have prompted him to exploit the numerous opportunities for comparative study that the diffusion of the Westminster model created. Political scientists interested in studying institutions often bemoan the fact they cannot abstract those institutions from the highly specific conditions under which they developed in order to examine their performance when the surrounding circumstances change. The diffusion of the Westminster model created just such an opportunity. The powers of the Prime Minister or Parliament, the role of political parties, and all the other basic questions asked about the British political system could be studied in settings as different as Canberra, New Delhi and Ottawa as well as Westminster. Ironically, as Leon Epstein has noted,[3] British political scientists turned inward just as the intrinsic importance of studying the British political system declined along with Britain's relative standing in world politics. Just as British governments failed to maintain British influence in now independent former colonies, so the British intelligentsia turned its attention away from the former empire, including its politics. Far from seizing the opportunity to study the essentials of their system of government in different settings, British political scientists were even less willing than in the past to look outwards. Most courses on British politics in British universities – and even in other countries – are taught as if the Westminster model existed only in Britain.

If we say that the Westminster model is indeed found in countries other than Britain and if we wish to analyse its performance in other settings, we need to abstract its essential elements from features of British politics that are merely contingent. We have already encountered one element in British political practice (having a hereditary element in the legislature) that is not part of the basic Westminster model; 'Westminster' countries other than Britain survive without it. The monarchy is perhaps another element that is not essential. Were Canada or Australia to replace the Queen with a retired politician as a presidential head of state, they would still, like India, be basically 'Westminster' polities.

What, then, are its basic elements? The most basic is that the party that after an election can command a majority in the lower House of Parliament is entitled to form the government. British experience with minority government in the 1970s could be interpreted as meaning that once a government has been formed, it can remain in office until it is defeated in a vote on a motion that the House has (has not) confidence in the government; contrary to what many undergraduates had been taught over the years, the Callaghan government proved that it is possible for a Westminster government to remain in office legitimately even after it has suffered defeats on major legislation that it has proposed. Implicit in this basic requirement is that there are elections, and indeed that there are political parties. It is, otherwise, almost easier to mention the numerous familiar characteristics of British politics that are not in fact necessarily part of the model.

A *career civil service* is generally found in Westminster model countries. Even in India, the civil service has been able so far to withstand attempts to use government posts as a form of patronage. Yet a career civil service that constitutes the primary source of policy advice and evaluation for ministers (what I have termed elsewhere a *Whitehall model*) is not basic to the Westminster model. Ministers might choose to rely – and Mrs. Thatcher herself showed many signs of wanting to do this – on advice from ideologically sympathetic political appointees of members of think-tanks rather than permanent officials, without calling into question the operation of the Westminster model. Indeed, most Westminster model countries do not have as extreme a dependence of elected politicians on permanent officials as does Britain; political appointees are more common and more important in, for example, Canada.

Programmatic political parties are also not necessary for, or are not necessarily the result of, a Westminster model system. Again Canada is a suitable example. The Liberal and Conservative Parties that dominated Canadian politics from the British North America Act until the very recent past were examples of 'catch-all' parties more commonly associated with the United States than Britain.[4] No clear ideological or class differences existed between the parties. Even the regional bases of support for the Liberals and Conservatives have been unstable. Thus within the last twenty years, both the Liberals and the Conservatives have scored stunning successes in the Quebec ridings in elections to the federal Parliament. The Congress Party, though not perhaps what it once was in Indian politics, remains one of the world's major examples of a 'catch-all' party whose ideology is inchoate and whose support again comes from very different classes and regions.[5]

Cabinet government can be counted a feature of the Westminster model. In all 'Westminster' countries it is the cabinet that is supposed to provide central co-ordination and policy coherence. Were ministers to refuse to accept collective responsibility for government policies other than their own departments' as a matter of routine, then the Westminster model would not operate.

Yet even here, there are important qualifications to be made. In Britain itself, collective responsibility has taken some telling blows. The 1974–9 Labour government was perhaps an extreme example of a divided government. Not only were members of the cabinet allowed to take different sides publicly on an issue that was arguably the most important of the day for Britain's future (membership of the European Community) but a group of left-wing ministers led by Anthony Wedgwood Benn made clear their opposition to the government's basic economic strategy. The successor Thatcher government, though led by a very forceful figure, contained ministers who made clear their disdain for their prime minister. The prime minister in turn described one member of her cabinet as 'semi-detached' because of his dubious loyalty.[6] As Blondel himself has demonstrated better than anyone, the nature of cabinets and ministers also varies considerably.[7] Important differences can be found even among nations that are examples of the Westminster model. Thus the Canadians expect their cabinets to be extremely large (around 40) and geographically balanced. The British in contrast operate with a relatively small cabinet (around 22) that is balanced more ideologically than regionally (though Scotland and Wales always receive some representation). No informed Canadian would seriously expect policy direction or ideological coherence from the cabinet.

The *relationships between parties and the cabinet* are also more varied than the British might expect. One of the most basic powers of the British prime minister is to choose whom to include and whom to exclude from the cabinet. Callaghan, as noted earlier, decided it was wise to include Benn in his cabinet in spite of serious policy disagreements. Thatcher at first was surrounded in her cabinet by a non-Thatcherite majority.[8] But even in these cases, British prime ministers have been able to minimize the numbers of their critics in the cabinet and to confine them to less damaging posts. In contrast, Australian practice has obliged prime ministers to work with a cabinet elected by the parliamentary party, a practice no recent British prime minister would have relished.[9] The Canadians in a sense go even further. Their 'semi-American' parties select the party leader and therefore prime minister in primaries instead of leaving the task to the parliamentary party. As was the case with the selection of Brian Mulroney as leader of the Conservative Party and thus prime minister, the party leader chosen may well come from outside the ranks of the parliamentary party. Thus, in some countries the Parliamentary party can be stripped of even its function as permanent electoral college – which some writers have seen as the residual role left to backbenchers in the Westminster model.

Judicial review has been viewed in Britain with the mixture of fascination and horror reserved for practices associated with the United States. One of the basic features of the British political system has been that once legislation is passed by Parliament (and signed into law by the Sovereign) it cannot be invalidated by judges. (Laws that conflict with the laws of the European Community may be an exception to this doctrine.) Yet judicial review is not absent from Westminster model countries. On the contrary judicial review, though rarely practised as enthusiastically as in the United States, is found in all Westminster model countries except Britain! Judicial review is probably inevitable in any country with a formalized constitution even if, as in the case of Canada until the 1980s, the constitution is in form merely an Act of the British Parliament. Ironically given the avoidance of judicial review in Britain itself, the Judicial Committee of the Privy Council in London occasionally played an important role before the 'patriation' of the constitution in settling important political and constitutional issues such as the power of the Canadian federal government to create a welfare state. Canada provides an interesting example of a widespread trend toward increased use of judicial review. The Canadian Charter of Rights is one of the most explicit attempts to combine judicial review of legislation that threatens basic rights with the Westminster stress on parliamentary sovereignty.[10]

The British political system has also been in general a *unitary rather than a federalist* system. Arguably Northern Ireland had the status of a state within a federal system until Stormont was suspended. But the suspension of Stormont, no matter how justified, showed the limits of federalism as a constitutional doctrine in Britain. In contrast, many of the attempts to export the Westminster model have created federations. Canada, Australia, Nigeria, the defunct federations of the West Indies and of Rhodesia and Nyasaland or of South Africa show how geographically widespread have been the attempts to couple the Westminster model with federalism.

For all these differences, a fundamental feature of the Westminster model is indeed shared by all the nations that use it. At its heart is the unity of the legislature and executive secured through a disciplined political party. The party that controls the legislature thereby controls the executive branch too; its control of both legislature and executive is conditional upon not losing that control of the legislature to another party or alliance of parties. This combination of legislative and executive power in the hands of the government party is the basic feature of the Westminster model.

The Appeal of the Model

The Westminster model, if poorly specified, has been much admired. No doubt some of this has been due to aspects of British politics that are not aspects of the Westminster model itself. For example, left-wing Americans who believe (often incorrectly) that British elections offer voters a more meaningful choice between parties than their own, are admiring a feature of British politics, not of the Westminster model. The Canadian example shows that catch-all, non-ideologically differentiated parties can dominate Westminster model polities. Yet leaving aside this conflation of aspects of British politics with the Westminster model, the Westminster model itself has had a significant number of admirers around the world.

Its chief attraction is an apparent suitability for mass democracy. A crucial problem here has been how to offer voters an opportunity to make clear and decisive choices about who should rule them. In Westminster democracies, as in all others, this process is complex and problematic. Parties may well take refuge in ambiguity, or in emotionally powerful but essentially meaningless gestures (as when Mrs Thatcher kissed a calf for the television news). Parties may make convincing promises that they cannot keep or have little intention of keeping. New problems or crises may arise as soon as the election is over that have not been discussed in the campaign. But in Westminster model countries more than in other types of democracy, voters are at least able to make a crystal clear *retrospective* judgement.[11] In the United States, blame for unpopular public policies can be diffused among different branches of government (often controlled by different political parties). A large literature has grown up on 'divided government', the situation in which the Democrats generally control Congress, the Republicans the presidency. Although, as this literature shows, the game of divided government is complex, there can be little doubt that it obscures responsibility for government successes or failures. In contrast, the Westminster model leaves little doubt where blame or praise should go. If things have gone wrong the legislature cannot be blamed; if the chief executive has erred, his or her party cannot avoid electoral blame unless it can convince voters that circumstances such as the world economy absolve all politicians from responsibility. Thus, in Westminster model countries, at least retrospective voting ensures clear accountability.

The Westminster model may increase the chances of campaign promises being turned into public policy. McKenzie may have gone too far in his celebrated work in suggesting that the distribution of power in the British Conservative and Labour Parties was almost identical.[12] Yet there can be little doubt that the Westminster model imposes a need for unusually strong discipline on parties. This discipline in turn enhances the probability that electoral promises will be fulfilled. No strong-minded committee chairs or legislative manoeuvring will stand in the way if the party wishes to keep its promises.[13]

A second advantage of the Westminster model in the eyes of its admirers was precisely that it encouraged strong parties. The extreme importance of maintaining a majority in the legislature has helped to ensure that the discipline of parties in Westminster model countries is nearly always total. Voters in turn are so conditioned to expect party unity that signs of disagreement within a party are regarded as reasons for not voting for it. Why should strong parties be regarded as an advantage? Largely because disciplined political parties are probably the most effective way that has been found for electorates to control their rulers. For all the claims in countries such as the United States that weaker parties allow voters to choose individuals rather than voting robotically for anyone nominated by a party, the reality is that few voters have the information or inclination to evaluate individual candidates carefully; the only (and partial) exception to this rule is in contests for the American presidency.[14] Voters are, however, fully capable of making accurate assessments of where parties stand in relation to each other on policy issues. Even more valuably, voters are able to guess accurately how parties are likely to react to future crises or problems; voters have sufficient interest and knowledge to be able to guess that *ceteris paribus* the centre-left party is less likely to cut welfare in a budget crisis than a centre-right party. Thus, Westminster model systems, by encouraging the development of strong parties, encourage the institutions best suited to mass democracy. As Rose and McAllister have pointed out, British voters increasingly choose between parties in terms of their policies and past records; it does not follow that British voters would be any more capable than American voters of evaluating carefully the record of their individual legislators if party discipline had broken down.[15]

Admirers of the Westminster model have generally liked the limits it sets on the political power of interest groups. Interest groups do flourish in Westminster model systems, and have often enjoyed sufficient economic leverage to compel governments to make major concessions to them or enter into neo-corporatist relations with them. Occasionally, an interest group has been able to suggest that it was a crucial swing group in elections; British farmers in the 1940s and 1950s and British Leyland workers in the 1970s were highly subsidized in part for such reasons. But claims to be the decisive voting bloc in elections have generally been unconvincing. The Westminster model has inhibited most institutionalized forms of interest group political power.[16] The model provides no scope for the 'iron triangles' that were once thought to give American interest groups the power to control their policy area; the log-rolling so evident in distributive policy-making in Congress is much less likely to happen. Thus, while allowing interest groups to operate freely and often work very closely with government departments, Westminster arrangements seemed to offer a very effective check on their power.

A fourth advantage of the Westminster model was thought to be decisiveness in policy-making. Unencumbered by the need to steer legislation through a separate, potentially recalcitrant legislature, political leaders in Westminster model countries could pursue policies that could be promulgated speedily and that would be coherent. These advantages were thought to be particularly important in economic policy-making. The capacity of governments to make speedy, coherent policy changes was of particular advantage during the Keynesian era. The capacity of a British chancellor of the exchequer to vary taxes almost immediately was contrasted with the long-drawn-out battle with Congress that the Kennedy administration faced when it wished to cut taxes in the 1960s in order to stimulate the economy. By the time the American tax cut had been decided upon and implemented, it stoked the fires of inflation in the later 1960s rather than counteracting recession at the start of the decade. In contrast, Westminster model countries were institutionally well equipped to steer their economies, changing policy quickly to take account of changing economic conditions.

The Decline of the Westminster Model

The number of countries governed under the Westminster model peaked in the 1960s. Thereafter, the descent into tyranny of many of Britain's former colonies reduced the number sharply. This decline in numbers coincided with a sharp decline in intellectual standing; Leon Epstein noted a similar and related decline in the prestige of the British type of political party.[17] What brought these associated developments about?

Partly, no doubt, the answer was the comparative economic decline of the most prominent Westminster model country, Britain. Even more damaging was the suspicion that this was due in part to the workings of its political institutions. A large literature emerged that ascribed Britain's economic difficulties to features of the Westminster model.[18] Several competing arguments were advanced to support this claim. The very features of the Westminster model that had facilitated democratic control of policy were blamed for creating economic problems.

As we have seen, a fundamental feature of the Westminster model is that it gives tremendous power to elected governments. Westminster model systems have great difficulty in insulating issues or policy areas from political decision-making. For this reason, civil libertarians have always had doubts about the degree to which such countries safeguard basic rights. The British Parliament can – and does – strip away fundamental civil liberties if in its view circumstances (such as IRA terrorism) seem to warrant the step. The recent Canadian attempt to combine guarantees of rights with the supremacy of the legislature has not entirely succeeded; the 'not withstanding' procedure for legislating contrary to the Charter opens a loophole that so far has been exploited by provinces, not the federal Parliament, but the latter may use it in the future.

Monetarists also have seen the extensive power of elected politicians in Westminster model countries as a major problem unless that power is checked by some discipline such as the gold standard. It is now conventional wisdom among European governments – articulated, for example, at the Maastricht summit of the European Community – that central banks can operate effectively in controlling the money supply only if they enjoy considerable autonomy from politicians. The Bundesbank's success in steering the Germany economy has been ascribed to the greater degree of independence it possesses than the American Federal Reserve Board, which in turn is more autonomous than the Bank of England. The Bank of England may indeed be one of the least autonomous central banks in the world, and this lack of autonomy is a direct result of the emphasis on the dominance of elected politicians that the Westminster model creates more generally. Monetarists believe that politicians will almost always misuse their power, manipulating the money supply in order to secure their own re-election rather than stable growth in the money supply.[19]

The cynicism about the use Westminster politicians make of their capacity to make speedy decisive changes in macroeconomic policy is by no means limited to monetarists. Even during the peak of Keynesianism's dominance of economic thought, doubts had been raised about the capacity of the Treasury to diagnose sufficiently quickly and accurately changes in economic conditions for it to take effective corrective action. Changes in economic policy may have inadvertently exacerbated inflation and unemployment because policy-makers lacked the information necessary to react to upturns or downturns at the appropriate point in the economic cycle. Even worse, the Westminster model would provide no institutional limits on governments that wanted to use their power to engineer pre-election booms followed by post-election retrenchments that would destabilize the economy. The 'stop–go' cycle that was such a feature of the British economy after the Second World War was due at least in part to the unrestrained power over economic policy that the Westminster model gave politicians. The much admired capacity for decisive action that it provided was perhaps a failing.

The greatest difficulty the Westminster model has experienced around the world has not been in economic policy-making, however; probably all democracies have an imperfect record in that area. The greatest difficulty has been in coping with ethnic and racial divisions, and in providing for the peaceable politics of what Young calls 'cultural pluralism'.[20] Most of the countries in which cultural pluralism has broken down have been countries in which a Westminster model has reinforced or exacerbated pre-existing tensions between regions or tribes. The demise of the federation of the West Indies, the frequent coups in Nigeria and the replacement of the Westminster model with one-party tyrannies in many of Britain's former colonies all reflect this problem. The standard justification for one-party rule in Africa, for example, has been the need to avoid exacerbating tensions between different tribes that generally support different, competing political parties. So general has the problem been among British colonies that have achieved independence since the Second World War that it is the great exception, India, the world's largest democracy, that demands an explanation for its survival that cannot be explored here. The reasons for the survival of the Westminster model in India in the face of appalling difficulties deserves extensive research.

It should be noted that the Westminster model's difficulties with cultural pluralism are by no means confined to the Third World. The antagonism between anglophone and francophone Canadians has been more bitter since the late 1960s than for the previous hundred years. A more tragic conflict has raged in Northern Ireland. In the course of various attempts to settle this bloody conflict, British governments have admitted that the Westminster model cannot work in Northern Ireland. All the proposals for power sharing have involved the abandonment of the Westminster model Stormont Parliament that governed Northern Ireland from 1922 until 1972 and the creation of institutions that differ sharply from the rules and practices of the Westminster system.[21]

What is it about Westminster model systems that has created such difficulty in adapting to conditions of cultural pluralism? Once again, the problem has been the obverse of the advantage long claimed for the Westminster model; it generates clear winners and clear losers. When politics is based primarily on class division and conflict (as was by and large the case in Britain), this can be tolerated; class division can usually be compromised, and class conflict, contrary to Marx, involves the formation of complex unstable coalitions so that the balance of power between social classes can shift. Primordial loyalties to one's race, ethnic group or region are less easily compromised, though the consociational nations have shown that such compromise is possible. But the Westminster model tends to generate clear winners and, so long as politics revolves around ethnic or racial loyalties, the winners will always be winners, and the losers will always lose. This was, of course, the major problem in Stormont. The Catholic minority had no prospects of becoming the majority and under-standably failed to generate much allegiance to the Northern Irish state. Similarly, the ever victorious Protestant majority had few incentives to accommodate the interests or wishes of the minority. The long period of Conservative rule over Scotland while Scotland overwhelmingly rejects Conservative candidates has produced another difficult because uncom-promised situation.

American practice provides an interesting comparison here. After the Civil War the South was a defeated, alienated region. Yet (and given its treatment of African Americans, unfortunately) the South was soon fully incorporated into the political system, because it was allowed to dominate Congress; and through the workings of the seniority system retained a disproportionate influence there until the 1960s. Though we may dis-approve of the purposes to which this power was put, such as blocking civil rights legislation, the compromise was useful in terms of rebuilding national unity after the Civil War. A potentially disaffected region was given a major share of national power.

The capacity of the American system of separation of powers to give favoured minority regions a share is well known. It has been much harder to secure this in Westminster model countries. Canadian political practice has been to make strenuous efforts to secure representation for all of the nation's regions. The unusually large Canadian cabinet (generally contain-ing over 40 ministers) owes its size and composition to the attempt to include and balance politicians from all the regions. Canadian prime ministers spend as much time thinking about the regional balance of their cabinets as British prime ministers spend on ideological balance. Yet even the Canadian genius for accommodation has proved to be incapable of resolving the Quebec issue. When political divisions are as profoundly based as those between anglophone and francophone Canadians, the Westminster model's tendency to generate an unambiguous political result becomes a major problem. Both the Canadian parties compete for Quebec's votes, but Canadian institutions do not provide an institutional base from which the Quebecois could play, and perhaps as importantly could see themselves playing, the sort of role in national politics that the South played through its congressional base in American national politics. As in Northern Ireland – though fortunately without violence – Canadian experience suggests that the tendency of the Canadian system to produce clear, relatively unfettered winners is problematic in deeply divided societies. The outcome of the Quebec crisis in Canada is uncertain. We do know, however, that the Westminster model has been discarded in most of

Britain's former colonies precisely because of its inability to cope with regional divisions.

The Future of the Westminster Model

We should not disparage the Westminster model. Its advantages, described above, are very real. It continues to provide a degree of clear democratic accountability unmatched by the main contending models. Neither the American system of sharing powers between different institutions, nor the continental European multi-party systems, come close to providing as clear and effective a way of holding rulers answerable to the ruled as it does. Both also obscure the answer to basic questions about who is responsible for public policy. The Westminster model makes the answer clear. Nor can we say that it has been relegated to insignificance. It continues to provide the basis for the government of the world's largest democracy, India, for Britain, and for the 'white Commonwealth'. The Westminster model has some claims on the basis of population to be the world's major democratic political system.

Yet with the interesting anomaly of India, Westminster-type arrangements have been confined to relatively homogeneous nation states, which may themselves be a thing of the past. The vast movement of populations around the world in the second half of the twentieth century has made all nations more multicultural than they used to be. All the European countries have significant minority populations now that will not be as easily assimilated as, for example, successive waves of immigrants were into Britain until the 1950s. (One might compare the rise of Jean Blondel within British political science to the similarly dramatic rise of immigrant industrialists such as Mond or retailers such as Sief or Cohen.) British or French Muslims, for example, are likely to remain a separate element in their societies for the foreseeable future, with a culture and religion that sets them aside from their fellow citizens.

The nation is thus threatened from both above and below. The creation of the European Community is the clearest example of the transfer of sovereignty and power to a supranational level. Simultaneously, and in apparent contradiction to trends towards supranationalism, the revival of nationalism across Europe in the last quarter of the century has revived the claims of old nations such as Scotland, Euskadia, Catalonia, Corsica and Flanders to some degree of autonomy. The nation state that was the fundamental unit of political life from the eighteenth century until the present will have to cope with the claims of more diverse societies, and demands to share sovereignty at several levels. The political systems of the next century will be more complex, so the advantages of a model that provides neat, clear government, offering clear democratic accountability, will rarely be in demand.

This is particularly true in the case of new democracies in Eastern Europe and Latin America, which are generally ethnically heterogeneous and which need to accommodate and conciliate their various minorities rather than to give all power to the majority. We turn to a direct consideration of these systems in the following chapters.

Notes

1 Committee on Political Parties, American Political Science Association, *Toward a More Responsible Party System*, *American Political Science Review* 44 Supplement (September 1950).

2 For the best of this writing see Leon Epstein, *Political Parties in the American Mold* (Madison: University of Wisconsin Press, 1986).

3 Leon Epstein, 'Books for Teaching Politics' *British Journal of Political Science* 17 Part 1 (January 1987) 93–108.

4 Peter Aucoin, *Party Government and Regional Representation in Canada* (Toronto: University of Toronto Press, 1985); Keith Archer, 'On the Study of Canadian Political Parties' *Canadian Journal of Political Science* XII (June 1989) 389–98.

5 Atul Kohl, *India's Democracy: An Analysis of Changing State–Society Relations* (Princeton NJ: Princeton University Press, 1988); *Democracy and Discontent: India's Growing Crisis of Governability* (Cambridge and New York: Cambridge University Press, 1990).

6 For a number of interesting examples, see Peter Hennessy, *Cabinet*, (Oxford: Basil Blackwell, 1980).

7 Jean Blondel, *World Leaders: Heads of Government in the Postwar Period* (London and Beverly Hills: Sage Publications, 1980); *The Organization of Governments in the Contemporary World* (London and Beverly Hills: Sage Publications, 1985).

8 For a stimulating discussion of how Thatcher was constrained by and manoeuvred within the constraints of a cabinet dominated by adversaries, see Anthony King, 'Margaret Thatcher: The Style of a Prime Minister' in Anthony King (ed.), *The British Prime Minister* (Raleigh: Duke University Press, 1985).

9 David Butler, *The Canberra Model* (Oxford: Oxford University Press, 1973) not only describes this practice but provides one of the few books on the Westminster model in comparative perspective.

10 Clare Beckton and Wayne MacKay, *The Courts and the Charter* (Toronto: University of Toronto Press, 1985); David Elkins, 'Facing Our Destiny: Rights and Canadian Distinctiveness' *Canadian Journal of Political Science* XII (1989).

11 On the general importance of restrospective voting see Morris Fiorina. *Retrospective Voting in American National Elections* (New Haven: Yale University Press, 1981).

12 Robert McKenzie, *British Political Parties* (London: Heinemann, 1955).

13 On the surprising frequency with which campaign promises are kept, see Ian Budge, David Robertson and D.J. Hearl (eds), *Ideology, Strategy and Party Change: Spatial Analyses of Post-War Election Programmes in 19 Democracies* (Cambridge: Cambridge University Press, 1987) Chapter 1.

14 For a defence of voter rationality in presidential contests see Benjamin I. Page and Robert Y. Shapiro, *The Rational Public* (Chicago: University of Chicago Press, 1992).

15 Richard Rose and Ian McAllister, *The Voters Begin to Choose: From Closed Class to Open Elections in Britain* (London and Beverly Hills: Sage Publications, 1986; but see Bruce E. Cain, John A. Ferejohn and Morris P. Fiorina, 'The Constituency Basis of the Vote for US Representatives and British Members of Parliament' *American Political Science Review* 78 no. 1 (1984) 110–25 for arguments that British MPs do indeed owe some of their vote to their own as opposed to their parties' records.

16 For an interesting exchange on this point, see J. Roland Pennock, 'Pressure Groups and Parties in Britain' *American Political Science Review* 56 (1962); and Brian Barry, 'Comments on the "Pork Barrel" and Majority Rule' *Journal of Politics* 33 (1971).

17 Leon Epstein, 'What Happened to the British Model?' *American Political Science Review* 74 no. 1 (1980) 9–22.

18 See Samuel Brittan, 'The Economic Contradictions of Democracy' *British Journal of Political Science* 5 (1975) 129–59; for a critical review of these arguments see Brian Barry, 'Does Democracy Cause Inflation? The Political Ideas of Some Economists' in Leon Lindberg and Charles Maier (eds), *The Politics of Inflation and Economic Stagnation* (Washington DC: Brookings Institution, 1985) 280–317.

19 Brittan, 'Economic Contradictions'; for a good review of the literature on central bank autonomy see John Woolley, 'Central Banks and Inflation' in Lindberg and Maier, *The Politics of Inflation* 318–48.

20 Crawford Young, *The Politics of Cultural Pluralism* (Madison: University of Wisconsin Press, 1976).

21 On Northern Ireland see Richard Rose, *Governing With Consensus* (London: Faber and Faber, 1971); A.T.Q. Stewart, *The Narrow Ground Aspects of Ulster 1609–1969* (London: Allen and Unwin, 1977); on Quebec see Richard Handler, *Nationalism and the Politics of Culture in Quebec* (Madison: University of Wisconsin Press, 1988); David Bell, *The Roots of Disunity: A Look at Canadian Political Culture* (Toronto: McClelland and Stewart, 1979); Kenneth McRoberts and Dale Postgate, *Quebec: Social Change and Political Crisis* (Toronto: McClelland and Stewart, 1986); André Bernard, *What Does Quebec Want?* (Toronto: James Lorimer, 1978).

12

Democratization and Constitutional Choices in Czechoslovakia, Hungary and Poland, 1989–1991

Arend Lijphart

Among the most important constitutional choices that have to be made in democracies are the choice of the electoral system, especially majoritarian election methods versus proportional representation (PR), and the choice – which we have just discussed in terms of the 'Westminster model' – of the relationship between the executive and the legislature, especially presidential versus parliamentary government. Political scientists disagree about which of the alternatives are preferable, but they are in agreement that the choices made by democratic constitutional engineers can have far-reaching effects on how well the democratic system operates (see Hermens, 1941; Lakeman and Lambert, 1955; Finer, 1975; Lijphart and Grofman, 1984; Linz, 1990; Horowitz, 1990, Lijphart, 1992). Moreover, these choices strongly influence the basic orientation – majoritarian or consensual – of the democracy that is being created: presidential government and electoral rules like the first-past-the-post (plurality) method promote the former, and PR and parliamentary government the latter orientation (Lijphart, 1991).

For democratizing countries, these choices are particularly important because the many non-institutional conditions for viable democracy – social, cultural, historical and international – are much less amenable to change by political fiat. In addition, if the new democracy does prove to be viable, the initial choices are likely to last for a long time. Seymour Martin Lipset and Stein Rokkan (1967) have pointed out that the party system established at the beginning of a country's democratic experience tends to become virtually 'frozen'. This applies even more strongly to the fundamental constitutional structure: drastic changes in electoral systems and shifts from presidentialism to parliamentarianism or vice versa are extremely rare in established democracies.

How and why do the constitutional engineers in democratizing countries choose one or the other of the basic alternatives? This is the question that I shall try to answer in this chapter. My point of departure will be Rokkan's suggestion that the logic of the democratization process itself is a critical explanatory factor. On the basis of a comparative examination of the three most promising new democracies in Eastern Europe – Czechoslovakia, Hungary and Poland – I shall formulate several qualifications and refinements to Rokkan's thesis as well as a number of additional explanations.

The Rokkan Hypothesis

There is no general theory on transitions from communism to democracy that is directly relevant to our enterprise. Fortunately, we do have some indirectly applicable theory, based on earlier democratic transitions: Stein Rokkan's discussion of the adoption of PR in continental European countries at the end of the nineteenth and the beginning of the twentieth century. Rokkan (1970, p. 157) explains that shifts to PR came about 'through a convergence of pressures from below and from above. The rising working class wanted to lower the thresholds of representation in order to gain access to the legislatures, and the most threatened of the old-established parties demanded PR to protect their position against the new waves of mobilized voters created by universal suffrage.' Barbara Geddes (1990, p. 29) finds a similar pattern in Latin American political history: 'Shifts to proportional representation in the larger Latin American countries have all taken place at the time of major changes in the distribution of political power . . . Parties expecting to decline . . . want proportional representation as a means of insuring that they can continue to exercise some degree of influence.'

This is what nowadays would be called a 'rational choice explanation': given the inevitability of democratic universal-suffrage elections and based on a realistic – and, to be on the safe side, slightly pessimistic – assessment of their electoral chances, both the ruling conservative parties and their challengers needed PR to protect their interests. The old parties that would necessarily lose at least some of their representation and power wanted to make sure that they did not lose everything, and the new parties wanted a guarantee that they would gain at least a substantial share of representation and political power.

The frequent use of the bicameral compromise exhibits the same logic of power-sharing: one fully democratic chamber in which the new parties would have the best chance, but a second chamber in which the old parties would still be favoured by means of a continuation, perhaps only temporary, of more restricted voting rights and/or the over-representation of rural areas with stronger than average conservative support. The power-sharing logic can be extrapolated similarly to the choice of parliamentary or presidential forms of government: presidentialism means separation, and separate election, of executive and legislature and hence, assuming at least slightly different chances for the old and the new parties (or groups of parties) in these elections, another possibility of safeguarding the interests of both sets of parties.

These logics are equally applicable to the East European democratic transitions around 1990. For Rokkan's 'old-established parties' read ruling communist parties, and for his 'rising working class' read the new democratic forces.[1] And they add up to the expectation that in Eastern Europe PR and presidentialism should be the prevalent new constitutional structures.

At first blush, this hypothesis does not appear very promising as a general social-science explanation. Even in Western Europe, the area covered by Rokkan, it runs into an awkward deviant case: if the process of democratization entails the logic of power-sharing by means of PR, why didn't this logic operate in the UK, which democratized without turning to PR? Also, presidentialism (or semi-presidentialism) has remained rare in Western Europe. On a worldwide basis, the hypothesis suggests that we should find PR and presidentialism to be the normal constitutional pattern: all contemporary democracies were non-democracies once, and hence had to go through the process of democratization at some point. Instead, there is only one large area of the world characterized by PR presidentialism: Latin America. Elsewhere we find PR and parliamentarianism (continental Western Europe), presidentialism and plurality elections (the United States and the countries it has influenced, especially the Philippines), and the combination of parliamentarianism and plurality (the U.K. and those of its former colonies that are now democracies in Africa, Asia, Australasia, the Caribbean and North America) – a geographical pattern with only a few minor exceptions (Blondel, 1969, p. 319; Powell, 1982, p. 67).

Nevertheless, the Rokkan hypothesis has great heuristic value since it provides a theoretical point of departure for a theory-starved subject matter. More importantly, when several qualifications, which are already logically implied by the Rokkan hypothesis itself, are added, and in conjunction with a few other explanations, it turns out to have strong explanatory power after all. The most important of these additional explanations – the problem of ethnic division and minority representation – can also be derived from Rokkan's work. I shall discuss this second Rokkan hypothesis at greater length below.

Constitutional Patterns in Three East European Democracies

Czechoslovakia, Hungary and Poland form an attractive set of cases for our comparative examination, because they clearly differ from each other on both the electoral system and the parliamentary–presidential dimensions. In fact, if these dimensions are represented as continua with four basic positions – as they are shown in Figure 12.1 – the three cases show almost perfect variation for the purpose of empirical analysis. With regard to the electoral system, they range from extreme PR (Poland) to a moderately majoritarian system (Hungary); only the fully majoritarian position, exemplified by the United Kingdom, is not occupied. On the

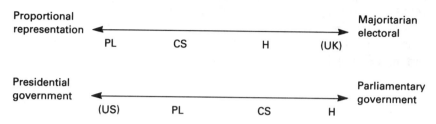

FIRST ROKKAN HYPOTHESIS

CS, Czechoslovakia; H, Hungary; PL, Poland; UK, United Kingdom; US, United States

Figure 12.1 *Constitutional choices by three new (and two old) democracies, plotted on the proportional-representation/majoritarian and presidential/parliamentary continua*

presidential–parliamentary continuum, the range is from semi-presidentialism (Poland) to full parliamentarianism (Hungary), with only the full presidential form of government, as in the United States, unrepresented.

A few words need to be said to justify the placement of the countries on the two continua. The system adopted for Poland's October 1991 parliamentary elections is generally seen as one of extreme, even irresponsible, PR. For instance, *Newsweek*'s Warsaw correspondent speaks of its 'zany rules' leading to the 'politics of the bizarre', and describes the election result as 'a laboratory demonstration of proportional representation gone wild' (Nagorski, 1991a, p. 14; 1991b, p. 28). This description is vastly exaggerated. For the lower house (Sejm), the electoral formula was indeed one of the most proportional that PR countries use (largest remainders with the Hare quota), but the average district magnitude, that is the number of deputies elected per district, was not unusually high (10.6), and 15 per cent of the seats were set aside as bonuses for the larger parties (those receiving more than 5 per cent of the total vote). This is certainly not 'bizarre' by comparative standards.

The system did yield a very high degree of party fragmentation: nine parties with more than 5 per cent of the seats in the Sejm (the largest of which won only 13.5 per cent of the seats), and an additional twenty smaller parties. But fragmentation in the Senate, elected by plurality, was almost the same: even more parties elected, a total of thirty-one, including as many as seven with at least 5 per cent of the seats.[2] Clearly, PR was not the only culprit. Nevertheless, in the conventional dichotomous classification of PR systems as moderate or extreme PR, Poland comfortably fits the extreme category, mainly because of the absence of an effective barrier for small parties: the 5 per cent rule was used to give the larger parties a bit of an advantage rather than really to hurt the smaller ones.

The rules for the 1990 elections in Czechoslovakia fit the moderate PR

category. The electoral formula was slightly less proportional than the
Polish one (largest remainders with the Droop or Hagenback-Bischoff
quota), but there were much larger district magnitudes (with the Czech and
Slovak republics serving as the final two election districts). The crucial
difference with Poland, however, was the 5 per cent minimum which
parties had to meet in either the Czech or the Slovak district. Even if the
allied Czech and Slovak parties are counted as separate parties, only eight
parties won parliamentary seats, and the allied Civic Forum and Public
Against Violence won clear majorities in both chambers (Wightman,
1990).[3]

Hungary's law for the 1990 elections is much more complicated than its
Czechoslovak and Polish counterparts and also much more complicated
than almost all of the electoral laws in the established Western democracies
– and hence far too complex to be described in detail here. However, its
essential elements can be summarized easily: a combination of majoritarian methods (a two-ballot system in single-member districts) for 45.6 per
cent of the parliamentary seats, and PR rules for the remaining 54.4 per
cent of the seats, with a 4 per cent threshold (for further details see
Körösényi, 1990; Kukorelli, 1990; Szoboszlai, 1990). These rules bear a
superficial resemblance to those of the German system, but they differ in
that the disproportionalities of the single-member district elections are not
compensated by the PR results. Unlike the German system, therefore,
which is in the final analysis basically a PR system, the Hungarian system
can truly be called a combined or mixed majoritarian-PR system.

Its results were also far from proportional. John R. Hibbing and Samuel
C. Patterson (1992, p. 436) state that 'Hungary's electoral system, like
practically all known in the world, hurts smaller parties and helps larger
parties' – ignoring the fact that, by comparative standards, this tendency
was extreme. The largest party won 42.5 per cent of the seats with 24.4 per
cent of the voters' support, as measured by the PR votes (Hibbing and
Patterson, 1992, pp. 436, 450). Since the second party was also over-
represented to some extent, the total percentage of over-representation
amounted to more than 20 per cent – a higher percentage than the average
in the highly disproportional British elections from 1974 to 1987![4] Another
indicator of the majoritarian nature of the electoral system is that the
largest party, with the same 24.4 per cent vote share, would have won
about 29 per cent of the seats under hypothetical list PR rules (with a 4 per
cent threshold) but 48 per cent under hypothetical British-style plurality
rules: the actual result, 42.5 per cent of the seats won, is much closer to the
hypothetical plurality than to the hypothetical PR result (Ilonszki, 1991,
p. 15). Clearly, while the Hungarian system is not a fully majoritarian one,
it belongs on the majoritarian side of the continuum in Figure 12.1.

The placement of the three countries on the presidential–parliamentary
continuum requires less extensive commentary. Poland has a semi-
presidential system 'modelled on the Fifth French Republic' (Pelczynski
and Kowalski, 1990, p. 347): a popularly elected president with substantial

powers, but also a prime minister and cabinet subject to parliamentary confidence. Czechoslovakia and Hungary have basically parliamentary systems. Their presidents are elected by parliament, and they serve mainly as ceremonial heads of state. The one important qualification is that Czechoslovakia's president, Vaclav Havel, derives considerable political influence from his huge popularity. His position may be compared – though not quite equated – with that of President Charles de Gaulle in his first term of office from 1958 to 1965. Like de Gaulle during this period, Havel's democratic legitimacy and prestige are so great that he does not require popular election to confirm them. In short, while Czechoslovakia remains basically parliamentary, it is at least slightly more 'presidential' than Hungary.[5]

Refining the Rokkan Hypothesis

Figure 12.1 shows that the Rokkan hypothesis is supported by only half, three out of six, of the basic constitutional choices made by the East European democracies, and only one case – Poland – is completely in accordance with it. On the other hand, the Polish case does not merely fit the hypothesis, but provides a well-nigh perfect illustration of it. Semi-presidentialism and extreme PR emerged as the result of the round table agreements of early 1989 and the subsequent attempt by the Communist Party to retain at least a small share of political power. During the round table negotiations, the position of the Communist Party was still strong and Solidarity had to consent to conservative compromises because of the fear of Soviet intervention. A strong president was created, elected by the two chambers of parliament but not subject to its confidence; it was tacitly agreed that General Wojciech Jaruzelski would be elected president – providing a guarantee of continued communist power. A further guarantee of this kind was that in the June 1989 elections, 65 per cent of the seats on the Sejm (lower house) were reserved for the Communist Party and its allies and that only 35 per cent of the seats would be freely elected. On the other hand, in the newly created Senate, all seats could be freely contested (Pelczynski and Kowalski, 1990, pp. 347-51).

Solidarity's overwhelming election victory ushered in the second phase of constitutional reform. Having created a strong and independent presidency, it was logical to make this office a popularly elected one – won by Lech Walesa in late 1990. And the chastened communists now insisted on a pure form of PR for the next Sejm elections in order not to be driven from power altogether.

In short, the logic of power-sharing as a result of democratization operated exactly as suggested by Rokkan: shared power by means of PR, by the separation of executive and legislative power, and even by a bicameral legislature. Why didn't this logic determine a similar outcome in Czechoslovakia and Hungary? Rokkan's hypothesis requires three qualifications.

The first and most critical qualification that needs to be made to Rokkan's hypothesis is that it is dependent on the 'old-established parties' retaining sufficient power and legitimacy to negotiate a relatively favourable compromise. The logic of power-sharing only operates if the new constitutional structures are the outcome of a genuinely negotiated agreement. Round table conferences between Communists and democrats took place in all three countries, and the outcome, termed a 'negotiated revolution' by László Bruszt (1991) in the Hungarian case, can be similarly described in the other two countries.

The big difference is that Poland was the first country to begin the democratization process, and that, by the time of the Hungarian and Czechoslovak round table conferences, the threat of Soviet disapproval had receded. Another difference is that in Poland and Hungary so-called reform communists, less tainted by the non-democratic past, played an increasingly important role, while reform communism was crushed in Czechoslovakia after the Prague Spring in 1968. Since the old-style Czechoslovak Communist Party lacked both raw political power, provided by the external threat, and internal legitimacy, it continued to take part in the round table talks, but 'the course of events was largely determined by its political opponents' (Wightman, 1990, p. 319).

Hungary was in an intermediate position with regard to the power and legitimacy of the 'old-established parties'. It is significant that, similar to the situation in Poland and in accord with Rokkan's thinking, the Hungarian communists wanted 'a semi-presidential system in which a popularly elected president', presumably the well-known reform communist leader Imre Pozsgay, 'could counterbalance the parliamentary opposition majority' (Szoboszlai, 1991, p. 203). The compromise reached at the round table was that the first president would be elected directly, prior to the election of the new parliament. However, two of the new democratic parties refused to sign this agreement and initiated a referendum, narrowly approved by the voters in late 1989, which stipulated that parliamentary elections take place first and, by implication, that the president would be elected by the new parliament. This was indeed the constitutional arrangement that the newly elected parliament approved in 1990: a straightforward parliamentary system. The reform communists still did not give up and once more proposed, by means of a referendum of their own in the summer of 1990, that the president be popularly elected; the referendum failed because of a very low turnout.

Another assumption made by Rokkan is that both old and new parties are not only rational maximizers of their self-interest, but also capable of making a realistic assessment of their future electoral potential. This assumption is not necessarily correct, and, to the extent that it is incorrect, it may affect the validity of the Rokkan hypothesis.

The Hungarian and Polish cases provide several examples of unwarranted optimism as well as pessimism. The Polish communists were much too optimistic at first, and they were stunned by Solidarity's victory in 1989.

They then became too pessimistic about their political future, and insisted on an extreme form of PR for the 1991 parliamentary election which would enable them to survive, if only barely, another electoral disaster. As the election result showed, moderate PR would have served this purpose just as well: they became the second largest party, winning about 12 per cent of the vote.

In Hungary, the communists were consistently too optimistic – and their opponents too pessimistic. Although it was never put to a test, the expectation that reform communist leader Pozsgay could win a direct presidential election was probably not realistic; he ran in a single-member parliamentary election district in 1990, and was defeated. In the negotiations about the electoral system for parliamentary elections, the communists also behaved as if they expected to remain a major party. They held out for a mixed but predominantly majoritarian system: 75 per cent of the deputies elected in single-member districts and only 25 per cent by PR. The other parties wanted to reverse these proportions, and the round table compromise was to have approximately equal proportions. However, the old parliament, in which the communists still held greater power, had the final word and decided to increase the number of single-member districts (Szoboszlai, 1991, pp. 203–4; Kukorelli, 1990, pp. 139–44).

Moreover, in the debate about the electoral threshold, the reform communists argued in favour of a relatively high 5 per cent threshold, in contrast with the 3 per cent barrier advocated by the new parties; the predictable compromise was 4 per cent. With about 10.9 per cent popular support in the March 1990 election (as measured by their PR votes), they won an almost proportional 8.5 per cent of the seats. A higher threshold would not have hurt them, but having 75 per cent of the seats filled in single-member districts, as they had originally proposed, would have hurt badly: they were saved by their opponents!

The final qualification concerns Rokkan's assumption that parties are the main political actors in the democratization process and are expected to remain so in the new democratic system. In all three countries, the deep distrust of the Communist Party appears to have spread to all organizations called 'parties'. Hungarian MP József Szájer (1991, p. 42) writes that 'the three p-words – parties, parliament, politics – are held in low esteem by the public'. As a result, politicians have a strong incentive to emphasize personalities instead of parties. This has had several effects on the choice of electoral system and the parliamentarianism–presidentialism debate.

In Hungary, an additional reason why the communists favoured a semi-presidential system was that they believed that Pozsgay's personal popularity would be able to overcome the unpopularity of the party label. In Czechoslovakia, President Havel's personal popularity, and the political influence based on it, are already high by absolute standards, but they are further magnified by, and relative to, the low reputation of the political parties.

As far as electoral systems are concerned, the distrust of political parties has tended to weaken the case for PR, since PR almost always means party-list PR.[6] This gives party organizations the responsibility to compose the lists of candidates – and hence a great deal of control over who gets elected. Moreover, to the extent that parties believe that their individual candidates are considerably more attractive than the parties as collectivities, they have a strong reason to opt for majoritarian elections in single-member districts instead of PR elections. Both factors played a major role in Hungary's decision not to adopt PR.[7]

In Poland, these considerations were also important, but instead of leading to a decision against PR, they resulted in the adoption of the kind of list PR used in Finland. In this system, the voter must choose both a party and an individual candidate in the party; the winning candidates are simply those that have received the highest number of individual votes. This reduces the power of party organizations considerably, and it stands in sharp contrast to the so-called 'closed-list' system, used, for instance, in Germany and Israel, in which the order of the candidates on the list fixed by the party cannot be changed by the voters.

Additional Explanations

So far, I have focused on Rokkan's hypothesis concerning the effects of democratization on constitutional choices, and I have tried to refine and strengthen it by pointing out the conditions under which it is more or less likely to operate. However, the comparative examination of the three East European countries also reveals a number of *additional* explanations – unrelated to the logic of the Rokkan hypothesis.

First, Rokkan himself states the most important of these other explanations: the problem of ethnic and religious minorities. It provides a strong reason to adopt PR, because PR guarantees minority representation and can counteract potential threats to national unity and political stability. Rokkan (1970, p. 157) writes that 'it was no accident that the earliest moves toward proportional representation (PR) came in the ethnically most heterogeneous countries' of Western Europe. In Latin America, too, a second important reason for shifts to PR was that it served 'as a means of limiting competition which . . . in the past resulted in violence and military intervention' (Geddes, 1990, p. 16).

When we make Rokkan's and Geddes's second explanation into a general hypothesis and apply it to Eastern Europe, it works especially well for the case of Czechoslovakia. Its use of PR was decisively influenced by the fact that it is a deeply divided binational state. In fact, its PR is an integral part of what may well be called a textbook example of consociational democracy (Lijphart, 1977). Proportionality is one of the four basic principles of consociationalism, and Czechoslovakia is also thoroughly consociational in the other three respects: (a) it has a power-sharing cabinet including representatives of both the Czech majority and the

Slovak minority, as well as a Czech president and a Slovak prime minister; (b) it is a two-unit federal system consisting of autonomous Czech and Slovak republics with their own governments; and (c) it has a mutual veto in the form of a concurrent majority requirement stipulating that constitutional amendments and major legislation require not only approval by extraordinary legislative majorities but also by such majorities in the upper house among Czech and Slovak representatives voting separately.

Clearly, for Czechoslovakia PR was a deliberate choice and part of a comprehensive package of measures designed to alleviate ethnic pluralism. Moreover, the consociational principle of executive power-sharing virtually rules out presidential and semi-presidential forms of government. While it is not completely impossible to have consociational democracy under such systems, their concentration of executive power in the hands of one person is inimical to the basic idea of shared power – in sharp contrast with the collegial sharing of power in cabinets in parliamentary systems.[8] Because Czechoslovakia is characterized by such a thorough and comprehensive application of consociational democracy, its parliamentary form of government must also be regarded as part of the total consociational syndrome of constitutional arrangements – and hence also, like PR, as one of the effects of the country's deep ethnic divisions.

Ethnic pluralism was also a concern, although not at all to the same extent, in the Polish decision to opt for PR. For instance, the 1991 electoral law specifically exempted ethnic minority parties, such as the German Minority Party, from the 5 per cent requirement for taking advantage of the bonus seats for large parties. The minority-protection explanation gains further plausibility from the fact that Hungary – the one country that opted against PR – while certainly not completely homogeneous, has fewer ethnic problems and less politicized ethnicity than the other two countries.

A second further explanation of the choice of electoral system is that majoritarian electoral systems, applied in single-member districts, may have a special quality that makes them attractive in addition to their strategic advantages for large parties and for parties which believe that they have especially appealing individual candidates: the direct link between the voter and the voter's individual representative. This factor has played an important role in preserving majoritarian election systems in the United Kingdom and most other English-speaking countries.

It also appears to have been a factor of considerable importance in Hungary. The main reason was that the old system was a single-member district system, and that it was already being slowly reformed into a genuinely representative system before 1989. Although the 1985 election was still a one-party election, about forty independent candidates were elected (Körösényi, 1990, p. 337; Szoboszlai, 1990, pp. 121–2). And in 1988 and 1989, recall elections, which had long been a formal possibility, were actually and successfully used on several occasions – increasing the legitimacy of the single-member district form of representation.

Thirdly, my earlier references to Poland's adoption of French-style semi-presidentialism and of the Finnish form of list PR raise the general question of the influence of foreign models. In the above two instances, the choices were much more strongly determined by internal political considerations than by external models. On the other hand, these foreign models served as more than mere after-the-fact rationalizations: they gave the advocates of semi-presidentialism and open-list PR the useful ammunition of specific empirical precedents in their arguments in favour of these alternatives.

A slightly stronger facilitating influence was exerted by the foreign example of an electoral threshold of about 4 or 5 per cent. All three East European democracies adopted such a threshold (although in Poland only for the allocation of bonus seats). Among the Western democracies, West Germany pioneered the 5 per cent threshold in its very first federal election in 1949, but in more recent years 4 per cent thresholds were also adopted by Sweden as part of its 1970 constitutional reform and in Norway for the 1989 election. Germany also uses the 5 per cent threshold for its European Parliament elections, as does France; and the Netherlands uses a 4 per cent threshold in the election of its European representatives. These percentages may appear rather arbitrary, but the approximately 4 or 5 per cent level is now widely seen as the judicious level at which small parties are effectively discouraged, while the principle of proportionality remains basically intact.

Another example of the borrowing of a specific constitutional device is Hungary's adoption of the German constructive vote of no confidence, designed to increase executive stability and the prime minister's power. It is tempting to attribute the impact of these German precedents to geographical proximity. But it should be remembered that the other major instance of the introduction of the constructive vote of no confidence occurred in more distant Spain, and that the most ambitious proposal to adopt a German-inspired electoral system was made, in 1986, by a royal commission in even more distant New Zealand!

Fourthly, a model that is likely to be more influential than any foreign model is a democratizing country's own previous model of democracy. Czechoslovakia provides an almost perfect example: except for its federal structure and the 5 per cent electoral threshold, the new Czechoslovak democracy is very similar to that of the inter-war First Republic. Hungary and Poland were mainly governed by authoritarian regimes during the inter-war period and hence lack the kind of democratic background that could have served as an influential model for their new democratic structures. Of course, to the extent that earlier democratic models have a significant impact on contemporary institutions, it becomes important to inquire into the determinants of these earlier forms of democracy. To do so in detail is beyond the scope of this chapter. However, in the case of Czechoslovakia it is clear that the First Republic was already deeply influenced by the need to accommodate ethnic divisions and that, as a result, it already operated largely along consociational lines.

Tentative Conclusions

This analysis runs into the usual problem of comparative research: a large number of relevant explanatory variables, but only a small number of cases. Hence my conclusions can only be tentative. Nevertheless, a rather clear pattern has emerged, and Rokkan's theoretical insights, with the various extensions and qualifications that I have added, are by and large vindicated. The two most important explanations of the choice of electoral system and presidential or parliamentary government are precisely the two suggested by Rokkan in the context of the earlier democratization of Western Europe: the logic of the democratization process itself – with the crucial proviso that the old and new parties have approximately equal bargaining power and need to reach a genuine compromise – and the problem of ethnic division and minority representation.

The other influences – distrust of political parties, attachment to single-member district representation, the examples of foreign and previous democratic experiences, and incorrect assessments of parties' electoral chances in free electoral competition – appear, at least in our three cases, to be of secondary importance. However, the last of these factors *could* have a major impact: for instance, if the old and new parties were both far too optimistic and felt confident of winning an outright victory, the pressure for PR and presidentialism would vanish. In our cases, the unwarranted optimism and pessimism of the parties merely reinforced already existing tendencies (in Poland) or cancelled each other out (in Hungary).

Together, these factors explain the placement of the six constitutional choices in Figure 12.1 very well. The Polish choices are completely in line with the first Rokkan hypothesis. Since the communist parties were weak negotiating partners during and following the Hungarian and Czechoslovak round table conferences, the first Rokkan hypothesis also explains why three of their four constitutional choices were *not* PR and presidential; the most dramatic illustration is Hungary's adoption of parliamentary government, pushed through by two of the new parties against the strong communist preference for, and the initial agreement on, a directly elected president. The basic constitutional choices made by Czechoslovakia – PR and parliamentarianism – are perfectly accounted for by its adoption of a thoroughly consociational system for managing its ethnic divisions, in line with the second Rokkan hypothesis. It also explains the Hungarian choice of a mainly majoritarian electoral system quite well – in terms of the *absence* of major ethnic divisions.

These basic tendencies predicted by Rokkan's two hypotheses were reinforced but not, in my judgement, fundamentally determined by the attachment to single-member district representation and the distrust of political parties (Hungary), the influence of an earlier democratic model (Czechoslovakia), the salience of a foreign model (French semi-presidentialism in the case of Poland), and unwarranted communist pessimism (Poland). Conversely, but in only one case, one of these secondary factors has weakened a primary influence to some extent: the distrust of political parties has increased the trace of presidentialism in Czechoslovakia's mainly parliamentary government.

Prospects: the 'Freezing' of Initial Choices?

Another reason why my conclusions can only be tentative is that the constitutional choices indicated in Figure 12.1 may not be final. How likely is it that major shifts will take place in the foreseeable future?

Czechoslovakia appears to face the greatest uncertainty: will it remain one state or will it be partitioned along ethnic lines into separate Czech and Slovak sovereign states? Maintenance of political unity will probably require an increase in the already strongly federal and consociational character of the system. President Havel's December 1991 proposal that the popular election of the upper (federal) house be changed to its election by and from the two republic legislatures, and that this new chamber meet in the Slovak capital of Bratislava instead of Prague, is symbolic of this trend. But Slovak pressures for outright secession and Czech impatience with Slovak demands are growing. On the other hand, if Czechoslovakia does remain a single sovereign state, it is highly likely that it will retain PR and parliamentarianism – the latter notwithstanding President Havel's popularity and political ambition. It is instructive to recall that the parliamentary First Republic also had an extremely popular and activist president, Tomás Masaryk, who was unable to effect a lasting shift into a more presidential direction.

Hungary is the least likely of the three countries to change its basic constitutional choices. The extremely complex electoral rules may be simplified to some extent, but their majoritarian character will probably not be affected. Majoritarianism favours the two largest parties, and these parties are, understandably, not eager to abandon this advantage; this is the same mechanism that has tended to maintain the plurality method in two-party systems like the United Kingdom, Canada and New Zealand. The parliamentary form of government also appears to be strongly anchored in the Hungarian constitutional system – reinforced by the fact that the presidential alternative is closely identified in the public mind with the former Communist Party.

In Poland, PR is likely to be maintained but the larger parties – those above the 5 per cent level – are likely to introduce an electoral threshold to make it into a more moderate PR system, unless, of course, public opinion surveys predict a drastic loss of support for these parties. Polish semi-presidentialism appears to be the least stable of the six basic constitutional choices. President Walesa's repeated suggestion that he also become prime minister – uniting the presidency and prime ministership in one person – entails the abandonment of the essence of semi-presidentialism and has the potential of inducing a permanent shift either to full presidentialism or to full parliamentarianism. Among other new democracies, semi-presidentialism has not proved very stable either: Portugal and, to a more limited extent, Greece adopted a strong French-style president when they democratized in the 1970s, but they both abandoned this innovation in the earlier 1980s, shifting to conventional parliamentary forms of government. Another reason why Poland may shift to parliamentary government is its extreme multi-partyism in which no party, unless it has an unusually popular leader, can realistically expect to win presidential elections by itself; there are therefore no strong partisan self-interests in maintaining the powerful, directly elected, presidency.

These forecasts are obviously speculative, but they are not, in my judgement, overly conservative. Of the six basic constitutional choices in the three East European countries, only one appears to be subject to a major modification, confirming another Rokkan-inspired proposition: the 'freezing' of political and constitutional structures in the immediate aftermath of democratization.

Notes

I am very grateful to the many politicians and social scientists in Budapest, Prague and Warsaw, who were so kind to discuss this subject with me during my visits in November and December 1991. My research was supported by a grant from the Center for German and European Studies, University of California, Berkeley, and the first draft of this chapter was written while I was a fellow of the Science Centre, Berlin. I should also like to thank these two centres for their invaluable support. Finally, I should like to express my appreciation for the helpful comments I received from Atilla Agh, Tun-jen Cheng, Ellen Comisso, Ghita Ionescu, Frangano Ledgister, Matthew S. Shughart, György Szoboszlai, and the participants in two meetings at which I presented earlier versions of this chapter: the Seminar in Political Decision-Making, Graduate School of International Relations and Pacific Studies, University of California, San Diego, on 27 January 1992, and the conference on 'Institutions and the Democratic Process', Focused Research Program on Democratization, University of California, Irvine, on 22 February 1992.
This article was written before the break up of Czechoslovakia in 1993.

1 I shall use the term 'communists' and 'reform communists' generically to refer to parties that, in both the pre-democratic and democratic phases, may have used different formal names (such as the old Hungarian Socialists Workers' Party, the new Hungarian Socialist Party, the old Polish United Workers' Party, and the new Polish Democratic Left Alliance), and although the reform 'communists' eventually restyled themselves as social democrats on the West European model. At the time of the 1990 elections, the Czechoslovak communists still formally called themselves the 'Communist Party' in both parts of the country.

2 Professor Jerzy Wiatr of the University of Warsaw (and a newly elected member of the Sejm) kindly supplied me with the final election results.

3 As Ellen Comisso (1991) has pointed out, however, these 'parties' in the 1990 election were social movements rather than parties as usually defined; future elections may therefore well produce greater party-system fragmentation.

4 This percentage of over-representation is the commonly used Loosemore-Hanby index of disproportionality (see Loosemore and Hanby, 1971; Taagepera and Shugart, 1989). The election results on which I based my calculations are given in Szoboszlai (1991, p. 209).

5 Attila Agh (1991, p. 22) goes so far – too far, in my opinion – as to include Czechoslovakia in the semi-presidential category together with Poland.

6   As György Szoboszlai has reminded me, however, the 176 single-member district elections in Hungary yielded 170 winners who were party candidates and only 6 independent winners – indicating that the negative feelings toward political parties should not be exaggerated.

7   The alternative of the single-transferable-vote form of PR, in which voters vote for individual candidates instead of parties, appears not to have been seriously considered in any of the three countries.

8   Because semi-presidentialism entails a measure of shared power between president and prime minister and because it also has a collegial cabinet, it is less inimical to consociational democracy than pure presidentialism. Nevertheless, a semi-presidential president is normally still the pre-eminent executive officer – which hurts the possibilities of forming broad governing coalitions.

References

Agh, Attila. 1991. *The Parliamentary Way to Democracy: The Case of Hungary*. Budapest Papers on Democratic Transition, no. 2. Budapest: Hungarian Center for Democracy Studies Foundation.

Blondel, Jean. 1969. *An Introduction to Comparative Government*. London: Weidenfeld and Nicolson.

Bruszt, László. 1991. '1989: The Negotiated Revolution of Hungary', in György Szoboszlai, ed., *Democracy and Political Transformation: Theories and East-Central European Realities*. Budapest: Hungarian Political Science Association.

Comisso, Ellen. 1991. 'Political Coalitions, Economic Choices', *Journal of International Affairs*, vol. 45, no. 1 (summer), pp. 1–29.

Finer, S.E. 1975. *Adversary Politics and Electoral Reform*. London: Anthony Wigram.

Geddes, Barbara. 1990. 'Democratic Institutions as a Bargain Among Self-Interested Politicians', paper presented at the annual meeting of the American Political Science Association, San Francisco, 1990.

Hermens, F.A. 1941. *Democracy or Anarchy? A Study of Proportional Representation*. Notre Dame, Indiana: The Review of Politics.

Hibbing, John R. and Samuel C. Patterson. 1992. 'A Democratic Legislature in the Making: The Historic Hungarian Elections of 1990', *Comparative Political Studies*, vol. 24, no. 4 (January), pp. 430–54.

Horowitz, Donald L. 1990. 'Comparing Democratic Systems', *Journal of Democracy*, vol. 1, no. 4 (fall), pp. 73–8.

Ilonski, Gabriella. 1991. *An Introduction to the New Hungarian Parliament*. Budapest Papers on Democratic Transition. Budapest: Hungarian Center for Democracy Studies Foundation.

Körösényi, András. 1990. 'Hungary', *Electoral Studies*, vol. 9, no. 4 (December), pp. 337–45.

Kukorelli, István. 1990. 'The Birth, Testing and Results of the 1989 Hungarian Electoral Law', *Soviet Studies*, vol. 43, no. 1, pp. 137–56.

Lakeman, Enid and James D. Lambert. 1955. *Voting in Democracies: A Study of Majority and Proportional Electoral Systems*. London: Faber and Faber.

Lijphart, Arend. 1977. *Democracy in Plural Societies: A Comparative Exploration*. New Haven: Yale University Press.

Lijphart, Arend. 1991. 'Constitutional Choices for New Democracies', *Journal of Democracy*, vol. 2, no. 1, (winter), pp. 72–84.

Lijphart, Arend, ed. 1992. *Parliamentary Versus Presidential Government*. Oxford: Oxford University Press.

Lijphart, Arend, and Bernard Grofman, eds 1984. *Choosing an Electoral System: Issues and Alternatives*. New York: Praeger.

Linz, Juan J. 1990. 'The Perils of Presidentialism', *Journal of Democracy*, vol. 1, no. 1 (winter), pp. 51–69.

Lipset, Seymour Martin and Stein Rokkan. 1967. 'Cleavage Structures, Party Systems and Voter Alignments: An Introduction', in Seymour Martin Lipset and Stein Rokkan, eds, *Party Systems and Voter Alignments*. New York: Free Press.

Loosemore, John and Victor J. Hanby. 1971. 'The Theoretical Limits of Maximum Distortion: Some Analytic Expressions for Electoral Systems', *British Journal of Political Science*, vol. 1, no. 4, pp. 467–77.

Nagorski, Andrew. 1991a. 'Politics of the Bizarre: Democracy Is Running Wild in the Polish Elections', *Newsweek*, 28 October, p. 14.

Nagorski, Andrew. 1991b. 'Taking a Lesson from Poland', *Newsweek*, 11 November, pp. 28–9.

Pelczynski, Zbigniew and Sergiusz Kowalski. 1990. 'Poland', *Electoral Studies*, vol. 9, no. 4 (December), pp. 346–54.

Powell, G. Bingham, Jr. 1982. *Contemporary Democracies: Participation, Stability and Violence*. Cambridge, Mass.: Harvard University Press.

Rokkan, Stein. 1970. *Citizens, Elections, Parties: Approaches to the Comparative Study of the Processes of Development*. Oslo: Universitetsforlaget.

Szájer, József. 1991. 'Political Differentiation During the Democratic Transition', *Uncaptive Minds*, vol. 4, no. 2 (summer), pp. 40–3.

Szoboszlai, György. 1990. 'From a Paternalistic to a Pluralistic Electoral System: The Case of Hungary, 1985–1990', in György Szoboszlai, ed., *Váltók é Utak*. Budapest: Magyar Politikatudományi Társaság.

Szoboszlai, György. 1991. 'Political Transition and Constitutional Changes', in György Szoboszlai, ed., *Democracy and Political Transition: Theories and East-Central European Realities*. Budapest: Hungarian Political Science Association.

Taagepera, Rein and Matthew S. Shugart. 1989. *Seats and Votes: The Effects and Determinants of Electoral Systems*. New Haven: Yale University Press.

Wightman, Gordon. 1990. 'Czechoslovakia', *Electoral Studies*, vol. 9, no. 4 (December), pp. 319–26.

13

Popular Political Organization and Democratization: a Comparison of Spain and Mexico

Joe Foweraker

It is odd that most research on democratic development in the countries of Southern Europe and Latin America ignores popular politics and focuses almost exclusively on elite initiatives. The ambitious scope of past paradigms of political change made this almost inevitable. The modernization approach[1] supposed that urban industrial growth would promote democracy by expanding popular participation, while the bureaucratic-authoritarian thesis[2] replied that it was precisely this expansion which most threatened democracy. But the final focus was always on the holders of economic and political-military power. More recently, the largest and most systematic attempt to assess democratic advance in these countries[3] again privileges elite pacts and constitutional prescriptions at the expense of popular organizations. It is true that lip service is paid to the 'resurrection of civil society' (O'Donnell et al. 1986: 26), but this society is treated abstractly, and little attention is paid either to political parties or to the rise of popular movements.

A new literature is emerging, however, which reflects more accurately the increasing importance of popular movements in democratic development. These movements include neighbourhood associations, church networks, human rights groups, peasant organizations and independent trade unions or union 'tendencies', to mention only some; and recent studies, both by senior scholars in Europe[4] and mainly younger scholars in the United States,[5] have established the force of these movements in virtually every social sector and region of the countries in question. There is now more information both on the social composition of these movements and on the prevalent forms of popular protest, not to mention an enhanced sense of the democratic potential of popular politics.

Yet this new research still stops short of a systematic inquiry into the political principles of popular organization and strategic choice, and so fails to pursue the connections between popular politics and processes of institutional change within political regimes. Consequently neither of the two main approaches to popular politics and democratic change proves capable of delivering an integrated account. On the one hand, there is the 'transitions' literature, which infers from general observations that civil society does indeed condition elite accommodation,[6] but leaves the reified social forces of this society outside of the political analysis proper; on the other, there are the grass-roots studies which defend but do not demonstrate the importance of popular political organizations for democratic advance. In short, there is a 'top-down' and a 'bottom-up' approach, but 'ne'er the twain do meet' because they do not explore and explain the linkages between popular political actors and the changing institutions and policies of central government. Hence surprisingly little is really known about the popular contribution to making democracy.

This general conclusion applies *a fortiori* to the cases of Spain and Mexico. The almost forty years of Francoism prevented all research into popular politics in Spain, so that the world remained largely ignorant of what might be happening at the grass-roots of Spanish civil society. Linz's early characterization of the 'limited pluralism' of Spanish authoritarianism (Linz, 1964) referred uniquely to elite actors; while the main studies of popular politics under Franco published since his death are restricted to peak organizations and national leaderships, and do not address the relationships between grass-roots struggle and regime change (Maravall, 1978; 1982; Preston, 1976; 1986; Tusell, 1977; Vilar, 1976). Similar strictures apply to research on Mexico where the 'standard account' (Roxborough, 1984) of the regime of the Revolutionary Institutional Party has portrayed it as the supremely assured political manager of an immature and fragmented civil society. In this account popular political organizations are either coopted or dispersed by government action, and so have quite failed to influence the institutional configuration of the most stable political regime of Latin America (Foweraker, 1988). In both cases an explicable empirical bias is compounded by the kind of conceptual blinkers which would anyway make popular political history almost invisible except at moments of spectacular or violent manifestation.

The purpose of the present inquiry is to compare the impact of popular politics in Spain and Mexico, and so provide a corrective to an exclusive emphasis on elite pacts and constitutional changes. The intention is not to deny the facts of formal negotiation and political engineering, but to complement them. Thus, there is no doubt that Spain democratized through a *transición pactada*, but only after the ground had been prepared by at least twenty years of popular struggle; while the democratic outcome of a similar period of such struggle in Mexico has recently been prevented by an elite and constitutional pact between the ruling party and its traditional right-wing opposition (the PRI and the PAN). The evident ability of elite actors to both promote and prevent 'democratic transitions' is sufficient reason to address the independently popular contribution to developing democracy, whether or not it achieves a change of regime. To do so I will look first at the new forms of popular political organization to emerge in these countries, before examining their political and strategic context, and especially their links with the institutions of central government and the ways they work to change those institutions.

Popular Political Organization

The main organizational innovation in the popular politics of these two countries was to combine labour union and social movement into a combative 'new unionism' or popular movement. Such movements were successful in extending independent popular organization in seemingly adverse conditions. Spanish workers discovered in the workers' commissions a *sui generis* style of organization, which emerged from small pockets of resistance in the workplace to spearhead the political struggle against the Franco regime; while the 'democratic tendencies' amongst the electrical workers and teachers in Mexico led the way in constructing a new kind of popular movement in that country. These were not the only opposition organizations. By the early 1970s democratic opposition in Spain included church groups and their youth sections, student organizations, intellectual caucuses, neighbourhood associations and even some proscribed political parties, not to mention resurgent nationalisms in Catalonia and the Basque country. Civil society in Mexico also contained a range of opposition parties, as well as urban popular movements, student groups and peasant organizations of different kinds. But in both countries it was the union movements which catalysed other forms of popular politics, and these same movements which discovered the key strategies of popular political struggle.

The movements were led by 'natural leaders' who had been born to a particular political generation. In Spain it was the children of the Civil War, who came of age in the 1950s. In Mexico it was the generation of the student movement of 1968. The white terror in Spain left no family of this generation intact. The student massacre of 1968 precipitated a diaspora of young activists to every sector and region of Mexico, so spawning a plethora of new movements and 'fronts' during the 1970s. Thus these were leaders born of repression and schooled in generic traditions of struggle, rather than in particular doctrines. Communists and Catholics organized side by side in the workers' commissions; while communists, 'Cubans', Maoists, Trotskyists and left Catholics all joined the Mexican diaspora. The movements themselves acted as schools of democracy, which prevented cooptation by close accountability; but directly democratic mechanisms exacerbated the internal tensions occasionally created by competing convictions or personal ambitions. Hence, the early movements in both Spain and Mexico were better at mobilizing than organizing; and building more permanent organizations continued to be difficult in clandestine or repressive conditions.

There is no doubt that activism in the new movements led to political learning, and many activists attest to the progressive discovery of their own social and political selves (as, in their own language, they changed from being objects to subjects of their own history). But the initial demands of the movements were not political, and had really nothing to do with democracy writ large. On the contrary, they were typically 'bread and butter' demands concerning wages and conditions of work. Yet it was making demands at all which mattered (Castells, 1983), and, in retrospect, it is clear that the roots of democratic struggle are to be found in these incipient union-popular practices, and not in the rediscovery of a democratic tradition or the reassertion of democratic values. In neither Spain nor Mexico is it possible to discern any initial commitment to an 'imagined' liberal democratic polity, which motivated popular actors because it appeared desirable (with Spain's democratic experience being conflicted and truncated, and Mexico's quite absent). Still less did any party political programme of the left have any appeal. In fact, political parties could only begin to play a positive role in the democratic struggle by offering logistical support to the movements, as in Spain, or by persuading the movements to join them in the electoral arena, as in Mexico.

The real process is one of demand-making, and it is this process which makes the Spanish experience of successful transition comparable with the frustrated struggle in Mexico. For only by putting their economic and social demands do popular actors discover the legal and institutional constraints of the authoritarian regime, and so begin to imagine the political conditions for effective demand-making, and the political changes which might see their original demands satisfied. In other words, what popular leaders most require is a certain *capacidad de gestión*, or the kind of ability to get the results which legitimate their own position and cement their own organization; and this means effective political representation. Hence, the movements begin to press demands which relate increasingly to the nature and forms of their linkage to the system overall, and it is this process which translates economic to political demands, and union struggles into political projects. It is a process which is driven by popular mobilization but catalysed by institutional controls, and so cannot be understood without a sense of the institutional context.

Institutional Context and Strategic Choices

The union movements under comparison all emerged from within the central corporatist institutions of their respective regimes. Their birth and development were stimulated by 'statist' (Schmitter, 1974) corporatist initiatives. Thus the first commissions in Spain were self-elected from the factory committees of Franco's Vertical Syndicate. These new leaders had gained union experience on the committees, where they discussed conditions of work, social security and job classification; and the most combative workers used the relative freedom of election to secure committee posts first at factory and later at provincial and national levels.

Similarly in Mexico, the most successful movements have organized within the state-chartered union corporations of the ruling party, which, like the Syndicate in Spain, provide a formal framework of legal and institutional constraints and opportunities. The movements in Mexico have often been able to organize openly, if with difficulty: the constitution only sanctions a single accredited union per sector. The illegal commissions, on the other hand, had to act simultaneously as legal factory committees to escape direct repression. But in both cases the movements took advantage of the representational forms of the state corporations to achieve autonomous organization and pursue their own objectives. The political trajectory of the movements therefore highlights the linkages between popular organization and central government, and their struggles often express incremental attempts to 'renegotiate' their relations with central institutions of representation and regulation.

It must be recognized that these corporatist institutions are not mere appendages of the regimes in question, but command the high ground of the legal and institutional terrain linking state and civil society. The massive pyramidal structure of the Vertical Syndicate aspired to control every workplace in Spain, and until 1966 its *apparatchiks* were confident they could coopt the commissions and subject them to reason of state. The state structure of Mexico is much more complex, but, in similar fashion, the union sectors of the ruling party and its Labour Congress have sought to bind all organized labour to the corporate bias of government, and have offered lucrative careers to compliant labour leaders. In both regimes government has deployed a range of vertical and clientelistic controls through formal corporatist structures, so that legal constraints are combined with legal chicanery and corruption to confuse and demoralize opposition, and delay or prevent authentic representation.

In this connection it may appear strange that popular organizations developed a close and symbiotic relationship with these corporatist institutions. But it was precisely the state attempts at control and cooptation which catalysed the distinctive strategic discoveries of the new movements (the strategic moment always being the moment of engagement with the political environment). Indeed, the decision to develop the movements both inside and outside state institutions was itself a strategic choice of the first importance, which confirmed the key strategic combination of legal and extra-legal struggle. The Spanish commissions had to launch strikes to back their demands, but in conditions of clandestinity this was only possible by maintaining the effective fiction of a legal separation between striking workers and commissions' representatives on the factory committees of the Syndicate (when in fact it was the commissions themselves which had launched the strike). In this way even repression, or the fear of it, could be turned to good strategic account. In Mexico autonomous organization had to advance against the deceptions and administrative repression of *charrismo* (the corrupt bossism of the state-chartered corporations), but attempts at legal advance often had to use illegal means (so that the origins of many urban popular movements were an illegal act of land invasion for which they nevertheless sought legal and political sanction). Just as the Spanish commissions used strikes as an integral part of their legal/extra-legal negotiating strategy, so union movements in Mexico would always mobilize and negotiate simultaneously, in a strategic thrust which Mexico's teachers graphically described as 'war in Vietnam, negotiations in Paris'.

Hence, the new forms of popular organization discovered their own strategies. Movements in Mexico were especially suspicious of political parties, and would accept no strategic orientation from them. The support given to the commissions by the Spanish Communist Party was logistical but derivative in so far as it formalized and disseminated the strategic discoveries of the labour movement (and for these purposes the party's pragmatism and opportunism were entirely appropriate). And as the legal and political constraints complicated and condensed, so the strategic opportunities multiplied. The Spanish commissions used the 1958 Law of Collective Contracts to advance their own demands through the legal form of the Syndicate, while developing their real relationship with employers far beyond the confines of Francoist legality.

The combination of legal and extra-legal struggle allowed Spanish commissions and Mexican movements to infiltrate the Vertical Syndicate and colonize the union corporations of the ruling party. In Spain the legal fictions had to be maintained intact, while in Mexico popular leaders could at least aspire to legal control of the delegational and sectional committees of the union corporations. This process of infiltration allowed the Spanish commissions to use the institutional resources and legal cover of the Syndicate to coordinate their own activities and build a horizontal organization despite vertical impositions. In Mexico the national scope of union corporations like the state teachers' union (SNTE) finally favoured the extension of inter-regional and cross-sectoral alliance strategies, and the construction of national-level 'coordinating committees', which were partially successful in combating the transformism of the ruling party (Foweraker, 1988) and assuaging the negative effects of institutional linkage. Such effects were everywhere evident in both Spain and Mexico, for infiltration and colonization occupied exactly the same strategic space as cooptation and corruption, and many movements succumbed to the blandishments of state power. Hence the effectiveness of popular strategy depended on the trust which reposed in natural leaders, and the tight personal networks woven during years of grass-roots struggle in authoritarian circumstances. It was only such networks which could bind together the legal and extra-legal fields, and so allow popular movements to traverse the institutional boundaries of the state with relative impunity.

The vertical impositions on popular organization were so irksome and damaging that popular leaders came to insist on the need for organizational autonomy of authoritarian controls. But it is clear that such autonomy could never be a real goal or objective of popular organization, but was rather the tactical or strategic condition of effective representation. For the main requirement of popular politics continued to be the kind of *capacidad de gestión* which could get a proper response to immediate and concrete demands, which meant that popular movements sought engagement with state agencies and insertion into the political system overall. To allege that such representation was not 'real' because it was conditioned by vertical manipulation is to miss the point. It was real to the degree that demands were satisfied, and to the degree that popular organization achieved the conditions for satisfying further demands. Thus, popular strategy was both *institutionalist* in seeking to project grass-roots change into the political system, and *legalist* in its awareness that only legal forms and statutory procedures could secure these changes. This may not seem a very romantic vision of democratic struggle, but it does suggest the heroism of daily survival and advance under authoritarian regimes. Legalism tended to broaden the base of resistance to continuing violence and repression, and institutionalism itself did not imply either conformism or lack of conflict.

Popular Organization and Political Change

The new forms of popular political organization clearly imply political changes in civil society of the kind which Dahl might characterize as associationalism (Dahl, 1971). Moreover the political learning which takes place through political and strategic choices creates a new kind of knowledge which is itself essential to popular advance in what Gramsci calls the 'war of position' (Gramsci, 1971). But there are no guarantees that political changes in civil society will bring about institutional changes at the level of political regime, still less a regime change itself. Indeed, the inherent intractability of the authoritarian regime and its reluctance to recognize popular initiatives means that the search for institutional linkage has constantly to be impelled by mobilization, popular protest and strike activity. Even then it is apparent that such linkage is only achieved piecemeal and precariously. Nonetheless, it is precisely through seeking and shaping linkage, and through demanding more effective forms of representation, that popular organizations finally achieve changes in the institutional configuration of the regime, and in the broader political culture.

The key to understanding the general dynamics of this process is to understand that the vertical controls of the Syndicate in Spain and the corrupt bossism of union corporations in Mexico both acted to deny effective popular representation and prevent institutional linkage. Hence, the very search for such linkage challenges and undermines the vertical assumptions of Francoism, the pervasive clientelism of union corporations in Mexico, and the particularism of power relations in both regimes. Although this popular challenge is specific, gradual and differentiated it does achieve important general results. In Spain it progressively undermined the institutional cornerstone of the whole regime, and precipitated the subsequent disintegration of the Francoist project. In Mexico it similarly subverted the coherence of the regime's union corporations, and, by extension, its corporate control of the electoral arena which has for so long assured the ruling party's electoral dominance. Furthermore, as traditional mechanisms of political control decomposed the regime was obliged to install more centralized and 'concerted' forms of political mediation and regulation, which then impaired the coherence of the ruling party itself. Federal administrative and bureaucratic initiatives inevitably removed powers of patronage from regional power-brokers within the party, which led to intra-elite splits at regional level long before the Democratic Current split from the party at national level and contested the general elections (see below). In short, the popular challenge to union bossism provoked splits in the party apparatus and finally promoted the first effective electoral challenge to the system in several decades.

As a corollary to these developments the popular challenge, as much in Spain as in Mexico, contributed to create a *de facto* tradition of free collective bargaining by increasingly autonomous union movements, despite the worst intentions of the regimes. In Spain this was critical to the success of transition itself, as the governments of the transition and post-transition periods drew on the tradition to promote the social 'concertation' which underwrote the fledgeling democratic constitutional arrangements. Even in Mexico the new tradition tended to reform the relations between civil society and regime, and to recover a measure of political initiative for popular organizations. This was apparent in the aftermath of the earthquake of September 1985 in Mexico City, when the government was obliged to abandon its own reconstruction plans, and recognize the alternative project presented by the urban popular movements. This successful challenge then carried over into the formation of neighbourhood committees, the election of popular representatives to the Neighbourhood Assembly, the dissemination of the demand for an elected government of the Federal District, and a clear electoral triumph for the opposition in the capital in the general elections of July 1988.

In these ways a slowly changing balance of political force within civil society could begin to impinge upon the operational capabilities of these regimes. But none of this would have been possible had not the popular organizations simultaneously developed their own capacity to deliver and sustain high levels of popular mobilization. In Spain the commissions and their allies maintained a widespread and insistent mobilization throughout the critical period of the transition (1976 and the first three or four months of 1977) until first political parties and then labour unions themselves were made legal. The importance of these protests was that they clearly conditioned the calculations by elite and state actors of the political costs of different policy and constitutional options, with the result that *continuismo* became not so much impossible as impracticable. Mexico, on the other hand, had experienced a rising rhythm of popular mobilization in its civil

society throughout the 1980s which extended from protests against government austerity policies to yet broader and angrier protests at electoral
fraud. The 'civic stoppages' of earlier in the decade brought hundreds of
thousands of Mexicans on to the streets, but they look insignificant
compared with the electoral mobilization of 1988, and the mass protests
which followed the July elections. Yet, despite the most public and
universal challenge ever, the ruling party stood firm, and replied with a
politically repressive war of attrition against the opposition coalition. In
this instance it appears that popular organization and protest had not so far
altered elite calculations as to impel a change in the rules of the political
game.

   A different conclusion is also possible, which is that the outcomes of this
form of popular and democratic struggle are indirect and contingent, and
do not necessarily conform to either the immediate or the long-term
objectives of popular actors. Indeed, it is difficult to deny that the political
aspirations and objectives of popular organizations in Spain and Mexico
have been the contingent result of union demand-making and mobilization. Contingencies are clearly present if only because popular objectives
are mediated by the interaction or opposition of contending or contradictory organizations, and are multiplied at the moment of engagement with
the political environment. In similar fashion, strategic choice itself may
indicate intentionality, but it cannot assume a unified agent with a singular
rationality because all such choices are influenced *inter alia* by political
organization, leadership, factionalism, ideology, legal and institutional
constraints, and the many faces of political repression.

Popular Politics and Democratic Development

These observations make it impossible to think of democratic projects as
historical personalities, or even as the result of historical imagination. On
the contrary, the emergence of a recognizable project will mean that
certain strategic choices have accumulated and crystallized into some
systematic organizational and ideological expression. But even in such
contingent cases there are comparable benchmarks, as when union and
popular demands begin to be stated in terms of *rights*. In Spain this
moment was reached in 1966 when the commissions opted for open
struggle and the communists for a mass party. These decisions reflected
their sense of their rights to organize autonomously and assemble and
speak freely. They were rights which integrated the political conditions for
winning their demands, but the principal demands now focused on
democratic liberties. Finally it was the formation of clearly inter-class
organizations like the Junta Democrática and the Plataforma de Conver-
gencia Democrática in 1974 which marked the definitive broadening of the
union movement into a popular struggle for democracy.

   In Mexico the challenge to union bossism had led to an insistence on labour and professional rights (which were anyway inscribed in the constitution of 1917), and to many battles for the political control of union corporations. This was because any notion of civil and legal rights plainly ran counter to the particularism which made all power non-normative and implicitly rejected all juridical authority. But until the late 1980s popular movements had remained suspicious of political parties and the ruling party's manipulation of electoral politics, and their belated entry into the electoral arena and the beginning of their struggle for fair elections can best be understood as an extension of their traditional struggles in the corporatist arena. In the past they had struggled for legal rights against clientelism and *charrismo*. Their struggle now was also for political rights and against the clientelist control of elections in Mexico's 'corporatist democracy' (Aziz, 1987). The principle of continuity was indeed the rule of law, but there were signs that democracy itself had become a value, and the primary objective of popular political organization.

The Democratic Current, which went on to form the opposition electoral coalition of the National Democratic Front (FDN), had split from the ruling party in response to the Democratic Electoral Movement, which was pledged to defend the revolutionary promise of 'effective suffrage' by setting up a national organization of poll-watchers to oversee general elections. Moreover, there is no reason to doubt the force of the unprecedented presence of popular movements in this coalition. The year 1988 had begun with the first demonstration in the capital of the National Front for Mass Organizations, and 1988 is also the first year that the movements were openly prepared to ally with political parties at national level. But this shift to electoral politics may not yet indicate a direct demand for liberal democracy so much as a strategic choice to forge new alliances in the electoral arena and thereby extend the scope of popular struggle, while continuing to build sectoral and union movements and to press immediate and concrete demands.

But what does this matter if, even after several days of agonizing 'electoral alchemy' after the elections of July 1988, the ruling party barely secured an absolute majority? And may in fact only have secured a narrow plurality? The ruling party's vote had anyway been in secular decline, and with the austerity policies of the 1980s the opposition vote had anyway been assuming a plebiscitary character (Cammack, 1988). Add to these tendencies the abstention rate of almost 50 per cent, and it is most likely that the National Democratic Front benefited most from the vote of the disaffected middle classes in the cities. If this is so, then the influence of Mexico's popular movements on the electoral results may have been more indirect than direct, and achieved by the political wedge they have driven into the corporatist flank of this 'corporatist democracy'. The state-chartered union corporations which used to mobilize the vote and control the voting booths can no longer be sure of doing so; while popular mobilization itself has raised the costs of electoral fraud and made it more difficult to accomplish. In these ways popular movements have dramatically reduced the ruling party's ability to manage the electoral arena, but not necessarily by invading it. The Front certainly attracted many votes from popular organizations in July of 1988, but more recent elections seem to indicate that this is not a permanent result, and that democracy is still hovering on the horizon of the historical agenda in Mexico.

Nonetheless, both the Mexican and the Spanish cases do indicate the ways in which popular political organizations may come to spearhead the struggle of civil society against authoritarian controls and for the development of a democratic regime. But note that in both cases the importance of union movements to this process is itself contingent on the corporatist characteristics of their regimes. Franco's corporatism was a global and uniform strategy for organizing and disciplining the whole of Spain's economically active population. The corporatism of the Mexican regime is far more variegated and uneven, with its various union corporations inserted differentially into both the sectoral organization of the ruling party and the regional and federated systems of power-holding and power-broking. Furthermore, the Mexican regime has also managed to maintain the appearance of electoral-democratic politics by extending elaborate mechanisms of corporatist-clientelist control into the electoral arena. These differences evidently make the regimes more or less 'susceptible' to different forms of popular strategy. The combination of legal and extra-legal struggle in Spain, and the comprehensive infiltration of the Vertical Syndicate, was successful in subverting the regime's corporatism; and, since the regime could offer no alternative representational arena, this severely damaged the coherence of the regime itself. Similar strategies in Mexico, and the *ad hoc* pursuit of political alliances, have proved partially successful in discomposing the regime, which has nevertheless been able to divert popular protest into the alternative electoral arena, which it has traditionally managed with assurance and sang-froid. Despite the danger signals of July 1988 and the months which followed it now appears that the regime has again recovered the political initiative.

The popular contribution to developing democracy requires explanations of relatively *longue durée*. It tends to be a protracted process which recurrently redefines the relationships between civil society and regime. There is a varying threshold of separation and proximity between the two, which is the result of varying dispositions of social force in different moments: an unstable frontier between the forces which exercise state power and which attempt to expand their basis of political support by incorporating and regulating private organizations; and the forces of civil society which acquiesce in or resist such incorporation and regulation, and attempt to articulate their own strategies for extending the field of their autonomous operation. The shifting terrain of this difficult frontier is germane to democratic struggle. Indeed, were there an immanent and fixed divide between state and civil society no such struggle would be possible. Moreover, it is this institutional instability which creates the characteristic ambiguity of democratic struggle in authoritarian contexts, where popular political actors must engage in a complex game of constantly changing strategic options: new political spaces may be created even within the institutions of the regime, but some degree of autonomy may thereby be lost; ways may be found to use the legal cover and resources of state agencies for extra-legal and independent activities, but democratic actors may be coopted or democratic goals distorted; repression of democratic initiatives may promote greater internal coherence within and among opposition groups, but their own organizations may simultaneously become more authoritarian in style. Far from constituting a political disadvantage for popular politics under authoritarian regimes, this ambiguity is the very stuff of democratic struggle, which cannot advance by appeals to absolute values, however liberal or democratic, but only by painstaking strategic calculation.

Finally, and perhaps unfortunately, nothing here should be taken to suggest that new forms of popular political organization can alone achieve democracy against authoritarian odds. However great their courage and however sophisticated their strategies, Spain's commissions could not have impelled a 'pacted transition' to democracy in that country had not nearly every sector of the Spanish bourgeoisie either accepted or actively promoted a newly democratic regime (Fraser, 1976; Foweraker, 1987). Their incentive was clear. The European Economic Community stipulated the democratic pre-conditions for entry, and Spain's entrepreneurs knew that their only future lay in Europe. In Mexico, on the contrary, the recent constitutional pact between the ruling party and its conservative opposition (the National Action Party, or PAN) guarantees future regime stability even were the ruling party to win a mere 35 per cent of the national vote. This stability is seen as essential to successful negotiation of Mexico's entry into the North American Free Trade Area, which, differently from the Community, carries no democratic pre-conditions. There is no doubt that the United States administration also prefers stability to democracy in Mexico, having known this particular devil for many decades. Thus, the regime will continue, and so will its popular opposition. The force of this opposition fluctuates, and is presently in decline. An imminent transition to democracy in Mexico appears improbable.

Notes

1   The best succinct account of modernization theory is to be found in Randall and Theobald (1985). For its theoretical underpinnings, see Smelser (1968). A typical application of the approach to Latin America is Johnson (1958). The most sophisticated statement of the position, which is also critical of some of the assumptions, is Huntington (1968).

2   See O'Donnell (1978; and also 1973). For an overview, see Collier (1979); and for a similar approach, which nevertheless operates with different assumptions, Malloy (1977). For further arguments see Foxeley (1983) and Ramos (1986).

3   O'Donnell et al. (1986). Two other studies which are broadly similar in their general perspectives are Baloyra (1987) and Malloy and Mitchell (1987).

4 See, for example, the collection by Slater (1985); Touraine (1987); as well as the collection by the senior North American scholar Susan Eckstein (1988).

5 See Mainwaring and Viola (1984); Mainwaring (1987); Keck (1989); Rubin (1987); Fox (1986); Cook (1990); as well as the essays and authors in Foweraker and Craig (1990).

6 See O'Donnell et al. (1986); and the critique by Levine (1988). For a recent restatement of the elite-oriented view of democratic transitions, see Karl (1990). A more balanced and comprehensive view, which adopts a historical and institutional approach, is found in Diamond et al.(1989); while a more politically radical analysis, which places formal emphasis on the popular sector, is pursued by Munck (1989).

References

Aziz, Alberto. 1987. 'Electoral Practices and Democracy in Chihuahua, 1985' in A. Alvarado, ed., *Electoral Patterns and Perspectives in Mexico*. Center for U.S.–Mexican Studies, UC, San Diego.

Baloyra, Enrique ed. 1987. *Comparing New Democracies: Transition and Consolidation in Mediterranean Europe and the Southern Cone*. Westview, Boulder, CO.

Cammack, Paul. 1988. 'The "Brazilianization" of Mexico?'. *Government and Opposition*.

Castells, Manuel. 1983. *The City and the Grassroots*. Edward Arnold, London.

Collier, David ed. 1979. *The New Authoritarianism in Latin America*. Princeton University Press, Princeton, NJ.

Cook, Maria Lorena. 1990. 'State–Union Conflict and the Emergence of Democratic Union Movements'. PhD dissertation, Political Science, University of California, Berkeley, CA.

Dahl, Robert. 1971. *Polyarchy: Participation and Opposition*. Yale University Press, New Haven & London.

Diamond, Larry, Juan J. Linz and Seymour Martin Lipset eds 1989. *Democracy in Developing Countries. Vol. 4: Latin America*. Lynne Rienner, Boulder, CO.

Eckstein, Susan ed. 1988. *Power and Popular Protest: Latin American Social Movements*. University of California Press, Berkeley, CA.

Foweraker, Joe. 1987. 'The Role of Labor Organizations in the Transition to Democracy in Spain' in R. Clark and M. Haltzel, eds, *Spain in the 1980s: the Democratic Transition and a New International Role*. Ballinger, Cambridge, Mass.

Foweraker, Joe. 1988. *Transformism Transformed: the Nature of Mexico's Political Crisis*. Essex Papers in Politics and Government, no. 46, Department of Government, University of Essex.

Foweraker, Joe and Ann Craig eds. 1990. *Popular Movements and Political Change in Mexico*. Lynne Rienner Publishers, Boulder, CO.

Fox, Jonathan. 1986. 'The Political Economy of Reform in Mexico: the Case of the Mexican Food System'. PhD dissertation, Political Science, MIT.

Foxeley, Alejandro. 1983. *Latin American Experiments in Neo-Conservative Economics*. University of California Press, Berkeley, CA.

Fraser, R. 1976. 'Spain on the Brink'. *New Left Review*. No. 60. March–April.

Gramsci, Antonio. 1971. *Selections from the Prison Notebooks of Antonio Gramsci*. eds Q. Hoare and G.N. Smith. Lawrence and Wishart, London.

Huntington, Samuel P. 1968. *Political Order in Changing Societies*. Yale University Press, New Haven.

Johnson, J.J. 1958. *Political Change in Latin America: the Emergence of the Middle Sectors*. Stanford University Press, Stanford.

Karl, Terry Lynn. 1990. 'Dilemmas of Democratization in Latin America'. *Comparative Politics*. Vol. 23, no. 1.

Keck, Margaret. 1989. 'The "New Unionism" in the Brazilian Transition' in Alfred Stepan, ed., *Democratizing Brazil*. Oxford University Press, New York.

Levine, Daniel, 1988. 'Paradigm Lost: Dependence to Democracy'. *World Politics*. Vol. XL, no. 3.

Linz, J.J. 1964. 'An Authoritarian Regime: Spain' in E. Allardt and Y. Littunen, eds, *Cleavages, Ideologies and Party Systems*. The Academic Bookstore, New York.

Mainwaring, Scott. 1987. 'Urban Popular Movements, Identity, and Democratization in Brazil'. *Comparative Political Studies*. Vol. 20, no. 2, July.

Mainwaring, Scott and Eduardo Viola. 1984. 'New Social Movements, Political Culture, and Democracy: Brazil and Argentina in the 1980s'. *Telos*. No. 61, fall.

Malloy, James. 1977. 'Latin America: the Modal Pattern' in James Malloy, ed., *Authoritarianism and Corporatism in Latin America*. University of Pittsburgh Press, Pittsburgh.

Malloy, James and Mitchell Seligson eds 1987. *Authoritarians and Democrats: Regime Transition in Latin America*. University of Pittsburgh Press, Pittsburgh.

Maravall, J.M. 1978. *Dictatorship and Political Dissent*. Tavistock, London.

Maravall, J.M. 1982. *The Transition to Democracy in Spain*. Croom Helm, London.

Munck, Ronaldo. 1989. *Latin America: Transition to Democracy*. Zed Books, London.

O'Donnell, Guillermo. 1973. *Modernization and Bureaucratic Authoritarianism: Studies in South American Politics*. Institute of International Studies, Berkeley, CA.

O'Donnell, Guillermo. 1978. 'Reflections on the Patterns of Change in the Bureaucratic Authoritarian State'. *Latin American Research Review*. Vol. 13, no. 1.

O'Donnell, Guillermo, Philippe C. Schmitter and Laurence Whitehead eds 1986. *Transitions from Authoritarian Rule: Prospects for Democracy*. Johns Hopkins University Press, Baltimore, 4 vols.

Preston, P. ed. 1976. *Spain in Crisis*. Harvester, Hassocks.

Preston, P. ed. 1986. *The Triumph of Democracy in Spain*. Methuen, London.

Ramos, Joseph. 1986. *Neo-Conservative Economics in the Southern Cone of Latin America, 1973–1983*. Johns Hopkins University Press, Baltimore.

Randall, V. and R. Theobald. 1985. *Political Change and Underdevelopment: a Critical Introduction to Third World Politics*. Macmillan, London.

Roxborough, Ian. 1984. *Unions and Politics in Mexico*. Cambridge University Press, London.

Rubin, Jeff. 1987. 'State Policies, Leftist Oppositions, and Municipal Elections: the Case of the COCEI in Juchitan' in Arturo Alvarado, ed., *Electoral Patterns and Perspectives in Mexico*. Monograph 22, Center for US–Mexican Studies, San Diego.

Schmitter, P. 1974. 'Still the Century of Corporatism?'. *Review of Politics*. Vol. 36.

Slater, David ed. 1985. *New Social Movements and the State in Latin America*. CEDLA, Amsterdam.

Smelser, N.J. 1968. 'Toward a Theory of Modernization' in NJ. Smelser, ed., *Essays in Sociological Explanation*. Prentice-Hall, Englewood Cliffs, NJ.

Touraine, A. 1987. *Actores Sociales y Sistemas Politics en America Latina*. PREALC, Santiago de Chile.

Tusell, X. 1977. *La oposición democrática al franquismo*. Planeta, Barcelona.

Vilar, S. 1976. *La oposición a la dictadura: protagonistas de la España democrática*. Ayma, Barcelona.

PART FIVE

NEW DEMOCRACIES:
ASSESSMENTS AND PROGNOSES

14

Democracy and the Rule of Law in Latin America

Christian Anglade

Between 1974 and 1990, more than thirty countries in Southern Europe, Latin America, East Asia and Eastern Europe shifted from authoritarian to democratic systems of government. This 'global democratic revolution' is probably the most important political trend in the late twentieth century.[1]

This assertion is more controversial than Huntington had intended, for the evidence offered by several 'new' democracies shows that a move away from authoritarian rule is not necessarily a move into democratic rule. Since problems of definition and meaning are involved, a consequence of the trend described by Huntington has been to reactivate the debate over what democracy is about. Huntington – among others – equates democracy with the holding of 'competitive elections in which the bulk of the population can participate'.[2] A contentious definition, since – without denying the key role of elections in a democratic process – many would question whether elections (and procedures in general) are sufficient to define democracy. In an attempt to break the impasse of the debate over a procedural versus a substantive definition, the suggestion was also made that democracy should be understood in strict political terms, and that *political* democracy should be kept distinct from both *social* and *economic* democracy, assumed to be secondary.[3] But such a clear-cut distinction is easier to hypothesize than to substantiate and it tends to lead to inconsistencies in the argument. After asserting that the term 'democracy' was meant 'to signify a political system, separate and apart from the economic and social system to which it is joined',[4] Diamond and Linz later recognize that democratic stability is highly dependent on economic performance, understood not only as sustained growth but as promoting social mobility and 'steady and broad improvement in popular well being'.[5] This contradiction in their argument merely illustrates the difficulties involved in breaking down democracy into sub-categories and in keeping those sub-categories separate from each other.[6] Another aspect of the current debate concerns the meaning of 'political democracy': is it to be understood in the broad liberal democratic sense of equal individual civil and political rights and obligations; or is it to be more narrowly focused on forms and procedures as in the earlier definition given by Huntington?

In the Latin American context, this twofold debate has led some authors[7] to argue that the social and economic inequalities pervading in the area are incompatible with the democratic principle of equal rights and equal participation; unless those inequalities are redressed, the minimum social conditions necessary for a meaningful political participation will not be met and the Latin American democracies will remain at best pseudo-democracies. This 'substantive' approach is criticized by a second group of academics,[8] who accuse the first of confusing democracy with equality and who argue that simply to pretend that the two are in any way connected only serves to confuse the issues. For the latter, it is theoretically unsound and empirically unfounded to see social and economic conditions – or anything else for that matter – as a prerequisite for democracy; they even argue that the causal relationship between the two – if there is any – might be working the other way round, with democracy improving social and economic conditions.[9] But for them, even though a reduction of inequality might be desirable in itself, it is a separate issue from democracy. The democratic nature of a government and its authority to rule are determined only by its procedural origins.[10]

It is the issues involved in this debate that I will discuss in this chapter, first by examining the different theoretical traditions of liberal democracy which have inspired the debate, and then by setting a minimalist liberal democratic paradigm which will be used for an evaluation of the contemporary Latin American democratic record.

The Theoretical Approach

For the liberal democratic tradition, democracy is defined by the two combined principles of equal individual rights and accountability of the rulers to the ruled. For this tradition ranging from Tocqueville to Rawls,[11] democracy is not merely a question of forms and procedures; it is also a question of substance, i.e. – and this appears to be its bottom line – of equal rights to individual autonomy and liberty, those equal rights including equal obligations.

Another tradition – more recent and more unified – has its origins in the writings of Schumpeter, Dahl and Huntington.[12] From an observation of the way liberal democratic regimes have developed, it asserts that the tendency for individuals is to pursue their interests not individually but as members of groups through which they try to maximize their rights in a competitive fashion shaped by the market. The plurality of those groups and their influence in the political process constitute the best possible protection of the individual rights of their members; accountability is guaranteed by the periodic holding of elections through which those who govern can be kept either in or out of office by the governed, with the interest groups representing the latter playing a key role in that process.

From a previous definition emphasizing means and ends, we have moved to an institutional definition of democracy, and in so doing, we have moved also – so we are told – from a hypothetical, idealistic and normative definition of democracy to one that is empirical, realistic and descriptive. 'Democracy has a useful meaning only when it is defined in institutional terms',[13] i.e. as means, thus avoiding the normative bias. But since means are by definition instrumental, sooner or later an instrumental definition of democracy will raise the issue of purposes which the institutionalists precisely wanted to avoid. The question of what democracy is about has been merely delayed in the process. If the answer is that democracy is about free and competitive elections, then institutions are no longer simply instrumental and they become an end in themselves. The reason for avoiding a purposeful definition of democracy was that any such attempt was bound to be normative. But why should the assertion that democracy is about free and competitive elections be less normative than the assertion that democracy is about equal civil and political rights? All definitions of democracy are necessarily normative, and the institutionalists' concern for 'neutrality' has led them to draw an artificial distinction between means and ends which has introduced some confusion in their theoretical argument.

This confusion has been compounded by the ethnocentric bias of the pluralist approach, which has reduced the universality of the liberal democratic principle of equal rights. For pluralism, individuals entrust the defence of their political rights to the groups that represent them. This 'delegation' leaves them freer to maximize their other – mainly economic – interests in a market society, and it can even generate declining levels of individual participation in the political process without affecting the democratic quality of the whole process. Hence the pluralist assumptions that silence means satisfaction and that, on balance, all social and economic groups exert equal political influence. Both assumptions are unwarranted, even in advanced democracies, since 'pluralism may tacitly condone in practice the reproduction of the power relations that obtain in the social and economic realm.'[14] As a result, pluralism not only tends to reproduce social and economic inequalities, but also, by 'realistically' recognizing that such inequalities exist, introduces them as 'systemic features', thereby 'justify[ing] the status quo by redefining democracy in these terms'.[15] The significance of this tendency for democracy is directly proportional to the level of those inequalities and to the percentage of the

national population that they affect. On both accounts, its impact is likely
to be much stronger in the 'new' democracies of the Third World.

The validity of the pluralist/institutionalist approach must also be
questioned on more general grounds, since there appears to be some
evidence that silence and political apathy can also mean dissatisfaction. For
instance, should political apathy in Colombia (measured by the rate of
electoral abstentions) be taken as an indication of satisfaction of the
Colombian electorate? Since the answer to this question can only be
qualified, it means that the same outcome (a low participation in competitive elections) can sometimes express satisfaction and sometimes not. It
also means that procedural origins are an insufficient measure of democracy and that – when separated from their substance or from their context
– the formal institutions of democracy are meaningless. Another consequence of the pluralist approach derives both from its ethnocentrism and
from the elitist theory of democracy to which it is attached. It concerns the
other basic democratic principle of accountability. For the pluralists, as we
know, accountability is guaranteed by regular elections; once elected,
governments should be left to govern, first because they know best and
secondly because they will periodically be subjected to elections, which
should be enough to convince office holders that they have a vested interest
in doing what is expected of them. The argument that elections guarantee
accountability is based on the assumption that the electoral process is the
result of free, competitive and meaningful elections. Yet in the case of
Latin America, this issue is often treated as a zero-sum game: it is assumed
that elections are free and competitive unless the evidence to the contrary
is so overwhelming as to make an obvious farce of the whole electoral
process. But, short of extreme cases, the category is used so extensively as
to call its validity into question.[16] It is curious that those who place so much
importance on the procedural origins of a government as the source of its
authority should pay so little attention to the actual conditions that
surround electoral outcomes. How free and competitive elections really
are is a *substantive* issue, particularly – but by no means exclusively – in the
Latin American context.

The other general principle behind democratic accountability is that
governments have to abide by certain rules of law which have been
democratically agreed to. Yet, as we will see in the next section, Latin
America offers again little evidence to support the assumption that, if
governments (or other state institutions) act unconstitutionally, the mechanisms that make them accountable will be set in motion. Like electoral
accountability, constitutional accountability is a *substantive* issue, and the
mechanisms that establish accountability cannot be assumed to work
simply because they have a formal constitutional existence.

Interestingly, it is modern liberal theory which reminds us that form can
be misleading, and that a substantive – and normative – definition of
democracy is unavoidable. For Pennock, '[t]he context by which the
fairness of governmental procedures should be judged involves an evalu-

ation of the *ends* to be achieved, including the recognition of fundamental rights.'[17] Forms and procedures are merely instrumental for achieving the ends of democracy. If the fundamental rights that constitute those ends are not promoted and protected by those formal arrangements, the latter are not fulfilling their function which, as it is merely contingent upon doing so or not, cannot define democracy.

The democratic character of the rule of law is defined both by its *form* and by its *substance*. To rely simply upon the formalism of the rule of law, or indeed to emphasize that it is this formalism which defines democracy, as Letwin does in the Kelsenian tradition,[18] is politically dangerous for it can end up justifying virtually any regime which upholds a formally consistent rule of law. This is why the rule of law is 'a poor criterion [of democracy]; many repressive regimes have relied upon a strict but consistent judicial system to maintain power, including Nazi Germany'.[19] Authoritarian regimes often keep the laws which they inherit from the democratic regimes they have overthrown and which they use to their advantage by claiming to be the new recipients of a basically unchanged rule of law. It could be argued that this is an usurpation of the rule of law. Yet if the formalism of the rule of law allows it to be usurped in this way, surely it must be a poor criterion of democracy.[20] This is why, since all modern systems of government – whether democratic or not – formally adhere to the principle of the rule of law, what defines a democracy is not the law as it is, but what the law *says*, that is its substance, and the extent to which that law is *implemented*.

It is this concern for the dangers of the formalism of institutional procedures in general and the rule of law in particular that presides over Rawls's contribution to democratic theory.[21] For him, democracy requires that the rule of law be made and administered within a context of substantive – as opposed to formal – justice, and resting on the two basic principles of equal liberty and fair equality of opportunity. He does not identify equality with the democratic principle but – and this is perhaps his most significant contribution to the study of 'new' democracies – his argument on the relevance of social and economic conditions for the democratic principle is a bottom line argument. Contrary to what Gould argues,[22] Rawls does advocate equal rights to minimal means of subsistence, and he makes this clear when he discusses the chain connection of his difference principle, aimed at 'maximiz[ing] the expectations of those most disadvantaged'.[23] Pennock too finds it difficult to justify restricting the liberal agenda to civil and political rights: 'what is at stake is not whether formal democracy is in principle justifiable; rather it is the extent to which the democratic ideal demands that it minimize economic inequality.'[24]

The liberal democratic agenda does not argue for equality, nor does it argue for socioeconomic modernization – however defined – either as conditions of democracy or as their outcome. It argues for a bottom line beyond which inequality is no longer compatible with democracy. For the purpose of this chapter, that bottom line will be measured by the proportion of the national population which falls below the poverty line. Minimum socioeconomic rights are not attainable for those who are below the poverty line, measured by the incapacity to cover basic social needs in a given society.[25] Absolute levels of poverty determine social exclusion which in turn is indicative of political exclusion in two ways: (a) the basic socioeconomic conditions required for a level of political participation compatible with democracy are not met; but also – and crucially for a democratic system of government – (b) the ignoring of basic social needs by governments is a reflection of the lack of political representation of the interests of those who are socially excluded.

In other words, socioeconomic exclusion not only restricts the autonomy – and the meaning – of political participation, but is also evidence of political exclusion, of which it is a direct consequence. It can thus be argued that, in those political systems in which institutional arrangements depend on the outcome of elections, socioeconomic exclusion is indicative of political exclusion which, in turn, is incompatible with democracy.

An overall bottom line – or minimalist – liberal democratic agenda is thus inspired by a Rawlsian approach to the rule of law, stressing substance as well as form, and including (a) equal civil and political rights; (b) minimum socioeconomic rights; and (c) accountability. It is the contemporary Latin American record on this minimalist agenda that I will assess in the next section.

Democracy and the Rule of Law in Latin America

Rights and obligations are closely related to each other in liberal democratic theory. Those who hold governmental and other institutional positions have the same rights and obligations as ordinary citizens, but as incumbents of those positions, they also have institutional responsibilities for which they are accountable. They have the obligation to abide by the constitution as well as to ensure that the rule of law is implemented, even enforced if necessary.

These notions of rights, obligations, implementation and accountability are conceptually different, but they are so directly connected in their application that it is difficult to keep them separate when looking at their effects on the democratic process. For instance, what is at stake if civil rights are regularly violated is (a) that these rights are not efficiently protected; (b) that the mechanisms that are supposed to protect them do not work; and (c) that the institutions which are responsible for checking that these mechanisms work are not properly accountable for failing to do so. In other words, the same particular issue (in this case, the violation of civil rights) is equally relevant for evaluating rights, the implementation of the rule of law and institutional accountability. It is important to keep this in mind when we assess the Latin American record on the general issues of the liberal democratic theory of democracy.

The Issue of Rights

The liberal democratic distinction between civil and political rights and socioeconomic rights is increasingly giving way to the notion of human rights, probably more useful because potentially more comprehensive and more mobilizing as well. But since the liberal democratic tradition has more modest requirements on socioeconomic rights, it represents an adequate minimal benchmark to assess democratic rule in Latin America.

Civil Rights

The classical civil rights (speech, publication, association and assembly) are formally recognized everywhere, but the extent to which they are protected varies across the Latin American 'democracies', from high in countries like Costa Rica, Uruguay, Chile, Argentina, Brazil and Venezuela to low in Colombia, Peru, Guatemala, El Salvador and Honduras.[26] The fundamental civil right overriding all others in the area is that of personal security: its most minimal expression – right to habeas corpus – is included in all constitutions, but it is routinely violated in most countries.[27]

The justification sometimes given to the restriction imposed on civil rights in general, and on the right to personal security in particular, is that states have the right as well as the duty to protect democracy against terrorist attacks and insurgency. This may be a valid principle, but its exercise must be carefully monitored in order to avoid abuses. First, the initial declaration of the state of emergency has to be justified, a criterion so widely ignored in Latin America that even the Inter-American Commission on Human Rights has kept absolute discretion on this issue.[28] Secondly, the government is expected to remain in control when it has decided to suspend civil liberties. Yet, in all those Latin American countries where there is some degree of insurgency (Colombia, Peru, El Salvador and Guatemala) – and whether a state of emergency has been formally declared or not – the armed forces seem to be able to detain people without even notifying the civilian authorities and they generally act in ways demonstrating a near complete independence from the governments.[29] In addition, the right to personal security is also violated in countries where there does not seem to be any evidence of insurgency, such as Brazil and Honduras. But in these countries as well as in those of the previous group, all of which are formal democracies, there are hundreds of disappearances and extra-judicial executions every year; death squads, including both uniformed and off-duty members of the security forces, the army and paramilitary groups, target peasants, trade union leaders, human rights workers, lawyers, academics, and minor delinquents (including children). Those responsible are usually known, but the authorities do little to bring them to justice. In fact, most cases of serious human rights violation remain unresolved. Without being so bad, the record of disappearances and extra-judicial executions in Ecuador, Mexico and Venezuela is also indicative of an inadequate protection of basic civil rights. Perhaps the most significant aspect of this trend from the perspective of the rule of law is that those who commit those gross violations appear to operate with total impunity. In the few cases that are brought to justice, judicial irregularities and delays are frequent.

The civil rights of those people who are simply detained are also routinely violated: cases of arbitrary detention, ill-treatment and torture are frequent, and they also occur – albeit less often – in Argentina, Chile and Uruguay. In these countries, those violations are perhaps due to the survival of undemocratic practices inherited from previous military regimes, but the high degree of continuity in the police and armed forces and in the judicial personnel from one regime to the other is in itself a very significant indication of the restricted scope of their democratic processes.

Another fundamental principle of democratic justice is that those whose rights have been violated under a previous government have the right to initiate a judicial procedure against those who perpetrated those violations. Yet, judicial enquiries into the violation of civil rights under previous military governments have been notoriously ineffective under any of the civilian governments that followed. Even in Argentina, Chile and Uruguay, where those violations had been the most widespread, one of the first decisions taken by the newly elected civil governments was to ask Congress to vote a law of amnesty. This represents perhaps the clearest evidence that – as we will see later – the military are effectively unaccountable in Latin America.[30]

Political Rights

These concern the right to participate in free and competitive elections.

Freedom refers to the conditions surrounding both the campaign and the voting process: how free is the information available, how readily available is that information to the electorate at large, how open is the access to the various media for all political parties, how fair is voting and the counting of votes? etc. The Latin American score on the guarantees of freedom of the electoral process cannot be taken for granted and it varies roughly in line with each country's record on civil rights. For a majority of countries in the area, this means that elections are only partially – or very partially – free. To recognize that in some elections there were 'widespread allegations of fraud, high levels of military influence over political institutions, limited opposition participation, and outside political intervention'[31] and yet to include those elections in a list designed to survey the outcome of *democratic* elections in Latin America in the period 1982–90 makes one wonder what criteria would have to be met for *any* election not to be seen as democratic by some institutionalists. The danger of formalism in that approach can hardly be more clearly demonstrated.

Competitiveness refers not only to the number of political parties present in the election, but also to the extent to which the parties competing for the electors' votes offer meaningful choice to the electorate, in that the range of programmes and policy alternatives they stand for is broadly representative of the range of interests present in society at large, not merely among the elites. If and when large numbers of electors have interests which are not – or which are only marginally – represented in the party system, the competitiveness of the electoral process tends to be rather formal: the more limited the representativeness of the parties, the more limited the competitiveness of elections.

The evaluation of party representativeness is a complex issue since it inevitably involves a value judgement at some point not only in our own perception of the 'objective' interests of particular social groups or classes, but also in our appreciation of the extent to which those interests are represented by specific parties. The more programmatic the party, the easier it is to see what interests it represents. Programmatic does not mean class-based, but neither does it mean that most of the 'catch-all' or 'multi-class' parties we find in Latin America are programmatic, in the sense that they are in any way comparable to European social democratic or Christian democratic parties. With few – and partial – exceptions (the Peronists in Argentina, the Christian democrats in Chile and to a lesser extent in Venezuela, the National Liberation Party in Costa Rica and perhaps the Blancos and Colorados in Uruguay) catch-all parties are elite-dominated and – contrary to what Dix argues[32] – they cut across classes only in so far as they manage to attract non-elite votes. That is precisely what they are designed to do while continuing to represent elite interests whose stability they enhance in the process. To consider the traditional parties of Colombia, as Dix does,[33] as multi-class and non-elite–dominated is tantamount to using these notions as catch-all categories themselves, so broad that they become meaningless, or worse, misleading. The social unrepresentativeness of the Colombian conservative and liberal parties is borne out by the consistently high level of abstentions that characterize Colombian elections, whether presidential, congressional, gubernatorial, municipal, or even for a constituent assembly. The recent record is very telling, with abstentions reaching over 54 per cent in the 1990 presidential election, 66 per cent in the 1991 congressional and gubernatorial elections, 65 per cent in the 1992 municipal elections and 75 per cent in the 1990 election for a new constituent assembly.[34] This last figure is particularly significant, since it reveals not only the lack of representativeness of the Colombian parties but also the extent to which the Colombian electorate is disillusioned with the formal institutions of democracy.

The Colombian situation is not unique, and high rates of abstentions are an indication of the unrepresentativeness of political parties in many other Latin American countries. In Guatemala, 43.7 per cent abstained in the first round of the presidential election in 1990 and 57.1 per cent in the second round in 1991. In the Dominican Republic, 40 per cent abstained in the 1990 presidential election. In Peru, there was a 36 per cent abstentions rate plus 15.5 per cent blank and invalid votes in the 1989 presidential and congressional elections. In Venezuela, in spite of voting being compulsory for national elections, there was an 18.15 per cent abstentions rate in the 1989 presidential elections and 70 per cent in the 1989 provincial and municipal elections, at which voting is not compulsory. In Brazil, the Electoral Tribunal reported that in the 1989 congressional and guber- natorial elections, and in spite of compulsory voting, 60 per cent of the voters had either made a 'mistake' with ballot papers or had not voted at all. In Paraguay, in a 1991 election for a new constituent assembly, abstentions ran at 48.3 per cent.[35]

Outside Argentina, Chile, Uruguay and Costa Rica, a pattern of high abstentionism is common in Latin America. That pattern is indicative neither of 'satisfaction', as pluralist theory might be tempted to argue, nor of a half-hearted support for democracy among electorates sometimes portrayed as having a double loyalty, to democracy but also to 'Bonapar- tism'.[36] For the Latin American electorates, a rejection of the formal institutions of democracy that they know does not imply a rejection of democracy *per se*. Where those institutions are more congruent with the fundamental principles of democracy, as in Costa Rica and Chile, support for them is higher and abstentions lower. On the contrary, it could be argued that the unrepresentativeness of parties and the poor record of political institutions in most Latin American countries are so much in contradiction with democratic principles that to condone them as they are would be indicative of naïve and easily manipulated electorates. Their rejection of those parties and institutions rather shows a much higher degree of political maturity than they are usually given credit for.

Socioeconomic Rights

As can be seen from Table 14.1, the Latin American record on basic socioeconomic rights – measured by the poverty line – is incompatible with the minimum requirements of democracy in most countries. Four comments are called for.

First, in view of the patterns of poverty prevailing in Bolivia, the Dominican Republic, Haiti, Nicaragua and Paraguay, their inclusion in the table would certainly make the overall picture even worse. Secondly, only Uruguay and Costa Rica managed to maintain in the 1980s absolute levels of poverty which, although substantial in their own right, were relatively modest by comparison with the other countries of the region. Thirdly, countries like Brazil, Colombia, Guatemala, Honduras and Peru showed consistently high records of poverty throughout the 1970s and 1980s, and this is also true for Ecuador and El Salvador, for which no statistical series are available here.

Fourthly, perhaps the most significant pattern is that of Argentina and Chile, and to a lesser extent, Venezuela. The first two have experienced a so-called 'Latin Americanization' in the social conditions of a large percentage of their population between 1970 and the late 1980s to early 1990s, owing to a combination of the economic crisis of the 1980s and of

Table 14.1 *Percentage of the population below the poverty line in Latin America*

	1967	1970[1]	1979[2]	1980[2]	1981[2]	1986[2]	1987[2]	1988[2]	1989[3]	1990
Argentina		8.0		9.0		13.0				44.0[4]
Brazil		49.0	39.0							50.0[5]
Chile		17.0					40.0 / 38.0 / 44.4[6]			
Colombia		45.0		39.0		38.0				40.0[7]
Costa Rica		24.0			22.0			25.0		
Ecuador									22.0	
El Salvador							55.0[8]			
Guatemala				65.0		68.0				61.4[3]
Honduras	65.0								76.3[3]	77.5[3]
Mexico		34.0			45.0[9]		50.9[9]			
Panama		50.0	36.0			34.0				
Peru						52.0				54.4[3]
Uruguay					11.0				15.0	
Venezuela		25.0			37.0[10]	15.0			65.0[10]	

Sources:

[1] CEPAL, 1990, p. 45.
[2] CEPAL, 1991, p. 18.
[3] International Labour Office data published in *Latin American Regional Report (LARR): Mexico and Central America Report*, 1992, no. 1.
[4] *Latin American Weekly Report (LAWR)*, 1990, no. 16.
[5] *Pesquisa Nacional por Amostra de Domicilios* direct estimates.
[6] Data from a CEPAL study quoted by the Chilean Planning Minister Sergio Molina and published in *LAWR*, 1990, no. 43.
[7] From data published in *LAWR*, 1991, no. 42.
[8] Santos, 1989.
[9] Data from *Programa Nacional de Solidaridad*, published in *LAWR*, 1990, no. 31.
[10] Data quoted by G. Marquez from the *Instituto de Estudios Superiores de Administración* and published in *LARR: Andean Group Report*, 1992, no. 1.

the neo-liberal policies introduced by the military and pursued by civilian governments. In Venezuela, the distribution of the oil rent to buy social peace came to a virtual halt in the late 1980s, which provoked the food riots of 1989, the high poverty figure for 1989 and a general situation of discontent and instability which help to explain the attempted military coup of 1992.[37]

The Issue of Obligations

In democratic regimes, it is expected that – once elected – governments will uphold the rule of law and will also have the means to ensure that citizens do so. This implies that government authority and accountability are well established and that both governments and citizens are law abiding. It is doubtful that these expectations would be reasonable in Latin America, where citizen or government compliance in abiding by the rule of law, and government authority in enforcing it, can be assumed no more than the accountability of the latter if it fails to fulfil its constitutional responsibilities.

This raises some important general issues concerning the legal culture of Latin America, by tradition formally hyper-legal and yet one in which the law is to be obeyed in principle though not necessarily complied with in practice.[38] Such an apparent paradox can be explained only by reference to norms and values inherited from the patrimonialist societies of the nineteenth century, in which attempts to reconcile the Spanish colonial heritage with the new liberal values inspired by European and American political theory had already produced significant differences between constitutional theory and institutional practice and between legal formalism and individual compliance with the law.

This is not the place to discuss the specific issues involved in this paradox and why that different legal culture began to emerge in sixteenth century Spain. But there is no doubt that the patrimonialist tradition does not establish the clear-cut distinction between the public and the private domains that is fundamental to liberal democratic theory.[39] In the patrimonialist tradition, the two domains are intertwined and the first is often seen as an extension of the second. This tradition persists in contemporary Latin America, where it leads frequently to forms of behaviour and institutional practices which are not easily compatible with democratic norms. The key issue here is not only that corruption will be encouraged and will therefore become more widespread, but also that the whole legal process will be weakened to the extent that it will not be able to guarantee the implementation of the rule of law.

For the rule of law to be applied, the *primary* rules contained in constitutional principles and in general laws require the adoption of *secondary* rules which will provide the detailed legislation necessary to carry out the broad indications given by the primary rules.[40] In democratic regimes, it is expected that (a) those secondary rules will closely follow the primary ones in time; that (b) when they do, they will be congruent with what the primary rules were designed to achieve; and that (c) once enacted, they will be implemented.

Violations of these three principles are common in Latin America. First, secondary rules are often unduly delayed for – as is usually argued – it is pointless to introduce a detailed legislation requiring budgetary resources without first seeing what resources are going to be made available for it. An example of this is in the area of legislation on agrarian reform, where the financial resources needed both to compensate expropriated landowners and to help the beneficiaries of land reform have to be properly budgeted before the details of the law can be worked out. Since the 1917 Mexican constitution, the Latin American legislative scene offers many examples of primary rules of agrarian reform waiting for secondary rules which have never been voted. If true, the budgetary argument is weak since it demonstrates a low degree of commitment of the political authorities to reform; it is also fallacious, since it appears that the real reason for the absence of secondary rules is the strong opposition of large landowners. Through their influence on the government and through the over-representation of their interests in Congress (resulting from electoral laws which tend to favour rural areas), they manage either to block agrarian reform or to reverse it if it has been enacted. Brazil offered an example of the first under the Sarney government, whose five-year programme of agrarian reform redistributed only 10 per cent of the land and resettled only 6 per cent of the population that had been originally targeted.[41] An example of the second is offered by El Salvador where the land confiscated from some of the largest landowners in 1981, and distributed to peasant cooperatives, was taken away from the latter in 1991 by President Cristiani.[42] There is a long tradition of both practices in Central America as well as in Mexico, Bolivia, Colombia, Ecuador, Peru, Chile and Venezuela. In a more general way, the fact that agrarian reform is sometimes not even a constitutional or legal issue in countries where land is very unequally distributed (as in Paraguay) bears evidence to the influence of landowning interests and to the unrepresentativeness of political parties. Attempts to promote agrarian reform have always either failed or backfired in Latin America (Mexico, Bolivia, Chile, Peru, Brazil, El Salvador, Honduras). Today it remains one of the most contentious issues in the area, and the veto power of landowning organizations is a major obstacle to democratization in many countries.

The area of social and labour legislation is another example of formal primary rules lacking secondary legislation. Most Latin American constitutions are quite progressive in these matters, guaranteeing wide cover to social rights and setting norms of labour law usually found in the more advanced European social democracies. This tendency is not new and it can be found as early as in the 1917 Mexican constitution. Its latest expression is in the new Colombian constitution of 1991, in which the social rights of old age, invalidity, sickness, maternity, work injury, unemployment and family allowances are again highlighted in the constitution of a country in which only 16 per cent of the population was covered by social security in the period 1985–8.[43]

Secondly, when secondary rules are enacted, they are often at odds with the goal of the primary rule. The basic principles of neutrality and universality of the law imply that, in the particular area of land and property laws, for example, the laws will aim at a just resolution of conflicts. But, in his analysis of land laws in Brazil, Holston argues that the law is instead 'an instrument of calculated disorder by means of which illegal practices produce law, and extra-legal solutions are smuggled into the judicial process'.[44] He convincingly demonstrates that the aim of that law is in effect 'the maintenance of privilege among those who possess extra-legal powers to manage politics, bureaucracy, and the historical record itself. In this sense, legal irresolution is an effective, though perverse, means of rule.'[45]

Thirdly, the enactment of secondary rules is no guarantee that those rules will be implemented. The non- or partial implementation of rules of law 'democratically' voted by congress is often attributed either to the same budgetary causes given to explain the absence of secondary rules or to the lack of proper institutional and administrative mechanisms to carry them over, or both. These problems are often brought up to explain the gap between law and law enforcement in the areas of legislation already mentioned. This is also the case for taxation which – together with agrarian reform – represents the core of the area in which the implementation of the rule of law is a key measure of democracy in Latin America.

Latin American tax laws are neither democratic nor progressive, since indirect taxes make up the bulk of tax revenues and since higher incomes are taxed at rates well below those set in advanced democracies.[46] In addition, the fundamental democratic principle of equal tax obligation for all is not fulfilled either, since both corporate and personal tax evasion is widespread. Among firms, the worst culprits are the large foreign firms which, besides the various loopholes in tax laws, also use the whole array of accounting mechanisms at their disposal (overbilling, underbilling, etc.) to evade taxation illegally as well. As to personal income tax, few people pay it owing to the combination of three factors: (1) given the levels of poverty obtaining in the area, large percentages of the population are below income tax thresholds; (2) the rapid expansion of the informal sectors (by definition unregistered) since the 1980s has aggravated the loss in tax revenue; (3) tax evasion among high-income earners follows patterns similar to corporate tax evasion, with a mixture of loopholes and illegal mechanisms being used on a scale roughly proportional to income levels. The impact of these various factors on tax revenues makes Latin America the least taxed region in the world: tax revenue represented 11.2 per cent of GDP for Latin America in 1988, compared with 23.8 per cent for Africa and 32.8 per cent for the industrialized countries.[47] Although taxation has become a political issue for the elected governments which took over from authoritarian regimes in the early and mid 1980s, that issue has failed to materialize in higher tax revenues. These have even decreased as a percentage of GDP in many countries between 1985 and 1990 (Chile, Costa Rica, El Salvador, Panama and Venezuela), with a dramatic drop in Argentina (from 9 to 5.2 per cent), the Dominican Republic (from 15 to 10 per cent), Ecuador (from 16.7 to 7.7 per cent), Nicaragua (from 27.2 to 12.5 per cent) and Peru (from 12.5 to 7 per cent).[48]

In his review of tax reform in Latin America, Bird argues that 'throughout the region, [there] has been a move away from progressive income taxation [which] . . . appears to reflect the realization that such taxes have not been and probably cannot be effectively administered in most Latin American countries'.[49] 'The fundamental problem bedeviling direct tax administration in most of Latin America [is] the political impossibility of enforcing taxes on rich and powerful taxpayers.'[50] This incapacity of Latin American governments to enforce tax laws on the rich and the token nature of those cases of tax evasion which some of them bring to justice means that the implementation of the rule of law is defective in an area of legislation of high practical and symbolic significance for any democratic process. By restricting government revenue, it also hinders government performance in a way that can only have a negative impact on the consolidation of democratic rule in the area.

The weakness of the legal process is also reinforced by the lack of authority of supreme courts. 'With very limited exceptions, Latin American supreme courts have had the authority to measure only the form of legislation against constitutional norms. The substance has, in general, gone unrevised.'[51] The reasons why the supreme courts as well as ordinary tribunals are ineffective in implementing the judicial function have to do with issues of accountability which I will examine in the next section, but they are also related to factors such as the personal insecurity of magistrates (particularly in Colombia) and – more generally – to their fear of antagonizing the military when they are asked to review allegations brought against the latter for violations of civil rights under the military regimes. Yet, it is not only in countries like Argentina, Brazil, Chile or Uruguay, or in 'insurgency countries' like Colombia, Peru, Guatemala, or El Salvador, that tribunals shy away from these issues. In Venezuela, where civilian rule has been uninterrupted, the civilian courts declared themselves without authority to deal with cases involving serious violations of human rights by the army during the food riots of 1989 when several hundred people were killed, and they decided to transfer the cases to military courts.[52]

The Issue of Accountability

Accountability is a key principle of representative democracy, by which those institutions that have not been elected by direct popular suffrage are accountable to those that have been. In a presidential system of government in which both the president and congress are directly elected – which is the case throughout Latin America – the president is accountable to congress in most areas of government action, with the judiciary having authority to resolve conflicts between them. But the practice of account-ability is often less clearcut than constitutional theory assumes.

First, the president's accountability to congress is frequently complicated by the former increasingly resorting to ruling by decree in an attempt to bypass congress. This has led to growing tensions between the two, particularly in those countries (Argentina, Bolivia, Brazil, Ecuador, Peru, Venezuela) where presidents were elected on the promise that they would implement neo-Keynesian expansionist policies and where they now implement strict neo-liberal policies instead. Congress then sometimes reacts to try to reassert its constitutional authority. Yet the ensuing conflicts between the two are rarely solved by the supreme court, showing how little prepared it is to intervene in a decisive way. This is largely because the accountability of the supreme court – an unelected body – is not clearly established. Much depends on the respective weight of the president and congress in the nomination of judges. This does not mean that judges who owe their nomination to either of them will necessarily owe them allegiance as well, but it is an area where accountability tends to become nebulous. This is shown precisely by the indecision of supreme courts which have so far tended to confirm the authority of congress while allowing the president to pursue the policies which originated the conflict. Even when congress has authority to allow the president to rule by decree – as in the new Brazilian constitution – its power to control him is limited.[53]

Secondly, there is the issue of accountability of the military. In Latin America, this issue is already complicated by the inclusion in the constitu-tions of clauses which are in contradiction with common constitutional practice elsewhere. In one form or another, most Latin American constitu-tions attribute to the armed forces the role of guardian of the constitution and it is this role which has always been invoked by the military to justify their intervention in politics. One would have thought that the new civilian governments would have learnt this lesson. But the Brazilian constitution of 1988 attributes the same role to the armed forces, and the Colombian constitution of 1989 even goes so far as to give them the right to hold suspects for three days before turning them over to the judicial authori-ties.[54]

In addition, Latin American presidents have no authority in the appointment of defence secretaries or of the various ministers responsible for the armed forces. Again in contradiction with basic constitutional principles, those ministers have usually been military men themselves, chosen in order of seniority by the military hierarchy. Whenever a new president tries to assert his right to appoint ministers and military commanders of his choice, the military react openly, as happened in 1990 in Uruguay.[55] It is generally revealing of the extent of military account-ability to see that in those countries where they were still in power in the early 1980s the military now openly criticize the elected governments which replaced them. In Chile, incidents in which the army – and particularly General Pinochet – speaks out against President Aylwin have been frequent since his government was elected;[56] in Argentina and Brazil, rumours of coup-mongering alternate with the Brazilian military openly criticizing the government over pay issues.[57] In these and many other countries, as we saw earlier, the armed forces are also effectively unaccountable in all issues involving violations of human rights.

Whether the assumption of electoral accountability is reasonable for Latin America is also doubtful: there are too many limitations to the freedom and competitiveness of the electoral process and to institutional accountability in general for elections to perform that function in most Latin American countries. On the basis of my earlier examination of these issues, electoral accountability seems to exist to some extent in Costa Rica and Chile, possibly in Uruguay and Argentina, questionably in Venezuela and Peru,[58] and probably not in Ecuador, Bolivia and the Dominican Republic, and is currently out of the question elsewhere.

More generally, this examination of the Latin American record in the minimalist terms of the liberal democratic agenda does not leave much ground for complacency. Civil and political rights are routinely violated outside Costa Rica, and although the elected governments of Chile, Uruguay and Argentina are trying to reassert their authority over their armed forces, these are still a potent institutional anomaly in the building of a democratic process in all three countries, as well as an ever present menace in Argentina. The deterioration of the minimum socioeconomic rights of large sectors of the population in Argentina and Chile during the 1980s was yet another limitation to the democratic record of these two countries; they would have to address this issue as a matter of urgency if they intend to consolidate democracy. The challenge is not an easy one, nor will it be easy to curb a long tradition of military non-accountability in the three southern cone countries. Nevertheless, together with Costa Rica, these countries seem to have better prospects than most others.

The extent to which all elected Latin American governments will be able to enforce the rule of law in areas of long-standing slackness will be a measure of their success in improving their overall poor current democratic record. The relevance of a better civil rights record for democracy does not require any elaboration. But a more effective enforcement of tax and agrarian reform legislation is equally important, not only because of the fundamental democratic principle that nobody must be above the law, but also because it is the responsibility of elected governments to promote citizenship. If, in Huntington's own words, democracy is incompatible with high levels of economic inequality,[59] this means that those who are below the poverty line will have to be pulled above it. Although they now feature in neo-liberal policies, relief programmes to alleviate poverty do not promote citizenship; reforms in the way wealth and income are distributed do. A strict enforcement of tax and agrarian reform laws would be indicative both of the determination of elected governments to bring up reforms and of their capacity to implement them. It would also give these governments the fiscal resources that governments have never had in the region before, and this might help them to improve their democratic record.

Notes

1 Huntington (1991–2, p. 579).
2 Ibid (p. 580).
3 See Diamond et al. (1989, p. XVI); O'Donnell and Schmitter (1986, pp. 7–11).
4 Diamond et al. (1989).
5 Diamond and Linz (1989, p. 46).
6 Another example of such difficulty can be found in Burton et al. (1992).
7 See Lipset (1959); Malloy and Seligson (1987); Diamond and Linz (1989).
8 See Remmer (1991a); Karl (1990); see also Burton et al. (1992, p. 2).
9 Karl (1990, p. 5).
10 Remmer (1991b, p. 791).
11 Tocqueville (1961, vol. I); Rawls (1989).
12 Schumpeter (1943); Dahl (1971); Huntington (1984).
13 Huntington (1989, p. 15).
14 Gould (1990, p. 100).
15 Ibid, (pp. 9–10).
16 Remmer (1991b, p. 780).
17 Pennock (1989, p. 15).
18 Letwin (1989).
19 Barsh (1992, p. 122).
20 Letwin recognizes this danger herself when – at the end of her article – in an unexpected statement, which contradicts her strong emphasis on the formalism of the rule of law as a key criterion of democracy, she concludes that 'Though democracy is inseparable from the rule of law, the converse is not equally true; for it is conceivable that the rule of law may flourish, perhaps even more effectively, under other forms of government' (1989, p. 234).
21 Rawls (1989).
22 Gould (1990, p. 137).
23 Rawls (1989, p. 80).
24 Pennock (1989, p. 23).
25 There are some problems of measurement here, discussed in Cardoso and Helwege (1992), but, if anything, the CEPAL (1990) measurement of poverty, which I use for most of the data in my Table 1, tends to underestimate poverty.
26 See Amnesty International (1989; 1990; 1991a).
27 Ibid.
28 Farer (1989b, p. 508).
29 Amnesty International (1989; 1990; 1991a).
30 Ibid.
31 Remmer (1991b, p. 780).
32 Dix (1992, pp. 500–2).
33 Ibid. (p. 501).
34 All the data on abstentions come from Keesing (1989 to 1992).
35 Ibid.
36 Wiarda (1990, pp. 32–46).
37 See Latin America Newsletter, *Latin American Weekly Report* (*LAWR*) (1992, no. 6); *Latin American Regional Report* (*LARR*): *Andean Group Report* (1992, no. 2).

38 'Obedezco, pero no cumplo' ('I obey, but do not comply with') came to be a norm of individual legal practice in sixteenth century Spain, from where it spread to Latin America during the colonial period.

39 On these particular issues of patrimonialism, see Weber (1947).

40 See Hart (1961, especially chapter V).

41 *LARR: Brazil Report* (1990, no. 4).

42 *LAWR* (1991, no. 14).

43 Inter-American Development Bank (1991, Table 1, p. 186).

44 Holston (1991, p. 695).

45 Ibid (p. 722).

46 For recent evidence, see Bird (1992).

47 For Latin America, calculated from data in Inter-American Development Bank (1991, Table C-1, p. 284 and Table C-7, p. 287); for Africa and industrialized countries, International Monetary Fund (1990, pp. 104–5).

48 Calculated from Inter-American Development Bank (1991).

49 Bird (1992, p. 33).

50 Ibid (pp. 27–8).

51 Farer (1989a, p. 445).

52 See Amnesty International (1991b).

53 Owing to the various other 'exceptional' powers granted to the president: see *LARR: Brazil Report* (1990, no. 3).

54 See *LAWR* (1991, no. 28).

55 See *LAWR* (1990, no. 7).

56 See *LAWR* (1990, no. 40).

57 See *LARR: Brazil Report* (1991, no. 7).

58 The coup perpetrated in April 1992 against Congress by President Fujimori with the support of the army reinforces this point, particularly since his election had been widely interpreted in 1990 as yet another indication that democratic rule was well under way in some Latin American countries, with new political leaders – without any links with the traditional political class – emerging on to the political scene through a more open electoral process, and thus supposedly reinforcing democracy.

59 Huntington (1989, pp. 19 and 25).

References

Amnesty International. 1989, 1990, 1991a. *Amnesty International Report*, (London).

Amnesty International. 1991b. *Venezuela*, doc. AMR 53/02/91, June (London).

Barsh, R.L. 1992. 'Democratization and Development', *Human Rights Quarterly*, vol. 14, no. 1, pp. 120–34.

Bird, R.M. 1992. 'Tax Reform in Latin America: A Review of some Recent Experiences', *Latin American Research Review*, vol. 27, no. 1, pp. 7–36.

Burton, M., R. Gunther and J. Highley. 1992. 'Introduction: Elite Transformations and Democratic Regimes' in J. Highley and R. Gunther, eds, *Elites and Democratic Consolidation in Latin America and Southern Europe* (Cambridge: Cambridge University Press).

Cardoso, E. and A. Helwege. 1992. 'Below the Line: Poverty in Latin America', *World Development*, vol. 20, no. 1, pp. 19–37.

CEPAL (Comisión Económica para America Latina y el Caribe). 1990. *Statistical Yearbook for Latin America and the Caribbean 1990* (Santiago de Chile).

CEPAL. 1991. 'Nota sobre el desarrollo social de America Latina', *Notas sobre la Economia y el Desarrollo*, no. 511/512, July.

Dahl, R.A. 1971. *Polyarchy* (New Haven: Yale University Press).

Diamond, L. and J.J. Linz. 1989. 'Introduction: Politics, Society and Democracy in Latin America' in L. Diamond, J.J. Linz and S.M. Lipset, eds, *Democracy in Developing Countries, Volume 4: Latin America* (Boulder: Lynne Rienner).

Diamond, L., J.J. Linz and S.M. Lipset, eds 1989. *Democracy in Developing Countries, Volume 4: Latin America* (Boulder: Lynne Rienner).

Dix, R.H. 1992. 'Democratization and the Institutionalization of Latin American Political Parties', *Comparative Political Studies*, vol. 24, no. 4, pp. 488–511.

Farer, T.J. 1989a. 'Reinforcing Democracy in Latin America: Notes toward an Appropriate Legal Framework', *Human Rights Quarterly*, vol. 11, no. 3.

Farer, T.J. 1989b. 'Elections, Democracy and Human Rights: Toward Union', *Human Rights Quarterly*, vol. 11, no. 4.

Gould, C.C. 1990. *Rethinking Democracy* (Cambridge: Cambridge University Press).

Hart, H.L.A. 1961. *The Concept of Law* (Oxford: Clarendon Press).

Holston, J. (1991) 'The Misrule of Law: Land and Usurpation in Brazil', *Comparative Studies in Society and History*, vol. 33, no. 4, pp. 695–725.

Huntington, S.P. 1984. 'Will More Countries become Democratic?', *Political Science Quarterly*, 99.

Huntington, S.P. 1989. 'The Modest Meaning of Democracy' in R. Pastor, ed., *Democracy in the Americas: Stopping the Pendulum* (New York: Holmes and Meier).

Huntington, S.P. 1991–2. 'How Countries Democratize', *Political Science Quarterly*, 106.

Inter-American Development Bank (IDB) 1991. *Economic and Social Progress in Latin America* (Washington DC).

International Monetary Fund (IMF) 1990. *Government Finance Statistics Yearbook 1990* (Washington, DC).

Karl, T.L. 1990. 'Dilemmas of Democratization in Latin America' *Comparative Politics*, vol. 23, no. 1, pp. 1–21.

Keesing 1989, 1990, 1991, 1992. *Keesing's Record of World Events* (London: Longman).

Latin America Newsletter. *Latin American Regional Report (LARR): Andean Group Report* (1992), *Brazil Report* (1990) (1991) (1992), *Mexico and Central America Report* (1992); *Latin American Weekly Report (LAWR)* (1990) (1991) (1992) (London).

Letwin, S.R. 1989. 'The Morality of Democracy and the Rule of Law' in G. Brennan and L. Lomasky, eds, *Politics and Process: New Essays in Democratic Thought* (Cambridge: Cambridge University Press).

Lipset, S.M. 1959. 'Some Social Requisites of Democracy: Economic Development and Political Legitimacy', *American Political Science Review*, vol. 53, pp. 69–105.

Malloy, J.M. and M.A. Seligson, eds 1987. *Authoritarians and Democrats – Regime Transitions in Latin America* (Pittsburgh: University of Pittsburgh Press).

O'Donnell, G. and P. Schmitter 1986. *Transitions from Authoritarian Rule – Tentative Conclusions about Uncertain Democracies* (Baltimore: Johns Hopkins University Press).

Pennock, J.R. 1989. 'The Justification of Democracy' in G. Brennan and L. Lomasky, eds, *Politics and Process: New Essays in Democratic Thought* (Cambridge: Cambridge University Press).

Rawls, J. 1989. *A Theory of Justice* (Oxford: Oxford University Press, ninth impression).

Remmer, K.L. 1991a. 'New Wine or Old Bottlenecks? The Study of Latin American Democracy', *Comparative Politics*, vol. 23, no. 4, pp. 479–95.

Remmer, K.L. 1991b. 'The Political Impact of Economic Crisis in Latin America in the 1980s', *American Political Science Review*, vol. 85, no. 3, pp. 777–800.

Santos, E. 1989. 'Poverty in Ecuador', *CEPAL Review*, 38.

Schumpeter, J.A. 1943. *Capitalism, Socialism and Democracy* (London: George Allen and Unwin).

Tocqueville, A. de. 1961. *Democracy in America* (New York: Schocken Books).

Weber, M. 1947. *The Theory of Social and Economic Organization* (Oxford: Oxford University Press).

Wiarda, H. 1990. *The Democratic Revolution in Latin America* (New York: Holmes and Meier).

15

The European Community:
a Transnational Democracy?

Emil J. Kirchner

The EC represents a hybrid form between confederation and federation. A confederation signifies a condition where a group of nations (states) collaborate in economic, political and security matters without establishing a single central authority to regulate or adjudicate these matters. In contrast, a federation represents a condition where a group of nations (states) decide to establish a territorial division of government that endows a single centre with overarching authority while protecting the (limited) autonomy of the previously independent units.[1] By assessing EC developments against these two models, we can establish whether and why the EC is moving more in one direction or the other, whether and how democratic norms are observed in EC decision-making, and whether an intensification of EC integration can go hand in hand with democratization and geographic expansion.

In spite of extensive debates over a forty-year period, no clear blueprint has emerged about the EC's final form or how such a form would be achieved.[2] Rather, as one author has put it, the EC resembles 'a journey to an unknown destination'.[3] In the absence of a clear and shared definition of the dependent variable, scholars have focused on the process of integration rather than the conditions under which political union will be achieved. However, different actors and forces are identified by scholars as being important both for the process of integration and for taking this process towards an end result. These are vaguely defined in either confederal or federal terms. For federalists and neo-functionalists the growth of central institutions and the shift in the locus of authority from the national to the supranational level took on great importance, whereas for communication theorists economic and social transactions among different countries, together with attitudinal transformation, were of more significance.[4] While the former were concerned with state-building, the latter focused on nation-building.[5] Nation-building, although on a global scale in the form of 'communities of interests', was also a preoccupation of the functionalists.[6] Neo-realists and intergovernmentalists, in turn, relied on negotiations, bargaining and tradeoffs in interstate cooperation, in which gains and losses of national interest featured strongly. Federalists and neo-functionalists can be associated with federal models, whereas communication theorists are closer to the confederal model. Functionalists clearly aspire to federalism, but on a global rather than regional scale. Neo-realists and intergovernmentalists adopt the confederal model.

None of these theoretical approaches can explain the why and how of the Single European Act (SEA) of 1986, and all fail to capture the long-term dynamics of the European integration process.[7] This inability to explain is partly due to the way existing theories have concentrated either on the supranational level or the national level rather than on both levels simultaneously. Both the growth of central institutional competences and the use of intergovernmental practices occur simultaneously in EC decision-making and development. This makes demarcation difficult. What can be done, however, is to identify the areas in which either supranational or national competences predominate. The range and depth of central institutional competences tell us something about the presence or the extent to which each prevails in a given area of either the confederal or the federal model. Equally, the level of interstate cooperation (in such areas as foreign affairs and security and immigration policy), and the insistence on unanimity in EC decision-making, signify the extent to which confederal or federal tendencies prevail. The role played by the European Parliament (EP) in EC decision-making provides information on democratic accountability at EC level. The extent to which national administrations comply with EC policy implementation helps to shed light on the effectiveness of European integration and on the level of cooperation between national and supranational administrations. Another important consideration relates to the degree to which the public identifies and supports EC decisions and integration, perceives benefits from the working of the EC, and develops a sense of identity or 'we feeling' – as contrasted with a rigid separation of 'us and them' – among the different nationalities of the Community. Equally, there is a need to consider the extent to which citizens can hold multiple identities simultaneously, e.g. Bavarian, German and European.

In the following we will assess the division of competences held between national and Community institutions, examine attitudes and public opinion on EC integration, and then return to the question of democracy and the potential development of the EC also as a possible model for other areas of the world.

Decision-Making Competences

A variety of forms have emerged through which the EC takes decisions. In some areas, like foreign policy coordination, known as European political cooperation (EPC), member states take decisions with minimal involvement of either the Commission or the EP, and there is no recourse to the

Court of Justice. This signifies the presence of the intergovernmental model. In contrast, areas where EC treaty provisions prevail, such as in agriculture, external trade or the internal market, there is an interplay of all Community institutions, usually taking the form of the Commission proposing and the Council of Ministers deciding legislation. Certain provisions also enable the Commission to act alone, as in competition policy, where the Commission can issue fines in cases of unfair trading practices, control mergers and use discretionary powers over the granting of 'state subsidies'. Treaty provisions also allow the Court of Justice to arbitrate and to exercise judicial review. Through these provisions the Court of Justice has been able to play a crucial role in upholding and promoting Community objectives and identity.[8] There are, however, differences of opinion on whether the Court has always put Community objectives over national ones. The debate over the latter has centred mostly on the Cassis de Dijon case of 1978. In its landmark judgement the Court ruled that national standards should be mutually recognized by member states so as not to inhibit trade within the Community. This principle of mutual recognition, which applies not only to goods but also to services (e.g. mutual recognition of diplomas), has found its way into the SEA. The principle is particularly noticeable with regard to the completion of the internal market programme and to subsidiarity, which stipulates that decisions should be taken at the level of government most appropriate, and which stimulated the 1991 Maastricht negotiations. The issue in question is thus whether the Court in its Cassis de Dijon case conceded more to national interests and national protectionism than it did to Community interests and free trade.[9] Whilst in one sense the Court has deviated from its federalizing aims, the instrumental federal objectives are still apparent. In other words, whilst it has upheld national preferences, and its decision as disguised intergovernmentalism, it has also promoted the free circulation of goods and services which, most likely, will promote cooperation within the EC and may result in strengthening it further institutionally.

Unlike decisions reached intergovernmentally, decisions based on treaty provisions and passed by the Council of Ministers, the Commission, or the Court of Justice are directly binding on member states or individual companies. However, a distinction must be made between regulations and directives: the former are binding with regard to both specified ends and means; the latter are binding with regard to ends but leave member states to choose the means whereby the ends can be reached. In those areas where treaty provisions prevail, EC law is supreme over national law. This makes the EC different from international organizations. Hence, the EC is not simply an extension or conglomeration of national democratic systems but also sets its own rules. In addition, Community provisions about free trade, free location and free migration limit the powers of states over their citizens. This, as will be shown below, was reconfirmed with regard to the Irish authorities in 1992, who had tried to prevent a girl travelling to the United Kingdom for an abortion.

But the existence of a legitimate system for the resolution of conflict and for the making of authoritative decisions for the group as a whole does not imply that the EC has a single locus of supreme authority. Rather the emphasis within the EC is still on negotiation among member states. These negotiations are based, as Helen Wallace points out, on common jurisdiction, a system of collective rule, and a firm contract to collaborate on an expanding agenda.[10] Thus, there is neither a monopoly of coercion, nor a single locus of supreme authority, nor a separation of powers. In practice the Community's institutional framework has been sufficiently elastic to allow different concepts of political organization and hierarchy to survive and coexist.[11]

Many checks and balances operate to underpin the basis on which the member states are prepared to exercise collective decision-making. Member states seek to safeguard sovereignty and therefore try to minimize the use of majority voting. This can be seen in part in the role of the Council presidency and in part in the voting method practised in the Council of Ministers.

The system of the Council presidency, whereby member states on a six-monthly rotation preside over the activities in the Council of Ministers and the European Council, creates an opportunity for making an impact on common arrangements, while at the same time allowing the state to appear as a distinctive power within the system and in relations with outsiders.[12]

EC decisions and agreements are passed or ratified in a variety of forms. The two dominant forms relate to majority and unanimity. Both the Commission and the EP take nearly all their decisions by majority vote, but this can involve qualified majorities; each commissioner or MEP, respectively, has one vote.

The extreme cases of unanimity can be seen in EC treaty amendments and in the veto in the Council of Ministers. Unlike national constitutions, EC treaties can be amended only on the basis of the unanimous consent of member governments and parliaments. Though only used occasionally in an open form,[13] the potential of a veto still prevails in the Council of Ministers; neither the SEA nor the Treaty of Union, agreed at Maastricht, has altered this.

Although the SEA opened the way for greater use of majority voting, in practice most EC decisions are taken by unanimity. When majority voting takes place in the Council of Ministers it is based on weighted (block) votes whereby each state is given a number of votes ranging between 2 and 10. Hence, out of a total of 76 the required qualified majority is 54. This weighted voting deviates from most national practices but resembles voting in the German upper house (the Bundesrat) and in a number of international organizations.

Qualified majority voting can most easily be applied to decisions involving the mutual recognition of national norms. This marks an important departure from the previous practice of standardization (insistence on uniform Community norms) or harmonization (stipulation of minimum or maximum criteria). However, even where majority voting is possible, the use of weighted votes often produces blocking minorities.

Maastricht and Beyond

The Maastricht agreement of December 1991 signifies a significant qualitative shift in the use of majority voting by bringing important and sensitive areas of policy-making under EC remit. For example, as early as 31 December 1996 and as late as December 1998, the heads of state and governments will decide by qualified majority which countries have met the convergence criteria and thus are eligible to enter the third stage of European monetary union (EMU), which envisages the introduction of a single currency and the establishment of a European central bank.

Qualified majority voting has also been specified for some aspects of environmental policy and for some of the 'new' policies like development, health, consumer protection and trans-European networks. Unanimity has been retained for other environmental matters (fiscal, land use, energy), for most social policy items, for the research and development programme, for fiscal harmonization, for the common foreign and security policy, and for the review of the structural funds.

Political integration has moved forward in fits and starts. The outcome of the Maastricht summit is a case in point. The summit did not signify a great leap forward and may be disappointing to those with federalist aspirations, but it did make definite progress with regard to policy and institutional expansion and it did set specific deadlines on the road to further integration. In addition, the effects of the Maastricht agreement on EMU can be expected to be even more far-reaching than those of the internal market programme. As Joly Dixon points out:

> the primary effects of the latter are through the commercial and industrial world. EMU will have its effects through this channel, but it will also have a more immediate effect on each and every individual; and an even greater implication for the development of the Community.[14]

The overall agreement at Maastricht consists of three pillars. The first one brings a number of new policies under EC treaty jurisdiction, of which economic and monetary union is the main one. The second and third pillars represent intergovernmental arrangements respectively in the fields of foreign and security policy, and immigration policy (including issues of visa, asylum and policing). In both these fields decisions can be vetoed by a single government because of the unanimity requirement.[15] The common foreign and security policy (CFSP) covers all matters relating to the security of the member states, and therefore the eventual framing of a common defence policy which might in time lead to a common defence. Where the Community countries' foreign and defence policy decisions have defence implications, the Western European Union (WEU) will be asked to implement them. Member states which are members of NATO shall, however, continue to comply with their obligations under NATO, and foreign and security policy shall therefore be compatible with NATO's security and defence policy.

Four items feature prominently on the EC agenda in the 1990s: financial transfers and reforms; geographic enlargement; economic and monetary convergence; and the intergovernmental conference in 1994. The way these issues are settled will have profound implications for moving between a confederal and a federal model and for democratic control of its decision-making process. Though these issues are interrelated, for analytical reasons they will be treated separately.

First, a cohesion fund for the poorer EC regions of Southern Europe was established in 1993. Its introduction raises tricky questions about costs and benefits, Germany's preponderant net contribution to the EC budget in the face of internal economic difficulties, and the tradeoffs between subsidies to Mediterranean countries as compared with Eastern European countries.

Secondly, there were pending applications from Austria, Cyprus, Finland, Malta, Norway, Sweden and Turkey for EC membership by 1993; a further application was expected from Switzerland. Though the EC had reached association agreements with Czechoslovakia, Hungary and Poland, applications for full membership from these and other Central and Eastern European countries were also expected during the later 1990s. EC enlargement raises a host of questions, such as its implications for the internal market programme, EMU timetable and EC developments generally. It also heightens concerns over whether full membership of Central and Eastern European states would strengthen the German position within the EC, both in economic terms (because of trade and financial links) and in voting terms (creating a 'blocking minority' in the Council of Ministers).[16] There were of course also a number of technical issues to be settled such as the number of official languages, the size of the EC institutions, especially the EP and the Commission, and the rotation of the six-monthly Council presidency. Most critically, it would add pressure for more majority voting in EC decision-making. Effects on the elected EPs' ability to affect community decisions are uncertain.

Thirdly, majority voting will be an important factor in determining which countries meet the criteria of economic convergence as a precondition for entering stage three of EMU which entails the introduction of a single currency by 1 January 1999 at the latest. The convergence criteria relate to price stability, budget deficits, exchange rate stability and interest rates. Between December 1996 and December 1998, the Community's heads of state or government shall decide by qualified majority whether the majority of the member states (i.e. at least seven of the present twelve member states) fulfil the necessary conditions. Meeting these criteria might be a tough hurdle for some countries such as Italy, Portugal and Greece. There might also be considerable controversy over the interpretation of these criteria and subsequently whether or not a given country has met them. The European Monetary Institute, which is to coordinate monetary policy from 1994, might contribute to clarification of these questions.

Fourthly, some of these issues may surface in the new intergovernmental conference, scheduled for 1994, which ostensibly will review the two pillars of immigration policy and of CFSP. In particular, ambiguities surrounding the role of WEU have to be cleared up, e.g. is WEU to be a bridge between the EC and NATO, could it be the EC's defence arm, or could it formulate EC defence policy? France interprets the Maastricht accord as signifying an EC which is more self-reliant in security matters, whereas the United Kingdom interprets the same accord as signalling a confirmation of NATO's primacy and a subservience of EC and WEU policies to those of NATO.

Clarification of these considerations coincides with a general and fundamental review of the whole concept of security which has been provoked by the disappearance of the former Warsaw Pact, the disintegration of the former Soviet Union and the ethnic conflict in Eastern European countries, especially Yugoslavia. As Schmitter says, the 'very existence of what constitutes security is shifting from protection against a military based threat to physical existence to protection against an economic based threat to well-being'.[17] Whilst this points to an increasing intertwining of security and economy, any move towards a common defence strategy has implications both internally and externally. Within the Community, it challenges the concept of the EC as a 'civilian power'. With regard to potential new member states who have so far pursued neutrality as their foreign policy objective, EC defence commitments pose an additional hurdle to membership.[18]

Discussions over a strengthening of EC immigration policy will prove no less controversial. As Smith and Woolcock point out, the EC and by extension the European Economic Area including the EFTA are committed to free movement of citizens, but the EC exists in a broader Europe which is likely to produce major unplanned and involuntary movements of population during the 1990s. This will raise issues not only of domestic security and order but also of stability for the wider Europe.[19]

Besides the sensitivity of the issues raised, the intergovernmental conference of 1994 might also see an increase in the complexity of the negotiations – particularly in the shape of national parliaments and regional entities. The latter might be particularly noticeable in the case of the German *Länder* who have expressed considerable anxiety that the Maastricht agreement has opened the way to an unprecedented shift of authority to the Community level. To maintain their leverage, the state heads have linked their approval of the two treaties to a change in the German constitution that would give the *Länder* a say, along with the government, on any transfer of powers to supranational organizations. Preferably, the states want to be able to decide in conjunction with the government whether the economic conditions for EMU have been fulfilled by all, or the majority of, member states intending to go on to the final stage; and whether political union has been strengthened by, among other things, increasing the powers of the European Parliament.[20]

Decision-Making and Democracy

An increase in EP powers, though helpful, is in itself not sufficient to eliminate the existing democratic deficit in EC decision-making.[21] In general terms this democratic deficit relates to the inability of either national parliaments or the EP to influence significantly the outcome of EC decisions.[22] With few exceptions (Denmark) governments do not present policy issues or negotiating stands to national parliaments prior to approval by the Council of Ministers. The reason given is that such information and exposure would weaken governments' negotiating positions within the Council of Ministers. However, when a government introduces the full conclusions of the Council of Ministers, they are presented as the 'best deal' achievable and their acceptance by parliaments is often interpreted as a vote of confidence in the government. As a result, the measures usually receive the customary approval or 'rubber stamp'. By both keeping their own powers and deriding the EP as impotent, while providing or controlling key economic, social and security sectors, national governments succeed in maintaining citizen support and loyalty. The EP is neither an active broker in EC decision-making nor an effective agent for imbuing citizens with Community interest and loyalty. The EP has only limited ability to influence EC decisions via the cooperation procedure, the codecision procedure and the assent procedure.[23] In contrast, the Council of Ministers plays a dominant role in EC decisions. In turn this affects the ability of citizens or voters to use elections for the EP as a means of holding the EC accountable for its actions. Moreover, since members of the EP are mostly elected according to party-list systems rather than through constituency ties, the EP is seen as remote and associated more with European-wide interests than with local ones. Relatively low voter turnout in the three direct elections to the EP underscore this feeling of remoteness and irrelevance.[24]

Yet it would be wrong to concentrate unduly on EP inabilities or inadequacies. The Commission was for a long time seen as hugely bureaucratic, highly inefficient, mostly self-serving, and unnecessarily interfering. Even the Court of Justice, which has perhaps done more than any other institution to augment Community values and promote the mobility and rights of citizens throughout the Community, is seen as too legalistic and too remote from daily concerns. This is particularly surprising since Court judgements have direct applications to citizens and provide the possibility of individual remedial action, e.g. individuals have the right to take their complaints to the Court of Justice in cases where there are perceived clashes of interest between national and Community law.

The internal market programme has helped to create a more favourable public perception of the EC generally and the Commission particularly. This has opened prospects for a direct relationship between the Commission and the citizenry and may provide the Commission with an opportunity to build an independent power base for legitimizing its policy initiatives. To inform citizens more fully, the Commission has launched an 'internal market information campaign', which complements national publicity, to stress the main objectives of the programme for individuals, i.e. freedom of movement and social dialogue. But it must be realized that the EC has limited financial means for satisfying citizens' demands. The EC budget amounts to only 2 to 3 per cent of member states' total public expenditure, even though in volume it is not trivial and in sectors such as agriculture it predominates over national contributions.[25] Also, the EC budget has grown at a considerably faster rate than those of member states in the last two decades. On the whole, as Helen Wallace suggests, the EC resource transfers do take place systematically, with some deliberately redistributive purposes, but at a modest and contested level. For Helen Wallace, 'the really rewarding potentialities of the welfare state for building loyalties remain firmly entrenched in its national-member bureaucracies.'[26]

Nonetheless, there are possibilities for the Commission to strengthen links with citizens either directly or indirectly. First, the Commission intends to promote greater participation of sub-national units in the distribution of structural funds. The aim is to give more discretion and power to sub-units (e.g. local and regional governments) in the planning process. Whilst this will not by-pass the national level directly, it will give sub-units a greater share in these kinds of negotiations and will increase access and increase information flow. It may also pave the way for coalition formation between the two, *vis-à-vis* national governments. These potential developments might also be enhanced by the establishment of the Committee of the Regions, which is an advisory committee consisting of 189 representatives of regional and local authorities.

Whether such arrangements can protect sub-national entities against centralizing tendencies in the shape of trade standardization (via the single market) or monetary policy (via the proposed European central bank) remains to be seen. In the past, attempts to place the locus of authority even further from the domain of the individual and small group and which threaten them with even more standardized treatment have often engendered resistance and demands for greater autonomy.

There is of course also the wider question of whether sub-national units use the EC as a (temporary) instrument to obtain greater regional autonomy *vis-à-vis* national governments. Similarly, if the EC contributes, willingly or unwillingly, to such regional aspirations, this may have a destabilizing effect not only on the nation state but also on EC integration generally.

Secondly, besides the use of structural funds, the Commission may affect individuals and working conditions in other ways. To appreciate this point more fully it is helpful to consider Majone's distinction between social policy and social regulation.[27] Social policy is seen as involving social insurance, public assistance, the health and welfare services and housing policy. Social regulation, in contrast, refers to the quality of the working environment, health and safety, gender equality and consumer protection. Whereas the establishment of a European-wide social policy is seen as requiring large EC financial support, which is both absent and difficult to raise, no such financial resources are needed to set up social regulations, since the costs of most regulatory programmes are borne directly by the firms and individuals who have to comply with them. Majone suggests that 'as the new concerns about risk, consumer protection and civil rights replace the old class struggle over the division of the national product, the Community should play a pioneering role in the development of the new social regulation'.[28]

The European Social Charter of 1989 raised some interesting points in this respect. It has brought to the fore the potential of the Commission, via EC legislation, to reach groups and individuals more directly and in ways certain governments find unacceptable. The stand taken by the United Kingdom government on the European Social Charter and on the Maastricht negotiations, where it forced the other eleven to conclude a special deal amongst themselves and outside the Maastricht accord, is one of the most significant expressions of disapproval. Meantime, the strong campaign by the British TUC and Labour Party for the acceptance of the social dimension by the UK demonstrates how certain groups can be won over by EC action and may become potential allies against their own national governments.

Thirdly, a link exists between the considerable interest which the single market programme has provoked in citizens, especially in employment and prosperity terms, and the various schemes which the Community has launched or is just about to introduce to promote mobility. These schemes affect workers, students and academics (the ERASMUS project), professions and tourists, and improve transnational transport and communication networks. The introduction of a single currency will stimulate further interest.

Fourthly, the concept of European citizenship, launched at the Maastricht summit, provides citizens with the right to vote and stand as a candidate in municipal elections and EP elections in the member state in which they reside. All citizens of the EC shall have the right to petition the EP and apply to the Community ombudsman. The EC may also be increasingly used on human rights issues, as in the case of the fourteen-year-old Irish girl who had been raped and was initially prevented from travelling to the United Kingdom for an abortion.

Moves toward a European citizenship seem to presage a federal future. However, there is as yet no European nation nor is there a significant aspiration by citizens for such an identity. Public attitudes on the level and degree of identification with European ideals appear ambiguous. This can be seen in the contradictory evidence of public opinion and in the potential danger of public opinion being hijacked by national governments. Whereas up to two-thirds of interviewees declared themselves in favour of the United States of Europe in 1987,[29] there is also evidence that only 16 per cent thought of themselves as Europeans.[30] In the absence of clear evidence, it is probably safe to agree with Barry Hughes who suggests that European identity will grow but that national identity will not be replaced by a European identity.[31] There is even a danger that national identity will be strengthened. Governments might become increasingly inclined, like the Italian one, to blame the EC, either for causing 'unnecessary' economic hardship in efforts to reach the economic convergence criteria for entering phase three of EMU, or for interpreting convergence performance differently from national governments and thus preventing entry into the single currency. As a consequence, and together with a general flaring-up of ethnic divisions in EC countries, national identity, rather than Community identity, might be on the rise.

Conclusion

Deep-seated and long-standing national differences, of which language is only one, have not and will not disappear in Europe. However, just as many of the existing nation states gradually assimilated diverse ethnic groups into larger entities over a prolonged period, so the EC may succeed in promoting cooperation among former enemies by instilling a degree of mutual responsiveness and trust and by creating a European identity. The EC has indeed already contributed to peace, stability and economic prosperity in the region. There is also a growing belief that the EC can respond more effectively to economic, political and security challenges in Europe and in the international environment than individual member states can. The EC is now on the brink of establishing economic and security policies which have serious implications for national sovereignty.

Nonetheless, the EC has to be wary of a reassertion of national interests. Treaty provisions, however noble, about EC ideals (peace, stability, prosperity and democratic norms) have to be translated into practice, where they can conflict with national interests, customs and prejudices. Strong national stands have been taken with regard to treaty amendments. Attempts to go beyond the narrow confines of the treaty provisions too quickly, as was the case in the early 1990s with regard to CFSP, have resulted in failures. However, whilst national differences will continue to be a significant factor, consensus building and coalition formation have been and will be the basic ingredients of EC success and its cumulative development.

The excessive centralization implicit in Jacques Delors's prediction in 1988 that 80 per cent of economic legislation within the EC will be decided by a federal/central authority in ten years' time, seems unfounded.[32] Both the development of monetary policy and the introduction of the principle of subsidiarity suggest a different outcome. Whereas the European central bank will be in charge of setting interest rates and has an overriding commitment to price stability, the Council of Finance Ministers will determine the exchange rates and will be responsible for the stability of the financial systems. Under the principle of subsidiarity, which has been written into the Maastricht treaty, the Community will take action only where the objectives can be better achieved by the Community than by the member states.

In spite of these developments, the governing capacity of the state is diminished by external constraints, both by other states and by a myriad of non-state actors. This generates a substantial readjustment in relations among states and between states and the EC. Philippe Schmitter foresees the EC establishing functionally specific authorities to regulate the conditions for the exchange of goods and services. It will, however, agree to govern their impact through a territorial redistribution of benefits, rather than resorting to the ultimate sanction of coercion, and without relying on some exclusive and overarching sense of loyalty.[33] Similarly, Barry Hughes concludes that we should look at the EC not as an embryonic superstate or supernation, but as one organ in a system of complex governance, consisting of multi-tiered, geographically overlapping structures of government and non-government elites.[34]

There is certainly an increasing degree of cooperation, in vertical terms between different government levels, and in horizontal terms among several groups of actors.[35] Cooperation in this sense thus implies two closely linked patterns of administrative interaction: the way state administrations develop their national policy-making style horizontally, and the way several national and international administrations shape common policies vertically. These trends are mutually reinforcing. They do, however, foster corporatist tendencies rather than democratic accountability. Moreover, the view that the EC was elite inspired and is elite driven still has a certain validity, though the time of the 'permissive consensus' of the masses is clearly over.[36]

The EC effectively combines national and supranational institutional competences, decision-making structures and administrative bodies in policy-making. Depending on the issue area involved, either the national or the Community dimension is more pronounced. However, in most circumstances there is a high degree of shared decision-making competences and responsibilities between the two layers; joint tasks rather than zero-sum transfers of authority from the national to the Community level are often the preferred form. This reflects deep-seated concerns about the loss of national sovereignty on the one hand, and a profound awareness of the prevailing high levels of economic and social interdependence among EC member states on the other. Both reflections have their origin in the legacy of the Second World War – in particular the post-war economic recovery programme, and the subsequent success of transnational economic, security and social cooperation.

Rather than forging ahead in either a federal or confederal direction, the EC appears to be stuck, for the time being, between the two forms. This may change more in the direction of federalism if current plans for the establishment of a single currency and a European central bank come to pass by the late 1990s. Meantime, the EC represents a unique form of transnational democracy which effectively combines national and Community norms, working habits, responsiveness and identity. Its very looseness and tentativeness may render it an attractive model of international association for countries further to the east, who do not want to submerge their new national democracies in highly centralized arrangements, but who recognize social and economic imperatives for cooperation with their neighbours and indeed between overlapping and disparate ethnic groups within their own borders.

Notes

1 For a more elaborate definition and treatment of these two concepts see Philippe Schmitter, 'The European Community as an Emergent and Novel Form of Political Domination', Estudio/Working Paper 1991/26, Centro de Estudios Avanzados en Ciencias Sociales, Instituto Juan March de Estudios e Investigaciones, September 1991.

2 Even when specific attempts were made such as through the Tindemans Report in the mid 1970s, or the Treaty of Union (Maastricht agreement), no clear consensus emerged on a definition for the end-state of the EC.

3 Andrew Schonfield, *A Journey to an Unknown Destination*, Harmondsworth: Penguin Books, 1973.

4 See Karl W. Deutsch et al., *Political Community and the North Atlantic Area: International Political Communities*, New York: Anchor Books, 1966, pp. 1–92, and Ron Inglehart, 'Public Opinion and Regional Integration', *International Organization*, vol. 25, 1971, pp.764–95.

5 See Barry B. Hughes, 'Delivering the Goods: European Integration and the Evolution of Complex Governance', paper presented at the Annual Meeting of the American Political Science Association, Washington, DC, August 1991.

6 See David Mitrany, *A Working Peace System*, London: The Royal Institute of International Affairs, 1943.

7 Philippe Schmitter, 'The European Community'.

8 See Joseph Weiler, 'Community, Member States and European Integration: Is the Law Relevant?', *Journal of Common Market Studies*, vol. XXI, 1982, pp. 39–56.

9 See Angelo M. Petroni, 'Views on a European Constitution', paper presented at the Karl Brunner Symposium, Interlaken, Switzerland, 20–24 May 1991.

10 Helen Wallace, 'The Europe that Came In from the Cold', *International Affairs*, vol. 67, 1991, p. 651.

11 Ibid., p. 655.

12 See Paul Taylor, 'The European Community and the State: Assumptions, Theories and Propositions', *Review of International Studies*, vol. 17, 1991, p. 122. For a more general treatment of the Council presidency see Emil J. Kirchner, *Decision-Making in the European Community: The Council Presidency and European Integration*, Manchester: Manchester University Press, 1992.

13 The German stand on the proposed decrease of cereal prices in 1985 is one of those rare examples where the veto was explicitly used. See Emil J. Kirchner, 'The Federal Republic of Germany in the European Community', in *The Federal Republic at Forty*, Peter Merkl, ed., New York: New York University Press, p. 428.

14   Joly Dixon, 'The Maastricht Conclusions on EMU', paper presented at Workshop of the European Community Studies Association, Chicago, 26–27 February 1991, p. 1.

15   However, in the case of specific joint action in the foreign and security field the Council of Ministers may unanimously decide that decisions in some areas may be taken by qualified majority.

16   A blocking minority within the current twelve EC member states consists of twenty-three votes.

17   Philippe Schmitter, 'The European Community', pp. 15 and 16.

18   Sweden has pointed out that its neutrality would not prevent it from acceding to the Maastricht agreement in respect of common foreign and security policy. See Juliet Lodge, 'Blindfolded by the F. Word', *Times Higher Educational Supplement*, 27 December 1991, p. 9.

19   Michael Smith and Stephen Woolcock, 'The United States and the EC: Confronting the Challenge of Political and Security Order', paper presented at the International Studies Association Convention, Atlanta, Georgia, April 1992.

20   See John Eisenhammer, 'German States Demand Role over EC budget', *The Independent*, 14 March 1992.

21   This point is made by, amongst others, Wolfgang Wessels, 'Administrative Inter-action', in *The Dynamics of European Integration*, William Wallace, ed., London: Pinter, 1990, p. 238.

22   A fuller treatment of the 'democratic deficit' is provided by Shirley Williams, 'Sovereignty and Accountability in the European Community', *Political Quarterly*, vol. 61, July–September 1990, pp. 299–317.

23   For further details on the various EP procedures, see Francis Jacobs and Richard Corbett, *The European Parliament*, Westview Press, 1991.

24   For an explanation of the relatively low turnouts to the EP elections in 1979, 1984 and 1989, averaging around 60 per cent of the electorate, see Juliet Lodge, ed., *The 1989 Election of the European Parliament*, London: Macmillan, 1990.

25   Helen Wallace, 'The Europe that Came In from the Cold', p. 652.

26   Ibid.

27   Giandomenico Majone, 'The European Community between Social Policy and Social Regulation', paper presented at the Workshop of the European Community Studies Association, Chicago, 26–27 February 1992.

28   Ibid., p. 12.

29   *Eurobarometer*, EC Commission, Brussels, March 1987.

30   *Eurobarometer*, EC Commission Brussels, October 1988.

31   Barry B. Hughes, 'Delivering the Goods', p. 4.

32   See Albert Bressand, 'Beyond Interdependence: 1992 as a Global Challenge', *International Affairs*, vol. 61, 1990, p. 54.

33   Philippe Schmitter, 'The European Community'.

34   Barry B. Hughes, 'Delivering the Goods'.

35   See Wolfgang Wessels, 'Administrative Interaction', p. 238.

36   The term 'permissive consensus' was initially coined by Lindberg and Scheingold and appeared relevant for the 1960s. See Leon Lindberg and Stuart Scheingold, *Europe's Would-Be Polity: Patterns of Change in the European Community*, Englewood Cliffs: Prentice-Hall, 1970.

16

Democracy in Eastern Europe

Ronald J. Hill

The collapse of communist rule in Eastern Europe[1] during 1989–90 was as unexpected as it was dramatic. Students of the region and of communism assumed that the communist form of rule had become a permanent type of political system. A new sub-field of political science – comparative communism – was established in the late 1970s to study the evolving communist systems of government on a comparative basis. Politicians seemed to share this view. Communist leaders referred to the onward march of socialism, and politicians in the 'Western' world warned of the dangers of communism and devised such theoretical constructs as the 'domino theory', the 'Hallstein doctrine' and the 'Brezhnev doctrine' to support their opposition to communist rule. Yet, across the globe, former communist regimes have been overthrown by popular action or have initiated changes that have led to their own demise. So spectacular was this development that it led one commentator to interpret it in apocalyptic terms as 'the end of history', since the inevitability of democratization seemed certain as socioeconomic modernization advanced.[2]

A central focus for such an argument is East-Central Europe: the countries that acquired communist regimes in the wake of the Second World War, resulting from either the activities of local communists or the presence of Soviet troops on their territory as the war ended (or, indeed, both). The creation of so-called 'people's democracies' was the first stage of the construction of 'communism', and broadly speaking entailed the application of measures established in the Soviet Union in the 1930s. The system as it existed is well known, and there is no need to elaborate it here.[3] The crucial elements were the exercise of control over society by a ruling Marxist-Leninist (communist) party, acting in pursuit of 'communism' as defined in the ideology. 'Politics', seen as a process of bargaining over interests and values, was 'ruled out'.[4] It was replaced by 'mobilization', whereby citizens were encouraged to participate in a variety of regime-sponsored activities, intended to inculcate devotion to Marxism–Leninism and to the party that claimed to be guided by it in ruling for the common good. Over four and a half decades, that system was maintained, in some well-known cases by military force, and in all cases by the presence of various security and control agencies that effectively permitted no opportunities for the expression of interests through the political process.

Developing Democracy

From 1989, however, 'democracy' has been proclaimed following the collapse of communism in the revolutions that struck the region with great force and drama. President Václav Havel of Czechoslovakia, harassed and repeatedly imprisoned for his 'dissident' views, expressed the aspirations of practically all the citizens of the region when he told his people that power had returned to them.[5] That emotional sense that the building of democracy – 'government of the people, by the people, for the people', in the simple but eloquent words of Lincoln's Gettysburg Address – could now be attained, and that, accompanied by the restoration of a market economy, it would rapidly improve the fortunes of former captive nations, inspired whole peoples – a whole continent – as Europe began to search again for common values in overcoming the ideological division.[6] However, great optimism at the prospect of democratization – the institutionalization of freedom, as Adam Michnik expressed it[7] – gave way within two or three years to greater realism about the complexity of the process; it is not yet clear that the fragile democratic institutions will everywhere manage to withstand the pressures to which they are subject.

Political Institutions and Democratization

A standard twentieth century view of the political process refers to the authoritative resolution of conflict among competing interests. From Bentley's 'process of government' through Truman's 'governmental process' to modern theorists of the state and political action, politics has been distinguished from war and civil strife as a mechanism for conflict resolution in a *peaceful* manner.[8] A conventional view of 'democracy' places an elected legislature at the centre of the institutional framework: a representative institution that takes binding decisions according to established procedures.[9]

Communist regimes ostensibly possessed such an institution: the Sejm in Poland, the Volkskammer in the German Democratic Republic, the Skupstina in Yugoslavia. It was vested with nominal authority and referred to with apparent respect amounting almost to deference. Yet nowhere did it function as the supreme organ of state power, as communist constitutions described it. The infrequency of its sessions (typically it met for a few days twice a year), the essential amateurism of the deputies (who retained their regular occupations), the control by the executive authorities (who set the agenda and restricted the deputies' function largely to voting in favour of the motions or draft laws), and, most of all, the dominating position of the Communist Party (under whatever name it chose) in the political system and the society at large – these and other recognized weaknesses rendered the parliamentary institution incapable of playing the role accorded to it in democratic theory.[10] While these institutions were rather more than the 'rubber stamps' of the widely held stereotype,[11] they were essentially docile instruments of rule. Democratization demands their conversion into an effective forum for the aggregation of interests in the process of law-making.

That evolutionary process entails both internal and external changes. Internally, the development demands extending the sessions, recruiting professional representatives, and devising standing orders to foster a businesslike working atmosphere for representatives to question and challenge the executive's proposals and actions. Externally, the process involves establishing an effective electoral system, and efforts to persuade the public to support the new institution. The first of these most likely involves the creation of political parties; the second requires effective behaviour by the new institutions.

The internal changes were perhaps not too difficult to bring about. Evidence from 1980–1 in Poland had already shown that parliamentarians, even when selected under the communist authorities' careful scrutiny, managed to act responsibly as representatives in the confrontation with them. Moreover, some countries – notably Poland and Hungary – had an ancient tradition of a national assembly, even though liberal democracy had not become established; Czechoslovakia's experience of parliamentary government was even more salient. And across the region, the model looked to for inspiration in the process of reform was that of the wealthy, stable democracies.[12]

Even so, the difficulties cannot be ignored, as Hungary's recent experience shows.[13] Problems identified include the overwhelming preponderance of well-educated, well-to-do professionals: these may be competent to articulate the interests of their voters (as happens in many Western legislatures), but in post-communist societies a much broader degree of social representation is needed if the population is not to feel excluded and alienated. Thus, by April 1991, 26 per cent of Bulgarian voters believed the first Grand National Assembly to be 'incapable of effective operation' and should be dissolved immediately; 49 per cent believed the institution should adopt a new constitution and then dissolve itself; a mere 10 per cent identified the Assembly as one of the 'credible' state institutions. This was seen as evidence of 'impatience on a mass scale'.[14] In Poland, the Sejm elected in 1989 steadily lost public confidence, which fell from 90 per cent in November 1989; it was dissolved after 850 days.[15]

That sense of exclusion and frustration was already evident earlier, as the public observed inexperienced parliamentarians 'playing games': displaying extreme factionalism, switching allegiances, establishing new parties, defying their parties' whips and acting to the cameras.[16] That lack of businesslike behaviour has been exacerbated by the failure in some cases to agree on new standing orders to regulate the proceedings, and by the overwhelming legislative agenda. Given the simultaneous tasks of establishing the framework for a new economy based on private ownership and market relations, setting up new political institutions and relationships, weeding out the old *nomenklatura*, all at a pace to satisfy a public opinion whose expectations were raised in the heady days of 1989, it is perhaps not surprising that 'a vast legislative agenda is probably the greatest single obstacle to parliamentary efficiency'.[17] Thus, in 1990, the Hungarian parliament considered 104 major bills, all of which needed debate in plenary session and in committee. How well thought out were they? How much detailed and competent consideration were they given? And is such a parliamentary work-load reasonable?[18]

The fragmented party system, in which new parties have been elected to office after a relatively short gestation without acquiring secure social or ideological bases, likewise threatens stability. So does the tendency, in such circumstances, to regard the initial post-communist parliament as provisional, and to call for fresh elections.[19] As the principal democratic mode for the selection of representatives, elections play a crucial role in democratization. But they are a sophisticated political device, and their place in the system needs to be secured with care.

Elections and Democratization

In an established democracy, elections are a reasonably reliable and acceptable way of selecting representatives who command the respect of the citizens in whose name they adopt laws. Under communism, 'elections' were held regularly.[20] Observing the legal niceties and expending considerable effort, the regimes mounted campaigns to select deputies to serve in the legislature (and in representative institutions at lower administrative levels). Moreover, they always produced impressive statistics to demonstrate near-unanimous support for the favoured candidates. Turnout figures of almost 100 per cent were matched by votes of a similar order for the candidates: occasionally such astonishing participation levels were allegedly exceeded.[21]

Nevertheless, few observers accepted these events as indicators of democracy. Not only were the statistics so impressive as to arouse suspicions; more obviously the system was dominated by the Communist Party, which always secured a firm majority, even as it permitted non-party candidates and candidates of other parties to win seats. Electoral systems took account of specific circumstances, including the presence of other parties in countries such as Poland and the legal requirement of a plurality of candidates, plus a requirement to mark the ballot, in Hungary.[22] But principles such as 'passive voting' or 'inertia voting', whereby voters had to take positive action in order to vote against the approved candidates but voted in favour by dropping an unmarked ballot paper into the ballot box, discouraged dissident voting.[23]

The new regimes quickly introduced competitive elections following the collapse of communism. In Poland a referendum on economic reform, held in November 1987, when the electorate rejected the communist government's proposed measures, whetted the appetite. The Jaruzelski regime was obliged to introduce some choice in the June 1989 elections, and the

Solidarity movement swept the board in those seats which it was permitted to contest. Across the region, communist parties renounced their political monopoly, frequently changed their name in order to enhance their electoral prospects, and prepared to do battle on the hustings alongside newly organized rivals. The results varied: former communists retained control of parliament in Bulgaria, Romania and Albania, and they polled almost 14 per cent in Czechoslovakia (a creditable performance in the circumstances); but, in general, the 'forum' movements performed most impressively, a testimony to their popularity following their role in bringing about the downfall of communism.[24] These results, and the varied but impressive showing of other groupings, proved that the communist plebiscitary elections had not completely destroyed popular appreciation of electoral choice, even though the mechanics of casting the ballot might have changed.

There were, however, far more serious requirements if the legislature were to develop as the centrepiece of democratic politics. The principles of access to the electoral process needed to be enshrined in new legislation, and specifically the right to organize to seek and wield power had to be guaranteed through new political parties.

Political Parties and Democratization

Alongside an effective parliament, modern democratic practice recognizes political parties as central institutions through which competing interests organize to win power: in the classic phrase 'they organize the chaotic public will' and are 'the proper engine' for a continuous plebiscite.[25] A further principle asserts that they should compete on equal terms for the support of the electorate. They need not adopt identical internal structures and rules – indeed, that is not normal in Western party systems[26] – but they should be able to approach the electorate on a more or less equal footing. They need access to the electorate, through face-to-face encounters (through canvassing or in public meetings) or indirectly through the mass media, posters and other means. To this end some systems (the British, for example) restrict the amount that a candidate may spend in an election campaign (while not necessarily making the same stipulation as regards national campaigning). Furthermore, parties need the legal protection afforded to other organizations: the right to attract members, establish an office, raise funds and hold bank accounts, own property, and be protected from external interference or from the mismanagement of their own officers, with legal remedies in cases of malfeasance. They also need leaders and members capable of reliably carrying out such intra-party 'housekeeping' and especially of devising campaign strategies, practical policies and political programmes, and of functioning as effective representatives in a new parliamentary institution under their party's guidance.

Eastern Europe has not been slow to exploit the opportunities offered by the demise of the communist domination. Communist rule excluded political activity for all but an elite, so the right to establish new political parties represented the supreme prize for societies embarking on democratization: they took to it with relish.[27] Following the demise of the ruling party – which in several cases changed its name and split into competing organizations – a proliferation of revived old and newly established parties filled the vacuum in advance of the first competitive elections, basing themselves variously on European, North American and local traditions.[28] In the East German national elections of March 1990, for example, almost 30 parties and movements fielded candidates; in Hungary, 65 parties were registered at the time of the 1990 elections and a further 32 parties and political associations were identified; in Poland, about 90 parties campaigned in the parliamentary election of October 1991; in Bulgaria, 61 parties and political clubs fought the October 1991 parliamentary election.[29]

Such vitality shows the optimism with which the opportunities for political involvement and activism were greeted after the deadening experience of communist rule. However, for the creation of stable, democratic institutions it is not necessarily a case of 'the more the better'. A real danger of 'extreme pluralism' exists,[30] leading to fragmentation of power. Where a large party is supported in coalition by one or more smaller parties, the fear is that 'the tail might wag the dog', preventing the firmness of purpose and bold policy initiatives that may be required in the difficult circumstances facing Eastern Europe. The electorates of Eastern Europe have faced a bewildering array of parties of many political stripes; only some of these might be considered potential governing parties, yet they have all expended effort and resources that might have been more valuably deployed. The creation of 'sofa parties' (so tiny that their members can be seated together on a sofa) evoked some derision in various countries.

It is, of course, the prerogative of citizens in a democracy to seek election. In some well-known cases, such as the British pop singer Screaming Lord Sutch and his Teenage Monster Raving Loony Party (or other variations), whose intermittent pastime is to run for election, the exercise of that right is mildly diverting and does not shake the foundations of the political system. However, Eastern Europe does not yet possess secure democratic systems. In March 1990, 2534 East Germans voted for the German Beer Drinkers' Union, and in October 1991 3.27 per cent of the Polish electorate voted for the Polish Beer Lovers' Party and won 16 seats in the Sejm[31] – evidence of disillusionment with conventional politics even before democracy is firmly established.

Effective, stable democracy may be fostered by a relatively small number of strong parties, each containing a wealth of talent and expertise valuable in policy-making, and a wide range of contacts through which to tap into society for information and support. Poland's Solidarity and the 'forum' movements elsewhere probably represented such a broad coalition. However, their overriding goal attained, there was little to hold them together, and they split into separate parties and organizations after the first contested elections, undermining the stability of the initial post-communist governments.

The development of a stable party system can be promoted by the choice of an appropriate electoral system, as noted in Chapter 14. The simple majority system may encourage such a development once a number of parties or organizations capable of mounting a national campaign exist. Whether or not proportional representation is deemed to be desirable, unrestricted proportional representation in the presence of a multiplicity of small parties may encourage fragmentation. In such circumstances, a threshold of a certain percentage of votes would weed out marginal groups that commanded little support but that could disrupt orderly government.

In Bulgaria, a 4 per cent threshold restricted the parliamentary access of all but a small number of parties: 38 parties and groupings contested the 1991 elections, but only three were eventually represented in parliament; one group – the Constitutional Forum Political Club – polled spectacularly poorly, gaining not a single vote![32] In Czechoslovakia, a new electoral law, adopted in January 1992, aimed to strengthen parties that commanded the most support: only parties with at least 10,000 members could register, at least 60 days before an election, and voting was by party lists using proportional representation; a 5 per cent threshold in either republic was stipulated, with a threshold of 7 per cent for election coalitions of two or three parties, and 10 per cent for coalitions of four or more parties. The number of parties was expected to be reduced by this measure.[33] In such cases, unsuccessful parties could merge and pool their efforts in future elections, or convert themselves into different organizations – interest groups or pressure groups.

However, this too has its risks for the development of stable democracy. One is that the parties in parliament will not be sufficiently broad-based to serve as 'catch-all' parties such as characterize Western democracies, and significant social elements will not be represented.[34] In this connection, the failure of agrarian-based parties in Bulgaria to clear the 4 per cent hurdle, and therefore to secure parliamentary representation for 1.2 million voters (some 20 per cent of the electorate), led to the conclusion that the hurdle was too high: a threshold 1 per cent lower would have brought about a parliament of a quite different composition.[35]

Nevertheless, the experience of the first parliamentary elections and subsequent working in parliament, involving adjustment to the circumstances of governing rather than opposition, does appear to lead to a more or less conventional political spectrum, judging by the experience of Czechoslovakia. There, it has been argued, the break-up of the Civic Forum and Public Against Violence coalitions, after their success in ending communist rule, had led to the creation of parties with political philosophies ranging across the broad left–right spectrum, while marginalizing extremist parties and still finding a place for parties with narrower regional or ethnic agendas.[36] Poland, too, had by the end of 1991 acquired a broad range, in which the traditional left was reviving thanks to adverse economic conditions; it achieved success in September 1993.

However, without continuing firm support for centrist parties, this may not be sufficient to guarantee steady democratization, since a second, related difficulty lies in the potential for extreme parliamentary politics, reflecting polarized ('blue' and 'red') opinion in the electorate.[37] With two strong parties or coalitions facing each other, political stalemate may ensue – or a small third party may hold the balance. Whether this promotes the development of a democratic process is not clear: West Germany functioned democratically for many years with such an arrangement; the Republic of Ireland, likewise, has long had a 'two-and-a-half party' system. Equally significant for stable democracy, perhaps, are the secondary, non-party institutions that give voice to various social groups.

Non-Party Organizations and Democratization

In a functioning democracy, there are places for institutions of different types: parties, which seek control over the state's decision-making organs, and therefore devise policies over a broad range of public issues; and representative organizations of various kinds which articulate their members' concerns and attempt to influence parties and governments within their sphere of interest, without seeking power through election to the state legislature. In fact, such organizations are vital if the machinery of government is not to be overladen, since they act as 'gatekeepers', screening out issues that can be resolved at the non-governmental level, and adding their organizational support to issues that require governmental action.

East European communist systems possessed many 'social' or 'public' organizations, enabling citizens to satisfy their interest in sports or theatre or various hobbies, and participate in communal affairs. In practice, all these organizations, including the trade unions and political parties themselves, were controlled and usually sponsored by the Communist Party. Their officers were normally communists, nominated through *nomenklatura*, the party-controlled appointment system. They were, in short, part of the mechanism of Communist Party rule, and lacked the autonomy to represent their members' interests as they saw fit. A preliminary goal of democratization, therefore, is to convert such 'transmission belts' of communist authority or replace them with new organizations that enjoy the confidence of their members, that are effectively controlled by those members, and that can develop a public role representing their interests. This includes the whole range of professional bodies from trade unions to employers' associations, plus special interest associations that promote the activities of their members, from chess to hang-gliding (and they may eventually perform a regulatory function). Some of these bodies will establish links with the political institutions, to serve as a conduit to the policy-makers in seeking legislative or budgetary provision to support or regulate their activities. A lobby system, whereby certain broadly based groups such as employers' or workers' organizations can have direct consultative access to political decision-makers, can institutionalize the articulation of interests in the system.

Without such supporting institutions, democratization seems likely to enjoy only partial success: it will be restricted to a relatively small circle of 'professionals', leaving the population few opportunities for democratic participation. Intermediate organizations can support democratic institutions and actors by channelling information and permitting citizens to develop and articulate their interests in a communal institutional setting; they can also relieve political institutions and actors of some of the burden of striving to gain first-hand knowledge of the electorate's wishes. They are thus an indispensable element in the structures of a living democratic system.

In Eastern Europe, certain bodies already possess the potential to develop such a role. The old, communist-controlled organizations should not be written off, including the trade unions, which began to perform more actively to protect their members' interests once the state began to threaten unemployment and privatization.[38] Moreover, such organizations, in which millions of communists cut their organizational teeth, could permit them to deploy their expertise in the difficult conditions of the economic market-place. Likewise, business organizations, such as the Bulgarian Business Bloc and the Bulgarian Business Party, could establish a permanent body to promote their supporters' interests. In Hungary, too, parties such as the Alliance of the Poor and Exploited, the Democratic Pensioners' Party and the Hungarian Humanists' Party seem by their titles to be precisely the single-issue organizations that in Western democracy would constitute interest or pressure groups. Some agrarian parties might convert themselves into farmers' representative organizations and forge links with various parliamentary parties, government, various ministries, the press and so forth.

However, the effective functioning of all the institutions, and their capacity to respond to public opinion, requires the establishment of a further, fundamental principle of liberal democracy: broad freedom of information in the society at large. Without it, a reliable public opinion cannot be developed, and it is impossible to win public sympathy, particularly in times of difficulties. Generally speaking, the mass media of all kinds – broadcast and print – very quickly established their autonomy and independence. Press freedom appears to have been won relatively easily, although not everywhere have opposition papers been given a completely free hand: supplies of newsprint and access to the presses – in the past a Communist Party near-monopoly – have been restricted.[39]

The significance of this for democratization is easily appreciated, yet it relates to a frequently overlooked element of the political system: the *supports* that were an element in the basic 'black box' model.[40] 'Democracy' is often reduced to parties, elections and parliaments; equally vital for effective democracy, as noted in Chapter 14, is the development of public support for the institutions. There is a desperate need to develop public confidence in elections as a legitimate way of selecting representatives; in parties as organizations for winning power and effectively wielding it for the public good; in parliaments as institutions capable of effective decision-making, whose laws are respected and implemented. All of this presupposes the development of both a supportive *political culture* and a supportive *public opinion*.

Political Culture and Democratization

A real difficulty facing Eastern Europe is the absence, in most cases, of a democratic tradition. Apart from Czechoslovakia, the region had little experience of functioning democracy and suffered various forms of authoritarian rule before the communists came to power. They were, moreover, relatively poor, uneducated, unsophisticated peasant countries, ill-equipped as peoples to sustain effective democratic institutions. Certainly, if one assumes the rationality and sovereignty of the electorate, effective participation presupposes a high level of information and a developed capacity for making political judgements. Furthermore, notions of toleration and respect for opponents – again, essential features of pluralist democracy – were not well established in the minds of most citizens in those countries. In Poland, for example, the virtues of struggle against partition and occupation were more highly valued than those of tolerance and liberalism;[41] in Hungary, the tradition included 'a certain respect for legality and institutional politics', yet 'violence and arbitrary action' combined with 'complex and bureaucratic state procedures' and a low level of political literacy discredited the old parliamentary institutions;[42] Yugoslavia during the Second World War suffered at the cruel hands of fascist Croatian Ustase and the Serbian Chetniks, who left a bitter legacy;[43] Eastern Germany had experienced the weak Weimar republic and the disaster of Hitler's rule. In Czechoslovakia, alone among the successor states to the Austro-Hungarian Empire, an effective multi-party parliamentary democracy functioned for a generation, before the presence of the large German minority 'made it easy prey to Hitler's expansionist policies'.[44] Even there, however, it has been argued that the Slovaks 'had no opportunity to acquire elementary democratic habits' and 'people were increasingly inclined to submit passively to the authoritarian regime.'[45]

Such experiences of authoritarian rule did not exactly pave the way for a communist takeover by establishing a political culture conducive to acceptance of imposed rule: after all, a force of occupying troops or a determined band of individuals tends not to ask questions about political culture or the likely acceptability of their rule. Nor is the impact of such traditions on communist rule certain: in Poland the presence of a strong Roman Catholic Church caused the communists to act with some restraint, whereas Czechoslovakia's democratic traditions did not prevent the maintenance of one of the more odious and repressive communist regimes.[46]

Clearly, however, the experience of communist rule did little to overcome the absence of developed pluralist and liberal values. Where liberal and democratic values had existed, an ageing population took the experience to the grave; where the rising generations acquired such values through informal channels such as the family, they had no opportunity to reinforce them through practice. Ordinary citizens may have found abhorrent their rulers' definition of politics in terms of the Leninist principle of *kto kogo*? (who whom?); but with few opportunities to develop alternative political values, freedom became a somewhat abstract ideal, which now demands effective operationalization involving institutions and appropriate practices and values. In fact, given its propensity to treat disagreement as dissidence and opponents as enemies, communism may have undermined any confidence in parties, politicians and even politics as a mechanism for resolving conflicts. As noted above, confidence in the new institutions waned fairly steadily once the initial excitement dissipated.

In any case, the communist political ethic may indeed have been absorbed by populations acquiring modern education and experiencing urbanization and industrialization under communist rule, and *ipso facto* confronting politics for the first time. The idea of politics as a zero-sum game involving power and its deployment does not entirely contradict common-sense notions: the ideal of compromise as the goal of a political system is a sophisticated concept that has to be learnt by political leaders and followers alike. As a Bulgarian commentator observed, 'a democratic spirit . . . does not lie in the claim to a monopoly over democracy, but in the recognition that it is only a partner in the democratic system.'[47]

Further elements in the political culture may inhibit the establishment of democratic principles, posing problems that will demand some ingenuity in overcoming: specifically, Europe's ancient ethnic rivalries and animosities. The decline of the Turkish Empire followed by the collapse of Austria-Hungary in the First World War, and the creation of nation states whose boundaries did not respect the geographical distribution of ethnic groups, laid the potential for continuing conflict. Communism imposed a rough and ready peace over the region, but traditional suspicions remained. In the most complex case – Yugoslavia – despite attempts to wean citizens towards a common Yugoslav identity, only 5.4 per cent declared themselves to be 'Yugoslavs' in the census of 1981.[48] In the late 1980s hostility between Hungary and Romania over the position of the Hungarians in Transylvania led almost to a rupturing of relations between the two communist countries. Traditional rivalries between Czechs and Slovaks have resurfaced following the collapse of communism, as has the historic animosity of Bulgarians towards their country's Turkish minority. It was somewhat ironic that the first significant demonstration in post-communist

Bulgaria, in January 1990, sought to prevent the granting to the Turkish population of the full civic rights denied by the communists:[49] this shows both ethnic hostility and the absence of the appropriate liberal democratic value of tolerance. Across Eastern Europe, anti-Semitism has flared again.

These anti-liberal, anti-democractic sentiments have been exacerbated by economic and social pressures over the past decade or more. Mounting economic difficulties were a major contributory factor in the decline and eventual collapse of communist rule,[50] and the problems did not disappear when communism fell. Indeed, the chosen route to recovery – the switch to a market economy based on private ownership – threatened to exacerbate the situation. Rapid inflation, factory closures and unemployment, with their attendant social disruption and psychological disorientation, visited upon societies that had become accustomed to living without these pressures; the likely application of market principles to housing supply, education and health-care services, science and the arts and publications; and modifications to other features of communist rule, must all come as a shock to populations who had taken them for granted for most of their lives. Many depended on such state expenditures for their livelihood.

A reformist government can win temporary support by arguing that it is creating a new system and adopting a new approach. However, unless its policies improve the system fairly rapidly, disillusionment may set in, making it difficult for the new institutions to stabilize their support. This will result in alienation and withdrawal, and a declining evaluation of political institutions (as noted above), low voter turnout (as happened in Poland in October 1991, when the figure fell to 42.3 per cent, compared with 63 per cent in June 1989), and support for fringe and frivolous parties, such as Poland's Beer Lovers' Party. If the new institutions seem incapable of resolving the economic difficulties at a pace that satisfies public opinion, they become vulnerable. Citizens may express their opinions through strikes, demonstrations and other forms of social pressure, conceivably leading to a breakdown of law and order: the search for convenient scapegoats is a predictable response, alluded to above.

If the new system fails to cope because the government lacks the necessary resources, the lack of faith in conventional democratic politics is reinforced. Nostalgia for communist rule is perhaps unlikely in most of Eastern Europe. Nevertheless, elected governments may be tempted to revert to authoritarian methods from the communist past during which their political outlook was moulded. The Romanian National Salvation Front's reliance on the strong-arm tactics of mineworkers drafted into the capital to deal with protests and demonstrations in 1990 and 1991 is a clear example. President Walesa's demand for more powers in 1991 is a further indicator, as is the attempt by President Havel to introduce an anti-party electoral law. Alternatively, societies may be vulnerable to the promises of demagogues. As the Polish scholar and politician Adam Michnik has observed, 'This is the ideal time for demagogy. Demagogy that aggressively attacks the government may be successful, which must lead to destabilization. Destabilization elicits chaos. Chaos generates a new poverty and a new dictatorship.'[51] Following half a century of manipulation by the political elite, in the absence of an appropriate culture 'people are highly susceptible to appeals of the left and the right.'[52] Either way, the establishment of democratic political institutions and conventions is retarded.

The Prospects for Democratization

Further problems are being addressed, notably the choice between a presidential and a parliamentary model of democratic government (as in Chapter 12). The merits and drawbacks of both systems are being taken into account as political leaders gain experience and look elsewhere for their inspiration, and as they search for an authoritative institution to take the hard decisions demanded by circumstances, while recognizing that the particular institutional balance will remain after the present urgent problems have been resolved.[53]

The pessimistic scenarios outlined above are not inevitable, but neither is a smooth transition. All revolutions, including anti-communist ones, raise expectations that place burdens on the new regime. The commitment to democratic methods may suffer in the face of popular pressure: if the alternative is a breakdown of law and order, governments may opt for displays of authority, since their principal function is to maintain the system and preserve public order.[54]

The threshold of a perceived threat to public order may vary, in part reflecting political culture, and perhaps also reflecting perceptions of international response. In that respect, the support given by other democratic countries may materially affect the prospects for democracy in Eastern Europe. The post-communist governments manifestly look to the West for assistance, most particularly economic aid – cash, capital, expertise – to help overcome the immediate problems of economic crisis. But this cannot wholly solve their problems, if only because Western interests in this regard are contradictory. Political peace and universal democracy are, in principle, desiderata of all democratic regimes; but enhancing the former communist countries' competitiveness may not enjoy the electoral appeal in the West that it might attract in Eastern Europe. Given their low wages, a relatively well-educated workforce and proximity to the West European market, appropriate investment could turn those countries into powerful economic rivals of Western nations whose own democratic institutions could come under pressure.

Successful democratization in Eastern Europe is therefore not guaranteed. Those nations are struggling towards democracy, on the basis of relatively little experience, and in circumstances that are not the most propitious. The prospects seem better in some countries than in others, in the light of their own traditions and given appropriate support from the

West. But undue pessimism is out of order: 'exaggerated scepticism' can result from misleading interpretations of historical and present circumstances; appropriate support from the West could make all the difference, since 'the trend toward freedom and democracy seems now to be crystallized', and its reversal would entail 'a major political battle affecting the entire European continent'.[55]

Lucian Pye observed a quarter of a century ago that 'scholars are . . . confronted by the fact that they lack the knowledge necessary to give firm answers to such questions as how democratic values and modern political institutions can most readily be transferred to new environments'.[56] While this may still be substantially true, political science has a contribution to make, in helping both participants and observers to appreciate the complexity of the transformation, and to offer solutions to specific problems. Ultimately, however, each nation must find its own road to democracy, and create a form of democratic politics that suits its own spirit and genius.

Notes

1   For convenience this chapter uses the term 'Eastern Europe' to denote those countries that were ruled by communists from shortly after the Second World War until 1989–90: Poland, Czechoslovakia, the German Democratic Republic, Hungary, Romania, Bulgaria, Yugoslavia and Albania. Following the collapse of communist rule in all those countries, the older terminology – devised at a time when travel times rendered fine politico-geographical distinctions more significant than they are today – is returning into vogue: 'East-Central Europe', 'Central Europe', 'South-East Europe' and perhaps 'Eastern Europe': see Timothy Garton Ash, 'Eastern Europe: The Year of Truth', *The New York Review of Books*, 15 February 1990, p. 17.

2   Francis Fukuyama, 'The End of History', *The National Interest*, 16 (summer 1989), pp. 3–18. Fukuyama has presented an extended elaboration of his argument in his *The End of History and the Last Man* (London: Hamish Hamilton, 1992).

3   Among the works dealing with the communist experience across Eastern Europe the following may be cited: H. Gordon Skilling, *The Governments of Communist East Europe* (New York: Crowell, 1966); Ghita Ionescu, *The Politics of the European Communist States* (London: Weidenfeld & Nicolson, 1967); François Fejtö, *A History of the People's Democracies: Eastern Europe Since Stalin* (Harmondsworth: Penguin, 1974); Teresa Rakowska-Harmstone and Andrew Gyorgy (eds), *Communism in Eastern Europe* (Bloomington, IN, and London: Indiana University Press, 1979); Joni Lovenduski and Jean Woodall, *Politics and Society in Eastern Europe* (London: Macmillan, 1987). There have, in addition, been many studies of individual countries; a useful starting-point is the relevant volumes in the series *Marxist Regimes: Politics, Economics and Society*, published in London by Pinter from 1984 under the general editorship of Bogdan Szajkowski. An influential theoretical analysis of such regimes was the 'totalitarian' model, famously expounded in Carl J. Friedrich and Zbigniew K. Brzezinski, *Totalitarian Dictatorship and Autocracy*, 2nd edn (New York: Praeger, 1966).

4   See Ivan Krustev, 'The Illusions of Politics', *East European Reporter*, vol. 4, no. 4 (1991), p. 32; quoted in Michael Waller, 'Groups, Interests and Political Aggregation in East Central Europe', *Journal of Communist Studies*, vol. 8, no. 1 (1992), pp. 128–47 (p. 132).

5   In his New Year address to the nation of 1990, Havel said, 'Tvá vláda, lide, se k tobe navrátila', 'People, your government has returned to you': quoted as an epigraph in Timothy

Garton Ash, *We the People: The Revolution of '89* (Cambridge: Granta Books, in association with Penguin Books).

6   See, for example, 'The Year of Truth', ibid., pp. 131–56.

7   Quoted in Peter Frank, 'Gorbachev, Glasnost and Russian History', *Irish Slavonic Studies*, no. 12 (1991), pp. 1–10 (p. 7).

8   Arthur F. Bentley, *The Process of Government* (Cambridge, MA: Harvard University Press, 1967) (originally published in 1908); David B. Truman, *The Governmental Process* (New York: Knopf, 1951); J.D.B. Miller, *The Nature of Politics* (Harmondsworth: Penguin, 1962); Jean Blondel, *An Introduction to Comparative Government* (London: Weidenfeld & Nicholson, 1969).

9   See, for example, S.E. Finer, *Comparative Government* (London: Allen Lane, 1970), p. 66.

10   For a summary of the functioning of communist legislatures see Daniel Nelson and Stephen White (eds), *Communist Legislatures in Comparative Perspective* (Albany, NY: State University of New York Press, 1982), especially Chapter 1.

11   Stephen White ibid., pp. 191–5.

12   Jan Zielonka, 'East Central Europe: Democracy in Retreat?', *The Washington Quarterly*, vol. 14, no. 3 (1991), pp. 107–10.

13   The following analysis draws on Barnabas Racz, 'The Hungarian Parliament's Rise and Challenges', *RFE/RL Research Report*, vol. 1, no. 7 (14 February 1992), pp. 22–6.

14   Survey figures, reported in Antonii Todorov, 'Early to Red or Early to Blue?', *The Insider* (Sofia), no. 6 (1991), pp. 3–4 (p. 3).

15   'The First Free Parliamentary Elections', *Poland Today*, 1/92 (1992), pp. 6–7.

16   Vladimir V. Kusin, 'The Birth Pangs of Democratic Politics', *Report on Eastern Europe*, vol. 2, no. 1 (4 January 1991), pp. 45–50 (pp. 47–8).

17   Ibid., p. 47.

18   Racz, 'The Hungarian Parliament', pp. 24, 25–6.

19   Ibid., p. 25.

20   See, in particular, Alex Pravda, 'Elections in Communist Party States', in Guy Hermet, Richard Rose and Alain Rouquié (eds), *Elections Without Choice* (London: Macmillan, 1978), pp. 169–95.

21   In the Soviet Union Stalin obtained 'majorities' of more than 100 per cent: by obtaining a certificate permitting them to vote at any polling station, significant numbers of electors supposedly crossed into the constituency in which Stalin was a candidate and voted for the leader; in Albania in 1975 it was claimed that 100 per cent of the electors in the national election had voted. For these examples see George Barr Carson, *Electoral Practices in the USSR* (New York: 1955), p. 84, cited in Everett M. Jacobs, 'Soviet Local Elections: What They Are and What They Are Not', *Soviet Studies*, vol. XXII, no. 1 (1970), pp. 61–76 (p. 69), and Pravda, 'Elections', p. 176.

22   On elections in Poland under the 'hegemonic party system' see George Sanford and Martin Crouch, 'Sejm Elections in Communist Poland', *British Journal of Political Science*, vol. 8, no. 4 (1978), pp. 403–24. The Hungarian electoral system is discussed in Pravda, 'Elections'. The concept of the 'hegemonic party system' was advanced by the Polish scholar Jerzy Wiatr: see, for example, his article 'Political Parties, Interest Representation and Economic Development in Poland', *American Political Science Review*, vol. lxiv, no. 4 (1970), pp. 1239–45.

23   The term 'inertia voting' is suggested on the analogy of 'inertia selling', whereby a product is mailed to an addressee who is required to return it to avoid a demand for payment. Given the possible presence of agents of the political police at polling stations, the reluctance of voters to cross out names of unfavoured candidates is understandable; in any case, short of a coordinated campaign of such negative voting, the communist authorities' desired result was a foregone conclusion; even assuming such a campaign could be mounted without interference by the political police, there was no guarantee that the results would be acknowledged and honoured by the communists. For these and other reasons, the system favoured the results obtained.

24 For a broad examination of the first post-communist elections in Eastern Europe see the special issue of *Electoral Studies*, vol. 9, no. 4 (1990). In these generalizations, East Germany is a special case, in that West German party leaders were involved in the campaigning alongside GDR-based parties linked with their own, and there was a single overriding issue – unification of the two German states: see John Fitzmaurice, 'Eastern Germany', *Electoral Studies*, vol. 9, no. 4 (1990) pp. 327–36; Graham Timmins, *Democratic Transition in Eastern Germany* (Lorton Paper no. 3) (Manchester: Lorton House, 1991).

25 Sigmund Neumann, 'Towards a Comparative Study of Political Parties', reprinted in Jean Blondel (ed.), *Comparative Government: A Reader* (London: Macmillan, 1969), pp. 69–76 (pp. 71–2).

26 As Duverger showed some forty years ago: see Maurice Duverger, *Political Parties: Their Organization and Activity in the Modern State* (London: Methuen, 1959), Chapter 1; originally published in French in 1951.

27 An early examination of party formation is Sten Berglund and Jan Åke Dellenbrant (eds), *The New Democracies in Eastern Europe: Party Systems and Political Cleavages* (Aldershot: Edward Elgar, 1991).

28 Roumen Dimitrov, 'Formation of the Bulgarian Opposition, 1989–1991', *Bulgarian Quarterly*, vol. 1, no. 1 (1991), pp. 53–65 (p. 60).

29 For the GDR, see Timmins, *Democratic Transition*; for Poland, see George Sanford, 'Delay and Disappointment: The Fully Free Polish Election of 27 October 1991', *Journal of Communist Studies*, vol. 8, no. 2 (1992); also Frances Millard, *Political Parties and the Party System in Poland* (Lorton Paper no. 6) (Manchester: Lorton House, 1991); for Hungary, see Nigel Swain, *Hungary's New Political Parties* (Lorton Paper no. 5) (Manchester: Lorton House, 1991); for Bulgaria, see Dobrinka Kostova, 'Parliamentary Elections in Bulgaria: October 1991', *Journal of Communist Studies*, vol. 8, no. 1 (1992), pp. 196–203 (p. 201 and p. 199, Table 1). A recent compilation of information on the new parties in the Soviet Union and the countries of Eastern Europe is Bogdan Szajkowski (ed.), *New Political Parties of Eastern Europe and the Soviet Union* (London: Longman, 1992).

30 The term is Sartori's and is used in the East European context by Berglund and Dellenbrant, *The New Democracies*, p. 154–6.

31 'The First Free Parliamentary Elections', pp. 6–7.

32 For reports on the election of 13 October 1991 see *The Insider* (Sofia), no. 11 (1991), pp. 1–5; Kostova, 'Parliamentary Elections'. In the previous elections of June 1990, forty parties and coalitions had taken part, in a mixed electoral system that permitted four principal parties to gain parliamentary representation, two others to win a single seat each, and four independent candidates to secure election: see Stephen Ashley, 'Bulgaria', *Electoral Studies*, vol. 9, no. 4 (1990), pp. 312–18.

33 For an exposition and assessment of the new electoral law, see Jiri Pehe, 'Czechoslovak Federal Assembly Adopts Electoral Law', *RFE/RL Research Report*, 1, 7 (14 February 1992), 27–30. An unintended result was the break up of the country.

34 See Otto Kirchheimer, 'The Transformation of Western European Party Systems', in Joseph LaPalombara and Myron Weiner (eds), *Political Parties and Political Development* (Princeton, NJ: Princeton University Press, 1966), pp. 177–200.

35 *The Insider* (Sofia), no. 11 (1991), p. 2.

36 Jiri Pehe, 'Czechoslovakia's Changing Political Spectrum', *RFE/RL Research Report*, vol. 1, no. 5 (1992), pp. 1–7.

37 Such a danger was identified in Bulgaria following the election of October 1991: see Evgenii Dainov, 'Bulgaria: Politics after the October 1991 Elections', *RFE/RL Research Report*, vol. 1, no. 2 (1992), pp. 12–16; also Todorov, 'Early to Red'.

38 See Waller, 'Groups', pp. 136, 139–41.

39 See Kevin Devlin, 'Postrevolutionary Ferment in the East European Media', *Report on Eastern Europe*, vol. 1, no. 28 (1990), pp. 47–53.

40 See, for example, Blondel, *An Introduction to Comparative Government*, p. 17, Diagram 2–1.

41 This refers to perceptions of the 1791 constitution, 'Poland's first real attempt at

untrammelled parliamentary democracy': see George Kolankiewicz and Ray Taras, 'Poland: Socialism for Everyman?', in Archie Brown and Jack Gray (eds), *Political Culture and Political Change in Communist States*, 2nd edn (London: Macmillan, 1979), pp. 101–30 (pp. 102–3).

42   George Schöpflin, 'Hungary: An Uneasy Stability', in Brown and Gray, *Political Culture*, pp. 131–58 (pp. 132–5).

43   See, for a brief account, Fred Singleton, *Twentieth-Century Yugoslavia* (London: Macmillan, 1976).

44   Alex Pravda, 'Czechoslovak Socialist Republic' in Bogdan Szajkowski (ed.), *Marxist Regimes: A World Survey* (London: Macmillan, 1981), vol. 2, pp. 261–92 (p. 261).

45   Martin Bútora, Zora Bútorová and Tatiana Rosová, 'The Hard Birth of Democracy in Slovakia: The Eighteen Months Following the "Tender" Revolution', *Journal of Communist Studies*, vol. 7, no. 4 (1991), pp. 453–59 (p. 440).

46   Sten Berglund and Jan Åke Dellenbrant, 'The Evolution of Party Systems in Eastern Europe', *Journal of Communist Studies*, vol. 8, no. 1 (1992), pp. 148–59 (p. 150).

47   Roumen Dimitrov, 'Formation of the Bulgarian Opposition, 1989–1991 (Continued)', *Bulgarian Quarterly*, vol. 1, no. 2 (1991), pp. 43–52 (p. 52).

48   *Statistical Pocketbook of Yugoslavia, 1987* (Belgrade: Federal Statistical Office, 1987), p. 37.

49   As reported in, for example, *The Times*, 8 January 1990, p. 9.

50   See, for example, Martin Myant, 'Economic Reform and Political Evolution in Eastern Europe', *Journal of Communist Studies*, vol. 8, no. 1 (1992), pp. 107–27.

51   Quoted in Zielonka, 'East-Central Europe: Democracy in Retreat?', p. 108.

52   Lyubov Grigorova, 'Political Institutions and Stability', *Bulgarian Quarterly*, vol. 1, no. 1 (1991), pp. 66–77 (p. 66).

53   See Zielonka, 'East Central Europe: Democracy in Retreat?', pp. 114–15.

54   See, for example, Blondel, *An Introduction to Comparative Government*, p. 7.

55   Zielonka, 'East-Central Europe: Democracy in Retreat?', p. 119 and passim.

56   Lucian W. Pye, 'Introduction: Political Culture and Political Development', in Lucian W. Pye and Sidney Verba (eds), *Political Culture and Political Development* (Princeton, NJ: Princeton University Press, 1965), pp. 3–26 (pp. 4–5).

17

Problems of Democracy in Post-Soviet Russia

Peter Frank

Soviet totalitarianism was unique. While it bore certain resemblances to varieties of Western European fascism, its peculiar characteristics marked it off from similar systems elsewhere. Societies that chose to emulate the Soviet model (or, more likely, had it imposed upon them by force) rapidly assumed the salient features of the Soviet prototype.

The chief defining characteristics of a Soviet-type totalitarian system is that it is to be found in a society that has undergone a period of prolonged, mass, physical terror. In the case of the USSR, widespread terror was used by the Bolshevik regime virtually from its inception in October 1917, although it was to reach its apogee in the middle to late 1930s under Stalin.

Such was the frenzy of arrest, deportation, incarceration and execution in those years that for the mass of society what was happening seemed to have no rationale.

One night, 'they' would come to the block of flats where you lived and take away a neighbour. Then you remembered: he had once been a Menshevik, so perhaps he really was a saboteur. Soon after, someone else disappeared. Well, maybe she was an 'enemy of the people', too – after all she had once, you recalled, expressed sympathy for some of Trotsky's ideas. And so it went on. But when your workmate, whom you had always known to be a zealous communist and model citizen, was arrested and charged with being a 'wrecker', then you began to wonder. And what about all those 'Old Bolsheviks' – old not in years, but only in the sense that they belonged to the generation that had joined the party before the revolution, endured arrest and exile for their beliefs, and fought and won the brutal civil war that followed 1917: were they really 'spies' and '*agents provocateurs* of capitalism', as the secret police alleged, and thus deserved to be humiliated and shot?

By this time, there is no logic or rationale to explain what is happening. Yet it is in the nature of the human intellect to act rationally, and so your rational response to this seeming irrationality is to trust no one, to sever all those horizontal linkages that, together, join you to society. Instead, you become socially solitary, untrusting, suspicious; in short, society becomes atomized. And *that* is precisely the regime's rationale: to so atomize society as to make it terrified and submissive. It is true that reward plays its part in the totalitarian system, and not just fear. But however great the privilege, esteem and material benefits that accrue to the favoured individual, all can be taken away in an instant. Fear resides in everyone.

A brutalized society would be quite incapable of attaining the grandiose goals set for it by the regime if left in the atomized state to which it has been reduced by terror. Consequently, the next stage is to reconstitute society, to 'massify' it (that is to say, to mobilize people into mass social organizations that have no horizontal linkages with other institutions, but are instead subjected to strict vertical control). But that alone is not enough. There must also be a 'cement' that substitutes for informal, voluntary, horizontal linkages to give the new, vertically ordered society a spurious cohesion, direction and purpose, and that is the party.

By the end of the civil war in Russia in 1921, the Bolsheviks had eradicated all political parties other than themselves. First it had been the 'bourgeois' parties, such as the Constitutional Democrats; then the Mensheviks; then the Right Socialist Revolutionaries; and, eventually, the Left Socialist Revolutionaries, the Bolsheviks' erstwhile coalition partners. That, however, was not enough. As the decade drew to a close, the Communist Party, according to Stalin, had become 'monolithic' (which is to say that all fractions and opinion groupings within the party had been suppressed). By the mid 1930s, the Leader wielded awesome dictatorial power over society: the slightest whiff of dissent – even at the apex of the system – was ruthlessly suppressed.

Reinforcing the dictatorial power (which was exercised in the name of the Communist Party) was an exclusive ideology deriving from and couched in the language of scientific socialism. Strict censorship and control over information were also indispensable attributes of Soviet totalitarianism, as was the planned, centralized economy. Vital, too, was a judicial system in which due process was subordinated to political expediency. Finally, there was the mechanism which, after fear, did most to hold the new, atomized society together, the *nomenklatura*.

From top to bottom of society, at every nodal point of power, large or small, was a *nomenklatura* post filled by someone drawn from the appropriate party committee's cadres list. Be it the first secretary of a powerful regional party committee, or the head of a local transport undertaking; the commander of a military district, the editor of *Pravda* or the chairman of a collective farm; be it a member of the ruling CPSU Politburo, the rector of a university or the chief engineer in an industrial enterprise – all were *nomenklatura* posts and all were filled by persons selected or vetted and approved by the appropriate party committee.

To become a member of the *nomenklatura* was to enter the elite. There was material privilege: 'special' shops, canteens, rest homes, dachas and hospitals. Above all, there was power. Subservient to those who ranked higher in the hierarchy, even the most humble member of the *nomen-klatura* wielded enormous power over his (and, more rarely, her) subordinates. There was also enormous formal status and prestige, a sense of belonging, of being an insider, a part of the system: whatever other distinguishing features one might acquire, one was either non-*nomenklatura* or *nomenklatura*, and passing from one condition to the other was a veritable *rite de passage*, except that it was vouchsafed to only a minority of citizens.

One of the most frequent criticisms levelled against the totalitarian model is that it allegedly lacks dynamism. How is it, its detractors ask, that a system so terrorized and so atomized was able for much of its history to outdistance its pluralistic rivals? Surely, they say, such a society could never have industrialized in so short a time and in such a way as to be able to defeat the most formidable military machine Europe had ever seen, and still go on to match the West in terms of nuclear-weapons capacity.

It is a criticism easy to refute. First, much of the dynamism derived from fear. Terror supplied the motive force that drove Soviet society forward. But, in addition, Soviet totalitarianism was goal-oriented. The regime defined specific tasks for society (or these were defined for it from without). Each task was colossal: win the civil war, expel the foreign interventionists, collectivize peasant agriculture, crash industrialization, defeat the German invader, rebuild the shattered economy, develop an atomic bomb in the shortest possible time, attain nuclear parity with the West! All of these were staggering achievements.

To the extent that effectiveness may be defined as a system's capacity to attain its objectives, the Soviet totalitarian system must be one of the most successful known to history. It was brilliantly effective – yet, at the same time, prodigiously wasteful. The regime, having defined the next grandiose goal, was able to mobilize and coerce all its resources to realize that goal. And if that entailed enormous material waste, so be it. So be it, too, if there was enormous human waste: for example, what does it matter if millions of peasants are deported, starved to death or exterminated so long as collectivization is accomplished?

It was, therefore, the combination of mass coercion and dogmatic, goal-oriented leadership that gave Soviet totalitarianism its dynamism. And if further proof of this is needed it is only necessary to recall that once lesser, but more complex, goals are placed on the political agenda (such as Khrushchev's attempt to satisfy society's modest consumer needs at the same time as maintaining the USSR's great power status), the system proves to be incapable of attaining them. Similarly, to the extent that the incidence and intensity of terror diminish in society, so does dynamism decelerate.

To add shape and form to the system, a complex of interlinked interlocking and interdependent vertical structures was created. There was the military, with its highly centralized command structure; the related military-industrial complex, similarly organized and extending throughout the USSR; and the ideological apparatus that ensured a uniformity and unanimity of view at every level of society. The security apparatus, the

KGB, and the ministry of the interior (MVD) saw to the enforcement of the centre's commands by maintaining an undercurrent of fear, even when the grosser manifestations of Stalinist physical terror had been put in reserve. And at the heart of the complex was the party *apparat*, manipulating and overseeing the *nomenklatura*; what Milan Šimečka called 'the master link in the chain' (1984: 169).

For anyone living within this system, it seemed rock-solid and eternal. As Czeslaw Milosz, the Polish future Nobel prize-winner for literature, observed when Stalinism was still at its height in the early 1950s:

> What is happening in Russia and the countries dependent upon her bespeaks a kind of insanity, but it is not impossible that Russia will manage to impose her insanity upon the whole world and that the return to reason will occur only after two or three hundred years. (1985 [1953]: 71)

After 1953, physical terror as a mass phenomenon abated. It is true the 'inertia of fear' remained a potent and effective constraint on society, but, so long as the individual swam with the tide, life could be tolerable. Everyone knew her or his place. A certain, usually low, minimum of material well-being was guaranteed. Throughout most of the post-Stalin period, each year brought its slight increment of improvement in the standard of living – certainly enough to keep grumblingly quiescent a population accustomed to severe hardship and cut off from those parts of the world that would have provided unfavourable comparisons with their own lot. But the moral, intellectual and spiritual costs were enormous.

Probably the most cogent critique of Soviet-type totalitarianism and its moral consequences is to be found in Václav Havel's *Letter to Dr Gustáv Husák* written in 1975 at the height of the post-1968 'normalization' process in Czechoslovakia. In it, Havel describes Soviet totalitarianism as 'a system of existential pressure, embracing totally the whole of society and every individual, either as a specific everyday threat or as a general contingency'. It is, he argues, a system that leads to a universal mood of despair, and 'despair leads to apathy, apathy to conformity, conformity to routine performance' (1989: 3–35).

The result, says Havel, is that each person is driven into 'a foxhole of purely material existence'; deceit becomes the main form of communication with society. In such an environment, there is a gradual erosion of moral standards, the 'breakdown of all criteria of decency, and the widespread destruction of confidence in the meaning of any such values as truth, adherence to principles, sincerity, altruism, dignity and honour' (1989: 14–15).

In 1976, the year after Havel's devastatingly bleak assessment of Soviet-type systems, the then General Secretary of the Communist Party, Leonid Brezhnev, set out his view of the USSR. Addressing the twenty-fifth Congress of the CPSU, he declared:

> We have created a new society, a society the like of which humankind has never known. It is a society without crises, with a constantly growing economy, a society of mature socialist relationships, of genuine freedom. It is a society in

which a scientific, materialistic outlook prevails. It is a society in which there is firm confidence in the future, in bright communist perspectives. Opening up before it is boundless scope for further all-round progress. (1976: 113)

Time has given the lie to Brezhnev's bombastic, boastful claims. But in one crucial respect he told the truth: 'We have created a new society, a society the like of which humankind has never known.' Soviet-type totalitarianism *is* unique; it has no parallels; the damage that it wrought is incomparable. After decades, in spite of (and partly because of) the USSR's status as a world nuclear power, totalitarianism has created a wasteland. Physically, environmentally and, not least, morally and spiritually, country and society have been devastated. And it was this dreadful malaise that, in March 1985, Mikhail Gorbachev came to power determined to heal.

Mikhail Gorbachev was not a democrat, he was a democratizer; a reformer, not a revolutionary. To make such distinctions is not to belittle his courage and audacity in the early years of his term of office: to have expected more from him then would have been unrealistic. Appointed as CPSU general secretary by the narrowest of Politburo majorities, he had no alternative but to proceed by consent of his senior colleagues. Later, however, as he consolidated his power and as new forces (generated by his own reforms) offered the prospect of an alternative power base, Gorbachev, when presented with the choice of reform or transformation, always chose the more cautious option; for him, there was never any question of changing fundamentally the system that he had inherited and to which he was so emotionally and professionally bound. He was, and remains, a convinced communist. In the end, it was loyalty to a party that refused to adapt to the aspirations of society that brought about his, and that party's, downfall.

Although democrat and revolutionary Gorbachev was not, modernizer he was. By the early 1980s, it had become obvious that the Soviet Union had degenerated into a condition of acute inertia. One of the few justifications for the Soviet system had been that it was dynamic (and, indeed, for much of its existence it had achieved growth rates in certain selected areas of the economy that were spectacularly impressive). But as the then leader, Leonid Brezhnev, declined into senility, so did the Soviet economy exhibit signs of sclerosis and stagnation. The rapid demise of two more general secretaries made it inescapably obvious that economy and society were on the brink of catastrophe.

Gorbachev was to be the person who would lead the USSR away from that brink. He was young, tough, ambitious, intelligent and, it seemed, able and ready to lead. Also, he seemed to have ideas, albeit derivative from an informal circle of academics and advisers with whom for several years he had been meeting to discuss and analyse and seek remedies for some of the grosser ills from which the Soviet Union was suffering.

There was, however, to be one major constraint. Remedies could be radical and far-reaching; they could entail political risk; but they must always be bent towards restoring, refreshing and rehabilitating the system that had originated in 1917. Above all, Lenin's creation, the Communist Party of the Soviet Union, was sacrosanct. Whatever happened, the party's 'leading and directing' role should be preserved; the party must remain the 'core' of the political system.

The goal that Gorbachev defined for Soviet society when he came to office early in 1985 was that the USSR should attain the highest world levels of social productivity in the shortest possible time (implicitly, by the year 2000). Although deceptively simple to formulate, this was a colossally grandiose and ambitious target. Nor was there any clear formula for achieving it.

To begin with, the key word was 'acceleration'. Somehow, Soviet society was to receive an injection of dynamism that would propel, 'accelerate', the country towards the fulfilment of the stated goal. Probably Gorbachev believed that the power inherent in the office of general secretary would enable him to order a compliant party-state bureaucracy to carry out his instructions. At the same time, social discipline would be tightened up (the ill-conceived and ill-fated anti-alcohol campaign was one such measure); while, more practically, the crucial machine-building sector of the Soviet economy would be modernized, which in turn, it was hoped, would lead to a more general improvement in output.

To Gorbachev's dismay, these measures had little effect. The bureaucracy had become too used to a leader who had placed their interests above those of society: change for the *apparatchiki* was disruptive, it required effort, there was the danger that they might be judged by performance, rather than according to formal, time-serving criteria.

The people were inert because they were mistrustful of authority and cynical about promises of jam tomorrow in exchange for hard, conscientious work today. Industry was disinclined to adapt to new practices when old ones still served it well. This was not just a passing malaise, something that could be cured by prescribing mild palliatives. The Soviet system was in deep crisis – and it was getting worse.

It was at this juncture that Gorbachev began to turn seriously to the idea of *perestroika*, of restructuring the system. It is more than just semantics to point out that the term *perestroika* implies the refurbishment or reconstruction of an existing edifice. It does not mean destroying a structure and building something entirely different in its stead. Gorbachev was utterly consistent about this. Whenever he used the term, he made it quite obvious that what he had in mind was to prevent the disintegration of the system that had evolved since 1917. His purpose was, rather, to repair and strengthen it, perhaps to alter its shape and change its countenance. But, whatever else was done, the core of the structure was to remain the Communist Party – a party revivified and energized, yet always to be the load-bearing element in the overall design. To that extent, what was intended was something apparently different, yet fundamentally the same.

As mentioned earlier, the Soviet state rested upon massive, rigid supports: the party-state bureaucracy, the ideological apparatus, the KGB and military, the military-industrial complex and the massified, party-dominated public organizations. Connecting these otherwise apparently discrete supports was the *nomenklatura* mechanism. Taken together, it was a seemingly unshakeable structure.

But if *perestroika* meant anything at all beyond rhetoric, it was that it was a dynamic concept. Given the opportunity to express their thoughts within certain much-broadened limits, people would *give voice* (which is what *glasnost* really means) to their discontents and aspirations. At the same time, *demokratizatsiya* (meaning, essentially, electivity involving limited choice) would encourage citizens to feel engaged in the system, energize them and thus bring about that essential prerequisite for successful restructuring, psychological *perestroika*.

The trouble was, from Gorbachev's point of view, that either people remained inert (they were too demoralized by decades of Soviet rule to respond) or they seized the opportunities presented to them and began to agitate for more. They demanded not *glasnost*, but real freedom of expression; instead of democratization they insisted upon democracy; Gorbachev's socialist pluralism was rejected in favour of genuine pluralism. What they wanted was that the system be transformed into something qualitatively different, and not just a 'reconstruction' of the system that had devastated the country morally, physically and ecologically.

It was inevitable that sooner or later the dynamics of change that Gorbachev had part-intentionally and part-unwittingly unleashed would collide with the seemingly rigid, enduring supports that upheld the traditional Soviet political-economic system. And when that happened either the edifice would hold firm and the dynamic of change would be halted and turned back, or the current of change would undermine, overwhelm and sweep away the obstacles in its way and thus reform would become transformation, revolution.

The first sign that collision was imminent came in the late summer of 1990. A group of reformist economists led by Stanislav Shatalin had prepared a programme for change entitled 'The 500 Days Plan'. It was not just a set of proposals for dealing with the rapidly deteriorating economy; it was also a plan that would *inter alia* involve far-reaching political and social reforms. For its time, it was a bold project. Predictably, it was hated by the traditionalist forces that still dominated Soviet political structures. Nonetheless, Gorbachev (by now president of the USSR as well as CPSU general secretary) stated that it was the best option on offer and seemed to imply that he was ready to adopt the plan. A few days later, however, he performed a startling about turn, spurned the forces of democracy and threw in his lot with hardline reaction.

By early 1991, as the sixth year of Mikhail Gorbachev's project for *perestroika* was drawing to a close, the Soviet Union was in turmoil. Quasi-democratic institutions (themselves spectacular improvements on the old ones) had stimulated the formation of groups and movements that were anxious to go far beyond the limits envisaged by Gorbachev. Article Six of the Constitution had been amended to permit the formation of political parties. In the localities, broadly democratic movements were demonstrating against Communist Party hegemony. Workers struck to secure not just (indeed, not mainly) economic demands, but political demands, too. Entire nations were agitating for independence and secession from the Soviet Union. Yet, in the midst of it all, the CPSU remained implacably opposed to change: it had become the biggest single obstacle in the path of reform.

It was at this juncture that Gorbachev could have made a historic choice. Instead of swinging to the hardline, reactionary position, he could have entered into a *de facto* alliance with the democratic forces (by now headed by Boris Yeltsin), used his authority to appeal to the mass of people for their support over the heads of the old establishment, maximized the prodigious goodwill that he enjoyed abroad, and pressed forward along the path of transformation, a path that had been signposted initially by his own, limited reforms.

There were, I think, two main reasons for Gorbachev's behaviour in late 1990 and the first half of 1991. The first was that he did not trust the people. That is not to say that he did not care about them – but he did not trust them. Whenever presented with the opportunity to invest his power with authority, he turned away from it. Appointed initially as CPSU general secretary on a 4:4 vote in the Politburo (with Andrei Gromyko breaking the deadlock with his casting chairman's vote), he subsequently side-stepped a contest for the chairmanship of the presidium of the new Congress of People's Deputies of the USSR that he had set up (having in any case become a member of that body as one of the 'Party Hundred' nominated by the Politburo of which he himself was head). Then, having created the entirely new office of president of the USSR, he refused to stand in a contested general election and instead took his powers from the hands of a legislature whose democratic credentials were, to say the least, extremely doubtful. In the end, he had become a leader who, in formal terms, was invested with colossal power, but who had virtually no authority, lacking as he did the consent of the people on whose behalf he purported to rule; so that finally he found himself in the absurd position of constantly seeking (and obtaining) vastly increased powers on the grounds that they were needed to resolve the USSR's worsening crisis, while with every access of power the crisis deteriorated still further.

The other reason for Gorbachev's decision to run with the forces of reaction was that he was a deeply committed communist who intellectually and emotionally believed wholeheartedly in the communist ideal and who saw himself as a man of destiny who would restore the party to the health that, he believed, it had once enjoyed and thus secure for it and himself the place in history he believed it deserved. He refused to recognize that the party (and, by association, communism) was so discredited in the minds of the population that it could never be redeemed. Nothing could compensate for the suffering and cruelty and destruction that had been unleashed in dogmatic pursuit of an unrealizable ideal.

It was to protect socialism that Gorbachev consented (passively or actively is not yet known) to the violent attempt to subvert the constitutional authority in Lithuania. But all that happened was that the deaths in Vilnius were added to those in Tbilisi, Baku, Dushanbe and elsewhere and entered against the political establishment in Moscow. How, people asked, can we subscribe to *perestroika* if it has to be applied by force?

By late spring 1991, Gorbachev seems to have realized that the direction he had taken was leading to a dead end. *Perestroika* had degenerated into little more than a slogan; Gorbachev's own popularity had plummeted; lacking a popular mandate, his authority was almost non-existent. On the other hand, the democratic forces were rallying hundreds of thousands of people in Moscow, Leningrad and major industrial centres throughout the Union. The periphery was near to breaking away from the centre. Yeltsin was riding a wave of popularity that derived partly from his being perceived as a victim of the detested party (a party that he had already demonstratively abandoned), and partly from his own not inconsiderable political skill. So, it was against that background that in April 1991 Gorbachev performed another sharp turn, swung back towards the democratic wing, and began to prepare a new Union treaty that promised to loosen the bonds between the constituent republics and the centre (but stopping short of outright secession).

For the hardline establishment, it was the last straw. *Glasnost* and democratization had led to the erosion of the leading role of the party. Every assumption upon which the Soviet system had rested for over seventy years was being overturned. There was no sign of the onslaught's abating. Now it was the Union that was in peril. It was time to act.

If anyone had suggested to Yeltsin and his supporters on Sunday, 18 August 1991, that seventy-two hours later they would responsible for running the country, they would have been incredulous. Yet, there they were, on Wednesday evening, 21 August, in precisely that position. The bungled, but deadly serious, attempted coup by the self-styled State Committee for the Emergency Situation had collapsed. The eight leading conspirators (each one the head of one or another of the old totalitarian system's main supports) were either in flight, dead or under arrest. As one Russian commentator observed at the time: power had simply fallen from the skies, quite unexpectedly, into the hands of Yeltsin and his democratic supporters.

The ill-fated coup had been a desperate attempt to rescue the traditional Soviet political-economic system from otherwise certain demise. In the event, it simply hastened it. The conspirators had realized that if the Union were allowed to disintegrate, there would be no hope left of maintaining the system upon which rested their power, prestige and privilege. But, apart from their own incompetence, they, too, had underestimated how reviled the system was that they were seeking to preserve. It is true that the majority of citizens had gone about their daily business largely indifferent to the drama (and, at times, farce) that was being played out on the streets of Moscow and St Petersburg. But enough people did care sufficiently to rally to the democrats' support, while some soldiers placed their loyalty to the legally constituted authority above allegiance to a shadowy committee whose legitimacy was doubtful in the extreme.

Doubtless the conspirators had counted upon being able to win President Gorbachev over to their side: after all, he had come very close himself to imposing a state of emergency in March, and all the problems of which he had complained then had become even more acute by August. But they had not reckoned with Gorbachev's intense indignation at having his prerogatives as president challenged, nor upon Yeltsin and his supporters' meticulous insistence upon the observance of constitutional propriety (that is, the unconditional release of the president and his immediate restoration to office).

Gorbachev's position that Wednesday evening, 21 August, was that he was the general secretary of a party that had utterly disgraced itself. He himself had been responsible for appointing the conspirators to office (in several cases against the wishes of his own legislature). He was also still president of the Soviet Union; but it was now a Union at an advanced stage of decay (and, as it turned out, destined to survive for only another four months).

On the other hand, Yeltsin's conduct during the attempted coup had been irreproachable. He had not only shown considerable personal courage; he had demonstrated also wisdom and great political acumen. With some former republics (such as the Baltics) breaking away completely, and others asserting their independence *vis-à-vis* Moscow, Russia became in many respects the *de facto* successor state to the USSR. Yeltsin's responsibilities were now enormous.

Commenting early in 1991 on recent events in Central and Eastern Europe, Adam Michnik, the Polish historian and Solidarity activist, in a speech in Vienna had observed:

> In all these countries, dictatorship has lost and freedom has won . . . But that does not mean that democracy has won. Democracy means the institutionalization of freedom. We do not yet have a democratic order, and that is why our freedom is so fragile and shaky. (1991)

'Democracy is the institutionalization of freedom.' Behind this simple formulation lay a fundamental truth. Now people began to comprehend the magnitude of the task facing Yeltsin and his supporters. Russia was not facing a change of government, such as might happen in Britain or the United States following a general election. It was, rather, seeking to effect a transition from one type of system to another. Everyone knew precisely the nature of the system that was being left behind: Soviet totalitarianism was deeply embedded in every single individual's consciousness and behaviour. But no one had any clear idea at all of the precise nature of the system to which Russia was moving. Nor did anyone have any idea as to how the transition from one system to another might be made. There were no models, no precedents, no precepts to serve as a guide.

It is true that there were general aspirations to which the new leadership subscribed. It wanted to create a society that was economically and politically pluralistic, a society in which the rule of law would prevail and where government would be based upon choice and consent. Obviously, these are the broad principles upon which liberal democracies rest. But broad principles must be enshrined in institutions and implemented by political parties deriving from classes, social groups or constellations of interests which in turn operate within the framework of a party system. In the conventional sense of these terms, Russia had none of them.

Whether Yeltsin was overawed by the magnitude of the tasks confronting him, or whether, as he implied later, he was simply physically and mentally exhausted by his efforts during the coup, is hard to determine. But in the euphoria and rejoicing at the demise of the old order, the Russian leadership became peculiarly inert. For a whole month it did nothing. The country drifted. Desperately needed, unpopular measures that would have been accepted in the aftermath of victory were left undone. Old, hardline forces that were demoralized by failure were given time to catch their political breath. Meanwhile, the plethora of crises – ethnic, economic, social, political – festered.

It was at this juncture that an attribute of Soviet totalitarianism that had not been foreseen manifested itself. The central paradox of Soviet totalitarianism was that, while it was capable of achieving spectacular self-defined goals (and thus, in those terms, was highly effective), at the same time it was extraordinarily wasteful and inefficient. But probably because for most of its existence Soviet totalitarianism had seemed to be permanent and enduring, what had been overlooked was that in the event of its demise it bequeathed to its successors a truly devastated inheritance. Not only did it leave behind a country that was ravished and exhausted in its physical aspect, it left also a population that was spiritually and morally debilitated, and a system that in reality was not a system: in other words, an absence of successor institutions capable of restoring society to some semblance of physical and moral health.

It is this last circumstance that has made the prospects for democracy in Russia (and in the other successor states of the USSR) so bleak. Civil society as understood in Western liberal democracies was a weakly flower in Russia before the revolution of 1917 (although probably stronger than was imagined by many analysts, including the present writer, who were influenced by the steady drip of Soviet historiography). After 1917, civil society, such as there was of it, was systematically destroyed. Those myriad horizontal relationships that, together with the vertical linkages of the state, knit individuals together to form society had been deliberately, violently eliminated. Consequently, in Russia today there is nothing connecting the still largely atomized masses to institutions at the apex of society that, in any case, belong more to the old system than to the new. In short, there is a *political void*.

Similarly, because of the inadequacies of inherited institutions, together with the obstructionist power of personnel surviving in public office who are holdovers from the previous regime, there is also an *administrative void*. The government formulates policies; the president issues decrees; but in the overwhelming majority of cases it is impossible to ensure implementation at the local level. As a result, there is *proizvol*, arbitrary rule, or more likely, simply a power vacuum.

Thirdly, the Russian parliament (headed by its ambitious and flamboyant speaker, Ruslan Khasbulatov) and government were at loggerheads with each other. Unlike most pluralistic systems where the government *rests upon* a more or less solid party base (which in turn is rooted in a party system), in Russia (given the political void that exists between masses and the leading institutions) the government *depends from* the president, whose own power derives from an extremely amorphous electorate. At the same time, the quasi-democratic parliament (itself somewhat anachronistic, given that it is the product of the era before August 1991) is constantly at odds with the government and, indirectly, with the president. Consequently, there has developed in Russia a dysfunctional stalemate between the legislative and executive powers.

The presence simultaneously of a political void, an administrative void and a largely sterile stalemate between the two main branches of government (the judicial power is still extremely weak) is a recipe for instability. At the time of writing (May 1992), Russia is in a state of incipient crisis. A bold attempt at economic reform has reached a crucial juncture. The people's patience is wearing thin. There are fears of a so-called *nomenklatura revanche* and 'creeping restoration'. Russian statehood is in an extremely fragile condition and there is a distinct possibility that the Russian Federation might go the way of the old Union. New political formations are on the point of entering the political arena. Too much rests upon the wisdom and physical well-being of a single person, Boris Yeltsin (as even his fiercest political foes agree) who is the only politician who has a mandate from the people to govern.

Moreover, Yeltsin is a leader who is willing to lead. The broad trajectory of his political behaviour, so far, has been in the direction of economic and political pluralism. The youthful government that he has assembled is eager to govern. Both president and government are daring to court unpopularity. So far, despite manifest hardships, the people have endured the impact of reform and the widely predicted riots and violence have not materialized.

Cool, rational analysis of the prospects for democracy in Russia suggests a profoundly pessimistic outcome. It may take as long to exorcise the pernicious consequences of totalitarianism as it took to inculcate them – decades, rather than years. But Russia, despite the destruction wrought by seventy-four years of communism, is potentially a rich country. Its intellectual capital is substantial; raw materials are abundant. Objectively, there is no reason why it should not be as affluent as, say, the United States of America. The problem lies not so much in the physical aspect of Russia; it is, as ever was, a question of whether or not a system of government can be found that will stimulate and unlock the creative potential of peoples who have for so long been the victims of a grandiose, aberrant, dogmatic experiment. I suspect that eventually such a system will be found – but it may take a very long time.

References

Brezhnev, L. 1976. *XXV S"ezd KPSS, 24 fevralya – 5 marta 1976 goda. Stenograficheskii otchet, I.* Moscow: Politizdat.
Havel, V. 1989. *Living in Truth*. London: Faber & Faber.
Michnik, A. 1991. Quoted in *The Guardian*. 15 February.
Milosz, C. 1985 [1953]. *The Captive Mind*. London: Penguin.
Šimečka, M. 1984. *The Restoration of Order: The Normalization of Czechoslovakia 1969–76.* London: Verso.

PART SIX

DIAGNOSING AND IMPROVING DEMOCRATIC PERFORMANCE

18

Government and Private Censorship in Nine Western Democracies in the 1970s and 1980s

Kenneth Newton and Nigel Artingstall

The study of political communication should therefore be approached in the same way as the study of the political system as a whole, namely in terms of the interpenetration and reciprocal influences which exist between structures and behaviour . . . In the case of public communications, the mass media added a new range of structures; but these also act as constraints upon politicians. Newly created mass media can start developing independent tendencies which politicians may not easily control, unless these impose control on the media. This does of course also happen, but some aspect of legitimacy has then to be used in order to maintain this control. (Blondel, 1990, pp. 95–101)

In the Blondelian spirit of the study of comparative government this chapter investigates the relationships between structure and behaviour, and deals particularly with government and private attempts to impose controls on the flow of political information in nine Western democracies. In other words, it is concerned with political censorship, something which is covered by Blondel's phrase 'impose control on the media', but not spelled out. That it is touched upon only briefly in Jean Blondel's general book on comparative government is hardly surprising; specialists in political communications and the media have had remarkably little to say about political censorship in the West, even in their general textbooks, never mind their specialist research monographs and articles. In part this is because political censorship is so antithetical to democratic ideology in general. Nevertheless, it exists, and attempts to evaluate it depend first of all upon finding out about it, empirically and comparatively.

The chapter thus considers three general questions about censorship in Western democracies.

1 How and why does the amount of censorship vary among the democratic nations of the West? Are constitutional restrictions on governments the deciding factors, or are political or cultural factors more important? Perhaps there are differences between majoritarian and consensus forms of government (Lijphart, 1984), or between Anglo-Saxon and other democracies, or between socially heterogeneous and homogeneous populations?

2 Is the rate of government censorship increasing over time? One theory argues that modern society is becoming more pluralistic, more open, and more difficult to control, and that censorship is becoming more and more unacceptable to the general population. Another argues that the growth of technological and mass society, and in particular the growth of the secret state and the atomic state, makes it both more crucial for authorities to control the flow of information, and more possible for them to do so. Another approach argues that it is not censorship itself which is on the increase, but public sensitivity to the issue, and a willingness to report incidents, and to fight them.

3 To what extent does the government of the day help to create a climate of opinion which is followed by private interests and individuals? Do governments help to create a prevailing climate of opinion about censorship in which private individuals and organizations take their cue from public acts and government policy? Noelle-Neumann's theory of the spiral of silence (1974) is intended to explain shifts in public opinion, but the same sort of explanation might easily apply to censorship. In that case an increase in government censorship is likely to be followed by an increase in private censorship, and vice versa.

Attention in the chapter is focused on political rather than other forms of censorship. Although all forms of censorship are ultimately political, there are still theoretical and common-sense grounds for distinguishing between political and other communication. Preventing the broadcasting of news about war, defence, unemployment, homelessness, or the economy is one thing; censoring pornographic or violent films, or personal statements about private individuals, is another. In concentrating on political censorship we do not wish to make any deep, philosophical point about different sorts of censorship, but as political scientists we do want to simplify and limit a difficult and complicated research task.

Nor do we wish to argue that censorship is the only or even the most important way of managing and manipulating political communications in the modern state (see, for example, Keane, 1991, p. 90). As O'Neil writes, 'Worries about censorship are not groundless, but they are typically focused only on part of what we need to worry about if we take communicative obligations seriously' (O'Neil, 1990, p. 179). In a similar vein, Jansen (1991, pp. 7–8; see also Miller, 1962) distinguishes between constituent censorship which, because it is social and informal, is often not recognized even though it is pervasive in liberal societies, and regulative censorship, the formal and institutionalized version conducted by governments and officials. The latter is the concern in this chapter.

In some ways regulative censorship is the last resort for governments wishing to control the flow of information: it concerns attempts by governments to keep secret information which others know about and are trying to release. Most governments would rather prevent such matters getting even this far: they want the very existence of the information kept secret. They want to keep the cat in the bag, and the bag well hidden from public view. In this sense it may be useful to distinguish between three forms of government secrecy: concealment (keeping the very existence of information a secret); censorship (preventing the communication of information); and cover-up (concealing the act of censorship). This chapter will deal only with censorship and cover-up.

This however, brings us immediately to the difficult question of what is to be treated as censorship, how to distinguish between private and government examples of it, and how to collect information about censorship in the first place. Methodology may be the last resort of the failed theorist (or is it the other way round?), but, nevertheless, we will have to discuss questions of methodology.

A Methodological Detour

The term 'censorship', as used here, refers to restrictions placed upon the freedom to seek, receive or impart information and ideas. Government censorship involves restraint initiated by the government, or by an agency of the state or a public official directly responsible to government. Private censorship is a residual category of non-government censorship. Censorship involves an attempt by a first party to prevent a second party from releasing information to a third party – usually into the public domain. In other words, for censorship to occur, a government or private interest must try to prevent someone releasing information or opinion; the term does not include attempts to silence dogs which do not bark in the night.

The term includes successful and unsuccessful attempts to restrict the flow of news and opinion. This may be too inclusive for those who argue that a clear distinction should be drawn between effective and ineffective censorship. On the other hand, unsuccessful attempts to censor are important in advanced Western democracies, partly because they are an indication of intent, and because a high rate of attempted censorship tells us something about the prevailing political climate. Moreover, unsuccessful censorship may be a shot across the bows, which encourages people to think twice in the future, and which may encourage self-censorship. For the same sorts of reasons that political scientists are interested in the circumstances resulting in both coups and attempted coups, and that criminologists are interested in statistics for robbery and attempted robbery, so censorship and attempted censorship are included in this study.

Not every restriction on the free flow of information counts as censorship. Spies prevented from selling defence secrets to the enemy, and cabinet confidentiality in British government, do not involve censorship. Both are widely accepted as legitimate forms of secrecy, not censorship. Although it may be that secretive systems of government are also likely to be censorious, there is, nonetheless, an important difference between the two. The press laws which exist in one form or another in almost all societies do not necessarily amount to censorship (Article 19, 1991, p. 420) although in some cases they do, and in others they may promote self-censorship.

The term 'censorship' is morally loaded, and the activity is usually assumed to be bad. However, no moral worth, praise or blame, is attached to the term here. The principles of freedom of speech and expression elaborated in Article 19 of the United Nations Declaration of Human Rights are qualified (Article 29) by the rights and freedoms of others, and by the requirements of morality, public order and general welfare (see UNESCO, 1949, pp. 177–280; and Article 19, 1991, pp. 409–20). Censorship covers actions which seem justifiable in terms of the general good and the public interest, and others which seem to be straightforward examples of undemocratic action.

The figures on which this study is based are taken from the publication *Index on Censorship* which has been compiled and produced since 1972 by a non-profit-making body in London. The *Index* is independent of all governments and parties. Published ten times a year, it contains a section called '*Index* Index' which is 'A record of censorship, incorporating information from Amnesty International, Article 19, Interrights, Campaign for Press and Broadcasting Freedom, International PEN Writers in Prison Committee (UK), Reporters Sans Frontières (France), and the Committee to Protect Journalists (US).'

The '*Index* Index' presents brief accounts of current censorship activity in a large number of countries. The figures in the tables that follow are based upon these reports. They are prepared by independent experts who are well informed about their own countries, and whose reports can be checked and verified against other sources. This is because the nine countries covered in this study all have a relatively open system of government and a reasonably free press which is able to report censorship activity. The study could not cover authoritarian or totalitarian systems, and it would not make sense to try to compare them with Western democracies.

Perhaps the best way of illuminating the treatment of censorship here is to provide an illustrative list, albeit in brief form, of examples of government and private censorship in Britain since 1972.

Government censorship

1972 Commons Select Committee on Science and Technology criticizes government for declining to publish a government inquiry.

1977 Philip Agee, an American journalist working on a book about the CIA in Europe, is served with a deportation order.

1977 John Berry, Duncan Campbell and John Crispin arrested under Section II of the Official Secrets Act.

1981 Harriet Harman, legal officer of the National Council of Civil Liberties, arrested for disclosing documents the contents of which had already been read in open court.

1982 Adolfo Perez Esquivel, Argentine winner of the Nobel Peace Prize, 1980, refused entry into the UK.

1984 Clive Ponting arrested for leaking documents about the sinking of the battleship Belgrano.

1986 The government tries to prevent the British publication of *Spy-catcher*.

1990 A police report on the Wapping (*Times*) demonstrations finds that the police sought to frustrate members of the media by obstruction or violence.

Private censorship

1974 The Newcastle University Union Society withdraws an invitation to Martin Webster (of the National Front) to speak in a debate on freedom of speech.

1977 A fire started at the headquarters of the Socialist Workers Party by pouring petrol through the letter box and igniting it.

1981 BBC decides not to transmit a lecture by Professor Michael Pentz on the nuclear arms race.

1985 Two accredited journalists expelled from the Labour Party Conference.

1990 BBC admits cutting an interview with a medical officer who stated that there are health risks in living near overhead power cables.

Because the definitions and methods used by *Index* respondents may not be as systematic and explicit as those required by professional social scientists, the entries for one country, the UK, were checked against independent newspaper reports. It was not possible to check all sources or every newspaper for the 1972–90 period because this would, in itself, be a massive task, so two months of *The Times* were checked (February and August) every second year from 1978 to 1988, and the results compared with the *Index* figures. Two conclusions emerged from this validation exercise: first, all major incidences of government censorship reported in *The Times* appeared in the *Index*; secondly, while there were some differences in the statistics produced from the two sources, these did not vary by more than 7 per cent of each other, except on two occasions. In these cases, *The Guardian* and *The Daily Telegraph* were also checked and their reports were consistent with those in the *Index*.

Confidence in the reliability of the figures based on *Index* reports is further increased by another, entirely independent source of figures on the different but related matter of phone tapping in the UK. As we will see later, Home Office figures on phone tapping show the same pattern as the *Index* based figures for government censorship in the UK in the mid 1980s. While it may be pure coincidence that the *Index*, *The Times*, and the Home Office figures present the same pattern, it is more likely that they reflect events in the real world.

There is still a fundamental methodological problem, which involves the distinction between concealment and censorship. Does a low censorship figure suggest an open society in which information flows freely, or does it, on the contrary, suggest a government which is so powerful that it has no need of censorship? Does a high censorship figure suggest that the government has such a tight stranglehold on politically sensitive views and information that it has no need of censorship, or does it indicate the reverse? The answer is that we cannot tell, and that ultimately (as in some other fields of political science such as elite decision-making or power studies) it is a matter of opinion. However, it should be noted that there is a real difference between totalitarian dictatorships, with the capacity to conceal, and Western democracies, where the power to conceal is more limited, and where the interest in some quarters in at least some aspects of censorship is intense.

Another methodological problem is that censorship figures may reflect not so much what actually happens in the world, but the political sensitivities of people in different countries. Like crime statistics, the figures may tell us more about what people feel is important and are willing to report, than about what governments are actually doing. Thus countries which are insensitive to the problem may have a high incidence of censorship, but not report it; countries which are alive to the issue may have low rates, but report every minor incident. In this case, the figures will suggest the reverse of what is actually going on. We will also return to this problem later.

Because of the labour-intensive nature of combing through the *Index* and compiling tables, we had to choose between taking a relatively small number of countries over a long time period, and taking a large number of different nations over a shorter time. A pilot study for the UK showed a good deal of trendless fluctuation from one year to the next, so it was decided to maximize the time period in order to average the figures over a few years. This inevitably meant restricting the number of nations.

Nine nations are covered here. Besides the UK (the initial focus of interest) we chose: the USA (as the champion of democracy and freedom of speech, with all or most of the constitutional devices to protect them); France, West Germany, and Italy (European countries comparable with the UK); Australia and Canada (Anglo-Saxon democracies comparable with the UK and the USA); and Denmark and Sweden (which have a reputation for open government and freedom of expression).

At the same time as being comparable as liberal democracies, the nine nations represent a relatively wide range of political and social conditions among Western nations: large and small; socially homogeneous and heterogeneous; unitary and federal; world powers and minor states; old and new nations; Anglo-Saxon and others; Catholic and Protestant; and consensus and majoritarian. In this sense, the nine nations represent a good laboratory of 'most different systems' (Przeworski and Teune, 1970, pp. 34–39) among Western democracies, and to this extent constitute a good natural laboratory.

Government Censorship in Theory

Previous attempts to understand and explain government censorship – or closely related matters such as secrecy, confidentiality, or government privilege – have not been notably successful. For example, Chapman uses the distinction (borrowed from Heine) between monarchist and republican countries and suggests that the latter tend to be more open and participatory than the former (Chapman, 1959, pp. 308–22). Yet France, as an example of the republican style, has a reputation for government secrecy and control of the means of political communication (Manor, 1977, pp. 234–46).

Another approach argues that the social and political tensions produced by ethnic, religious, linguistic, and cultural diversity tend to create a need for secrecy, compared with homogeneous nations which can afford to be more open. However, Britain stands out as one of the more homogeneous and (by reputation) less open systems in the West. Another theory suggests that coalition governments have a greater need of secret negotiating and decision-making (Lijphart, 1968, p. 131). However, while both Sweden and Denmark have reputations for open and participatory government, Sweden has had the longest surviving single-party government in the West, and Denmark has had an unbroken history of coalition government for most of the twentieth century (Einhorn, 1977, pp. 264–5).

A different approach emphasizes the importance of international relations and questions of national defence and security. One might, for example, expect big differences between Norway or New Zealand, on the one hand, and a country like Israel on the other. The more a nation is threatened, and the closer its enemies are to its borders, the more it will tend to protect itself by secrecy and censorship. However, it is difficult to explain Britain's reputation in this way.

The most careful, elaborate, and illuminating treatment of the subject is Galnoor's discussion of government secrecy in ten Western nations (Galnoor, 1977, pp. 275–313). Basing his approach on the basic but inherently contradictory requirements of 'government privilege to conceal'

(GPTC) and 'the people's right to know' (PRTK), he groups the countries into two clusters:

> those oriented toward PRTK in their attitudes and laws (Sweden, U.S.A., Denmark, Norway and the Netherlands), and those oriented toward GPTC (the Netherlands, Germany, Canada, Israel, France, and Great Britain). We can now compare the similarities between the countries in each cluster, in such terms as size, population density, federal v. nonfederal systems, presidential v. parliamentary executives, social homogeneity, political stability, and so on. Without undue elaboration, even a casual survey demonstrates that the characteristics listed above are not significantly related to secrecy or openness. For instance, within the 'more open' cluster, the U.S.A., on one hand, and the Scandinavian countries and the Netherlands, on the other, form two distinct groups with regard to most of the above characteristics. More importantly, the U.S.A. is considered to be closer to the Anglo-Saxon political systems of Great Britain and Canada than to the systems of the Scandinavian countries. Even more perplexing are the differences between the five countries in the 'less open' cluster discussed in various parts of this chapter.

In spite of the best efforts of political scientists, therefore, the study of secrecy and censorship has not made a great deal of progress. What much of the discussion and theory lacks, however, is systematic data – national data, never mind comparative material. This chapter is an attempt to break into the subject again in a comparative way, and we will start at the beginning by mapping out some exploratory theory.

Censorship, like the classic crime novel, requires both motive and opportunity. In the case of government censorship in a Western democracy, the motive is likely to be provided by a wish to avoid blame or loss of political support or popularity resulting from the release of harmful information or opinion. In democratic political life, the motive to censor is likely to be related to two further considerations: the accountability of governments, and the scope of the activities for which they are accountable (for a similar approach see Robertson, 1982).

First, the clearer the lines of accountability and responsibility in a political system, the greater the incentive to censor material potentially harmful to the government. Conversely, where accountability and responsibility are confused, or where the rules of the political game are unclear, the greater the chances of diluting blame, or passing it on to another unit or level of government, and the less the need to censor.

Secondly, the greater the government's range of activities, and the wider its scope of responsibilities the greater its motive to censor information (Einhorn, 1977, p. 263). Conversely, the less a government does, and the narrower the range of its duties and responsibilities, the less likely it is to have a need or motive for censoring information. In other words, a government with minimal caretaker functions may have less occasion to censor than a government with a broad range of powers and duties.

One major factor affects this second consideration. Censorship usually involves matters of high politics (defence and key issues of domestic and foreign policy) rather than low politics. Since almost all modern governments take responsibility for the majority of high political matters, all may be pretty much in the same boat so far as censorship is concerned. To put it simply, the fact that some governments are involved with such things as sport, the arts, and keeping streets clean, is not likely to do much to the censorship figures.

More importance may be attached to the distinction between governments which are powerful and important in the international system, and those which play only a minor role in world diplomacy. The former are likely to have more secrets to keep than the latter. In terms of the nine countries covered in the present study, the United States clearly comes out at the top of the league, and might be expected therefore to have greater need of censorship than, say, Australia or Denmark. Similarly, nations which are at war, or which are threatened, especially by near neighbours, may have a greater motive to censor than those which are at peace with the world.

To return to the crime story analogy, censorship requires an opportunity as well as a motive. So far as opportunity for political censorship is concerned, the main factor is likely to be the constitutional position and powers of a government. A political system with a clear separation of powers, a written constitution, a bill of rights, a narrowly and precisely defined realm of official secrets, and with effective freedom of information legislation, gives its government far fewer censorship opportunities than a political system without any or most of these features. It seems reasonable to hypothesize that these must be the overwhelming factors determining government censorship rates in different nations. After all, they are at the very heart of the centuries-old drive towards limited and constitutional government, and they are, in the final analysis, the main determinants of the powers and capacities of democratic governments.

Besides the opportunities presented or prevented by such constitutional arrangements, the other main determinant of opportunity is the power of the government itself. In this respect there are two equally plausible but contradictory propositions. The first suggests that strong and popular governments may not have a compelling need or motive to censor: their strength means they need not worry about particular news items, and may have more to lose in the politics of the cover-up, than in the news itself. To the extent that they are weak, every little bit of good or bad publicity counts, and they may be inclined to indulge in a little 'news management' to help things. The converse may also be true: the stronger the government, the more confident it can feel in getting away with a bit of censorship and cover-up, and the more inclined it is to take the risk.

In totalitarian political systems, concealment is likely to be the most important form of government secrecy. As one writer puts it: 'The first rule of government secrecy is to keep secret the level of government secrecy' (Qualter, 1985, p. 152). Failing this, totalitarian government will use its power to censor. The power to cover up will be least important, since there is little need for it, the public being weakly organized and the norms of open government poorly developed. The more open and democratic the government, the more difficult it will find the job of concealment, and the more the emphasis will shift to censorship and cover-up. In the most democratic systems, the politics of the cover-up may be more important than the original act of censorship. Because public opinion is strongly mobilized in general against political censorship, cover-up becomes all the more important, and all the less acceptable if found out. Perhaps the best example is Richard Nixon, who suffered as much, if not more, from the entanglements of the Watergate cover-up, as from the comparatively minor, though illegal, burglary which started it all.

To summarize this brief theoretical section, it is suggested that government censorship in a democratic political system is likely to be a function of two main factors: motive and opportunity. Motive is likely to depend upon several considerations: the degree to which a government is accountable and responsible for its actions; the scope of activities for which it is responsible; the military and diplomatic role of the country in the world; whether it is in conflict or at peace with other nations, especially its neighbours; whether the nation is relatively homogeneous or fragmented; and whether its government is strong enough to take the risks involved with censorship, or, alternatively, weak enough to feel a compelling need to do so. The opportunity to censor depends upon having the legal or constitutional powers of censorship, and a position of political strength (or is it weakness?) both to censor and to cover up the act of censorship.

Factors which might affect rates of censorship may be grouped under five headings. First are *international factors* such as the size and geopolitical importance of the nation, and whether it has enemies, particularly enemies close to its borders. Second are the *constitutional mechanisms* for limiting the powers of government, including the presence of a written constitution, a bill of rights, freedom of information legislation, the separation of powers and federal or unitary forms of government. Third are *political considerations* such as two- or multi-party government, the scope of government activities, and traditions of ministerial and cabinet responsibility and of crown or executive privilege. Fourth, there are *social and cultural considerations* such as the presence of a homogeneous or heterogeneous population, and of a participatory or authoritarian political culture. And fifth, there are considerations relating to the nature of *elites and governing parties*, and the extent to which they are authoritarian and illiberal.

The five are placed in this order to reflect their hypothesized influence over censorship rates: it is hypothesized that the most powerful influences will be macro and structural features relating to geopolitical and constitutional variables, that political and social/cultural factors will have a smaller effect, and that the least powerful will relate to the particular characteristics of parties and leaders. Geopolitical and international relation variables relate primarily to the motive for censorship, while constitutional ones bear more directly on the opportunities.

Government Censorship in Nine Countries

The first preliminary observation about government censorship figures is that in most countries for most of the time there is a good deal of trendless fluctuation. In some countries the reported incidents are few and scattered; in Denmark there were only two for the 1972–90 period, and they occurred in 1980 and 1982. There were none in Australia between 1974 and 1978, followed by three years with one each, and another four years with none or one. In other countries, such as France and the USA, the rate is somewhat higher, but rises and falls in an apparently random fashion from one year to the next.

Because the figures are often small and variable, they are averaged over a period of years. For the sake of convenience we will average the figures out for the whole 1972–90 period, but also divide them into an eight-year period in the 1970s (1972–9) and an eleven-year period in the 1980s (1980–90).

Table 18.1 *Population size and government censorship, 1972–1990*

Country	Population 1980 (million)	Incidents of government censorship	Incidents of government censorship per million population
USA	227.7	134	0.59
W. Germany	61.6	13	0.21
Italy	56.1	11	0.20
UK	55.9	162	2.90
France	53.7	45	0.84
Canada	23.9	15	0.63
Australia	14.6	8	0.55
Sweden	8.3	1	0.12
Denmark	5.1	2	0.21

Table 18.1 presents figures for the total number of censorship incidents in each country, 1972–90. However, it may be misleading to analyse these (absolute) figures, in the same way that it would be foolish to compare the total GNP of, say, the USA and Denmark. The USA has approximately forty-five times the population of Denmark, and approximately forty-five times its GNP. For comparative purposes it makes sense to use per capita figures. However, whereas the most cursory inspection of absolute GNP figures shows the need to standardize by population size, the figures in Table 18.1 suggest no such thing for censorship. On the contrary, there is no relationship between total government censorship incidents and population size. (On the relationship between population size and government secrecy see Galnoor, 1977, p. 180.) Italy, with a population three times Canada's, has a marginally smaller total of censorship incidents. The UK, with only a quarter of the USA's population, has a substantially higher censorship rate.

The first conclusion, therefore, is that large nations do not generally have higher censorship rates, in either absolute or per capita terms, any more than smaller ones. Factors other than population size have an overwhelmingly greater influence on censorship. Therefore, there is little or nothing to be gained by standardizing for population size, as against dealing with absolute figures. The analysis which follows, therefore, will be in terms of raw or absolute figures in their simplest form. Table 18.2 presents them.

Table 18.2   *Incidents of government censorship, 1972–1990*

UK	162
USA	134
France	45
Canada	15
West Germany	13
Italy	11
Australia	8
Denmark	2
Sweden	1

This table also disposes of some of the propositions discussed earlier. The UK and the United States have easily the highest rates of censorship, followed, though at a lower level, by France. The lowest rates are found in Denmark and Sweden, but with Australia and Italy, and then West Germany and Canada, not much higher. This means that there is little difference between countries according to their constitutional forms. The unitary and the federal systems, the majoritarian and consensual systems, and the Anglo-Saxon and other systems, are all mixed together. For example, the unitary states rank 1, 3, 6, 8 and 9 on the list, and the federal systems rank 2, 4, 5 and 7. The Anglo-Saxon democracies rank 1, 2, 4 and 7. The majoritarian systems (Lijphart, 1984, p. 216) are numbers 1, 8 and 9, the majoritarian-federal systems 2, 4 and 7, and the consensual 3 and 6.

However one arranges, categorizes, or ranks the figures they do not vary according to differences of a constitutional or institutional nature. The second major finding of the study, therefore, is that in spite of all the importance attached to the constitutional requirements of limited, democratic government, these do not seem to explain variations in government propensity to censor. Given the central importance of freedom of speech and the right to information in the modern democratic state, and given the significance attached to constitutional devices for maximizing these rights and freedoms, the finding seems to run against the grain of conventional political wisdom.

There is, however, one immediate qualification to be made to this sweeping conclusion, and it concerns the figure for the UK. In particular, it is often said that Britain is one of the most secretive states, if not *the* most secretive in the Western world (see for example Seymour-Ure, 1977, p. 157; Qualter, 1985, p. 152), in which case rates of government censorship are also likely to be high. There is a fair amount of theorizing about why this might be the case (Robertson, 1982), and no lack of recent case-history discussion (see for example Peele, 1988, pp. 144–75), but the evidence is largely journalistic or impressionistic, and it is rarely if ever comparative or systematic.

When systematic figures are collected from the *Index* they confirm that Britain does, indeed, take its place not merely at the top of the international censorship league table, but head and shoulders above the rest. The reasons seem to revolve around the UK's rather special constitutional and political features, which are probably unique in combining most, if not all, of the preconditions creating both the motive and the opportunity for government censorship. These include (on the motive side) clear lines of accountability and responsibility leading from the electorate through the political parties into parliament, and from there to the government, its cabinet, and the prime minister. This, in turn, rests upon a complex of related features, including: a centralized and disciplined two-party (or two-and-a-half-party) party system; a simple majority electoral system; single-party government; collective cabinet responsibility; individual ministerial responsibility; and the general characteristics of a majoritarian political system. The broad scope of government responsibilities, and the fact that these (especially the matters of high politics) are carried overwhelmingly by central government, contributes further to the motive for central government censorship.

The British system also creates the opportunity to censor. With no written constitution, no bill of rights, relatively new and weak freedom of information legislation, plus the principle of parliamentary sovereignty, the government is relatively free to act compared with many (most/all?) other Western democracies. Indeed, the British Official Secrets Act, in either its new or its old form, is more draconian than its equivalent in almost any other Western nation. And the fact that government powers are not clearly divided between executive, legislature and judiciary adds to central government's opportunity and motive to censor.

In other words, to return to the comparative analysis, it is probable that formal constitutional and legal features of government do limit government power, at least to the extent that the British figures are higher than in other countries. This line of argument cannot be extended to explain variations among the other countries, however, where there is nothing to choose between unitary or federal systems, two-tier or three-tier systems, Anglo-Saxon and other systems, or majoritarian and consensual systems. In sum, formal and constitutional considerations are only a small part of the explanation, and probably serve mainly to distinguish Britain from the rest.

Perhaps, then, it is a matter of culture rather than structure – of religion, or tradition, or culture. Unfortunately, cultural factors do not seem to explain much either. The English-speaking Anglo-Saxon countries have mixed scores, and so also do those with strong Catholic or strong Protestant influences, and those in the north and south of Europe. The most homogeneous nations (Britain, France, Sweden, and Denmark) are distributed throughout the league table, and nor do two of the most mixed and fragmented ones (the USA, Canada) have much in common.

However, there may be something in the theory which says that censorship is partly a function of the military role a nation plays in the world. Britain and the USA are at the top of the list, Denmark and Sweden at the bottom, with Australia and Italy not much higher. The middle-ranking nations (West Germany, France and Canada) fall in between, although it is also true that the French figure is much higher than the other two. It may also be no coincidence that the two main winning nations in the Second World War (the USA and the UK) have easily the highest figures, whereas the two losing nations (Germany and Italy) have relatively low ones. France, a losing nation on the winning side, falls in between. It is possible, therefore, that losing a war (after a great deal of censorship and propaganda, in the case of Italy and Germany) makes a population suspicious of their government, and results in a restriction of the powers of censorship.

There may be a combined effect in which nations with a history of military success and an important military role in world affairs (the two are likely to be related, as in the case of the UK and the USA) have high rates of censorship, compared with nations which were either recently defeated and/or which play a smaller military role in the world (such as Germany, Italy, Denmark and Sweden).

Is Censorship on the Increase?

One interpretation of the politics of modern democratic states suggests that governments are finding censorship more difficult to accomplish, and more dangerous even to try. As technical expertise and skill spreads, as populations become more literate and educated, as the means of broad-casting news and views become cheaper and easier to master (local radio and television, desk-top publishing), as sources of news proliferate nation-ally and internationally, and as the democratic demands and expectations of citizens develop, so it becomes more difficult to control the flow of information centrally, and more counter-productive for democratically elected governments to try to do so.

Another approach – the more pessimistic theories of totalitarianism, authoritarianism and elitism – suggests, on the contrary, that the growth of technological society, of mass communications, of the nuclear/nerve-gas/germ warfare state and of international tensions and terrorism, all combine to make it more probable that political authorities will try to control the flow of politically sensitive information and opinion, and make it (technically and politically) easier for them to do so. Although there are many different ways in which political authorities can manage and manipulate the flow of information, examining changes in the rate of censorship over time is one way of testing the strength of democratic and pluralist theories against authoritarian and elitist ones.

At first glance the figures for changes in censorship over time suggest that the totalitarian theorists have it. Between 1972 and 1979 the incidents of government censorship each year averaged 1.3 per nation, but in the 1980–90 period this rose to 3.0. In the first period the nine nations together were averaging 11.63 incidents per year; in the second decade this almost trebled to 27.0.

However, closer analysis on a country by country basis suggests rather different conclusions (Table 18.3). The increase turns out to be largely due to dramatic and sustained increases in Britain and the USA. The increases are sudden and large, and found in both countries, which suggests that they are not simply an artifact of the way the evidence is collected in the first place. In Britain the figure rose from an annual average of 3.9 incidents in the 1970s to 11.8 in the 1980s. In the United States the equivalent figures are 3.25 and 9.8. This means that Britain and the United States, easily ranked first and second in the censorship tables for the 1970s, still managed to triple their figures in the 1980s.

The other seven nations register a much lower increase, from a combined total of 4.5 incidents per year during the 1972–9 period to 5.36 in the 1980–90 period (see Table 18.4). In fact, by far the largest proportion of the increase in the 1980s is recorded by the three nations with the highest censorship scores for the 1970s – that is Britain, the USA, and France. Between them these three show a 166 per cent increase compared with 9 per cent in the other six nations. By comparison, both Canada and Germany show a decrease in censorship, while Australia, Denmark, and Sweden show small increases from a low or zero baseline.

This leaves the pluralist versus authoritarian debate in a somewhat ambiguous position. Perhaps it depends on how the figures are interpreted. On the one hand, there *is* an undeniable increase in censorship in seven of the nine nations, and no matter how small, it may be taken as evidence supporting the authoritarian argument. On the other hand, there is no general pattern among the nine Western nations. Three of them (Britain, the USA, and France) show a substantial increase over the nineteen-year period, four show a smaller increase on low or zero base figures, and another two show a decrease. This seems to suggest not so much a single and general development towards either pluralism or authoritarianism, so much as different lines of development among different groups of Western nations (see Goldthorpe, 1984, pp. 315–43).

The British and American cases are worth closer attention, if only because they account for such a large proportion of the total for all nine nations, and show by far the largest increases. The figures from 1972 to 1990 are shown in Table 18.5. In Britain they fluctuate substantially from

Table 18.3   *Government censorship in the 1970s and 1980s*

	Government censorship incidents 1972–9	Annual average 1972–9	Government censorship incidents 1980–90	Annual average 1980–90	Percentage increase/ decrease 1972–9/1980–90
UK	31	3.88	130	11.82	+204.6
USA	26	3.25	108	9.82	+202.2
France	16	2.0	29	2.64	+ 32.0
Canada	7	0.88	8	0.73	− 17.1
Germany	6	0.75	7	0.64	− 14.7
Italy	4	0.50	7	0.64	+ 28.0
Australia	3	0.38	5	0.45	+ 18.4
Denmark	0	0.0	2	0.18	−
Sweden	0	0.0	1	0.09	−
Total	93	11.63	297	27.0	+132.2

Table 18.4   *Changes in government censorship in the UK, the USA, France and other nations, 1972–1979/1980–1990*

	Annual average 1972–9	Annual average 1980–90	Percentage increase/decrease 1972–9/1980–90
UK and USA	7.13	21.64	+203.46
Other 7 nations	4.50	5.36	+ 19.19
UK, USA and France	9.13	24.27	+165.86
Other 6 nations	2.5	2.73	+ 9.09

year to year between 1972 and 1985. In 1986, however, they rise to a new high, increase sharply in the next two years and remain at this unprecedented level for the rest of the 1980s. This confirms journalistic and impressionistic evidence about the Conservative government in the late 1980s (cf. Dworkin, 1988, pp. 7–8; Buchan and Sumner, 1989; Article 19, 1989, p. 3) when there was a series of headline-hitting cases such as *Spycatcher*, 'Real Lives', 'Death on the Rock', Zircon, a new Official Secrets Act in 1990, a broadcasting ban on Sinn Fein and other politicians in Northern Ireland, and bans and cuts in TV programmes, as well as government attacks on BBC news coverage of the Falklands and the bombing of Libya (see also the list earlier). The figures in Table 18.5 make it clear that these were not isolated incidents but part of a trend sustained over a five-year period.

At this point we will make a small methodological detour concerning the different but closely related subject of phone tapping. Official figures for phone tapping, published by the Home Office, show a sharp increase in activity in 1986 and a pattern in subsequent years similar to censorship figures in Table 18.5 (Newton and Mitton, forthcoming). In other words,

Table 18.5 *Annual incidents of government
censorship in the UK and the USA, 1972–1990*

	UK	USA
1972	1	3
1973	3	7
1974	0	0
1975	3	3
1976	3	2
1977	10	2
1978	5	2
1979	6	7
1980	9	3
1981	1	5
1982	4	4
1983	7	10
1984	4	6
1985	5	1
1986	12	2
1987	20	1
1988	34	21
1989	18	30
1990	17	25

two independent sources show the same trends in the different but related activities of censorship and phone tapping, and although this may be coincidence, it is more reasonable to interpret the figures as a reflection of something happening in government.

In the USA the annual figure also fluctuates randomly, usually in single figures (none in 1974, ten in 1983), until 1988, the year President Bush is elected, when they also rise to more than double the previous highest figure since 1972, and stay at unprecedently high levels for the final two years of the decade. In fact, in 1989 and 1990, the USA shows every sign of overtaking Britain as the league leader for censorship, even exceeding the totals for Thatcher's later years. In another few years it will become clear whether this level of activity has been sustained in the United States, and whether Thatcher's departure in 1991 resulted in a fall in the British figures.

In the 1950s, Edward Shils suggested that security consciousness was something new in the United States (Shils, 1956, p. 43), but it now appears to be part of the fabric of government (see Rourke, 1977, pp. 113–28). Certainly the evidence suggests a need to revise the general view of 'secretive' Britain and 'open' America; by the standards of the nine nations examined here, both now have secretive and censor-prone governments. Rather than a slow but steady erosion of government powers, or at least a progressive disinclination to use them (Seymour-Ure, 1977, p. 175), there seems to be an accretion of them.

Though the pattern of a steep increase followed by high and sustained levels of censorship in the UK and the USA is clear in the late 1980s, there are still puzzling aspects of the figures which will have to wait for more detailed research. Most notably the increase in Britain comes in the last year of Thatcher's second term, and is maintained in the third term. Similarly, in the USA, the increase occurs in the last year of Reagan's second term, and is maintained by Bush in 1989 and 1990. The British figures may be part of a more general picture in which the Conservatives gain a firmer grip on the machinery of government, and a greater willingness to use their power, but why should the American figures take off to new heights in Reagan's last year? The explanation requires a closer look at the USA, something which cannot be done here, for reasons of space.

Meanwhile, the British and American figures suggest a third pre-condition for censorship – the will to act. To return to the crime story, it may well be that many people have strong motives and favourable opportunities to commit crimes, but the great majority are unwilling to act. Similarly, prime ministers and presidents before Thatcher and Bush had ample motive and plentiful opportunity to censor, but were unwilling to use their powers. What marks off Thatcher and Bush from their predecessors, and possibly from many other Western leaders, is not so much the political, legal and constitutional constraints on their particular governments, but their willingness to use the political powers at their disposal.

This, in turn, reinforces the conclusion that we should be cautious about placing too much reliance on the formal and constitutional devices to control governments and to protect freedom of speech and information. In spite of major constitutional differences, the two countries have far higher censorship rates than other Western nations, and similar steep increases in the late 1980s. Some of the other nations share features of the British political system, some are more like the USA, but all have far lower censorship rates than either the UK or the USA. The figures suggest, as Karl Popper once put it, that the open society is like a fortress: it must be well designed and constructed, but it must also be well manned by people who believe in it and are motivated to defend it.

The findings also cast a little light on the theory that only weak governments will resort to censorship, and that strong ones have little need of it. In the British case the Thatcher government was strong in terms of parliamentary majority, public opinion ratings, and self-image. The government used its powers to censor not because it was driven to extremes to protect itself, but, on the contrary, because it had a firm grip on government and was willing to use its considerable powers.

Private and Public Censorship

The analysis so far has concentrated on government censorship, but there are also instances of private censorship which involve no government or public official: trade unions refusing to print news stories, bookshops refusing to sell publications, teachers refusing teaching materials, self-censorship on the part of the media, authors and speakers being threatened because of their views and writings, or courts of law placing limitations on political speech or publication. As with government censorship a good many of these cases are extremely complicated, and certainly not simple, black and white moral issues. The point of this analysis is not that these acts are right or wrong, good or bad, but that whoever commits them and for whatever reason, they constitute acts of censorship. According to some writers private censorship is at least as important, if not more so, than government censorship (Qualter, 1985, p. 149).

The term 'private' in this context means that governments are not involved, but only organizations, agencies and individuals who are not electorally and constitutionally accountable in the way that governments and their officials are. In the great majority of cases the incidents of censorship involve purely private individuals and organizations, but in a few cases they involve judicial bodies which are formally and actually separated from government.

How do figures relating to private censorship activities compare with government censorship: are they unrelated or do they covary? What proportions do each contribute to the total national figures? Do different nations vary in this respect? Do governments set the mood for private censoring activity? In which case, is an increase in government censorship likely to be followed by an increase in private censorship activity? Conversely, is a spiral of openness likely to be created by a government which opposes the use of censorship powers (even its own)?

The figures in Table 18.6 suggest that patterns of government and private censorship covary across time and across nations. The rank ordering of the nine countries according to incidents of government censorship is almost exactly the same as the rank ordering for incidents of private censorship. This holds across time for both the 1972–9 and the 1980–90 periods. In other words, countries which head the table for government censorship in the 1970s and 1980s head the table for private censorship as well.

There are two exceptions to this pattern, but the first, Canada, is a minor one. It deviates rather from the general pattern in the 1970s, but returns to it in the 1980s. The second, Italy, is more significant: in both periods the contribution of the government towards the total number of censorship incidents is substantially lower than that for the other nations. To put it the other way round, private censorship activity is more predominant in Italy than in the other eight countries. Possibly the special role of the Catholic Church has something to do with this, but the question will have to wait for more detailed research.

With this exception, however, the international pattern is fairly consistent – governments generally contribute between a third and a half to the total censorship incidents. When one considers the possible range – from a

Table 18.6 *Incidents of government and private censorship, 1972–1979, 1980–1990, 1972–1990*

	Total			Government			Private			Government as % of total		
	1972–9	1980–90	1972–90	1972–9	1980–90	1972–90	1972–9	1980–90	1972–90	1972–9	1980–90	1972–90
UK	99	286	385	31	131	162	68	155	223	31.3	45.8	42.1
USA	58	248	306	26	108	134	32	140	172	44.8	43.5	43.8
France	35	68	103	16	29	45	19	39	58	45.7	42.6	43.7
Canada	9	19	28	7	8	15	2	11	13	77.8	42.1	53.6
W. Germany	20	13	33	6	7	13	14	6	20	30.0	53.8	39.4
Italy	36	30	66	4	7	11	32	23	55	11.1	23.3	16.7
Australia	8	9	17	3	5	8	5	4	9	37.5	55.5	47.1
Denmark	0	3	3	0	2	2	0	1	1	0	66.7	66.7
Sweden	1	4	5	0	1	1	1	3	4	0	25.0	20.0
Total	266	680	946	93	298	391	173	382	555	35.0	43.8	41.3

small fraction of the total, to many times the private figure – this represents a notable consistency across nations and time. It also means that, whatever the cause and effect relationship, an increase in government activity is most likely to go hand in hand with an increase in private activity.

This brings us back to the theory of the spiral of censorship and the spiral of openness. The best test cases for this theory are the UK and the USA, which are the only countries to show a trend over time in the form of a major increase in government censorship. Did private censorship activity increase after the Thatcher and Reagan/Bush governments raised their governments' rate of activity? The answer is 'yes' (Table 18.7). After a long period of relatively high but randomly fluctuating figures, and one year after the government increase, the incidents of private censorship in the UK jump to a new high in 1988. The new high level of private activity is sustained in 1989 and 1990 with figures of 14 and 37.

Table 18.7   *Incidents of private censorship in the UK and the USA, 1972–1990*

	UK	USA
1972	8	4
1973	8	7
1974	5	0
1975	13	1
1976	5	7
1977	8	0
1978	13	6
1979	8	7
1980	10	4
1981	9	3
1982	11	2
1983	12	4
1984	10	5
1985	11	4
1986	13	8
1987	11	4
1988	17	39
1989	14	20
1990	37	47

The same thing happens in the United States. After a long period of trendless fluctuation in single figures, and in the same year that the government figure more than doubles its previous high, private censorship more than quadruples its previous high from 8 incidents in 1986 to 39 in 1988. And in the USA, private censorship also stays at an unprecedentedly high level in 1989 and 1990, with figures of 20 and 47.

In one way the British and American cases confirm the previous generalization that rates of private and government censorship follow or echo each other closely across nations and across time, but in another way the figures are puzzling. If governments help to set a climate of opinion about censorship, one would expect a time lag between government and private changes. This happens in the UK, where the private figure jumps to a new level a year after the government increase, but not in the USA, where the two changes coincide in 1988. In spite of the close association between the two sets of figures, therefore, and in spite of evidence supporting the spiral of censorship theory, the nature of the association between government and private censorship is far from clear, and must wait for further research.

Conclusion

If the study of political censorship is in its infancy, comparative study has scarcely been conceived. Sixteen years ago it was pointed out that 'the subject of government secrecy . . . has been neither researched intensively nor treated comparatively' (Galnoor, 1977, p. viii). This is still true. It is not difficult to understand why: apart from moral and evaluative problems, all the difficulties of definition, identification, operationalization and data collection are magnified by the demands of systematic comparative research, which then still leaves problems of interpretation.

The problems are not insurmountable. It is possible to collect comparative data, which are reliable to the extent that they are validated by an independent source – a newspaper – and which show a pattern of increase in Britain in 1986 which is replicated in Home Office phone tapping statistics. To this extent it is difficult to argue that the figures arc simply an artifact of the ways in which the raw material was collected by the *Index* in the first place.

Nor (to return to some of the methodological isues raised at the beginning) is it easy to explain away the figures as having more to do with public sensitivity to censorship than with rates of censorship activity. This is unlikely to explain the sudden and large increases in Britain and the USA in the late 1980s. Nor can it plausibly explain the low rates of censorship activity in Sweden and Denmark: these do not conceal real censorship activity which the Swedes and the Danes are either insensitive to, or afraid to report. Nor, in the light of all that has been been written, and all the hard evidence about the secret nature of the British state, can the British figures be the product of nothing more than a special sensitivity to censorship.

There is still the possibility that the Swedish and Danish figures show that these governments are particularly good at keeping their secrecy secret – that their low censorship figures show how effective censorship is in Denmark and Sweden. By the same token, it might be argued, British, American and French governments have to contend with leaky state apparatuses. This interpretation of the figures is difficult to sustain in the light of all the evidence about the five countries.

This leads to the further point that the censorship figures in the tables are consistent with conventional political scientific wisdom about levels of secrecy and censorship in Britain, France, Denmark and Sweden. In particular, the British figures are consistent with both the evidence and the theory about British government and politics, and with the late 1980s trend suggested by newspapers. It is not possible to accept these figures but to reject others because they happen to be inconvenient or counter-intuitive.

In other words, the statistics produced here cannot be easily interpreted as artifacts of the methods of data collection, or in terms of errors due to definition. They do seem to reflect actual censorship activity. It must be readily conceded that the figures are likely to be soft around the edges, but the fact that they are independently verified, and that it is difficult to sustain the obvious objections to them, suggests that they can support some generalizations.

To move on to substantive conclusions. The first concerns the rather secondary influence of constitutional differences in setting limits on government censorship activity. It is not claimed that formal, constitutional, or legal limits to the powers of government are irrelevant: the unique record of Britain and its particular features of government suggest otherwise. Nevertheless, the fact that two very different constitutional systems like Britain and the United States rank at the very top of the censorship tables, and that President Bush seems to have outdone even Mrs Thatcher's censorship record, suggests that government censorship requires the pre-conditions of motive and opportunity, but even more it requires politicians who have the will to act. Motive and opportunity are strongly influenced (or constrained) by the constitutional and political factors; the will to act has more to do with individual beliefs and ideology.

The second major conclusion suggests that neither the democratic/pluralist nor the authoritarian/elitist theories of the modern state are quite right so far as censorship is concerned. A comparison of the 1970s and 1980s shows that although there is a general overall increase in censorship activity by governments in the nine nations, this is notable in the cases of the USA, Britain, and France, and relatively slight in the cases of Italy, Australia, Denmark and Sweden. There is a decline in Canada and Germany. This suggests not a general developmental trend towards either pluralism or authoritarianism in the West, but developments in different directions by different nations.

The third set of conclusions concerns the close association between government and private censorship. With the exception of Italy, there is a uniform international pattern: countries with a good deal of government censorship have a good deal of private censorship as well, and vice versa. This covariance is found across nations and across time. Consequently, increases in private and government censorship seem to go together, at least in the case of Britain and the USA, which are the only two nations which register substantial changes over time. This, in turn, is consistent with the spiral of censorship theory, which argues that governments may well help to set the prevailing mood for private citizens and organizations.

In terms of the five different sets of factors which were earlier hypothesized as related to censorship, the results suggest that three are of importance, and two not. A country's international and geopolitical position (importance in the world system and defeat in war) seems to be of some influence in explaining the record of the UK, the USA and France. This, in turn, suggests that questions of defence and national security may account for a large proportion of government censorship matters – another topic which may merit further research. Constitutional mechanisms seem to explain at least part of Britain's record. Third, the presence of certain sorts of political leadership seems to be surprisingly important in the case of Thatcher and Bush (de Gaulle also, perhaps?) and capable, it seems, of overriding the constitutional provisions for freedom of speech. Other political factors, and social and cultural factors, do not seem to be of much significance.

However, it will take more work on more countries and over a longer period of time before we can be at all confident about these conclusions. In particular, the relatively constant relationship between government and private censorship is intriguing and needs further exploration, perhaps with a closer look at Italy as an exception to the general rule. Also an examination of the contribution of defence and national security matters to the total amount of government censorship might throw further light on their apparent importance. Lastly, a closer look at Britain and the United States over the past few years, and a follow-up after a further five years, will tell us more about why two such different political systems can be so alike.

Note

We are grateful to colleagues at the University of Essex, especially Kevin Boyle, Ivor Crewe, and Elinor Scarbrough, whose comments on a first draft of this chapter, presented to a departmental seminar, greatly improved the final version. We are also grateful to Colin Seymour-Ure whose thoughtful criticism also forced us to rethink, rework and rewrite the original version.

References

Article 19. 1989. *Liberty*. London:International Centre of Censorship.
Article 19. 1991. *Information Freedom and Censorship: World report 1991*. London: Library Association Publishing.
Blondel, J. 1990. *Comparative Government*. London: Phillip Allan
Buchan, N and T. Sumner. 1989. *Glasnost in Britain? Against Censorship and in Defence of the Word*. London:Macmillan.
Chapman, B. 1959. *The Profession of Government*. London: Allen and Unwin.
Dworkin, R. 1988. 'Devaluing Liberty'. *Index on Censorship* 17:7–8.
Einhorn, Eric S. 1977. 'Denmark, Norway and Sweden' in *Government Secrecy in Democracies*, Itzhak Galnoor, ed. New York: New York University Press.

Galnoor, Itzhak ed. 1977. *Government Secrecy in Democracies*, ed. New York: New York University Press.

Goldthorpe, John H. 1984. *Order and Conflict in Contemporary Capitalism*. Oxford: Clarendon Press.

Jansen, Sue Curry. 1991. *Censorship: The Knot that Binds Power and Knowledge*. New York: Oxford University Press.

Keane, John. 1991. *The Media and Democracy*. Oxford: Polity Press.

Lijphart, A. 1968. *The Politics of Accommodation: Pluralism and Democracy in the Netherlands*. Berkeley: University of California Press.

Lijphart, A. 1984. *Democracies: Patterns of Majoritarian and Consensus Government in Twenty-one Countries*. Newhaven: Yale University Press.

Manor, Yohanan. 1977. 'France', in *Government Secrecy in Democracies*. Itzhak Galnoor, ed. New York: New York University Press.

Miller, J. 1962. *Censorship and the Limits of Permission*. London: Oxford University Press.

Newton, K. and R. Mitton. Forthcoming. *Phone Tapping and Mail Interception in the UK, 1937–1990*. University of Essex.

Noelle-Neumann, E. 1974. 'The Spiral of Silence: A Theory of Public Opinion'. *Journal of Communication*, 24: 43–51.

O'Neil, O. 1990. 'Practices of Toleration' in *Democracy and the Mass Media*. J. Lichtenberg, ed. Cambridge: Cambridge University Press.

Peele, Gillian. 1988. 'The State and Civil Liberties' in *Developments in British Politics 2*, Henry Drucker, et al., eds. London: Macmillan.

Przeworski, A. and H. Teune, 1970. *The Logic of Comparative Social Inquiry*. New York: Wiley.

Qualter, Terence H. 1985. *Opinion Control in the Democracies*. Hong Kong: Macmillan Press

Robertson, K. 1982. *Public Secrets*. London: Macmillan.

Rourke, Francis E. 1977. 'The United States' in *Government Secrecy in Democracies*, Itzhak Galnoor, ed. New York: New York University Press.

Seymour-Ure, Colin. 1977. 'Great Britain' in *Government Secrecy in Democracies*, Itzhak Galnoor, ed. New York: New York University Press.

Shils, Edward A. 1956. *The Torment of Secrecy*. London: Heinemann.

UNESCO. 1949. *Human Rights*. London: Allan Wingate.

19

Enriching Democracy: Public Inquiry and the Policy Process

Anthony Barker

Government Decision-Making and Information in the Industrial and Post-Industrial Ages

If the context of this chapter were to be set with broad brush-strokes, they would simply outline the differences for public policy-making between industrial and post-industrial society. Industrial society generates social, economic and (thus) political problems requiring activist government, albeit in only a limited number of policy fields. The most important are material concerns such as food, housing and jobs, or minimal social security schemes against abject poverty or disease. Government must gather and organize enough mass support, whether or not through the ballot box, to create structures of policy and administration necessary for these great state projects. To attain them, the industrializing state requires systematic basic information, at least, about the condition of both the economy and the people. It obtains this knowledge directly, from censuses, tax returns or social insurance systems, and does not put much stress on either the sensitivity of its methods or the many aspects of society which fall outside its forceful, but limited, initiatives.

Government's main feature is its bureaucratic capacity to devise and deliver legislative programmes according to its particular radical or conservative ideology (Chapters 6 and 7): health and social services, anti-trade-union ('right to work') laws, or whatever. The conception, production and delivery of policies by government for the population is the dominant official *raison d'être*. Resources are always scarce, particularly if a left government is striving towards a welfare state. 'Gouverner, c'est choisir', declared the French socialist leader Jean Jaurès. 'Socialism is the language of priorities' echoed his Welsh counterpart, Aneurin Bevan, a generation later. For such socialists or other liberal progressives, the established power of the bourgeois state is to be captured and redirected, rather than analysed and transformed. The state machine, once captured, becomes an engine of war to collect taxes and to construct, legitimate and apply reformist policies. Any redesign or disarming of that engine would risk those policies which are to be imposed on the people in their own sovereign name. If the day ever comes when government can either morally justify or tactically afford to open its ranks to alternative analyses of the policy field and their official treatment, or to encourage a subtly interactive relationship between itself and civil society, that day has not yet arrived. Ideology, collective responsibility, party discipline, electoral loyalty and a firmly effective bureaucratic cadre in all sectors of state authority must remain dominant until it does arrive.

On such a historical stage, these self-confident imperatives of public power do not encourage a political climate featuring 'public participation' or its first cousin, 'public consultation and inquiry'. When government had to take on such great responsibilities as post-war economic recovery and the creation of a welfare state – perhaps combined with owning and running a huge public industry sector – it was not surprising that the proposition 'The gentleman in Whitehall knows best' was so persuasive and even obvious. Why winnow the hard-won harvest of policy proposals and plans into a possibly adverse wind of politics, vested interests and local sectionalism when those with the final responsibility for making these plans into a practical success can already see what should be done?

To say that senior government officials know best is no vague boast. In any advanced political system such as the leading Western democracies the statement contains several specific claims of great importance. The gentlemen in Whitehall and their international counterparts are trained and equipped to be well informed by having both the relevant materials and the brains to analyse them; they are trained to think properly about such materials and the issues they raise – and they are also trained to realize that they may not be adequately informed on certain matters. They are objective, impartial and analytical: a breach of any of these qualities would be a serious professional lapse. They work in a hierarchical group, processing a lot of written material with a high degree of peer control (or, at least, open sharing of arguments within a hierarchy) so that the collective view will probably prevail, subject to final ministerial authority. If the highest standards of professionalized public service are being practised, even greater benefits will flow because a judicious sense of fairness will also inform these civil servants' discretionary decision-making. This will affect administrative decisions as well as any quasi-judicial ones (where the courts may have a direct say in the procedures for reaching an official outcome).

This traditional pattern, providing government of the people and for the people but denying much direct involvement by the people, did not attempt to operate without external information. In the post-war era, Federal Germany, France and Britain – to mention only three states – have operated elaborate consultative networks, drawing in facts and opinions from a range of practitioners in fields which are, in the American phrase, 'affected with the public interest'. These formal consultees have usually been recognized and acceptable organizations. Their reporting is normally strictly confined to their own practical experience. Most of these firms,

trade associations, or other membership organizations are strongly conscious of the public standing bestowed on them as official consultees and
are glad to supply the government with information in return for it. Some
will have ambitions of moving beyond this exchange of information and
public standing to broader and more intimate roles as official advisers, and
more than a few have actually experienced this transition as part of the
neo-corporatist arrangements made by modern governments, notably in
Federal Germany, the Netherlands and Scandinavia. In Germany, indeed,
it has been suggested that the network or undergrowth of official advisory
sources (whether practitioner bodies or official standing advisory committees) is so dense that senior civil servants seek out their own unofficial
sources to get advice more quickly and privately (Murswieck, 1993). In this
event, all or parts of the official advisory structure could become merely
dignified or symbolic.

The 'strong government' style associated with the industrial age is
reflected in the method and assumptions of these traditional channels of
information and advice. The information required is highly practical and
factual; it is supplied responsively on the government's judgement of its
need to know, rather than actively by the reporting body; and it is
coordinated and related to other, wider issues only within government
itself so that its providers (the 'outside' bodies) do not influence or even
know about what use may be made of their own inputs. It is a useful, basic
relationship between insiders and outsiders, offering some legitimacy to
the official policies which may rest on the information received and some
public standing to its source organizations. But the distinction between
inside and outside is very strong: it is a simple case of the 'black box' of
official decision-making taking in, under its own complete control, such
material as it would find useful to make, or to legitimate, its policy and
casework decisions.

By contrast, the post-industrial, or post-materialist, form of political
system is supposed to have a broader issue agenda featuring new public
policy problems (Inglehart 1977; 1990). Even if traditional materialist
issues such as cheaper housing or economic recession persist, the agenda of
environmental standards, political or social dissent, or the quality of
government itself now seeks attention. As the interest and the political
resources of the public increase, so the government authorities are
expected to become more open and discursive in their dealings (Topf,
1993). More official functions – particularly at local government level –
become subject to public participation of some type or level. On national
questions this takes the form of richer and more negotiative exchanges
between the state and private (or semi-official) bodies, ranging beyond the
traditional supply of information and carefully controlled advice about any
particular aspect of national life.

Also by contrast, governments in the modern developed world have
growing areas of responsibility in which policy is not only hard to
operationalize and implement but also very hard even to design. The

technical knowledge base of policy fields becomes steadily more apparent and, quite often, harder to understand (Barker and Peters, 1993). In some, often highly publicized, policy fields, such as energy production and conservation, global warming or ozone depletion, it is a moot point whether the science involved in defining and understanding the problem is more daunting than the politics of doing something – nationally or internationally – to tackle it.

These novel and daunting challenges on the allegedly 'post-industrial' policy agenda have not sprung up of their own accord. Their political soil has been cultivated by 'post-industrial' individuals and organizations who deliberately press for both a new agenda and a new relationship between government and society as a better method of dealing with public issues (Topf, 1993). The goal is public participation in policy-making as well as in the actual design and delivery of certain other policies, notably of the practical, local kind such as public housing management, crime prevention or neighbourhood traffic and planning issues. For this, more demanding, approach by unofficial public interests to policy-making, the old 'information relationship' and the carefully controlled advisory processes initiated and managed by government in a largely unilateral manner are not sufficient. The positive discovery of new knowledge by means of various forms of research, surveys and inquiries is seen as essential in addition to the routines of basic factual data collection (Peters and Barker, 1993). The whole may be expressed as 'the spirit of inquiry', this being shared between the government, semi-government and private organizations involved in each particular policy field. This chapter explores the idea of 'inquiring' as the intellectual core of advanced and possibly, in some ways, post-industrial societies.

Conditions for Shared Inquiry

An ideal set of circumstances for a flourishing 'spirit of inquiry' to pervade any governmental and political system would be hard to achieve. Initially, the assumptions of free inquiry or research, free speech, free press and free broadcasting must be safely in place. Neither individuals nor organizations of any type (interest groups, firms, professional institutes, charities, membership organizations and the rest) will feel readily able to raise their heads in the public forum to offer the results of some report or inquiry unless they can assume a general right to be heard without fear of unreasonable or oppressive sanctions.

Secondly, an important contributor to this assumption is the state of the law on libel or slander where a 'public interest defence' is offered: that is, a claim by the defendant of a suit that any defamation is justified by the benefit of the public knowing of the matter in question. Thirdly, the law must also protect 'whistleblowers' within organizations who may well face both dismissal from their jobs and civil or even criminal legal actions as their reward for informing the legal authorities or the public at large of serious malpractices.

Fourthly, there must be in as many technically and professionally expert fields as possible a genuinely plural access to expertise so that no one sector – whether the state, a private industry or other vested interest – can prevent any rival experts from contradicting their own claims on some matter of public interest. In many fields there are four familiar sources of expert knowledge: the state (both central and local governments); the practitioners (whether in private or public sector industries); the professional institutes, which contain (or monitor) those practitioners; and the universities (or other higher education bodies) where experts teach and research in the field and are available to work on current issues or to offer independent checks and criticism on the work of these other groups. Ideally, in addition, there should be independent research institutes (which are separate from both industry-based and campus-based expertise) and, perhaps also (as in the cancer research field) research charities – or some overlapping of the two. The tax laws on individuals and firms should encourage donations to this independent research sector, particularly in Western Europe where universities and similar academic centres depend on state funds for their teaching or research support and where genuinely 'private' (financially independent) universities of any research standing are unusual or even unknown. Where (as in Britain) tax-exempt 'charitable' purposes are tightly defined in law, the need for tax-exempt research effort by acknowledged experts on work which is formally non-charitable, but very much in the public interest, is particularly marked. Similarly, almost all advanced countries lack a research expert tradition among local governments or among the huge modern array of quasi-official bodies, which therefore tend to look to central government, independent research institutes or the universities to undertake relevant research or specialist study on their behalf. The ideal would be that all sectors of society with executive capacity should accompany it with 'research' or 'inquiry' capacity of their own. In this way, all may become 'learning organizations' while also contributing to a broad public capacity.

A fifth requirement is implied by the fourth but deserves a separate and emphatic listing. This is simply the familiar idea of effective academic research freedom in the universities and other relevant colleges. It is often the last hope of one or other side in a disputed public policy issue – usually the side of 'David' rather than 'Goliath' – that an expert in academic life can be recruited to assist with technical scrutiny, advice or, possibly, further research. A government which applies political or financial pressures to prevent such help would be threatening a fundamental feature of the 'spirit of inquiry' – and, indeed, of a pluralist society in general. This threat may arise unintentionally, for example from a government in a country without private universities which forces the publicly funded ones to restrict research and scholarship in order to try to teach growing numbers of extra and unfunded students.

Sixthly, turning to the government system itself, this ideal model would, naturally, include a legal commitment to 'open government' in the executive's own operations. A strong freedom of information Act would be essential, based on the freeing of all information which is not specifically excluded (as in Scandinavia and the US) rather than leaving the presumption in favour of official secrecy, as amended here and there at the margin. On the legislature's responsibilities, our model would (seventhly) include a system of legislative committees which was fully in tune with the climate of continuing information gathering and policy review to be found outside its walls. This would, of course, apply to committees dealing with legislation and legal regulations as well as to committees scrutinizing the policy-making and administrative record of the executive government, not forgetting the effective management of the judiciary. Where a legislature has a tradition of individual deputies or senators bringing forward bills (as in the UK and the US, for example) they should enjoy the benefits of the wider system's commitment to information and inquiry by being fully supported through the legislature's research service and the resources of the committee system. Where there is no particular national tradition of individually promoted unofficial legislation, the value of encouraging its birth through procedural reform in the legislature should be carefully considered.

While such suggestions as these are familiar from the legislative reform debates of several advanced countries, one further proposition is more novel. This is that the ideal model would also include an interactive working relationship in the quest for policy-related information and analysis between the legislature's various specialist committees and the relevant 'outside' expert community. In the modern world, advanced political systems' legislatures cannot possibly hope to cover the full range of public affairs. Partnership with reliable and authoritative experts is essential. There is ample scope for joint ventures in research and inquiry without either side losing its independent judgement of the issues. As legislators should not (and, in practical terms, cannot) themselves conduct detailed investigations, the most likely relationship between them and established experts is sponsored research devised and funded jointly but conducted by the experts or a joint contractor on behalf of both of them. It could only strengthen the standing of elected legislatures in electorates' eyes to see them joining in the processes of research and inquiry on policy issues rather than merely reacting to such material put before them as evidence in their specialist committees (Barker, 1984).

The eighth and final characteristic in this checklist for an information-rich and 'inquiry-based' political culture is as radical and novel as these propositions about the legislature. It is that the executive itself would take on this same character of cooperating with the many expert and practitioner organizations in civil society to generate a flow of new information and analysis of public affairs. From the most formal and grand of royal or presidential commissions (found in numerous Western states) down to more humdrum technical reviews and surveys, there would be no reason to segregate all inquiry forms into either wholly public or wholly private responsibilities. While government and private interests will always wish to conduct some inquiries separately and under their own exclusive control, some others would be shared – again, as with the legislatures' joint efforts – probably on a joint commission basis. Thus, some official government inquiries and reviews would be done in-house; rather more by appointed commissions or committees of familiar type (reporting to the government alone); some would be commissioned from unofficial bodies of suitable standing such as universities, research institutes or professional institutions; and some, as suggested, would be joint efforts by government and non-government bodies, with each side being free to interpret the results as it wishes. As with the legislatures, modern governments would gain in public esteem if they seemed to move closer to policy problems by tackling their study more closely alongside the specialist bodies in that field. The interaction of the state authorities with organs of civil society would strengthen both sides and endorse the view that the state no longer stands separate and supreme in civil society but is its central mechanism for the determination of progress.

There has been little social science interest so far in the likely or prospective political scenery of so-called post-industrial or post-materialist political systems. Undoubtedly, what this chapter has called the 'spirit of inquiry' in public policy affairs is at the centre of such scenery because a political system of this kind would flourish or fail, very much depending on its capacity as a 'learning' or 'reflexive' system. Its modern economy alone would require that, and its political arrangements would find it hard to manage otherwise, given the sophisticated demands of its electorate. This outline checklist of eight broad propositions describing an ideal-type of 'inquiry-based' political system could be developed into a more detailed scheme. The result would be an essay in futurologist political studies, no doubt, but would also have a more current value. Like all ideal-types (if carefully devised) this one would allow each advanced political system to be measured, in broad terms, against its main features for 'openness', methods of inquiry or analysis of public affairs and – most radically – the questioning and erosion so far of the 'state–private' divide when the system as a whole sees a need for new information and study on a policy problem. Thus, one can see at a glance that the US and Scandinavia are closer to the model in certain important respects, at least. The dominant power of the First Amendment rights to free speech and press in the US, the entrenched role of the 'remiss' (petition) system in Sweden and the existence of freedom of information laws in both countries are the most obvious examples. The continuing absence of such laws in Britain, and the weakness of legislative committees or of the public inquiry element in land use planning in France, show failures to measure up to the model in two other countries. As with all analytical models, it matters not how far away from any given country's experience a post-industrial political system may still be. Nor is it necessary for all scholars to endorse every feature of a proposed model as necessary to the main idea. A model of some such type will help to make a map of advanced political systems' prospective features with regard to the essential theme of their capacity to absorb and mould new information for public policy-making.

Institutionalizing Public Inquiry

We must now turn from theoretical prescription or outline model-making on the 'spirit of inquiry' in any political system to the empirical question of how actual types of 'inquiry' forms may make up a pattern within that system. Figure 19.1 attempts to view all types of formal inquiry into public policy: governmental, legislative and private ('unofficial'). It tries to be universal in its categories and terms to suit any advanced system. It should be read from the top.

Within this overall scheme, the elements to be excluded from consideration are: 'all other advice and information' (because it is not based on inquiry forms) and 'formal inquiries conducted internally to the executive' (because they are not conducted in public, even in part, and do not normally publish any report). Having indicated the full canvas of all inquiries, one can look more closely at the various types of inquiry. Regarding the types of inquiry process, one can of course readily distinguish a government department's standing advisory committee on a policy field; an *ad hoc* committee of inquiry into a particular topic; or, of course, a public inquiry into a development scheme or into a policy disaster or major public scandal. These are institutional and legal distinctions (such as which inquiries have a statutory basis). Having classified these, one must attempt to make a functional analysis. One scheme would be to characterize inquiries' functions as follows (while noting that there will be overlaps whereby any particular inquiry would have more than one single function):

1 inquiries which discover or create new information or analysis;
2 inquiries which clarify and organize existing, confusing information;
3 inquiries which establish some new subject or approach in policy-making;
4 inquiries which legitimate and confirm information or policy already favoured by the government (or established opinion);
5 inquiries which reject or delegitimate such information or policy which is officially disfavoured;
6 inquiries which recommend a possibly controversial decision, including development and environmental issues;
7 inquiries which investigate serious 'system failures' ('policy disasters', major accidents, scandals).

Within any such scheme for inquiries' functions, the roles of principal participants must also be analysed in some suitably generalized form (cf.

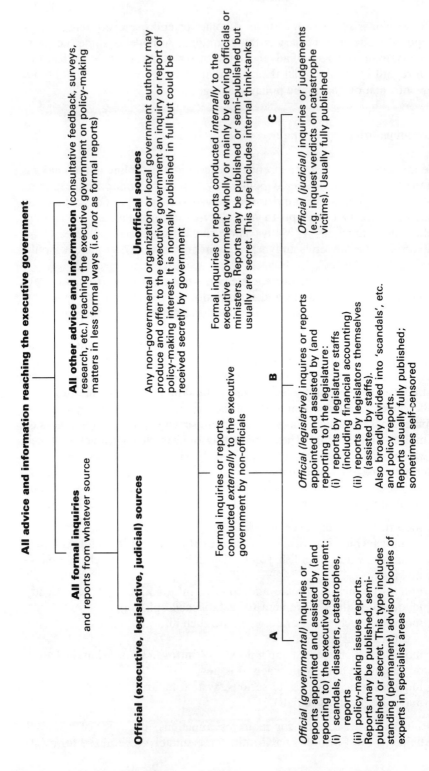

All advice and information reaching the executive government

All formal inquiries and reports from whatever source

All other advice and information (consultative feedback, surveys, research, etc.) reaching the executive government on policy-making matters in less formal ways (i.e. *not* as formal reports)

Official (executive, legislative, judicial) sources

Unofficial sources

Any non-governmental organization or local government authority may produce and offer to the executive government an inquiry or report of policy-making interest. It is normally published in full but could be received secretly by government

Formal inquiries or reports conducted *externally* to the executive government by non-officials

Formal inquiries or reports conducted *internally* to the executive government, wholly or mainly by serving officials or ministers. Reports may be published or semi-published but usually are secret. This type includes internal think-tanks

A

Official (governmental) inquiries or reports appointed and assisted by (and reporting to) the executive government:
(i) scandals, disasters, catastrophes, reports
(ii) policy-making issues reports.
Reports may be published, semi-published or secret. This type includes standing (permanent) advisory bodies of experts in specialist areas

B

Official (legislative) inquires or reports appointed and assisted by (and reporting to) the legislature:
(i) reports by legislature staffs (including financial accounting)
(ii) reports by legislators themselves (assisted by staffs).
Also broadly divided into 'scandals', etc. and policy reports.
Reports usually fully published; sometimes self-censored

C

Official (judicial) inquiries or judgements (e.g. inquest verdicts on catastrophe victims). Usually fully published

Figure 19.1 *A hierarchy of formal inquiries or reports available to executive governments on policy-making matters*

Wheare's 'seven characters' in official central and local government committee work: chairman, secretary, official, expert, layman, party man and interested party; Wheare, 1955). Table 19.1 sets out seven stages of public inquiry functions. These run from the inquiry's official appointment through to any final 'verdict' on its work and the problems of its field given by the generalist mass media and public opinion.

Actual Inquiries in One Democracy: Britain

In order to offer some actual examples of public inquiry practice and to put some flesh on the bones of these analytical models, the case of one political system (Britain's) will now be introduced. A systematic review of the British processes of formal inquiry into policy and administrative issues would go well beyond the small (and now rather old) literature about royal commissions and departmental committees of inquiry (Gosnell, 1934; Hauser, 1965; Wraith and Lamb, 1971; Bulmer, 1980; 1983) to include all other types of 'official' (central government appointed) inquiry or review exercises. Some of these are statutorily prescribed while others are discretionary within ministers' judgement of their needs. Local authorities establish discretionary external or public inquiries (as opposed to internal reviews) only very occasionally, and even these are often neglected or even formally boycotted by central government. This treatment and their rarity reduce them to a standing which is as low, or lower, than that enjoyed by the more numerous private or unofficial inquiries. Local authority examples include: Derbyshire County Council's inquiry into methane gas hazards; the London Borough of Haringey's inquiry (under Lord Gifford, QC) into the Broadwater Farm Estate riot (Gifford, 1986; 1988); and Liverpool City Council's inquiry (also under Gifford) into the policing of the Liverpool 8 district. Private or unofficial inquiries have included the Duke of Edinburgh's group's Inquiry into British Housing (one of the Rowntree charities); and the 'Death on the Rock' inquiry (by Lord Windlesham and Anthony Rampton, QC) for a television company (Windlesham and Rampton, 1989).

On the 'official' side of this range of inquiries, the institutions in question are mostly familiar. The departmental committee of inquiry has been somewhat neglected as a device since Mrs Thatcher's arrival in 1979 (Rhodes, 1975) and the *ad hoc* royal commission wholly so (until the Runciman Commission on criminal law procedures was appointed in 1991, after her departure). New forms of official inquiry have been preferred but not exclusively so. The 'ministerial reviews', notably of social security and health policies, have given ministers the greater personal control of the inquiry process which they wanted, while the external experts' 'short-order' inquiry, instructed to report back in weeks rather than months, is a less radical development – (a recent example was the Department of Education's fleeting committee on primary education, with its unprecedented steering by the then minister, Kenneth Clarke, apparently towards

Table 19.1 *Seven inquiry functions performed by system characters*

Functions performed	Inquiry system 'character' who performs it	Status of this 'character': lay (generalist) or expert (specialist)
1 Appointing the inquiry and receiving its report and recommendations	'Political executives' (ministers and senior civil servants)	Ministers: lay Administrative civil servants: lay Specialist grade civil servants: experts or semi-experts
2 Undertaking the inquiry (the 'inquirers')	Chairperson, members of commissions and committees of inquiry; inspector and assessors at public inquiries; (possibly coroner and assessors at certain policy-related inquests)	Chairperson: lay Members: both lay and expert Inquiry inspector: expert or semi-expert Inquiry assessors: expert Coroners: expert or semi-expert Inquest assessors: expert
3 Responding to being the subject of the inquiry (the 'inquirees')	Witnesses and interested observers in the field of inquiry: any individual, organization, organized group, professional or sub-professional group, academics or other experts, notably including any specialist journalists or publicists	Usually all are expert or semi-expert because all are fully involved in the field. But members of the general public may be 'inquirees' in policy disaster (including major accident) inquiries, e.g. football crowds, boat passengers or parents involved in child abuse accusations

his already preferred conclusions: (Adler, 1988). What of the quality of these governmental 'decision advice processes' (as they are best analytically labelled) and their optimum use? Former chairmen and members of pre-1979 commissions and committees such as Lord Rothschild, Lord Benson and Sir Andrew Shonfield have long since contributed some critical thoughts on how best to conduct this type of inquiry (Shonfield, 1980; Benson and Rothschild, 1982; Rothschild, 1983). Sir Frank Layfield, QC, has added some of his reactions to his tasks as the inspector inquiring into and recommending upon the Sizewell scheme for Britain's first PWR nuclear power station. And Professor Martin Bulmer has continued on these lines in his various books and other writings, notably on how commissions with social-science-based tasks deal with information and research (Bulmer, 1980; 1992). Clearly, therefore, a modern equivalent of Wraith and Lamb's *Public Inquiries as an Instrument of Government* of 1971 would need to be a good deal broader and more flexible than their institutionally based work if it is to capture the 'inquiry'-based aspects of official advice-taking in the British system.

Table 19.1 *continued*

4 Resonating within cognate or related subject fields – or within the relevant academic fields as a result of the inquiry process in the field in question	The equivalent range of persons and organizations in these other fields who feel affected by the processes of inquiry, evidence-taking, report and recommendations in the field in question	Less involved in this particular field, so less expert (although fully expert in their own field)
5 Providing further and wider information or opinions to the inquiry process (perhaps afterwards, at government decision time)	As for 3 and 4, but in further policy-making or knowledge fields which are not so much affected by the inquiry in question but who have some broader contextual information or opinion to offer	As for 4
6 Responding to the inquiry report and recommendations (and also to the government's own reactions)	As for 3–5, all of whom have some degree of interest in the inquiry in question and who form its 'reference group', perhaps including one or more 'advocacy coalitions' (Sabatier, 1987; 1988)	As for 3–5
7 Concluding the career of the inquiry by providing (i) the government's own response (ii) the wider general public response to its work	The 'political executives' (as in 1); laypeople among other political executives (in other government departments); more generalist journalists; legislators; the 'general public' (possibly responding via opinion polls)	As in 1 All: lay

On the 'unofficial' side of the inquiry spectrum, however, the map-making is much less easy because an almost unlimited range of private organizations can conduct and publish an 'inquiry' into some aspect of public policy-making. The problem of drawing a line between true 'inquiries' (with independent inquirers, public evidence-taking and a published report of recognized objectivity) on the one hand and the more self-serving review, survey or report produced by an 'interested party' (such as trade unions or trade associations) is a genuine difficulty.

Functional analysis is, quite clearly, the only sensible academic strategy. Detailed map-making or attempts at Linnaean classification are not sensible beyond a certain point: nor is the counting of specimens. In these respects, getting the analytical measure of official or unofficial ('public' or 'private') decision advice procedures is similar to the early work of twenty years ago on quasi-governmental and quasi-autonomous organizations

Table 19.2   *Twelve disastrous accidents, 1985–1989*

			Deaths
1	May 1985	Bradford football stadium fire	56
2	[May 1985	Heisel (Belgium) football stadium riot]	[38]
3	August 1985	Manchester airport: aircraft fire	55
4	November 1986	Shetland helicopter crash	45
5	March 1987	Zeebrugge ferry capsize	193
6	November 1987	London underground railway fire: King's Cross station	31
7	July 1988	North Sea oil rig (Piper Alpha) explosion	167
8	December 1988	Railway (South London) 3-train crash: Clapham	35
9	January 1989	Airliner crash on to M1 motorway	47
10	March 1989	Railway (South London) crash: Purley	5
11	April 1989	Sheffield (Hillsborough) football stadium: crowd surge	95
12	August 1989	London: *Marchioness* boat collision	51

Also, in December 1988, the terrorist destruction of Pan Am Flight 103 over Lockerbie, Scotland with 270 deaths. Although not an accidental disaster, this case has proved highly controversial in its policy implications.

(quangos). It was not their numbers or their details of design which mattered but their behaviour and functions in general and their practical relationship to the state and its agents in particular (Hague et al., 1975; Barker, 1982). Similarly, it is the function of 'public inquiries', as inclusively defined and as set out in some scheme similar to Figure 19.1, which is the object of study.

One type or group of public inquiries in Britain deserves notice here, to help to illustrate the empirical opportunities and difficulties of the 'inquiry' theme. These are mentioned in Figure 19.1 as type A(i): inquiry reports on scandals, disasters and catastrophes. As in all developed systems, serious charges of scandal in British government are supposed to attract an investigatory commission of some kind (although the notorious Profumo affair of thirty years ago was confidentially reviewed, in its alleged national security aspect, by a single senior judge: Denning, 1963). A specialized procedure, under the Tribunals of Inquiry (Evidence) Act of 1921, is available which carries High Court powers over witnesses and the risk of perjury, but it is now regarded as too cumbersome for practical use.

Public inquiries into disastrous accidents have been a very sad feature of the British 'inquiry' theme in recent years. Table 19.2 lists twelve. The list includes the Belgian football stadium riot which was caused by British members of the crowd and which occurred in the same month as the Bradford football stadium fire; public interest in Britain was therefore very high.

These administrative inquiries (together with any judicial ones established under the Tribunals of Inquiry (Evidence) Act of 1921) need to be related analytically not only to the judicial proceedings of coroners and inquest juries but also to any court cases which arise from these disastrous accidents. These cases may be criminal (such as the manslaughter charges brought following the Zeebrugge ferry and *Marchioness-Bowbelle* marine disasters) or civil (such as actions for damages or compensation by victims and relatives). The practical lack of logical relationship between public inquiries, court cases and the internal exercises of statutory inspectorates within the Health and Safety Commission and the Department of Transport was noticed by the government in the summer of 1991. An interdepartmental committee of officials is currently reviewing the question, apparently under Home Office chairmanship.

Another special interest in 'inquiry' research is the inquiry process into what might loosely be called 'policy disasters'. Here honest error, malpractice or worse has produced intense publicity and controversy or obvious failure and collapse to some branch of official public service or private commercial operations. A major example was the 'scandals' surrounding the professional findings of serious criminal sexual abuse of children by their parents or other adult relatives in Cleveland (north-east England), Orkney (Scotland), and elsewhere. Doctors, social workers, police and the subsequent judicial inquiring authorities (notably Lord Justice Butler-Sloss after 'Cleveland') were at odds on what had been true and correct action to protect the children.

There is no clear distinction between an inquiry into a major public tragic disaster and one into a 'policy disaster'. All accidents may ultimately be diagnosed as 'system failures' in the purist sense that all operating systems should preclude the risk arising from human error. In reality there is a spectrum on which, for example, one may place the Clapham train crash as having been a plainer 'policy disaster' than was the King's Cross fire. In this particular comparison the point would be that the signal maintenance task on Southern Region was manifestly failing for lack of properly qualified and remunerated staff, so that grossly excessive overtime hours had clearly been accepted as a routine feature of the system, when safety required that they should be no more than a rare emergency option. In London Underground's case, it may be fair to conclude that management's concern for the fire risk in underground stations had been to some extent displaced by the recent rise of the more novel and very disturbing risk of much greater use of the system causing crowds to surge down on to already crowded platforms during rush hours, and of passengers being pushed on to the rails. There were aspects of system failure at work (particularly following the earlier fire at Oxford Circus station) but the neglect of action to prevent a hypothetical disaster arising from a lighted cigarette end seems less culpable than the neglect of established operating standards caused by chronic staff shortages on signals maintenance work at Clapham. To use the common phrase, the Clapham case should have appeared rather more like 'an accident waiting to happen'.

A second and perhaps more contrasting pair (one a tragic accident and the other a 'policy disaster') might be the Piper Alpha oil rig explosion in the North Sea and the Cleveland child sex abuse case. According to the findings of the Scottish judge who conducted the oil rig public inquiry, this was a plain failure to follow safety standards – even if those standards could be considered adequate. So this was, like Clapham, a 'policy disaster' which happened to claim many lives. By contrast the Cleveland affair showed the policy system in full working order, so that the confident diagnoses of anal abuse made by two official doctors led to prompt statutory action by their social work colleagues forcibly to remove over 100 children from their homes. This system did not require police consent even though they would assemble the evidence to support the criminal charges which the Crown Prosecution Service would have considered bringing against the parents or other persons allegedly involved. The failure of the system in this case (as at Orkney and the other places) arises solely if the doctors were wrong or if the system was manifestly faulty in its design: and both of these possibilities remain contested even after a very full inquiry and continuing public and professional debate.

Clearly, some tragic public disasters are more plainly and directly the result of 'policy disaster' than others. Whether some number of people need to die in a resulting accident to make the event a 'public tragedy' is not the main analytical point. So all inquiries into either major tragic accidents or non-tragic 'policy disasters' are actually engaged in judging 'operating system failures' (whether on Clapham rail signals, police crowd controls at Hillsborough or the laws designed to prevent employers such as Robert Maxwell purloining their firms' pension funds). Research into the policy-making inquiry process should not drift into either a review of the risk of 'system failure' in general (such as Charles Perrow's *Normal Accidents* of 1984) or a study of regulatory regimes – whether in company and financial affairs or elsewhere. But those two themes are the substantive background to the general idea of 'inquiry' and form the basis of perhaps all inquiries' work. It is important to keep them in analytical focus but also to confine them to the background of this particular research theme.

In the British case, the theme for empirical research (within the eight-part, ideal-type framework outlined above) is this. There is a decidedly traditionalist and even somewhat brutish formal political system, based on the legitimacy of allowing the 'winners' of a general election to enjoy what has often been called 'unlimited power for a limited period'. As a result, there is rather poor legislative oversight of policy-making and adminis-tration and even weaker oversight of legislation itself. There is no freedom of information law or even a political culture which requires openness as a matter of conventional good practice. There is, instead, an opaque, centralized and still generally self-confident executive tradition which draws on a powerful heritage of royal prerogative powers and autonomous administrative initiative.

How can such a system manage to reach out into quasi-official and private civil society interests in order to gather information and advice for policy-making? When it fails to reach out for this purpose, how may interested elements in civil society 'reach in' to government to make some contribution to policy-making? The process of establishing formal or semi-formal 'inquiries' (whether by government or by non-government initiatives) is not, of course, the whole answer to these very broad questions. But it is a central and important part of the process of extending democracy by encouraging the engagement of the wider society in its political processes.

References

Adler, M. 1988. Lending a deaf ear: the Government's response to consultation on the reform of social security, in R. Davidson and P. White (eds) *Information and Government*, Edinburgh: Edinburgh University Press.

Barker, A. (ed.) 1982. *Quangos in Britain*, London: Macmillan.

Barker, A. 1984. Planning inquiries: a role for Parliament (Public lecture to the Royal Society of Arts), *RSA Journal*, August, 619–32.

Barker, A. and B.G. Peters 1993. Introduction: science policy and government, in A. Barker and B.G. Peters (eds) *The Politics of Expertise: Creating, Using and Manipulating Scientific Knowledge for Public Policy*, Edinburgh: Edinburgh University Press.

Benson (Lord) and Rothschild (Lord) 1982. Royal commissions: a memorial, *Public Administration*, 60, 339–48.

Bulmer, M. (ed.) 1980. *Social Research and Royal Commissions*, London: Allen and Unwin.

Bulmer, M. 1983. *Royal Commissions and Departmental Committees of Inquiry: the Lessons of Experience*. Report on a seminar, London: Royal Institute of Public Administration.

Bulmer, M. 1993. The royal commission and the departmental committee in the British policy-making process, in B.G. Peters and A. Barker (eds) *Advising West European Governments: Inquiries Expertise and Public Policy*, Edinburgh: Edinburgh University Press.

Denning (Lord) 1963. *Lord Denning's Report*, London: Her Majesty's Stationery Office.

Gifford (Lord) 1986. *The Broadwater Farm Inquiry* (Chairman: Lord Gifford, QC) London: London Borough of Haringey.

Gifford (Lord) 1988. *The Broadwater Farm Inquiry*, Second Report, London: London Borough of Haringey.

Gosnell, H.F. 1934. British royal commissions of inquiry, *Political Science Quarterly*, 49, 84–118.

Hague, D.C., W.J.M. Mackenzie and A. Barker (eds) 1975. *Public Policy and Private Interests: the Institutions of Compromise*, London: Macmillan.

Hauser, C.J. 1965. *Guide to Decision: The Royal Commission*, Totowa, NJ: The Bedminster Press.

Inglehart, R. 1977. *The Silent Revolution: Changing Values and Political Styles Among Western Publics*, Princeton, NJ: Princeton University Press.

Inglehart, R. 1990. *Culture Shift in Advanced Democracies*, Princeton, NJ: Princeton University Press.

Murswieck, A. 1993. Policy advice and decision-making in the German federal bureaucracy, in B.G. Peters and A. Barker (eds) *Advising West European Governments: Inquiries Expertise and Public Policy*, Edinburgh: Edinburgh University Press.

Perrow, C. 1984. *Normal Accidents*, New York, NY: Basic Books.

Peters, B.G. and A. Barker 1993. Introduction: governments, information, advice and policy-making, in B.G. Peters and A. Barker (eds) *Advising West European Governments: Inquiries Expertise and Public Policy*, Edinburgh: Edinburgh University Press.

Rhodes, G. 1975. *Committees of Inquiry*, London: Allen and Unwin for the Royal Institute of Public Administration.

Rothschild (Lord) 1983. The Royal Commission on Gambling, *American Behavioral Scientist*, 26(5), 623–42.

Sabatier, P. 1987. Knowledge, policy-orientated learning and policy change. An advocacy coalition framework, *Knowledge, Diffusion, Utilization*, 8(4), 649–92.

Sabatier, P. 1988. An adversary coalition framework of policy change and the role of policy-orientated learning therein, *Policy Sciences*, 2, 129–68.

Shonfield, (Sir) A. 1980. In the course of investigation, in M. Bulmer (ed.) *Social Research and Royal Commissions*, London: Allen and Unwin.

Topf, R. 1993. Conclusion: science, public policy and the authoritativeness of the governmental process, in A. Barker and B.G. Peters (eds), *The Politics of Expertise*, Edinburgh: Edinburgh University Press.

Wheare, K.C. 1955. *Government by Committee: an Essay on the British Constitution*, Oxford: The Clarendon Press.

Windlesham (Lord) and A. Rampton, QC 1989. *The Windlesham/Rampton Report on 'Death on the Rock'*, London: Faber and Faber.

Wraith, R.E. and G.B. Lamb 1971. *Public Inquiries as an Instrument of Government*, London: Allen and Unwin for the Royal Institute of Public Administration.

Select Bibliography of Blondel's Works

Books

As condiciónes da vida política no estado de Paraíba, Brazil, Fundación Vargas, 1955.

Voters, Parties and Leaders, London: Penguin, 1963 (numerous editions) (French and German translations).

Public Administration in France (with F. Ridley), London: Routledge & Kegan Paul, 1964, 1968.

Constituency Politics (with F. Bealey and P. McCann), London: Faber, 1965.

Comparative Government: A Reader, (editor), London: Macmillan, 1968.

An Introduction to Comparative Government, London: Weidenfeld & Praeger, 1969 (Spanish translation).

The Government of France. New York: Crowell, 1970.

A Workbook for Comparative Government (with V. Herman), London: Weidenfeld & Praeger, 1971.

Comparing Political Systems, London: Weidenfeld & Praeger, 1972.

Comparative Legislatures, Englewood-Cliffs, NJ: Prentice-Hall, 1973.

Thinking Politically, London: Wildwood 1976.

Political Parties, London: Wildwood, 1978.

World Leaders, London and Los Angeles: Sage Publications, 1980 (Japanese edition, 1984).

The Discipline of Politics, London: Butterworth, 1981.

The Organization of Governments, London and Los Angeles: Sage Publications, 1982.

Government Ministers in the Contemporary World, London and Los Angeles: Sage Publications, 1985.

Political Leadership, London and Los Angeles: Sage Publications, 1987.

Western European Cabinets (co-editor with F. Muller-Rommel), London: Macmillan, 1988.

Comparative Government, Oxford: Phillip Allan with Simon and Schuster, 1990.

The Profession of Government Minister in Western Europe (co-editor with J.L. Thiebault), London: Macmillan, 1991.

Articles

'Structures politiques et comportement électoral dans l'état de Paraíba (Brésil)', *Revue française de science politique*, vol. 5 (2), April–June 1955, pp. 315–34.

'L'évolution récente des colonies britanniques', *Revue française de science politique*, vol. 8 (3), Sept. 1958, pp. 576–602.

'The Conservative Association and the Labour Party in Reading', *Political Studies*, vol. 6 (2), June 1958, pp. 101–19.

'United Kingdom' in K. Lindsay, ed., *European Assemblies*, London: Stevens and Sons, 1960.

'Contemporary France' in D.G. Charlton, ed., *France: A Companion to French Studies*, London: Methuen, 1966.

'Local Government and the Local Offices of Ministers in a French Departement', *Public Administration*, Spring 1959, pp. 65–74.

'Politics in the Provinces: Somme' in D.E. Butler, ed., *Elections Abroad*, London: Macmillan, 1959, pp. 91–103.

'Newcastle under Lyme', in D.E. Butler and R. Rose, eds, *The British General Election of 1959*, London: Macmillan, 1960.

'The State and the Universities', *Sociological Review Monographs*, 7, Oct. 1963, pp. 31–43.

'Towards a General Theory of Change in Voting Behaviour', *Political Studies*, vol. 13 (1), Feb. 1965, pp. 93–5.

'Comportement politique face au pouvoir local dans deux communautes britanniques', (with R. Hall), *Revue française de sociologie*, vol. 7, 1966 (special), pp. 663–83.

'Conflict, Decision-making, and the Perception of Local Councillors', (with R. Hall), *Political Studies*, vol. 15 (3), Oct. 1967, pp. 322–50.

'Party Systems and Patterns of Government in Western Democracies', *Canadian Journal of Political Science*, vol. 1 (2), June 1968, pp. 180–203.

'Y-a-t-il une mutation politique en Grande-Bretagne?', *Revue française de science politique*, vol. 19 (4), Aug. 1969, pp. 773–92.

'Legislative Behaviour: Some Steps towards a Cross-National Measurement' (with others), *Government and Opposition*, vol. 5 (19), winter 1969–70, pp. 67–85.

'A Plea for Problem-Oriented Research in Political Science', *Political Studies*, vol. 25 (2–3), June–Sept. 1975, pp. 231–43.

'Types of Governmental Leadership in Atlantic Countries', *European Journal of Political Research*, vol. 5 (1), 1977, pp. 33–51.

'Dual Leadership in the Contemporary World' in D. Kavanagh and G. Peele, eds, *Comparative Government and Politics*, London: Heinemann, 1984.

'Le comparatisme' in M. Grawitz and J. Leca, eds, *Traite de science politique*, tome 2, Paris: PUF, 1985, pp. 1–26.

'Gouvernements et exécutifs, parlements et legislatifs', ibid., pp. 355–405.

'Political leadership in the Commonwealth: The British Legacy', in H.D. Clarke and M.M. Czudnowski, eds, *Political Elites in Anglo-American Democracies*, De Kalb, Ill.: Northern Illinois University Press, 1986, pp. 311–37.

'Dual Executive', 'Executives', 'Leadership', 'Political Succession', 'Politics', in V. Bogdanor, ed., *The Dictionary of Political Institutions*, London: Blackwell, 1987.

'Ministerial Careers and the Nature of Parliamentary Government: The Cases of Austria and Belgium'. *European Journal of Political Research*, vol. 16, (1) 1988, pp. 51–71.

'Cabinet Structure and Decision-Making Processes in Western Europe' (guest editor), *European Journal of Political Research*, vol. 16(2), 1988, special issue.

'Western European Governments in Cabinet Perspective', ibid., pp. 1–15.

'The Study of Western European Cabinets' (with J.L. Thiebault), ibid., pp. 115–123.

'Processus decisionnels, conflits et gouvernements de cabinets', *Recherches Sociologiques* (Louvain-la-Neuve), vol. 19(1), 1988, pp. 7–34.

'An Agenda for Comparative Government', *Scandinavian Political Studies*, vol. 11(1), 1988, pp. 1–20. This paper was based on the keynote address which was given to the Annual Convention of the Swedish Political Science Association, Gothenburg, October 1987.

'Decisioni di governo e vincoli partitici', *Rivista italiano di scienza politica*, vol. 19, agosto 1989, pp. 199–222.

'The Government of France' in M. Curtis, ed., *Comparative Politics*, New York: Harper and Row, 1984 (2nd edn fully revised, 1989).

'Are Ministers "Representatives" or "Managers", "Amateurs" or "Specialists"? Similarities and Differences across Western Europe' in H.D. Klingemann et al., eds, *Politische Klasse und politische Institutionen*, Opladen: Westdeutscher Verlag, 1991, pp. 187–207.

'Europe in the 1990s' in J. Beaumont, ed., *The New Europe: East and West*, Austrian Institute of International Affairs, 1991, pp. 12–22.

'Party Government: Normative and Empirical Aspects' in M. Wiberg, ed., *The Political Life of Institutions*, Jyvaskyla: The Finnish Political Science Association, 1991, pp. 889–109.

Index